Extraordinary Praise for T. J. English and *Where the Bodies Were Buried*

"Here's one way to tell that author T.J. English may be America's top chronicler of organized crime: Even the bad guys read his stuff. . . . In his fascinating new book, English indicts the federal criminal justice system in New England, accusing it of enabling an entire era of murder and mayhem. Thoroughly gripping and thoroughly depressing, *Where the Bodies Were Buried* . . . is a disturbing and addicting read."

—*Christian Science Monitor*

"In his first-rate new book he pulls back to expose a shocking panorama of institutional corruption stretching back generations. . . . English's outrage at the injustices perpetrated by the Department of Justice is palpable. It's matched only by his disgust that few responsible will ever be held accountable—and that the system is still operating today." —*Playboy*

"English goes into great detail and presents solid evidence that the demoralization of the Boston FBI and the Department of Justice (DOJ) allowed these men to terrorize New England. He demonstrates that the FBI went to great lengths to protect itself, and if innocent people were collateral damage, so be it. . . . This kind of insight into corruption in the FBI and the DOJ doesn't get published very often." —*Library Journal*

"*Where the Bodies Were Buried* is a searing narrative of the criminal underworld that reads like fiction, but unflinchingly exposes the truth about Whitey Bulger, his world, and the system that allowed him to flourish for years." —Huffington Post

"English does not tread lightly in presenting the intricate history of the web of machinations, as he reveals the interdependent, decades-long, corrupt relationship between the mob and the government. This is a candid and unflattering look at this country's broken criminal justice system. . . . As intriguing as it is revealing. . . . Illuminating, disconcerting, shocking, insightful and engaging as well. . . . Superbly written."

—Bestsellerworld.com

Praise for *Paddy Whacked*

"T. J. English, one of the great reporters of our time, has outdone himself with this amazing panorama of strivers and thugs. . . . A page-turner and a revelation."
—Luc Sante

"A fascinating combination of biography, ethnography, and social history. . . . Compelling, honest, startling."
—*Richmond Times-Dispatch*

Praise for *Havana Nocturne*

"A tight storyteller, English provides a juicy mix of true crime and political intrigue, all set against the sexy sizzle of Havana nightlife."
—*San Francisco Chronicle*

"[An] excellent new book. . . . [English] provides a detailed account of the personalities and elements that made up Cuban life. His well-researched descriptions of how business, gambling, politics, revolution, music and religion all played off each other give *Havana Nocturne* a broad context and a knowledgeable edge."
—*Washington Post*

Praise for *The Savage City*

"[T. J. English] returns with a swashbuckling, racially charged nightmare about New York City in the 1960s. This is one nightmare worth reliving because Mr. English so vividly recreates an era. . . . He graphically reconstructs a rampaging decade through three lives."
—*New York Times*

"Spellbinding and suspenseful. . . . The author masterfully re-creates [an] urban underworld. . . . [His] sympathy for his subjects and his decision to let them speak for themselves give the narrative immediacy and power."
—*Pittsburgh Post-Gazette*

"It's dripping with the kind of detail that's too good to make up."
—*Mother Jones*

WHERE

THE

BODIES

WERE

BURIED

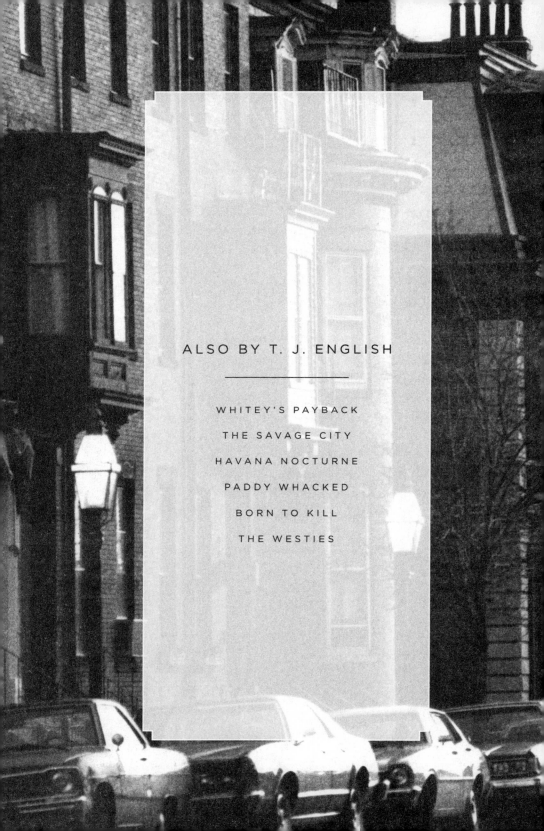

ALSO BY T. J. ENGLISH

WHITEY'S PAYBACK

THE SAVAGE CITY

HAVANA NOCTURNE

PADDY WHACKED

BORN TO KILL

THE WESTIES

WHERE THE BODIES WERE BURIED

WHITEY BULGER AND THE WORLD THAT MADE HIM

—————

T. J. ENGLISH

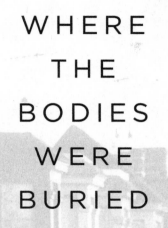

WILLIAM MORROW

An Imprint of HarperCollins*Publishers*

A hardcover edition of this book was published in 2015 by William Morrow, an imprint of HarperCollins Publishers.

FIRST WILLIAM MORROW PAPERBACK EDITION PUBLISHED 2016.

Designed by William Ruoto

Frontispiece photograph by Greg Derr/The Boston Globe via Getty Images
Part page photographs courtesy Tommy Colbert (Part I); public domain (Part II)

Library of Congress Cataloging-in-Publication Data has been applied for.

ISBN 978-0-06-229099-1

16 17 18 19 20   OV/RRD   10 9 8 7 6 5 4 3 2 1

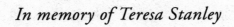

In memory of Teresa Stanley

First we feel. Then we fall.

—James Joyce, *Finnegans Wake*

CONTENTS

HE STROLLED INTO the café, an unassuming man with little indication that he had lived a life so far outside the norm as to be extraordinary. At age eighty-one, he still had a full, healthy mane of hair, though it was now completely white. He moved slowly but held his head high, and in the right light his blue eyes shined as bright as they had forty-six years ago when his life was first plunged into darkness. These days, he did not wish to be viewed as an aberration. He was a knockaround guy from the neighborhood, which is all he ever wanted to be. Back in the day, he was a handyman by trade, someone who helped people out for a modest sum. He did what he could to support his wife and four kids, until he got roped into one of the most outrageous miscarriages of justice in the history of the United States.

The man extended his hand. "Hi," he said. "I'm Joe Salvati."

We were standing in a café on Hanover Street, the central commercial street in Boston's North End, one of the last authentic Italian American neighborhoods in the country. Joseph Salvati was born here in 1933 and lived in the neighborhood most of his life—except for those years he was locked away deep within the belly of the beast.

I shook the hand of Joe Salvati. "I've been wanting to meet you for a long time," I said.

Salvati smiled a bit. He realized that he had gained a degree of notoriety in his golden years. It's nice to have a legacy, he figured, though he would rather be known as a good husband and father than as a man who got mon-umentally screwed by the U.S. Department of Justice (DOJ).

We had arrived in Café Pompeii, a venerable grappa and espresso joint on Hanover Street. We were there so that I might interview Joe Salvati about his life. Also, I wanted to ask him some questions about James "Whitey" Bulger.

It was late July 2013. The trial of Whitey Bulger—notorious gangster; longtime fugitive from the law; indicted on thirty-two counts of racketeering, including nineteen murders—had been ongoing in Boston for several weeks. I had been attending the trial on a daily basis and had not missed a moment of public testimony or in-court legal discussions among the various prosecutors, defense lawyers, and the judge. The trial was a major media event in the city and the nation based on Bulger's infamy as the last of a certain type of old-school gangster, with a criminal lineage that stretched back at least to the 1950s.

After we sat down and ordered some espresso, I said to Salvati, "I've noticed something about the Bulger trial."

"What's that?" he asked.

"Every time your name comes up, the prosecutors immediately raise an objection."

Again, Joe smiled—not a smile of mirth; it was a knowing smile, tinged with regret. "That's because when my name comes up, they know they're gonna have to talk about Barboza. And they don't wanna talk about Barboza."

Joseph "Animal" Barboza, a renowned mob hit man from the 1960s, was the man responsible for Salvati being sent away to prison many decades ago. At a Massachusetts state trial in September 1967, Joe Barboza, testifying on behalf of the U.S. government, fingered Salvati and three other men for a murder they did not commit. He did so with the acquiescence of many people in the criminal justice system, including field agents, prosecutors, and supervisors—all the way up to J. Edgar Hoover, director of the Federal Bureau of Investigation (FBI), who signed off on the framing of Joe Salvati. These men were more concerned with protecting the informant status of Barboza, who was being used as a federal witness against the Mafia in New England, than they were in safeguarding the civil liberties of four "nobodies" whom they knew were being wrongfully convicted.

All these years later, the web of duplicity that led to Joe Salvati serving thirty years in a maximum-security prison for a crime he didn't commit is still difficult to fathom. But it happened. Joe Salvati knows it happened, because he had to live it.

"At the time," he said, "it was the nightmare that wouldn't end."

Salvati speaks with a gravelly voice from another era, something out of the 1950s or 1960s, when he went away to prison. In fact, he sounds exactly like what he is: a street guy who was locked away decades ago and then abruptly released into the modern world with little preparation.

During the early weeks of the Bulger trial, the story of Joe Salvati's ordeal hung over the proceedings like a veil of smoke that lingers long after a conflagration has been brought under control. The grounds upon which the prosecutors objected each time Salvati's name was mentioned usually had something to do with "relevance." The prosecutors wanted to establish that the story of Salvati being framed by Barboza and many co-conspirators in the criminal justice system had no business being discussed at the trial of Whitey Bulger. It was ancient history, they contended, an admittedly shameful episode in the annals of justice in New England that had been rectified many years ago.

The prosecutors wanted it to appear as if what happened to Joe Salvati had nothing to do with Whitey Bulger.

Salvati had been victimized by Barboza and Barboza's handlers in the U.S. government. Afterward, some of Barboza's handlers in the FBI would go on to become the handlers of Whitey Bulger, who, like the Animal, was protected by the FBI and the U.S. attorney's office in New England. As a confidential informant, or CI, Bulger was the government's supposed secret weapon in the war against the Mafia, just as Barboza had been for a previous generation of agents and prosecutors. To allow the story of Joe Salvati to be told in court at the Bulger trial would directly link successive generations of corruption spanning half a century. It would suggest that perhaps the entire criminal justice system was a grand illusion; a shell game presided over by petty bureaucrats more concerned with promoting their careers and protecting their own asses than anything else. It would suggest that maybe the story of Whitey Bulger wasn't really even about Whitey Bulger; maybe it was more about the venal system of justice that had created Whitey, given him his power, and made it possible for Bulger to wreak havoc in Boston for twenty years.

I asked Joe, "How many reporters have come to interview you since Bulger was pinched?"

"Not many," he answered.

"How many since the trial got under way?"

"None."

Apparently, the local media didn't want to hear from Joe Salvati, either. Anything that Joe might have to say was a distraction from the main event, which had to do with burning Whitey Bulger at the stake. To ask questions about how Bulger came into being, to explore the historical antecedents that made Bulger possible, was considered to be doing the work of the defense lawyers. To the U.S. government and the media, it was all about Whitey, not about the universe that created Whitey.

At the trial of Whitey Bulger, there was no room for the big picture. There was no room for the story of Joe Salvati and how his ordeal, which began in 1967, had planted the seed for all that came later.

I asked Salvati, "What do you remember about the day you were arrested—anything?"

He said, "I remember everything from the day I was arrested till the day I come home."

I was skeptical: thirty years is a long time. "Tell me about it," I said.

It happened a block away from where we were sitting, at the corner of Hanover and Prince streets. "I was waiting for a guy to pick me up," said Salvati. "He'd bought a saloon on Washington Street; we were gonna go buy some stools for the bar. He was five or ten minutes late, so I told a kid there, 'If he comes, I'll be over at B.G.'s. I wanna bet a horse.'"

B.G. was a local bookie, and Salvati liked to bet the ponies. In fact, he placed so many bets that some people called him "Joe the Horse." Most everyone in the North End knew Joe Salvati was a hardworking guy; sometimes he unloaded fish down at the pier, or meat at the meat market. Sometimes he worked late as a doorman. In the North End, people knew who were the wiseguys and who were not; Joe Salvati was not a wiseguy, he was a citizen.

Sipping his afternoon espresso at Café Pompeii, Joe remembered it as if it were yesterday. "So I'm over there at B.G.'s," he said. "I bet a horse for twenty dollars. I go back to the corner, and I'm trying to get the race on the radio, because it was from a track in New Hampshire. When it started, I called to B.G., 'Hey, don't take no more bets. The race is off.' I turn around and I seen them coming, the cops. There must have been sixty of them. They were lined up and down the street.

"So I'm listening to the radio, and I win the race. I'm happy about that. Then the sergeant comes up."

Salvati knew the sergeant—Frank Walsh, head of an organized crime task force.

"He said to me, 'Joe, can I talk to you?' I said, 'Yeah, Frank, what's up?' He said, 'You may want to sit down for this. . . . I got a warrant with your name on it.' I said, 'A warrant for what?' He said, 'Murder.'

"Now, I knew Walsh, and he was always fucking with me, telling me who I shouldn't be hanging around with. So I says, 'Come on. Stop fucking with me. Murder! What murder?' He says the name Teddy Deegan. I says, 'Who the fuck is Teddy Deegan?'"

Walsh explained a bit about the murder charge. He didn't have to; it was a courtesy to Salvati, two guys chewing the fat. Then he mentioned that the case against Joe was based entirely on one person: Barboza.

"I had to sit down; I could hardly breathe. Walsh says, 'Go ahead, read the thing [the warrant].' I said, 'Read it? I can't even see it.' I was gasping. I was in fucking shock. Now, I'm looking at the thing. We're at the front door of B.G.'s. I'm looking out, thinking maybe I'm gonna run. Walsh read my mind, he says, 'Joe, don't even think about it. Don't try it.'

"I said to myself, Jesus, let me get my composure. I think I had a dollar and twelve cents in my pocket, because I just bet my last twenty dollars on the horse.

"I said to the sergeant, 'It's all a fuckin' lie. God only knows what they promised that fuckin' Barboza.'

"They locked me up, put me in station one. From there I went to Chelsea. They booked me in Chelsea, because that's where the murder was. From then on, the nightmare started."

The murder for which Salvati was being charged had occurred two years earlier. Salvati had no alibi because he had no idea where he had been on an anonymous night two years earlier. Probably home with his wife and kids. As the trial date approached, Salvati was certain the case would fall apart. First of all, he was innocent. Second, who would believe Joe Barboza?

Salvati knew all too well who Barboza was; back in 1965, Salvati had borrowed money from a friend named Tash, and this led him into the orbit of the Animal. "Tash was the nicest guy in the world; too nice to be a shylock," said Salvati. "I borrowed two hundred from him. Then, about a month later, I came back to borrow two hundred more. Tash said, 'I'll give you the money, but I'm with Barboza now.'

Barboza was a known hoodlum, a former professional boxer who had become a hit man for the New England Mafia. With his oversize head, dead eyes, and menacing demeanor, his name struck fear in the hearts of many in Boston. But Joe Salvati wasn't scared. He had boxed a little bit himself as a youngster and been around so-called tough guys his entire life. "I said to Tash, 'Okay, well, give me the money or not. I don't care who you're with.' He said, 'Yeah, but Barboza has to okay it.'"

Barboza was sitting in a nearby car, dressed in black, wearing dark sunglasses.

"So Tash went over there, spoke to Barboza. 'Bring him over here, I wanna talk to him,' said Barboza, meaning me. So I went over to the car. Barboza's looking at me, giving me the eye. He said, 'You want to borrow two hundred more?' I said, 'Yeah.' He told Tash, 'Give it to him.' Then he said to me, 'I hope you don't pay.' I looked at him. I'd fight him in a minute; he didn't scare me. . . . Well, that was it. Bad blood between us. That's how it all started."

Six months after being arrested by Sergeant Walsh on Hanover Street, Salvati went to trial. He was in a daze. He couldn't believe that he was going on trial, much less that he could be convicted. He was certain the whole case would be exposed as a fraud.

At first, Joe figured it was all being engineered by Barboza. It never crossed his mind that agents or prosecutors could be in on it. And then the trial began. Salvati went on trial for murder, along with five other defendants. Two of the men had been involved in the killing of small-time hood Teddy Deegan, but four of them—including Joe—were completely innocent of the crime. "From the beginning, it didn't look good," said Salvati. "The prosecutors were too confident, laughing and smiling like they already knew the outcome. And each day the courtroom was loaded with feds, FBI agents, sitting in the gallery. You think a third-base coach has hand signals; you should have seen those agents giving hand signals to Barboza when he was on the witness stand."

The trial lasted fifty days. All six defendants were found guilty as charged. On the day of sentencing, the judge told the first four defendants, "You are sentenced to die in the electric chair." The judge taunted the defendants, undulating his hands to illustrate the chair's 2,000-volt current, adding, "On the designated date, the electricity will run through your body until death."

Joe Salvati and another defendant came next. They had been found guilty as accessories to the murder of Deegan. Said the judge, "You are sentenced to Walpole prison for the rest of your natural life, without possibility of parole."[1]

Salvati was thirty-five years old.

"I still thought I was going to get out of there. The case was a joke. Barboza was their only witness. Everybody knew I was innocent."

His wife and young daughters came to visit him at the state prison in Walpole. "My kids couldn't really grasp what had happened. My daughter said to me, 'Daddy, what's the electric chair?' I said, 'What do you mean, what's an electric chair?' She says, 'The girls at school, the other kids, they say they're going to give you the electric chair.' My heart sank. I said, 'No, honey. Daddy's not getting the electric chair.'"

Decades later, at the café on Hanover Street, Salvati relates these memories from a great distance. He's been out of prison for sixteen years and told these stories before. But when I say to him about his daughter's question, "That must have broken your heart," the emotion comes rushing back. "I cried for two days," he said. And then he begins crying right there, an octogenarian who has never gotten over the grief of having seen the fear and confusion in the eyes of his family. He was and still is a broken man—broken in ways that can never be fully reversed.

Salvati tried to appeal the conviction. Barboza went on to testify the following year in a much bigger trial, a racketeering case against the boss of the New England Mafia. It resulted in the biggest conviction ever in the federal government's widely proclaimed war on organized crime. Decades later, it would be revealed that that case also was based on fraudulent testimony by Barboza, who would eventually be exposed as an inveterate liar and finally, in an act of revenge, be murdered by mafia assassins while he was living under a false name in the federal witness protection program.

Meanwhile, Salvati's case became buried deeper in the system. One year

[1]The judge at the Deegan murder trial was Felix Forte, seventy-three years old at the time. For a more detailed account of the trial, see: Jan Goodwin, "Justice Delayed: The Exoneration of Joseph Salvati," *Readers Digest*, March 2008.

became ten, and ten became thirty. He likely never would have been released at all were it not for Whitey Bulger.

I said to Salvati, "In a way, the Bulger case is the reason we're sitting here
today. His indictment is what blew your case wide open."

Salvati squinted his eyes; he knew I was being deliberately ironic. There
is no love lost between Joe and Whitey Bulger. Though Salvati never met
the man who was now a defendant in the biggest organized crime trial in
Boston since the Barboza years, he is, in many ways, a victim of the same
corrupt system that made Bulger possible. The same men who engineered
Joe Salvati's wrongful conviction were the men who laid the groundwork
for the Bulger era.

Talking to Joe Salvati was like being in the presence of a living ghost.
He was the link between what I had been observing daily at the federal
courthouse in Boston during the Bulger trial, and the historical quagmire
that had given rise to Whitey. For the first time, I realized that the trial
wasn't only about Bulger, it was about the vast network of people and events
that were wrapped up in a historical continuum that seemed to never end.

IN JUNE 2011, when it was first announced that James Bulger had been apprehended in Santa Monica, California, after sixteen years as a fugitive from
the law, it was a major international story. Whitey had always been a figure
of much conjecture and media attention in Boston, where he functioned
as an old-fashioned mob boss from 1975 to 1995. Among other things, he
was the older brother of perhaps the most powerful politician in the state of
Massachusetts, Senator William "Billy" Bulger, who served as president of
the state senate for sixteen years. Jim Bulger's criminal career did not hurt
his younger brother's political fortunes at all. In fact, it could be argued that
in South Boston, the Bulgers' home neighborhood, having a brother who
was reputed to be an "outlaw" was a badge of distinction. For a time, Bill
Bulger played the association for all it was worth. If a politician or media
outlet such as the *Boston Globe* mentioned Jim Bulger's name in relation to
the senator, they were accused of engaging in anti-Irish slander, a potent
accusation in a city where the Irish had risen from the gutter to control the
town.

The Brothers Bulger became a dominant topic of conversation and occasional source of criminal investigation in Boston. Of particular interest was the fact that their theoretical alliance as politician and gangster seemed to symbolize the connection between organized crime and the Democratic Party political machine that was at the heart of the Irish Mob going back at least to the Prohibition era of the 1920s.

All of this was to become a matter of supreme local attention in Boston, but Whitey Bulger never really became a national story until after he disappeared on the run. In January 1995, after receiving word from a contact in law enforcement that he was about to be indicted and arrested, Whitey fled along with Catherine Greig, a female companion. Many of Bulger's criminal associates were left behind to face the music. Some of these associates were arrested and cut deals with the government to tell all they knew about Bulger's operation in exchange for more lenient sentences and/or better conditions while they were incarcerated.

Most notable of those who would eventually cooperate with the government was Stephen J. Flemmi, who had been Whitey's criminal partner for twenty years. Flemmi was a lifelong gangster who had killed many people alongside Whitey and was a crucial link between Bulger's South Boston organization and the Italian Mafia based in the North End. Flemmi, an Italian American, had connections among nearly every criminal faction in the city, including, as it turned out, the FBI.

In 1997, attorneys for Flemmi were the first to drop the bombshell that both he and James Bulger had been operating as covert informants for the FBI since at least the mid-1970s. Many in Boston had suspected that Bulger had a "special relationship" with the FBI; it had been hinted at in the newspapers and was a source of frustration and anger among other law enforcement agencies that had, over the years, attempted to take down Bulger. Flemmi's lawyers revealed for the first time not only that Flemmi and Bulger were government informants but that they had, in fact, been protected by the FBI and others in the U.S. Department of Justice. It was part of Flemmi's defense that he could not be prosecuted for crimes that he had committed, because he and Bulger had been given immunity from prosecution in exchange for their serving as informants in the DOJ's war against the Mafia.

The judge presiding over Flemmi's case—Mark L. Wolf—eventually dismissed Flemmi's claim as being without merit, but not before calling for an evidentiary hearing that would become known as "the Wolf hearings." These hearings, which took place in a Boston federal courtroom in late 1997 and into 1998, were the local equivalent of the Nuremberg Trials. A generation of cops, federal agents, gangsters, political figures, and many others were compelled to testify under federal subpoena in what would go down as one of the most stunning public tribunals in the history of the city.

Along with Flemmi, a number of other Bulger associates had by then cut plea bargain deals with the government and begun cooperating with federal prosecutors. From the witness stand during the hearings, a generation's worth of murder and mayhem was revealed. Flemmi would eventually plead guilty to having committed eleven murders. Another Bulger associate, John Martorano, would admit to twenty murders. Bulger would eventually be charged with nineteen killings.

The high volume of dead bodies was one thing, but it went even deeper. The Wolf hearings revealed not only that Bulger and Flemmi had for years been protected by the FBI and others in the criminal justice system, but that the same FBI agents who originally recruited Bulger and Flemmi had played a role in framing Joe Salvati and his codefendants back in 1967. Those agents were given commendations from Director Hoover and received bonuses as part of the bureau's financial incentive program. On the prosecutorial side, others received promotions, and one key player went on to become a federal criminal court judge. These were men who had protected Joe Barboza and enabled his manipulations of the system, just as they and others would for Bulger and Flemmi. It was a cycle of complicity, if not outright corruption, that ran so deep, many in the system retreated into a state of denial that would continue right through the eventual prosecution of Whitey Bulger.

From the beginning, the prosecutors had a problem. It had been their intention to nail Bulger and his organization on an array of racketeering charges, but the Wolf hearings of 1997–98 had opened a Pandora's box of horrific crimes and law enforcement malfeasance going back nearly half a century. This rancid effluvia had threatened to infect the Bulger case, or, even more threatening to the reputation of the system, to wash aside the

Bulger case to reveal a broader sewer of criminal complicity on the part of many cops, federal agents, prosecutors, and other centurions of the U.S. Department of Justice.

The strategy that followed would play out over the next decade and a half. Certain journalists and book writers were cultivated as purveyors of information, and the cult of Bulger began to take shape. Flemmi and other former members of Whitey's inner circle began to give their versions of various murders and other crimes; this information was leaked to well-placed print, TV, and radio journalists in Boston, a city crawling with hungry and talented reporters. The Bulger legend took flight.

There were some who felt that the FBI and other representatives of the Justice Department had no real interest in finding Bulger. The speculation was that with all that Whitey knew, he could bring the system to its knees. Nonetheless, the Justice Department did take part in a wide-ranging public relations campaign to catch Whitey. Over the years, he was profiled nearly two dozens times on various television programs such as *America's Most Wanted* and *Unsolved Mysteries;* he was the subject of documentaries on the History Channel and the Discovery Channel. His reputation expanded to become part of popular American culture, culminating in his exploits being used as the basis for a character memorably played by actor Jack Nicholson in the movie *The Departed*. Directed by Martin Scorsese, the movie was a huge popular success and, in 2007, received the Academy Award for Best Picture.

Upon Bulger's capture, the media spotlight heated up once again. Only now, there would be a new element added to the saga: Whitey himself. Video images of Bulger, now in his eighties, handcuffed, in an orange prison jumpsuit, being brought back to Boston to face the music was all the populace needed to be drawn back into the Age of Whitey.

The prosecutors handling the case were the same men who had been pursuing Bulger since the early 1990s. Fred Wyshak and Brian Kelly were eager young prosecutors, both in their thirties, when they first began to build their case against Bulger, Flemmi, and others. That case, which had originally revolved around assorted illegal gambling charges, had grown over the years to include thirty-two criminal counts, including conspiracy, various racketeering charges, and nineteen murders. It would be a classic case under the Racketeer Influenced and Corrupt Organizations Act (RICO) in which Bulger would be charged as the leader of a racketeering enterprise. Those aligned to testify against Bulger included many former rank-and-file members of his organization, as well as three of his closest associates, including Steve Flemmi.

And yet, with all the evidence, testimony, and prosecutorial firepower accumulated over twenty years, the Bulger case remained a hot potato for the Boston U.S. attorney's office and a special challenge for Wyshak and Kelly. Though a lot of the pretrial machinations and publicity revolved around exalting Bulger's nefarious reputation as a psychopath and criminal mastermind, the prosecutors were never able to fully escape the nagging history of the case. Bulger's court-appointed attorney, J. W. Carney, sought to capitalize on this history by suggesting, on a number of occasions, that his client was going to take the stand and, for the first time, "tell his side of the story." The implication was that Whitey Bulger was going to blow the lid off forty years of dirt and deceit in the criminal justice system all the way from New England to Washington, D.C.

The central tension of the Bulger saga remained, and would continue throughout the trial. Was the Bulger story about one very crafty psychopath who had corrupted the system? Or was it about a preexisting corrupt system into which one very wily gangster insinuated himself and then played it for all it was worth?

For the prosecutors, this was the deluge they had been holding back for twenty years, the possibility that the Bulger saga might detour down a dozen different tributaries to reveal a generation's worth of dirty police work and institutional deception. The last thing Wyshak and Kelly wanted was for the government to be put on trial. It was their job to keep the focus on Whitey. It was a tall order. Prosecuting Whitey for his crimes was the easy part; the evidence was overwhelming. But presenting the evidence in all its ugliness and still containing the narrative of the trial required the efforts of skilled prosecutorial wranglers.

For the Justice Department, the dangers were clear: if the Bulger trial were to become about more than Whitey—if it were to establish, finally and definitively, the link between the Barboza era and the Bulger era—it could destroy all belief in the concept of criminal justice. It could discredit the reputation of the very office that was now prosecuting James Bulger, to an extent that it would be virtually impossible for the people to trust the institutional sanctity of the criminal justice system. There would no longer be good guys and bad guys, but rather one big criminal underworld in which the cops and the criminals were all merely co-conspirators in an ongoing effort to manipulate the universe to suit their needs and the needs of their overseers.

LIKE MANY PEOPLE who had fallen under the spell of the Bulger saga, I had been following the story for decades. My interest was first piqued in 1978 when I visited South Boston, or Southie, for the first time. I was twenty years old and had come from the West Coast to visit a former high school teacher of mine, now teaching at Cardinal Cushing High School, an all-girls Catholic school run by the Sisters of Notre Dame, then located at 50 West Broadway (the school closed its doors in 1992). At the time, Southie was only a few years removed from the civic maelstrom of forced busing, which had left many around the nation with the impression that the neighborhood was a haven for racism and parochialism. "The busing crisis," as those years became known, was characterized by blatant political demagoguery and violence in the streets, which was televised on national news programs and shown around the world. Badly tarnished by those years, feeling misrepresented and unfairly demonized by liberals, collectively the neighborhood had turned inward and was suspicious of outsiders.

The name of Whitey Bulger was not yet well known, even in the neighborhood. In law enforcement circles, it was common knowledge that Bulger was a key player in the Winter Hill Mob, a violent group of gangsters based in the city of Somerville, far from Southie on the other side of Boston and the Charles River. In Southie, Bulger was a shadowy figure. When it was first explained to me by a couple of students at Cardinal Cushing who he was, it was in the context of his brother, Senator Billy Bulger, who was a figure of renown.

For those in the know, the story was that the senator's brother was a protector of the neighborhood, a criminal, perhaps even a gangster, but he was "our gangster." Bulger's defenders argued that his activities were designed to help bring wealth and opportunity to the community. Furthermore, the local myth was that he kept hard drugs out of the neighborhood. This was an especially potent defense since some political and community leaders, including Billy Bulger, had argued that their resistance to busing was based on not wanting "undesirables" bringing drugs into their community.

In the 1970s, much of urban America was awash in heroin and marijuana and, in the years ahead, cocaine and crack. Southie residents took pride in the fact that they were a community that looked out for their own and allegedly kept the drug trade at bay, thanks, in part, to their benevolent gangster.

At Cardinal Cushing High, I talked with a girl—a senior—inside the school's gym, where a group of teenagers were practicing for a musical play that was being directed by my former teacher and friend. The student explained to me that Bulger was a kind of Robin Hood figure in the neighborhood: he stole from other criminals and took care of people in Southie. She spoke in a hushed voice, almost a whisper, as if it were not safe to talk about Whitey in mixed company.

Years later, I was startled to read in a book written by a criminal associate of Bulger that Whitey had set up a room in the local gym called the "dog room," where he spied on female Cardinal Cushing High School students as they undressed. It was also alleged that Bulger had sex with some of these girls and that, secretly, he had "dated" one of them when she was sixteen and he was a man in his forties. At the same time Bulger was having two simultaneous relationships with adult women, he purportedly picked up his underage "mistress" at the end of the school day and drove her to a neighborhood crash pad for sex.

Robin Hood? Whereas the merry bandit of Sherwood Forest stole from the rich to give to the poor, Bulger, it seemed, stole the virginity of underage girls to add to his list of conquests.

In early 2004, I was back in Southie, this time doing research for a book I was writing titled *Paddy Whacked: The Untold Story of the Irish American Gangster* (2005). The book was a sweeping overview of gangster history and folklore from the time of the Potato Famine to present day. The research took me to a number of cities, including New Orleans, New York, Chicago, and Boston, where the narrative of the Irish American gangster remained long after it had died out elsewhere. That history had become encapsulated in the personage of Bulger, who, at the time, was still on the run.

It was while researching *Paddy Whacked* that I first met Patrick Nee, a criminal rival and later an associate of Bulger. At the time, Pat Nee had only recently returned to Southie after a nine-year stint in federal prison on an armed robbery conviction. I interviewed Nee extensively and began with him a professional relationship that exists to this day.

The reason Nee had agreed to talk with me was a previous book I had published, *The Westies* (1990), an account of the rise and fall of the Irish Mob in New York City. The Westies were a loosely connected gang based on the West Side of Manhattan, in the neighborhood of Hell's Kitchen. They were known for their extreme violence, and, in particular, the manner by which they disposed of their murder victims: they dismembered the bodies, bagged the body parts, and dumped them in the river. The Westies were a terrifying wild card in the New York City underworld from the mid-1970s until 1988, when the core members of the gang were prosecuted and found guilty in a major racketeering trial in the Southern District of New York.

Nee read *The Westies* while incarcerated at the Danbury Federal Correctional Institution, in Connecticut. He remembered Bulger talking about the Westies gang back in the early 1980s. Whitey was familiar with some of the key players in the Westies story. In fact, according to Nee, at one point the leader of the Westies had reached out to Bulger in an attempt to establish a working relationship, but Whitey was reluctant based on the gang's reputation for wildness, and also, presumably, because he had at the time a "special relationship" with the FBI that might have been endangered had he formed an alliance with the Westies.

Over the years, via Pat Nee, I was introduced to a number of central players in the Bulger story, including Kevin Weeks, Bulger's right-hand man; John Martorano, a hit man for the Winter Hill Mob; Jim Martorano, John's brother, also a Winter Hill member; Teresa Stanley, Bulger's common-law wife for thirty years; and others. Through conversations and interviews with these people, and through my ongoing research on the Bulger years, I began to bend my mind around one of the most complicated and multilayered stories in the history of American organized crime.

When Bulger the octogenarian was finally apprehended in Santa Monica and brought back to Boston in June 2011, I was assigned by *Newsweek* magazine and its Web affiliate, the *Daily Beast,* to write a series of articles leading up to and including the trial. I wrote a half-dozen pretrial pieces in which, along with interviewing many of the people mentioned above, I tracked down and interviewed others, such as Joe Salvati—people who had been involved with or affected by traumatic events in the Boston underworld going back decades.

Among those I interviewed, the most crucial, arguably, was former FBI special agent John Connolly. From 1975 to 1990, Connolly had been the handler for Bulger in his role as a Top Echelon Informant. When, in the wake of the Wolf hearings, Bulger's informant status was revealed, Connolly became the focus of criminal investigations headed by prosecutors Wyshak and Kelly. In 2000, he was indicted and convicted on charges of fraud and obstruction of justice in the state of Massachusetts. While serving his ten-year sentence, he was indicted again by the prosecutors, this time in the state of Florida. The charge was murder, on the grounds that Connolly, while serving as Bulger's handler, had leaked information to Bulger's gang that led to the killing of a potential government witness.

I did not believe that Connolly was a totally innocent man. His relationship with Bulger and Flemmi had crossed the line in a number of ways. My own feeling was that the case in Massachusetts had resulted in a just verdict. But there was in the government's pursuit of Connolly the whiff of an attempt to make him the fall guy for the entire system's corrupt relationship with Bulger. Connolly was certainly a key player; he and Whitey had a close personal relationship—but Connolly did not create the Top Echelon Informant Program, nor was he a supervisor responsible for making decisions regarding internal policies that spawned the Bulger fiasco.

Connolly was in a position to present a version of the Justice Department's handling of Whitey that could endanger the careers of many government functionaries. At the time of the Wolf hearings, he had been a vocal public critic of the Justice Department, noting that everything he had done as Bulger's handler was authorized up the chain of command. In being so vocal, Connolly put a target on his back and became the focus of intense efforts by prosecutors to take him down, even if it meant stretching the bounds of legal propriety.

Specifically, it seemed as though the murder case against Connolly in Florida was an overreach, an attempt to discredit him for all time.

Since being convicted, the former FBI agent was buried away in state prison in the town of Chipley, near the Florida-Alabama border. Through mutual contacts, I was able to communicate with Connolly and request an interview. I made it clear that I was somewhat sympathetic with his predicament. The interview was done over the phone and lasted an hour.

Connolly struck me as a person who was still in denial about many things; he was unwilling to admit that he had done anything wrong, much less criminal in nature. But he offered some extraordinary details about Bulger's relationship with the criminal justice system. He described to me a meeting he set up between Whitey and the chief of the federal New England Organized Crime Strike Force, a man named Jeremiah O'Sullivan. The Strike Force operated under the umbrella of the U.S. attorney's office. Connolly was suggesting, for the first time, that the arrangement Bulger had with the government went beyond the FBI to the U.S. attorney's office and perhaps even higher up in the DOJ.

The article that appeared in *Newsweek* was an exclusive; Connolly had not spoken with any other journalist since Bulger's apprehension in Santa Monica. The article appeared under the headline "The Scapegoat" and created a stir. The U.S. attorney's office in Massachusetts was livid that Connolly had been publicly interviewed and allowed to make statements that were not beneficial to their case against Bulger. A spokesperson for the district attorney in Miami-Dade County publicly condemned the article. Prison authorities in Chipley were not pleased that Connolly had used the opportunity to call his murder conviction into question. Connolly was punished, thrown in "the hole" for fifty-one days of solitary confinement.

The incident reaffirmed something I had learned since I began writing about the government's various criminal prosecutions in relation to the Bulger fiasco. Any attempt to present a broader narrative of culpability that stretched above and beyond Bulger, Connolly, and the usual suspects would be met with resistance, if not outright malice, by representatives of the criminal justice system in the U.S. District of Massachusetts.[2]

THE BOOK YOU hold in your hand is an account of the trial of Whitey Bulger from a particular point of view. Like many reporters who have followed the Bulger story over the years, my conclusions are my own but have been shaped by the interviews I have done with people who were close to the events that led directly to Bulger's rise and fall.

As with other writers, I came to the trial with an "agenda" of sorts. It was my hope that the *People of the United States v. James J. Bulger* would be a final accounting of the entire Bulger scandal, not only laying out the full cast of characters that had enabled Bulger—all the way up the chain of command to Washington, D.C.—but also delving into the historical antecedents that had helped create Bulger in the first place. Even with all the articles, published memoirs, and many nonfiction books, television documentaries, and feature films based on the Bulger story, many important facts remained unknown. The trial represented an opportunity—perhaps a final opportunity—for a more complete picture of the Bulger scandal to finally be revealed.

From early June 2013 to mid-August, with a brief return in November, I attended every minute of every day of the trial and sentencing. Under federal law, cameras were prohibited from recording events in the courtroom, so the demand for seats was high for media people and spectators who hoped to view the proceedings live and in person. Some days I took in the proceedings from the actual courtroom where the trial took place, but mostly I watched from the media "overflow room," a separate room on a different floor in the courthouse.

Over the course of eight weeks, the trial unfolded like a casting call

---

[2]Connolly may yet get the final word on his conviction in Florida. In May 2014, the state's Third District Court of Appeal ruled that Connolly's conviction should be thrown out on the basis that the government used a gun possession charge against him that violated the statute of limitations. The government has appealed the decision. Connolly, age seventy-four, remained in prison during the appeal, but if the Florida Supreme Court affirms the decision, his second-degree murder conviction will be overturned and he will be released.

of characters from the Boston underworld spanning four decades. Along with the now-familiar turncoat trio of Flemmi, John Martorano, and Kevin Weeks, who had testified at many Bulger-related hearings and trials over the previous decade and a half, the supporting cast included assorted hoods who had never before been heard from in public. Though their testimony may not have shed much light on the central conspiracy of Bulger's informant relationship with the Justice Department, it did offer many pungent anecdotes and insights into one of the most rambunctious criminal underworlds in the United States over the latter half of the twentieth century.

In the pages that follow, wherever testimony from the trial is reproduced it is derived directly from the court transcript. Other events from inside the courtroom are re-created from my own notes and memory. Whenever possible, these events were further enhanced by follow-up conversations with the participants involved.

Seventy-one witnesses took the stand at the trial (see Appendix A). As far-reaching and devastating as the testimony appeared to be, it became clear as the proceedings unfolded that the evidence presented did not tell the full story. In some cases, witness testimony raised questions the details of which were deliberately being excluded from the proceedings by the prosecutors and the judge.

Thus, as well as attempting to give a daily narrative of the trial as it unfolded, this account is buttressed by historical asides and interviews away from the courtroom with some crucial observers, including people like Joe Salvati; Anthony Cardinale, a highly knowledgeable criminal defense attorney in Boston who has represented many organized crime figures; former FBI agent Robert Fitzpatrick, who was a controversial witness at the trial; and a member of the jury who was to become increasingly disillusioned as the proceedings unfolded.

The trial spawned many major news stories, with the defendant dramatically cursing out some of the witnesses, and one potential witness turning up dead while the trial was still ongoing. Locally, it was a front-page item most days, but the implications of the trial reached far beyond Boston.

Bulger and Flemmi had been recruited and used by the DOJ as part of the FBI's Top Echelon Informant Program. Though there had never been a full public accounting of this program—and there was little data available to the public on how many known criminals were involved, how much the program cost, or who exactly within the DOJ was responsible for its oversight—it was known that the TE program involved the recruiting and use of criminals all over the United States. How many "special relationships" with gangsters and drug lords had gone bad for the FBI? And who, if anybody, was ever held institutionally responsible?

These questions were especially pertinent because another scandal involving the Top Echelon Informant Program had flared up and died out just six years earlier. Around the same time it was first revealed that Bulger and Flemmi had been FBI informants, it came to light that a major mafia figure in New York, Gregory Scarpa, a capo in the Colombo crime family, had also served as a TE for the FBI. First recruited by the feds in the mid-1960s, Scarpa was believed to have committed as many as fifty murders while serving as a paid government informant.

In 1994, Scarpa died of AIDS without it ever having been publicly revealed that he was a federal informant for nearly thirty years. When it was finally revealed at a racketeering trial in Brooklyn, and as with the Bulger case, the Scarpa revelations led to federal charges being brought against the FBI agent who served as the gangster's handler. The case against the agent had been scheduled for trial in 2006 but fell apart when it was revealed that a key witness against the agent had lied under oath. On November 1, 2007, at the request of the government, a federal judge dismissed the charges against the agent; what had promised to be the first and most comprehensive public examination of the government's Top Echelon Informant Program had been thwarted.

Thus the Bulger trial took on added weight. Not only would the proceedings shed light on the criminal activities of the defendant, but they would provide, perhaps, a much-needed and unprecedented opportunity to bring clarity and accountability to a highly controversial method of law enforcement that had, without the knowledge or full understanding of the people, become a standard tactic not only of the FBI but also the Drug Enforcement Administration (DEA), the Department of Homeland Security's Immigration and Customs Enforcement (ICE) component, the Central Intelligence Agency (CIA), and other law enforcement agencies.

LIVING IN A studio apartment on Hanover Street, across from Café Pompeii—where I met and interviewed Joe Salvati—I walked Monday through Friday to the Moakley United States Courthouse to take in the trial. As I traversed the city, I could not help but notice how much the physical landscape of Boston had changed since the years of Bulger's reign. Boston was booming, with new buildings and ambitious commercial developments going up at a rapid pace. Cranes dotted the skyline. Young people of diverse nationalities populated the shops, restaurants, and drinking establishments once called bars, taverns, or saloons, but now more commonly referred to as lounges. Boston was becoming the diverse, culturally vibrant city some had always hoped it could be—a hope previously hindered by a parochial, insular, violent past that was encapsulated, most gruesomely, in the Bulger era and everything it represented.

That entire era was on trial. And before the city could completely break free, it would have to collectively look backward one last time at the skeletons in the closet.

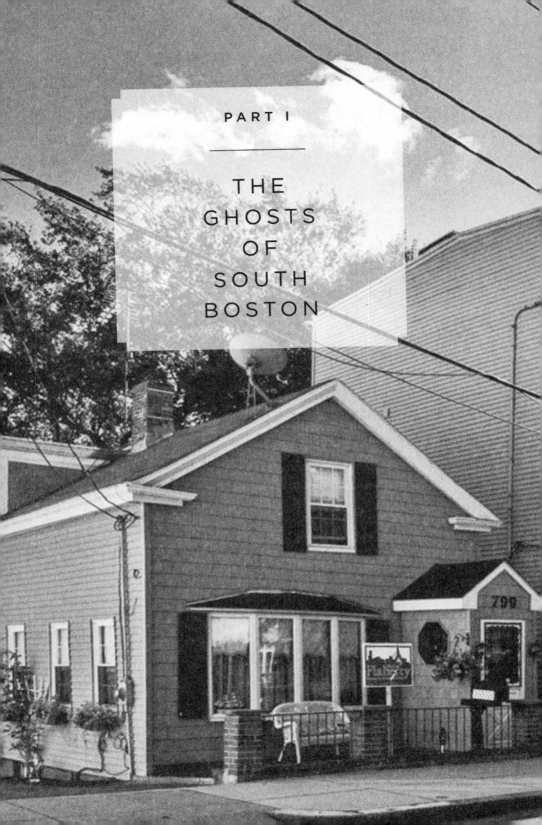

PART I

———

THE
GHOSTS
OF
SOUTH
BOSTON

1

THE HAUNTY

THE HOUSE AT 799 Third Street in Southie is modest in size, with a quaint architectural style. Unlike the triple-decker homes that traditionally dominate the neighborhood, lined side by side like pigs in a blanket, this one stands alone. A pyramid roof with asphalt shingles is complemented by classic wood siding and an extended vestibule in front of the house. Located in a quiet section of a venerable working-class community, far from any major thoroughfares, it is both out in the open and hidden away, a pleasant abode on a seemingly placid street in a quintessential corner of twenty-first-century urban America.

Pat Nee, formerly a criminal in Southie, was raised a half block from this house, at the corner of Third Street and Court Lane. When Nee was seven, he and his family emigrated from Rosmuc, County Galway, in the west of Ireland. Pat grew up on Third Street with three brothers, one of whom, Michael, would eventually become the owner of the house at 799.

The house had special meaning to the Nees. As kids playing on Third Street, they got to know the owner of the house, a former Harvard professor whom they knew only as "Mr. Sullivan." He was an older gentleman, with a patrician manner whose upper-class breeding made him an odd fit in the neighborhood. He was rumored to be friendly with the Kennedys, especially Joseph P. Kennedy, the patriarch of the most famous political family in the United States.

Mr. Sullivan was married but had no kids of his own, and he was friendly with the kids who played on that street, especially Pat Nee's brother Michael. When Mr. Sullivan passed away in the mid-1970s, he left the house in his will to Michael Nee.

In later years, Pat often visited Michael and his family at the house, sharing holiday meals and backyard beers, the small, everyday moments that keep a family together and form the backbone of a community.

Starting in the early 1980s, at the direction of Whitey Bulger, the house that had been bequeathed to Michael Nee was turned into a chamber of horrors.

"Miserable cocksucker," said Pat Nee at the mention of Bulger's name.

We were sitting in Nee's Jeep, parked on Third Street, across the street from the house. I had led Pat Nee back here to reminisce about how his brother's family home in Southie was turned into a place of entrapment, murder, and body disposal. Horrible things took place in this house—despicable things—some of which Nee heard about and others he is alleged to have participated in as a member of Bulger's organization.

Nee is known to some as a hard man, though now, at age sixty-eight, his tough-guy years are well behind him. He's mostly bald now, with a face that is weathered and a body that has been lived in. He is more likely to laugh and tell a joke than engage in gangster intimidation tactics. A grandfather who dotes over his two grandchildren as if they represent to him a new lease on life, Nee is a fixture in Southie, greeted with a friendly "Hey, Pat, how are ya'?" nearly everywhere he goes on his daily rounds in the neighborhood.

For much of his life, Nee was a professional criminal—a thief, a gun-runner for the Irish Republican Army (IRA), and a robber of armored cars. He is not particularly proud of his life of crime, but he makes no apologies, either. He did two separate stints in prison, totaling eleven years: he paid his dues. With the wisdom of passing years, he has come to understand that the codes and mores he grew up with in Southie played a crucial role in directing him along a path toward violence.

The first time I met Nee, in April 2004, he told me the story of another brother: Peter. In April 1969, Peter Nee was murdered in South Boston. Peter's death, and how Pat sought to avenge that killing through "street justice," as it is known in the neighborhood, became a defining moment for Nee.

Peter, the youngest of the four Nee brothers, was neither a gangster nor a troublemaker. He had served two tours of duty in Vietnam as a member of the U.S. Air Force's Strategic Air Command. Pat also served in Vietnam as a member of the U.S. Marine Corps.

On that fateful spring night in 1969, Peter and a group of friends got into a confrontation with some other neighborhood guys just returned from Vietnam. Outside the Coachman bar, down the block from Gate of Heaven Church on Broadway, Peter Nee was shot in the face and died at the scene.

There were many witnesses. But the code of the neighborhood was such that, if the assailant was also from the neighborhood, you did not go to the police. A witness, however, did inform Pat Nee that he saw the whole thing; he knew who killed Pat's brother. It was a neighborhood guy named Kevin Daley.

Nee asked around and confirmed that it was Daley who shot his unarmed brother in cold blood.

Nee knew Daley. They were both veterans of the Vietnam War with deep-rooted family connections in the neighborhood.

Having passed through an apprenticeship as a prominent member of the Mullen gang, a well-known youth gang in Southie in the early 1960s, Nee adhered to the codes of the street. He wanted revenge—not in a court of law, but by his own hands. Over a period of many months, he stalked Kevin Daley until the opportunity presented itself.

Back in April 2004, Nee drove me to the exact location in the heart of South Boston where the retribution took place. It was on East Third Street, just off Medal of Honor Park, near the Daley family home. As Pat described it:

The heavy rain made it difficult to see, which worked to our advantage. Me and my backup guy waited in an alleyway, laying down behind barrels and garbage cans. We had a third guy across the street with a shotgun loaded with buckshot. Daley's two brothers were Boston cops, living in that same house; we knew they might come running out once they heard gunfire. When they came out our guy was supposed to spray them with buckshot, chase them back into the house.

I heard Kevin Daley coming; he drove a Volkswagen with a bad muffler, so we heard him before we saw him. As luck would have it, there was a parking spot right there in the alleyway. I heard the engine turn off. With the rain pissing down, I crept up the alleyway.

I had a .38 automatic, which turned out to be a mistake. I was more comfortable with a rifle, but that would have been too big for such tight quarters. He was locking his car with the key. When he turned and saw me, I was no more than a foot away. I simply told him, "Now, it's your turn." And I started shooting. Hit him five times. After he went down, I kicked his teeth in and spit on him in the street.[1]

Nee went home that night believing he had killed Kevin Daley and avenged his brother's murder. A few days later, much to his surprise, he was arrested for assault with intent to kill and taken to the infamous Charles Street jail. Daley, apparently, had not died. "My brother got shot twice and died. I shot this guy five times—once above the heart, once below—and he lived. Go figure." Daley had not only survived; just as he thought he was about to expire, he had identified Pat Nee as his assailant.

Two months after the shooting, Nee was escorted into municipal court. Kevin Daley was brought in, in a wheelchair. Having miraculously and unexpectedly survived the brutal attack, Daley was now confronted with his deathbed statement, in which he had fingered Pat Nee.

"Does your client stand by his statement?" the judge asked Kevin Daley's attorney.

"Your Honor," said the lawyer, "my client now believes that the statement was made under duress, in a delusionary state, and we would like to rescind that statement. The truth is he did not get a good look at whoever shot and assaulted him on the night in question."

The judge was dumbfounded, and the court was thrown into disarray. Daley looked at Nee and nodded. It was a Southie thing. Daley had killed Pat's brother; Nee had shot Daley in the pursuit of street justice. Daley understood, and was signaling as much to Nee. Ostensibly, the score was now even. Nee was released from jail and the charges were dropped.

Decades later, the two of us seated in a car across the street from his brother Michael's old house on Third Street, the memories of Nee's attempts to avenge Peter's death seemed almost quaint. The moral certainty

---

[1]T. J. English, *Paddy Whacked* (New York: Harper, 2006), pp. 315–16, chapter titled "Irish v. Irish."

of what Pat had done back then—the use of violence as an honorable means to get even for a wrong that had been done—was replaced by allegations of what took place in this pretty little home. For years, Nee has maintained his silence, neither confirming nor denying the allegations. But these stories, which have been detailed and repeated at various trials and legal hearings over the years, take the former gangster back to his years with Bulger, which involved acts Nee participated in that still bring him feelings of regret and shame.

"I don't know how to describe it," he said, sitting in the driver's seat of his Jeep with the engine idling. "We all worked with Whitey at various things, but none of us knew the full extent of what he was up to. Then we found ourselves involved in things that were sick. Crazy. But when you're deep into something like that, the criminal life, making scores off of criminal activities, you get used to a life of secrecy, deception, the code of silence. The paranoia becomes part of it. You do things you don't want to sometimes because it's all part of the life you've chosen. It's not always possible to just say no and walk away. People get killed when they try to walk away from a situation like that."

"Does it bother you," I asked, "having your childhood memories covered over by the stories of what happened here on the street you grew up on, at this house?"

"I can't drive by here without thinking about it," said Nee. "It's a curse. I don't even want to be sitting here right now."

Between 1981 and 1985, on three separate occasions, three people were murdered and buried in the basement of the house on Third Street. Nee is alleged to have taken part in two of the burials. Years later, when Pat's brother Michael—who knew nothing of these killings and burials—put the house up for sale, it necessitated digging up the bodies, a gruesome task. According to trial testimony, Pat and another Bulger associate, Kevin Weeks, disinterred the bodies, which had decayed nearly beyond recognition. The stench was overwhelming, the bodies a mass of fluids, desiccated organs, and dismembered limbs. The severed head of one victim stared at them, as if in reproach. What was left of these bodies was wrapped up and transferred to another location for burial.

The macabre nature of how the murder victims were lured to the house, whacked, and interred under the basement floor led Kevin Weeks to nick-name the house "the Haunty." The abode was surely haunted by the ghosts of those who died there, but also by the spirit of Whitey Bulger, the neigh-borhood's seemingly untouchable mob boss who had orchestrated these un-seemly acts of murder.

Long ago, there had been rumors that Pat Nee would be charged with the crime of "accessory after the fact" for his role in the burials and disin-terments. But the federal statute of limitations on those crimes had passed long ago. Nee could not be charged.[2]

As Nee and I sat outside the Haunty and talked, a few miles away, at a courthouse on the South Boston waterfront, Bulger was about to go on trial. In various statements and legal motions filed leading up to the trial, it had become apparent that Bulger wanted to hurt Pat Nee, to entangle him in the legal consequences of a life they once shared as criminal associates. The reasons for this were buried deep in the relationship between the two Southie gangsters going back generations, but one clue is to be found in a book that Nee published in 2006, titled *A Criminal and an Irishman*. Mostly written by two coauthors, the book was published at a time when it seemed likely that Bulger would never resurface. Nee did not hold back his feelings: "Jimmy Bulger is a rat, a pedophile, a rapist, and a sociopath . . . and the man directly responsible for bringing drugs into South Boston."

When Bulger was arrested in Santa Monica, a copy of *A Criminal and an Irishman* was found on his bookshelf, right next to his bed.

Said Nee, "Whitey's gonna try to implicate me in criminal things he's done. If he takes the stand, he's gonna tell lies and try to get me indicted. He's used to having things go his way."

Nee glared at the house, as if its façade of civility were a duplicitous representation of the man himself: Bulger. Ever since Whitey's apprehen-sion, Nee had been concerned about how Whitey's trial might be used as an opportunity to seek revenge. Nee was worried about what Whitey might

---

[2]According to U.S. penal code, Title 18, Part 1, accessory after the fact is defined as "Whoever, knowing that an offense against the United States has been committed, receives, relieves, comforts or assists the offender in order to hinder or prevent his apprehension, trial or pun-ishment, is an accessory after the fact." The federal statute of limitations is five years from the time of the crime.

do, but he is also left with the bitter taste of things Bulger had already done and had others do in his name.

"Treacherous prick." Pat practically spit out the words. "Sure, I hope he gets convicted, but what I really want is to see him burn in hell. I'd put him there myself if I thought I could get away with it."

Kill Whitey.

This was a sentiment I had heard expressed frequently in Boston since I had arrived to cover the Bulger trial.

"Let's get out of here," I said to Pat. "This place gives me the creeps."

There was no argument from Nee. He slipped the Jeep's transmission into gear, and we eased down the street. The retired gangster seemed relieved to have the Haunty behind him—a toxic memory—framed squarely in the rearview mirror.

AT THE JOHN Joseph Moakley United States Courthouse, located at 1 Courthouse Way along the South Boston waterfront, the people gathered like a flock of hungry pigeons. They were hoping to catch a glimpse of Whitey's motorcade as it arrived from the Plymouth County Correctional Facility, where the city's most notorious criminal had been held during his incarceration.

A crowd of approximately two hundred spectators jostled for position. A gaggle of media personnel, with their cameras and boom microphones and mic stands forming a curbside gauntlet, were corralled behind a rope like paparazzi at a Hollywood award show. Keeping everyone in place was a cordon of cops and U.S. marshals dressed in SWAT gear.

The heavy security was not unexpected. Two months earlier, on Patriots' Day, April 15, the city had been rocked by the explosion of two homemade bombs planted at the finish line of the Boston Marathon. It was a shocking event that galvanized the attention of the entire country and the world. Three people were killed and an estimated 264 injured by the two pressure-cooker bombs packed with nails and hidden in a backpack left on the sidewalk near where many thousands of people gathered to welcome marathon runners as they crossed the finish line. The carnage was ugly, with images of burnt and bloodied victims that went viral via cable news reports and social media sites for days and weeks to come.

The bombers were soon identified as Tamerlan Tsarnaev and his younger brother, Dzhokhar, two Chechen exiles who had been living in the Boston area for more than a decade.

On the night of April 18—less than two months before the Bulger trial began—the brothers shot and killed a Massachusetts Institute of Technology police officer in Cambridge and initiated an exchange of gunfire with police in Watertown. In the ensuing chaos, Dzhokhar Tsarnaev, driving a stolen SUV, ran over and killed his brother, Tamerlan. Dzhokhar had been shot and injured but managed to escape. Law enforcement officers sealed off a twenty-block area in Watertown. They trapped and captured the alleged bomber, who was hiding inside a boat stored in a resident's backyard. Tsarnaev was bleeding and barely alive.

The bombing and subsequent manhunt was a seminal event for Boston, showcasing the city as a strong and cohesive community, with heroic officers of the law who always got their man. But once the triumph of the capture began to diminish, the city was left with the knowledge that this horrific act had been committed not by some invading force, but from within, by two young men who were largely indistinguishable from others who populated what was now an ethnically diverse metropolis. The security concerns that this caused—the fear of not knowing if the average person walking down the street was a terrorist bomber—was evident in the massive show of armed security outside the courthouse for the first day of the Bulger trial.[3]

At 7:30 A.M., a buzz went through the crowd. Bulger's motorcade was coming down the street. Five or six black SUVs, with dark-tinted windows, drove past the crowd toward a driveway leading to a restricted, underground entrance to the courthouse. It was impossible to tell which of the SUVs contained Bulger, but it didn't really matter. He was in one of those vehicles, wearing wrist and ankle cuffs, on his way to face his destiny.

Located on Fan Pier, jutting out into the harbor, the Moakley Courthouse was reflective of the new Boston—institutional, efficient, handsomely constructed. Designed by the firm of Pei Cobb Freed & Partners, based in

---

[3]On April 8, 2015, after a sixteen-day trial at the Moakley Courthouse, Dzhokhar Tsarnaev was found guilty of having perpetrated the bombing. Five weeks later, after deliberating more than fourteen hours over three days, the jury decided unanimously to give Tsarnaev the death penalty.

Manhattan, the building was completed in 1999 at a cost of $170 million. The courthouse building stands alone, across the street from a huge parking lot. The building has a wide entrance, with double glass doors and an undistinguished façade made of red brick. The front of the building, facing Seaport Street, is devoid of windows, so that it is not immediately clear what might be taking place behind the walls of this imposing urban monolith.

Despite the notoriety of the Bulger trial, which had all but guaranteed large crowds and high public interest, the trial was not being held in the largest courtroom in the building. In the interest of crowd management, *The People v. Bulger* was assigned to courtroom number eleven, a midsize room on the building's fifth floor. Media personnel and spectators who were unable to get a seat in the courtroom were diverted to overflow rooms on separate floors.

Inside courtroom eleven, spectators jockeyed for position. The various legal representatives gathered at large tables in the well of the room, two tables for the prosecutors and their legal assistants, two tables for the defense team. Everyone waited expectantly for the defendant to be brought in.

At around 8:45 A.M., a side door in the well of the courtroom opened up. Two U.S. marshals entered, followed by the short, lean figure of James J. Bulger.

Whitey had shaved off the full white beard he had at the time of his arrest and had maintained during his pretrial appearances in court. Without the beard, he looked slightly younger and more accessible—the type of old man you might see out for a brisk morning walk along the waterfront. He was wearing a long-sleeved kelly-green shirt known as a Hensley, much like a crewneck T-shirt but with three vertical buttons at the collar, along with blue jeans and white sneakers. Apparently, Bulger and his team decided that he go with a casual, workingman look as opposed to the dapper suit-and-tie presentation favored by many mobster defendants. Whitey was Irish American, not a Mafioso, and his choice of attire seemed designed to underscore the difference.

Nonetheless, he was a man of stature, and as he was led to his seat at the defense table, Bulger sought to do so with a certain swagger. He knew that he was being watched, not only by a courtroom full of onlookers but by hordes of reporters who would characterize his demeanor to the masses. Back in the day, his tough-guy strut no doubt served to reflect his standing in the city's underworld, but now, at the age of eighty-two, his swagger was circumscribed by the realities of his aged physical frame. As he positioned himself to sit down in the heavy oak chair, he almost stumbled.

The defendant sat with his back to the spectators' gallery and courtroom entrance, a disappointment to members of the public who had hoped that, by securing entry, they would get to stare the city's most notorious desperado in the eye. Instead, they were looking at the back of his mostly bald head.

"All rise," announced a court clerk. Everyone in the courtroom stood as Judge Denise J. Casper entered the room and took her place on the bench, an elevated perch that looked out over the entire courtroom.

An African American woman in her mid-forties, Casper was notable for her relative youthfulness. She had come into the case a year into its development, when the previous judge, Richard G. Stearns, had been removed on the grounds that there was a conflict of interest. Back in the 1980s, Stearns had served as an assistant in the criminal division of the U.S. attorney's office when James Bulger was covertly functioning as an informant for the government. The defense claimed that Judge Stearns, at the time, must have been aware of Bulger's informant status—a claim the judge denied. But he was removed from the case by an appellate court that ruled "the appearance of a conflict" was sufficient grounds to warrant bringing on a new judge.

Casper was the first black female judge to serve on the federal bench in Massachusetts. She had been a federal judge for only three years, a noticeably short tenure for someone presiding over such a high-profile case. But she had a sterling reputation for fairness and at least one other characteristic that made her appealing to both the prosecution and the defense: she had not been around long enough to be associated with or tainted by the district's problematic historical relationship with Bulger.

Casper greeted the defendant and all of the lawyers, which included Fred Wyshak, Brian Kelly, and Zachary Hafer for the prosecution, and for the defense, J. W. Carney and Hank Brennan.

There followed a brief discussion about the respective lengths of the opening statements. There would need to be a short morning and afternoon break, and a one-hour lunch break. The judge wanted to get a sense of how best to schedule these interruptions. After hearing from both sides, she asked the bailiff to bring the jury into the courtroom.

From a backstage door, eighteen citizens entered the courtroom and took their seats in the jury box. As with most juries, it was a collection of average-looking folk, more men than women, and predominantly Caucasian. Ultimately, twelve would serve as actual jurors; the other six were alternate jurors to be called upon only if something unforeseen happened to one of the original twelve that made it impossible for them to continue.

Among the members of the jury was Janet Uhlar, a fifty-five-year-old woman from Cape Cod, who had been selected from among three hundred people who were interviewed from among the jury pool. Uhlar had come into the case not knowing much about the story of Whitey Bulger. She was a retired schoolteacher and author of three books about differing aspects of the American Revolutionary War. Born and raised in Quincy, a city just south of Boston, she had nonetheless lived outside Massachusetts for thirty years. She had heard Bulger's name and knew that he had a brother who was formerly a powerful politician in the state. She was aware of something called the "Irish Mob" through references in popular culture. She had not seen *The Departed* or any other movies that were supposedly based on Bulger, and she had not read any of the many published books on the subject.

As Uhlar took her seat as juror number twelve, she looked out for the first time at the courtroom packed to the gills, the lawyers in their suits surrounded by boxes of evidence and stacks of legal documents. After weeks of filling out questionnaires; being interviewed multiple times by the lawyers on both sides; having sat through, the previous day, a long instruction to the jury by Judge Casper, the moment had finally arrived. After taking a deep breath, Janet Uhlar said to herself, "Sit back and enjoy the ride; this may be one of the big adventures of your life."

"IS THE GOVERNMENT ready to proceed with its case?" asked Judge Casper, directing her question to the prosecutors' table.

Co-prosecutor Brian Kelly stood and answered, "Yes, thank you, Your Honor."

Kelly walked over to a podium facing Janet Uhlar and the other jurors. His manner was dour and workmanlike as he began his opening statement.

"Good morning," he said, nodding to the jurors. "This is my chance to give you an overview of the case. It's a case about organized crime, public corruption, and all sorts of illegal activities ranging from extortion to drug dealing to money laundering to possession of machine guns to murder. Nineteen murders. It's about a criminal enterprise, which is a group of criminals, who ran amok in the city of Boston for almost thirty years. So you'll hear about crimes in the seventies, the eighties, and the nineties. And at the center of all this murder and mayhem is one man, the defendant in this case, James Bulger."

Kelly adopted the demeanor of the common man. At the age of fifty-two, balding and paunchy, he somewhat resembled the actor Paul Giamatti, and gave the impression of being a card-carrying member of the proletariat, but he was, in fact, a seasoned assistant U.S. attorney with a reputation as a tenacious trial lawyer. In the early 2000s, Kelly spent several years investigating financial fraud arising from Boston's infamous $14.5 billion Big Dig infrastructure project. The prosecutor recovered more than $500 million in fraudulent charges against the government, making him a darling among government accountants and a recipient of an Exceptional Service Award, the DOJ's highest honor. In the Bulger case, he had, over the years, proven to be a tough negotiator who enlisted the cooperation of many government witnesses via means that some defense lawyers characterized as highly coercive.

If judged by appearance only, Kelly could have been a Boston detective, or a deliveryman, or a ditch digger. His manner of addressing the jury was conversational. He was one of them, and, in theory, his outrage would become their outrage as he described the criminal methodology of the man now seated just a few feet away in his kelly-green T-shirt.

"Let's go back to the summer of 1983," said Kelly. "There was a man named Arthur Barrett; everyone called him Bucky. Bucky Barrett. By all accounts, a likable guy, wife, two little kids, owned a restaurant, and he had a fondness for stolen jewelry that he could resell for a profit. And it's this fondness for jewelry that proved to be his undoing. Because in the summer of '83, he was tricked into going to a small home in South Boston at seven ninety-nine Third Street. He was tricked with the false promise that there would be stolen jewelry there that he could assess and then resell for a profit. But, instead, when he got to that small house, he didn't see any stolen jewelry. What he saw was this man over here, James Bulger, sticking a gun at him, yelling at him to freeze. And Bucky Barrett froze."

As an experienced prosecutor, Kelly knew that opening statements were like the introduction to a book. You were expected to lay out your themes but also to hook the reader into your narrative. Kelly was attempting to position the jury into being led by the government's interpretation of the evidence. He would tell them a story, and they would be enraptured, like a group of scouts seated around the campfire listening to a yarn from their scoutmaster.

"And then Bucky Barrett was taken to a chair, handcuffed, and chained to that chair. And then for several hours he was questioned by this man over here, James Bulger"—Kelly pointed at Whitey, making the connection as explicit as possible—"and his criminal sidekick, Stephen Flemmi. And they questioned him about other criminals in the area, pumped him for information about their criminal competitors. . . . They asked him a lot of questions, but eventually they got around to asking him where he kept his money. He admitted that he had cash in his house. So they made him call his wife several times and try to get her to leave the house with the young kids so they could go over and take the money.

"Finally, she was able to do that. She didn't know why she had to leave the house; she just kept getting calls from her husband, Bucky. When she left the house, Bulger and Flemmi went to the house and helped themselves to over forty thousand dollars.

"Now, you will hear from Elaine Barrett herself. She's a witness in this case. She will tell you that that was the last time she heard from Bucky Barrett. Because Bucky Barrett, while Bulger and Flemmi were at his house stealing money, was back at the small house in South Boston, still chained to the chair, being watched by two other members of his criminal enterprise, one of whom was a guy named Kevin Weeks. Kevin Weeks watched [Barrett] as he said his prayers.

"Bulger and Flemmi got back to the house. . . . Eventually, Bulger led Barrett to the top of the cellar stairs, and they made a little joke to Kevin

Weeks. They said, Barrett's going downstairs to lie down for a while. As Barrett walked down the stairs, this man over here, James Bulger, shot him in the back of the head, killing him.

"This little house at seven ninety-nine Third Street didn't have a regular cement cellar. It was dirt. It was that dirt cellar where Bucky Barrett was buried. Bulger didn't get involved in the burial process; he let other gang members do that. He stayed upstairs and rested on the couch."

The jury sat in silence; Kelly had them. He could have continued for another hour on the Bucky Barrett murder alone, but there was much to cover.

A chart was projected onto large flat-screen monitors for the jury to see; it was a list of the thirty-two counts, or charges, in the indictment. Kelly led the jury through the various counts. Twenty-three were related to money laundering. Five related to illegal gun possession charges. There were numerous counts related to illegal gambling. Some of the most vivid testimony in the trial, Kelly noted, would stem from the extortion charges against Bulger. There were also many narcotics charges.

All of these charges came under the heading of racketeering. To be considered part of a racketeering enterprise, a defendant had to be found guilty of at least two racketeering acts. Bulger was charged with thirty-three.

Kelly rushed through the various counts in the indictment and focused primarily on the murders. He promised the jury that, along with hearing from Bulger's criminal associates who, in some cases, had taken part in these murders with Bulger, they would hear testimony from wives, children, and other relatives of the deceased. Some of this testimony would be heart-wrenching, Kelly promised. Then he dove back into his litany of violence, picking up with racketeering count number eight, the murder of John McIntyre.

As Kelly explained it, John McIntyre was believed to be an informant against Bulger and his gang. He was lured to the house on Third Street and, like Bucky Barrett, chained to a chair. The prosecutor painted the picture: "And then McIntyre was led downstairs to the basement at gunpoint and McIntyre was placed on a chair and then this man over here, the defendant, James Bulger, tried to choke him to death with a rope. But the rope was too thick, couldn't kill him, all it did was make him gag. So as he was gagging, Bulger asks him, You want one in the head? And McIntyre says, Yes, please.

And at that point Bulger shoots him in the head. And then, like Barrett, McIntyre is buried in the dirt floor."

Here Kelly paused to let the details work their way into the hearts and heads of the jury, then he was back at it with his Southie version of Grand Guignol theater: "Now, several months after this murder of McIntyre, Kevin Weeks was told by Bulger to go back to that house. They were going to meet Stephen Flemmi, Bulger's longtime criminal partner. Weeks was told that Flemmi was coming by with his stepdaughter, Deborah Hussey. At first, Weeks was relieved when he heard that Flemmi was coming by with his stepdaughter. He thought with her around, nothing bad would happen. But Weeks was wrong. Because years earlier, Hussey had been molested by Flemmi, and she had a tough life, and as you will hear in this case, a much tougher death—a death at the hands, literally, at the hands of Bulger. . . .

"So, Weeks was upstairs using the bathroom when he heard Flemmi and Deborah Hussey arrive. What does he hear next? He hears a big thud, like someone falling to the floor. Because, in fact, that's what was happening. Deborah Hussey was falling to the floor as James Bulger strangled this young woman to death. And then she, too, like Bucky Barrett, was buried in a dirt grave in the basement."

Bulger was a killer, but he was also a mob boss, a gangland figure of great renown; Kelly gave the jury a brief history of the Winter Hill gang and a thumbnail sketch of Bulger's criminal enterprise, noting how he was at times a partner and also a competitor of the Mafia in Boston. He gained an edge in the city's underworld, Kelly freely admitted, through "public corruption." He bought off cops and FBI agents and a key member of the Massachusetts State Police. Bulger became an informant for the FBI, who protected him as if he were one of their own.

Nowhere in Kelly's opening statement was there any mention of Jeremiah O'Sullivan or the role he and others from the U.S. attorney's office or Department of Justice might have played in protecting Bulger's criminal enterprise.

Eventually, the prosecutor turned his attention to one of his and Wyshak's biggest challenges. In their desire to nail Bulger, they would be calling to the stand men who were as bad, if not worse, than Bulger himself. One of those men, John Martorano, admitted to killing twenty people. Surely, defense attorneys would seek to convey to the jury that this was a case of the government making deals with the devil, and so Kelly, preemptively, put it out on the table.

"I've mentioned now two of Bulger's closest co-conspirators, John Martorano and Steve Flemmi." Here the prosecutor's voice hardened, letting the jury know that this was the part where they would have to eat their spinach. "Like the defendant, Bulger, they are killers. And they were part of Bulger's criminal enterprise for many, many years. They were prosecuted and pled guilty, and eventually both agreed to cooperate. They pled guilty to participating in murders, extortion, money laundering, racketeering. They will both testify in this case. They will admit to their crimes, and they will explain to you their friend Bulger's role in those crimes. . . .

"Flemmi and Bulger were partners in crime for many, many years. They extorted people, they killed people together. In fact, after several of the murders that Bulger and Flemmi committed together, Flemmi pulled the teeth out of the victims in the mistaken belief that it would somehow prevent the bodies from being identified, not anticipating DNA testing years later. So, clearly, Flemmi is a vicious killer, but just as clearly, the evidence in this case will show that he was James Bulger's partner for many years."

And if all this weren't enough for the jury to take in, Kelly finally got around to explaining that Bulger and Flemmi "were also partners in the informant business." They both met with FBI agent John Connolly and fed him information about criminal rivals. They both paid thousands of dollars in bribes to Connolly and others in law enforcement in exchange for inside information that would help them "escape prosecution from legitimate cops who were, in fact, investigating them."

Kelly's opening statement lasted nearly ninety minutes. At the end, he came back to the nineteen murders. He read aloud the name of each victim as an accompanying photo was shown to the jury on a monitor—usually a photo of the victim in the flower of his or her youth, vigorous, smiling, a family photo of a loved one. It was an effective device, with the names and faces of the dead lingering in the courtroom for weeks and months to come.

LATER THAT MORNING, the lead defense lawyer, Carney, stood to deliver his side's opening statement. Whereas Kelly was unfussy and down-to-earth,

Carney was formal and patrician. With his white beard and bald cranium, he somewhat resembled his client, though he was softer and far less intimidating in demeanor and presentation.

Carney was a court-appointed lawyer. Technically, his client was an indigent defendant. Back in 2011, when Whitey was apprehended in Santa Monica, they discovered $820,000 hidden in the wall of his apartment. The money was confiscated by the government. When Bulger was dragged back to Boston, he was taken before a magistrate judge who asked, "Are you able to afford an attorney?" Said Bulger, "I would be if you gave me back my money." It was an uncharacteristically funny line from Whitey, a man not known for his humor.

The belief by many in law enforcement—and some of Bulger's former associates—was that he had hidden money away in secret Swiss accounts and elsewhere, a bounty that had been estimated, in some accounts, to be in the tens of millions. Nobody could prove it, so Bulger, like all U.S. citizens, had the right to an attorney, paid for by you the taxpayer.

Jay Carney was a well-known figure in Boston legal circles. Like many defense attorneys, he had served time on the other side as an assistant district attorney, in his case for five years in Middlesex County. In 1988, after forming his own criminal defense law firm, he became associated with some high-profile cases, including the trial of John Salvi, who had committed murders at a number of Boston-area abortion clinics, and Tarek Mehanna, a terrorism case. Because of these clients and others, Carney had become known as "the Patron Saint of Lost Cases." As with the Bulger case, Carney's clients often faced seemingly insurmountable odds.

When first assigned the case, Carney claimed to know very little about Whitey Bulger. Although Bulger had been a major media story for two decades, like most lawyers who handled large, complicated criminal defenses, Carney kept his nose to the grindstone. Part of the reason the Bulger case took as long as it did to come to trial—two years from the time of Whitey's arrest to the opening of the trial—was that the defense needed the time to absorb not only the totality of the charges against their client, but also the criminal history surrounding his case.

Carney began his opening statement by introducing himself and his co-counsel, Hank Brennan, to the jury. "When we were appointed by a judge in this court to represent [James Bulger], we knew we had a challenging task. We hope when we present our case to you, you will see the results of all the work we have done to dig into this case and present to you what the truth is."

Carney's manner of speaking was deliberate, as if he were talking to a small child. He thanked the jury for their service, a common gambit among lawyers designed to give the men and women of the jury the impression that their service was highly valued.

Generally, trial lawyers are hyperattuned to the vagaries of human attraction. They know that jurors can be swayed simply by whether or not they like one particular legal advocate over another. In a trial that was expected to last many weeks, the lawyers and jurors in this case would be spending much time together. It was incumbent upon the lawyers to establish a rapport with the jury, to not alienate or grate upon an individual so as to turn them against your case simply because they didn't like you.

It was clear from the start that Carney was going to take his sweet time. In the weeks and months leading up to the trial, he had noticed, and frequently commented upon in court, that the strategy of the prosecution seemed to be to hold back information and then dump it on the court in large volumes at the last minute. At issue was what is known in the trade as "discovery material"—confidential documents, memos, internal law enforcement reports, court transcripts, etc.—that the government is obligated by law to turn over to the defense. The prosecution's strategy seemed to be to overwhelm with an avalanche of evidence anyone hoping to make sense of the charges against Bulger, an approach that Carney and Brennan, as a matter of principle, seemed determined to counteract.

"You know," said Bulger's public defender, "listening to Mr. Kelly's opening statement kind of reminded me of a restaurant and how when you go to a restaurant, you're served a meal, and the food has been prepared in the kitchen. By the time it gets to your table, there's a beautiful presentation. A lot of time has been spent on it, to make it look as appealing as possible. And that's sort of like what it is when the government presents a witness in the courtroom. They've spent a lot of time with the witness, they've done a lot of negotiating with the witness, things have evolved with the witness, and then it leads to the point where the witness is ready to come to the courtroom and testify, just like food when it's brought to your table.

"What Hank and I are going to do is try to show you what happens in the prosecutor's kitchen before this witness gets out here and tells you things that went on that Mr. Kelly didn't tell you, and the factors that shaped not just the witness, but more importantly, what the witness is going to be saying to you."

In keeping with the food and dining metaphor, Carney proceeded to set the table, which in his case involved laying out the historical framework that created the foundation for the Bulger years.

He began his narrative in the early 1960s, describing how FBI director J. Edgar Hoover had become obsessed with building criminal cases against the Mafia. Noted Carney, "This became a nationwide crusade on the part of every prosecutor and the majority of the FBI agents working for the federal government." Carney described how the FBI and the U.S. attorney's office—the agencies in the government that investigate and prosecute criminal cases—come under the heading of the U.S. Department of Justice, with its headquarters in Washington, D.C. At the time, said Carney, "The success of people working for the Department of Justice was often dependent upon how successful they were in getting indictments and convictions of the Mafia. If they were successful, they received pay increases, promotions, bonuses, awards. This was the number-one priority."

This mandate, noted Carney, is what led to the creation of the FBI's Top Echelon Informant Program. In Boston, a master cultivator of criminal informants was Special Agent John Connolly, and the man who benefited most from Connolly's efforts was Jeremiah O'Sullivan, the top organized crime prosecutor in town.

So far, so good: Carney was providing a historical context that would, perhaps, make it possible for the jury to comprehend Bulger's relationship with the criminal justice system. But then the defense lawyer segued into a couple of points that had longtime followers of the Bulger story reeling, as if they'd just been slapped in the face with a dead fish:

"Now, James Bulger never ever, the evidence will show, was an informant for John Connolly. There were two reasons for this. Number one, James Bulger was of Irish descent, and the worst thing that an Irish person could consider doing was becoming an informant, because of the history of the Troubles in Ireland. And that was the first and foremost reason why James Bulger was never an informant against people.

"The second reason was a practical one. James Bulger was not deeply tied to the Italian Mafia. You'll hear that La Cosa Nostra centered on people of Italian, in particular, Sicilian descent. They wouldn't let someone who wasn't of that background be knowledgeable about what was going on in their activities. They could pal around, they're like people who are in the same business, they can certainly be seen together and hang out together, but Bulger would never be provided with information that he could give, even if he wanted to. So Bulger was never an informant."

The argument that Bulger had nothing of value to give the FBI because he was not a member of the Mafia was at least conceivable. But to say that he could not be an informant simply because he was Irish sounded like a barroom boast, or a cruel joke, especially so to criminals currently incarcerated around the United States and in the old country who were there because an Irishman cut a deal with the authorities to save his or her own skin, and turned "state's evidence" against them. In the world of organized crime, becoming a rat is a survival mechanism unbound by race, color or creed.

The next bombshell that Carney threw out to the jury was to admit, on behalf of his client, to most of the charges in the indictment. "Yes," he told the jury, "James Bulger was involved in criminal activities in Boston. He was involved in illegal gaming, meaning selling football cards or other betting games and collecting the proceeds, which is illegal. It's called, in the business, bookmaking. He also lent money to people at very high rates. It's called loan-sharking. He was involved in drug dealing. These crimes, that's what he did."

Bulger had never before admitted publicly to any of these crimes, especially drug dealing. It was an astounding concession. It was not immediately clear why Bulger's defense team was making it, how they thought it would in any way enhance his chances for an acquittal, but Carney seized upon Bulger's admission of criminal wrongdoing to make a larger point. And that point was that for you to find Whitey Bulger guilty of anything, you would also have to find guilty his partners in crime—the U.S. Department of Justice.

The partnership started with John Connolly, said Carney, whom Bulger paid hundreds of thousands of dollars over the years for inside information on rivals in the underworld. Explained Carney, "Connolly was known nationwide as an extraordinary FBI agent, primarily because of the informants he developed. He had twenty Top Echelon Informants who were providing information against the Mafia in Boston and in Providence. He was able, with the assistance or the leadership of Jerry O'Sullivan, to obtain indictments and secure convictions. John Connolly was the FBI golden boy. . . . But what happened is that all of this acclaim, these raises, these promotions, these awards went to his head. John Connolly thought he was a rock star, and he became greedy."

To anyone who had closely followed the Bulger story, this was also surprising. It was always believed that Bulger and Connolly were close not only professionally, as a corrupt team, but personally, as friends. Some, including Connolly, believed that Bulger might even use his trial as an effort to exonerate his friend, who currently languished in prison on a murder rap. Already, on the first day of the trial, it was clear why the defense would not be calling "the Scapegoat" to the stand. It was their intention to use the disgraced agent as a tactical prop and throw him under the bus.

As Carney explained it, slowly and methodically, Connolly was not the sole underwriter of the partnership with Bulger; he was also its chief mythmaker. Carney explained to the jury how Connolly set about creating a fictional informant file to justify his relationship with Whitey:

"Procedures that were to be followed to set up an informant, as set up by the FBI, were never followed. There wasn't a contract signed by James Bulger. He didn't give his fingerprints and photograph to the FBI, as was required. But Connolly wanted people to believe that James Bulger was an informant. He never told Bulger, but he created a file, Connolly did, so he could point to it and say, This file contains the information I'm getting from James Bulger.

"The reason Connolly created this file was just to cover up the fact that he was being seen with Bulger so often, that he was meeting with him when Bulger would be providing him with money. His file grew to hundreds of pages. But when people, supervisors, in the FBI looked at this file, they said, the information in here is of little value. It's essentially worthless. Plus, it appears to be information, junk tips, that were provided to other FBI agents, because the information duplicated what was in these other FBI agents' files. . . .

"Supervisors would come from Washington and look at this and say, This person isn't a Top Echelon Informant. This information isn't valuable. The information in this file has not led to a single prosecution of anybody."

Part of Bulger's defense, Carney seemed to suggest, would be to show that whenever anyone in the Justice Department questioned the Bulger partnership, they were aggressively shut down by Connolly's organized crime squad. Thanks to Connolly, Bulger had protectors at the highest levels. Who were these protectors? Some would be named—Connolly's supervisor with the organized crime squad, John Morris; Jeremiah O'Sullivan, head of the New England Organized Crime Strike Force; and others. But the conspiracy was intentionally left open by Carney to form a gaping crater, into which could be thrown the names of Bulger enablers in the Justice Department who had since died or slinked off into retirement.

IN MAJOR ORGANIZED crime trials, juries and the public are sometimes shocked to discover that deals have been made with killers and criminals of the worst kind. In the United States, this is how criminal cases are routinely made. Since at least 1968, when the Organized Crime Control Act was expanded upon by the law-and-order president, Richard M. Nixon, the use of informants had been a staple of state and federal law enforcement. This technique of using criminals to convict other criminals was born out of a statute within the Organized Crime Control Act that led to the creation of a federal Witness Security Program (WITSEC), more commonly known as the witness protection program. Criminals who had been caught now saw themselves as having an alternative to prison: a new life with a new identity, hidden away in some remote recess of the country.

The witness protection program reinvigorated the era of the snitch. It began a long period in which traditional organized crime syndicates, most notably the American Mafia, were devastated through courtroom prosecutions.

In the Bulger case, the prosecutors would be showcasing at least two snitches whose body count was staggering. Steve Flemmi had pleaded guilty to ten murders, though observers with knowledge of the Boston underworld suspected there were more. The other most murderous witness was John Martorano, a gangster whose resume included twenty murders.

Carney and Brennan knew that the jury would likely be repulsed by these two men. In movies, gangsters are sometimes charismatic figures when played by actors like Robert De Niro and Al Pacino, but in real life, they are moral ciphers, a fact that defense attorney Carney would buff and shine and put on display for the jury to ponder as often as possible.

"At this trial," said Carney in his opening statement, "you will hear a lot about John Martorano. It would be fair to say he is the scariest criminal, violent psychopath in Boston history. He would kill people almost randomly, just as the mood befits him. He would kill people because they crossed him. He would kill people because he wanted to get their money. He would kill people because he didn't want to pay a gambling debt. He would kill people as easily as he would order a cup of coffee in a store."

For Carney and the defense, Martorano was the key to the government's case, even more so than Bulger's partner Steve Flemmi. Because Martorano had been the first former member of the Winter Hill Mob to come in and strike a deal. It was his cooperation that set off a chain of events that would lead, all these years later, to everyone currently sitting in a courtroom overflowing with spectators and media.

Martorano, Carney would allege, was the first to figure out what the government wanted and needed. "Remember," he told the jury, "at this point, Jim Bulger was gone. By this point years had passed . . . and there was a question if Bulger would ever be seen again. Rumors were that he had had plastic surgery, doesn't even look the same. There were other rumors of Bulger being hidden in a small village in Ireland where they're protecting him. Other people speculated that maybe he's dead of natural causes. But most people thought they'd never see him again.

"But the government had as its primary target John Connolly and had to find a way to get evidence against Connolly and tie Connolly to Bulger.

"And then Martorano was educated and learned that he could be the bridge from Bulger to Connolly."

Carney noted that Martorano had a problem: he had never met John

Connolly. How on earth was he going to link Connolly to Bulger when he'd never been in a room together with the two men? That was rectified when it was explained to Martorano by his attorney that if he testified about conversations he had with Bulger about Connolly, that could be introduced as evidence against both those men. "That became Martorano's ticket out of this mess," Carney told the jury. "The more corrupt that he could make Connolly and Bulger, the better the deal that Martorano could get."

The witnesses' state of mind, noted Carney, was all-important. In a criminal case, state of mind is more than idle speculation; it is often the most devastating evidence of all. Judges give fine-tuned instructions to juries on the legal ramifications of state of mind. What is a person thinking? What are they planning? What is on his or her mind as they set about to knowingly commit a criminal act?

With Martorano, his state of mind was informed by what he knew of how the game was played, and it was this knowledge, stated Carney, that would be the key to judging his credibility as a witness:

"John Martorano knew how a gangster could make a deal with the federal government and get extraordinary benefits if he were to provide testimony against others. He knew because he had a good friend who had gone through the process. His good friend was Joseph Barboza. Barboza was the mentor of Martorano. And so what Martorano wanted to do for himself was what Barboza did for himself. And like Barboza, Martorano was just as much a psychopath, a soulless killer without a conscience."

Barboza.

The name echoed throughout the courtroom and down through the ages, rustling the graves of dead mobsters throughout the region.

To anyone with a historical memory of Boston underworld crime, the name sent chills down the spine. Barboza was a thug and indiscriminate killer who, in the 1960s, made a deal with the FBI. He represented the Original Sin, the first mutant offspring of a law enforcement strategy that would later give birth to Bulger.

Barboza was the "rosebud" of the Boston underworld. If Carney and the defense team could link the Bulger case to the Barboza era, they would be cutting open the guts of the city's great whale of corruption. The innards would spew forth a legacy of dirty dealings within the criminal justice system in New England that would devastate the region's image of itself as a cradle of liberty and justice.

Carney sought to explain to the jury the history of Joe Barboza and his deal with the DOJ back in the 1960s. He explained how Barboza's criminal partner, Vincent "Jimmy the Bear" Flemmi, brother of Steve Flemmi, had initiated Barboza into the ranks of government informants. Jimmy Flemmi was himself a Top Echelon Informant. Together, Jimmy Flemmi and Barboza had committed a murder and then used their roles as informants to create a false prosecutorial narrative. To protect Jimmy Flemmi, Barboza lied in court. As part of his deal with the government, he admitted his own role in the murder but then framed four men who were innocent of the crime.

Carney was talking about the case that had led to the wrongful conviction of Joe Salvati. His presentation of these facts to the Bulger jury was clumsy and confusing, and it lacked the appropriate drama. The lawyer's bloodless delivery belied the shock of what he was saying: Barboza had committed the murder of small-time hood Teddy Deegan along with Jimmy the Bear Flemmi. Then, with the blessing of FBI agents, he took the stand and identified four innocent men. He committed perjury—lied on the stand—so that the government men would have their convictions.

For Barboza, it had been a sweet deal. He was allowed to lie on the stand to protect his criminal partner and friend. By doing the bidding of a corrupt system, he was set free. And his diabolical lie was kept buried for generations.

This, claimed Carney, was the lesson learned by John Martorano, an understanding of how the game was played based on historical precedent—the same historical precedent that lay at the heart of the Bulger prosecution.

The first day of the trial ended in midafternoon. The spectators, attorneys, and reporters spilled out onto the sidewalk in front of the courthouse. The microphones and cameras were in position to receive the various representatives of the case.

The trial was under a gag order, imposed by Judge Casper, which prohibited the lawyers from speaking with the press about the case. The prosecutors stayed out of the media glare altogether, but, occasionally, Carney or Brennan would stand before the microphones and offer innocuous statements, though mostly what they said was "I am prohibited from answering your question." It was a pointless exchange designed, perhaps, to expose the absurdity of the law, which the defense team had unsuccessfully sought to have rescinded by the judge.

Jay Carney stood before the media and basked in what he perceived to be the glow of a scintillating opening statement. Which was only partly true. For anyone who had followed the Bulger saga and hoped that the trial would tell the full story, Carney's opening statement had its moments. His detailing of the historical context for the charges against Bulger was potentially groundbreaking. His inclusion of Barboza and how the lessons of his deal with the government had not been lost on an entire generation of gangsters in Boston was the overarching narrative that many of us had been hoping would be brought to bear.

But outside the courthouse, in the scrum of commentary and specu-lation among observers that would become a post-trial ritual, what every-one wanted to talk about was Carney's "bombshell" that Bulger had never been an informant for the FBI. The veracity of this claim would be hotly debated in the weeks and months ahead, but what it had accomplished in the short term was to undermine Carney's opening presentation. The issue of whether or not Bulger had been an informant had little to do with the charges in the case, and it offered even less insight into the continuity of criminal negligence in the government's dealings with Barboza and Bulger.

In front of the media, Carney was smiling, but he shouldn't have been. A schizophrenic fissure in his case had been revealed, one that would grow more pronounced as the trial unfolded.

Carney had claimed that he and his co-counsel were going to reveal the dirty little secrets behind how the government prepared their prose-cutorial banquet, but instead, the defense lawyer misread the recipe and undercooked the main course, leaving the jury, paradoxically, both gaseous and malnourished.

2

CURSE OF THE COWRITER

ON THE EVENING of the trial's first day, I headed over to Southie to meet with Pat Nee and Kevin Weeks. I had arranged to meet them at Mirisola's, an Italian restaurant at the corner of L and East Eighth streets. I knew the place well. A year and a half earlier, I had met and interviewed Whitey Bulger's common-law wife, Teresa Stanley, at Mirisola's. The place is small and intimate, more like a diner than an actual restaurant. Teresa and I sat off in a corner, and she poured her heart out about Jimmy—never "Whitey"—and the relationship they had together for thirty years. Within months of that interview Teresa was informed that she had brain cancer; a few months after that, she was gone.

Every time I walked into Mirisola's I thought of Teresa, almost as if I could feel her presence. Few people had known Bulger as well or as closely as Teresa, though she remained blissfully ignorant of the full extent of his criminal activities when they were together. What she remembered most vividly was the night she found out about Catherine Greig. A mysterious woman had called Teresa and told her that they needed to meet. She went to an agreed-upon location and met the woman who introduced herself as "Jimmy's lover." Teresa had suspected that Bulger had other women on the side, temporary flings and one-night stands. She asked Catherine how long she and Jimmy had been together. When Greig told her "twenty years," she almost had a heart attack.

When Teresa recounted this episode to me at Mirisola's, many years after it had taken place, you could still see the hurt in her eyes.

She was seventy years old when I met her, still attractive, with a sweet and humble disposition. I could see she was not the kind of person who would have challenged Bulger, which was likely a requirement of any relationship he had with a woman. Teresa knew that Jimmy had done time in prison for bank robbery. She knew he was a bookmaker and probably a loan shark. But as with any long-term union between a woman and a known criminal, much of the relationship was based on her not asking questions and instead living in a state of denial.

That arrangement had made it possible for her to have a life of relative financial comfort for herself and her four kids, but in the end, she seemed shell-shocked. Before Whitey disappeared on the run, he told Teresa, "You'll hear many terrible things about me. Don't believe it. It's all lies." But because of the deception she had experienced with Bulger, a man who lived a separate and secret life with another lover for twenty years while he was also living with her, she had to admit that anything was possible.

When Teresa died on August 16, 2012, she went to her grave still haunted by the knowledge that the man she lived with all those years was quite possibly a psycho killer, or, at the very least, an inveterate liar who had deceived her and everybody else he knew for most of his adult life.

At Mirisola's, to my surprise, there was a small production crew in front of the place filming Pat Nee and some other guys as they entered the restaurant. Pat had told me there would be a crew from the Discovery Channel who were filming a reality show set in and around South Boston. The show was to be called *Saint Hoods,* and it would detail the activities of a group of bookmakers based in the neighborhoods of Southie, Dorchester, and Roxbury. Pat Nee was to be featured on the show, in which he would be identified as the crime boss of the neighborhood.

When I heard about it, I looked at Pat and asked, "Are you sure about this?" It seemed crazy to me that a person who was alleged to have been a professional criminal and was currently worried that he might be subpoenaed to appear at the Bulger trial would be taking part in a reality show in which he was being portrayed as a professional criminal.

Pat Nee is no dummy; he was aware of the risks. He explained, "This may be one of the last opportunities I have for a legitimate payday based on my connections in the neighborhood."

Nee was a consultant on *Saint Hoods* and had control over who was used as extras on the show and even locations that were used. He told the producers up front that he would not talk about Whitey Bulger or the trial on the show, and that they could not air the show until after the trial was over. According to Nee, the producers agreed to his conditions.

I still thought it was a bad idea, but who was I to tell a retired gangster with few options for making a living—legitimately—what did or did not make sense? I sat off to one side, not far from where I had interviewed Teresa Stanley, and waited until they were finished filming.

The production team was shooting a scene where Pat and his crew of bookies enter Mirisola's, take a seat, and engage in a spirited discussion about a group of rival bookies in Dorchester. Though it was supposed to be a reality show, much of the dialogue was scripted ahead of time. There was much tough-guy patter that seemed derived from an old Jimmy Cagney movie.

By the time they had finished shooting the scene and the production crew had begun wrapping it up for the day, Kevin Weeks arrived at Mirisola's.

I had known Weeks for seven years, having met him not long after he was released from prison after serving a five-year sentence on racketeering charges. By then, he had published a book called *Brutal,* written in collaboration with Phyllis Karas, which was an account of his years with Bulger. *Brutal* was an honest and unsentimental account of how Weeks became Bulger's right-hand man when he was still in his early twenties. Kevin was interviewed on *60 Minutes,* and his book became a bestseller, though he was restricted by law from receiving any proceeds.

As Bulger's "muscle," Kevin had done many bad acts, most of which were detailed in his book. Though he was not the kind of person to ask for sympathy or forgiveness, Kevin did admit that he had regrets. It had taken him years to come out from under the spell of Bulger, who was often described in the media as a "father figure" to Weeks—a description that Kevin did not agree with. "I had a father," he said. "I didn't need another one. Maybe he was like an uncle. He certainly was a mentor. He wanted to teach me things about life, so maybe he viewed me as a surrogate son. That is possible."

Not far from Mirisola's, Bulger and Weeks used to go for walks nearly every day at Carson Beach or Castle Island, two scenic spots along the South Boston waterfront. It was there that Bulger dispensed his underworld wisdom and they hatched schemes that kept money flowing in from various ongoing criminal rackets in the city. For a long time, it had been glorious, and then it all turned sour. "I won't bullshit you," Kevin told me when I first met him. "We had fun on the street. But so much of it was based on lies and deception. And then the lies start to get in the way of your personal life, your personal relationships. It's no way to live."

We shook hands and sat down at a table near the kitchen. I noticed from the handshake that Kevin could barely move his right arm and was in discomfort. He explained that he'd had an accident on his construction job that tore a muscle in his right shoulder, which required two separate surgeries. Presently, he had no feeling and little mobility with his right arm, but, again, he was not the type to complain. He insisted on shaking hands with his right hand, though it would have been much easier if he switched to his left.

Weeks had put on weight since I last saw him. In his youth, he'd been a Golden Gloves boxer. Now fifty-seven years old (born in 1956), he was less muscular than he used to be in his days on the street, but he was still formidable, with a straightforward, no-nonsense manner that had been part of his persona as Whitey's enforcer.

Pat Nee joined us, and we ordered a meal. Mirisola's is a Sicilian joint so unpretentious that you feel as if you are eating in someone's kitchen at home. Guy Mirisola, the proprietor, is a friend of both Pat and Kevin, who eat there frequently. He knows their tastes and makes suggestions. Though there allegedly are menus at Mirisola's, I have never seen one. The meal that arrives on your plate is usually the result of a personal consultation with Guy and his Sicilian mother, who is head chef.

As we awaited our order, I described to Nee and Weeks in some detail the day's opening statements, how Bulger sat in his kelly-green shirt as his attorney explained to the jury that he could not have been an informant for the FBI because he was Irish. They were both dumbfounded by this argument. Not only was it absurd, but it was an insult to the intelligence of the average criminal.

Nee was born in Ireland, and Weeks is of Irish and Welsh descent, born and raised in Southie. Nee did two years in prison on charges of smuggling guns to the IRA, due in part to various Irish informants. One of those informants, John McIntyre, an Irish American, was, as mentioned earlier, shot in the head by Bulger. In his book and at previous trials, Weeks detailed how both he and Pat had played a role in the disposal of McIntyre's body. Clearly, in the Irish criminal underworld informants were frowned upon—they were punished and often killed. But to say that someone could not be an informant because they were Irish defied logic and historical precedent.

This brought us around to a discussion of Bulger's defense, as explained by his attorney, that Whitey never was an informant.

Weeks shook his head in dismay. "What do you call it," he said, "when a guy meets with his FBI contacts every week, gives them information—names, locations, crimes—that goes right into their criminal files? What do you call that except being a rat?"

It had taken Weeks many years to bend his mind around what Bulger had done. For the longest time, like Teresa Stanley, he was in denial. Partly, this was because he was so deep inside the Bulger-Flemmi nexus that emotionally and intellectually he was incapable of acknowledging the truth.

In his book, Kevin recounted how retired special agent John Connolly, around the time of the Wolf hearings, came to him and attempted to give an elaborate justification for what had transpired. They met at the Top of the Hub restaurant, located in the Prudential Center tower, and Connolly had brought a mimeographed copy of Bulger's and Flemmi's FBI files.

As I read over the files at the Top of the Hub that night, Connolly kept telling me that 90 percent of the information in the files came from Stevie. Certainly Jimmy hadn't been around the Mafia the way Stevie had. But, Connolly told me, he had to put Jimmy's name on the files to keep his file active. As long as Jimmy was an active informant, Connolly said, he could justify meeting with Jimmy and giving him valuable information. Even after he retired, Connolly still had friends in the FBI, and he and Jimmy kept meeting to let each other know what was going on. I listened to all that, but now I understood that even though he was retired, Connolly was still getting information, as well as money, from Jimmy.

As I continued to read, I could see that a lot of the reports were not just against the Italians. There were more and more names of Polish and Irish guys, of people we had done business with, of friends of mine. Whenever I came across the name of someone I knew, I would read exactly what it said about that person. I would see, over and over again, that some of these people had been arrested for crimes that were mentioned in these reports. It didn't take long for me to realize that it had been bullshit when Connolly told me that the files hadn't been disseminated, that they had been for his own personal use. He had been an employee of the FBI. He hadn't worked for himself. If there was some investigation going on and his supervisor said, "Let me take a look at that," what was Connolly going to do? He had to give it up. And he obviously had. I thought about what Jimmy had always said, "You can lie to your wife and to your girlfriends, but not to your friends. Not to anyone we're in business with." Maybe Jimmy and Stevie hadn't lied to me. But they sure hadn't been telling me everything.[1]

To Pat Nee, Whitey being a rat had answered a lot of questions that had been nagging at him for decades. "He was very good at keeping us in the dark," said Nee. "He had all these different groups he did business with, and he made sure we didn't know what he was doing with the others. We knew he had Connolly on the payroll. We knew he was getting inside information from Connolly. But we didn't know he was giving the feds information about us. If we had, there's a good chance he would have gotten killed. We would have taken care of that."

The food arrived, and we ate. With Nee and Weeks, I sometimes felt bad asking so many questions about the Bulger years. It was an unpleasant topic for so many people in Boston—most especially those who had loved ones murdered by the Winter Hill gang—but it is also problematic for anyone who ever knew or did business with Bulger. In many ways, his former associates had been made to answer for his legacy, even though, in retrospect, it was clear they also were used and manipulated by Whitey.

Even if we had wanted to avoid the topic, it was not easy to do. As we sat eating our dinner, on a flat-screen television mounted on a wall a news

---

[1] Kevin Weeks and Phyllis Karas, *Brutal* (New York: William Morrow, 2007), p. 248.

report came on about the first day of the trial. A reporter summarized the day's events and talked about what was ahead; it was at this point that a photo of Weeks was shown superimposed over images of murder victims' bodies being dug up by federal investigators back in the early 2000s.

I looked across the table at Weeks, who could hear the TV but had been avoiding watching the report. He was sitting at the table; behind him, over his shoulder, was his face on the TV screen.

"Kevin," I said, nodding toward the TV. He turned around, looked briefly, and said, "Why they always have to put my face up there? There's going to be seventy-five witnesses at this trial and they always have to show me."

"Well," I said, "they have to show you because you're the only witness under the age of seventy at this trial, the only youthful face." It was a joke but also partly true. The witnesses from Bulger's era would mostly be old-time gangsters in their seventies. Kevin laughed, and Pat said, "Hey, I'm only sixty-eight."

I said, "Yeah, but you haven't been subpoenaed yet."

It was a prospect of considerable discussion whether or not Nee would be called by the defense to testify. He had already decided, under advisement from his attorney, that if he were called he would take the stand and invoke his Fifth Amendment right to not testify, on the grounds that he might incriminate himself.

This brought the conversation around to whether or not Whitey himself would take the stand. In the months leading up to the trial, Bulger's lawyers had stated publicly on a number of occasions that he would, that Whitey was anxious to tell his version of events in the courtroom. These proclamations, delivered both inside the courtroom, to the judge, and outside the courtroom, to the media, had contributed to the high level of advance publicity the trial had received all around the globe.

From the outset, I doubted Bulger would take the stand. I mentioned to Nee and Weeks that it was telling that during his opening statement to the jury, Carney had made no promises that Bulger would testify.

"Good," said Kevin. "He should keep his mouth shut."

I counterargued: "I'm hoping he takes the stand and names names of all the government people who facilitated his deal. I want him to get up there and lay it all out on the table." I was being a little provocative, knowing that this was not what Nee and Weeks wanted to see.

"Of course," said Kevin. "You're a writer. You want him to testify because that's a better story, but we have different concerns."

"We just want it to all be over," added Nee.

After we had finished eating, I asked Kevin directly, "So how are you holding up? Did you ever think you were going to see this day? How do you feel about it?"

It was clear that Weeks was conflicted and in a state of emotional discomfort about the trial and all that it entailed. "To me, it's sad," said Kevin. "To see Jimmy going through this. What's he doing? He could have copped a plea and avoided all this. Just seeing him so old, so diminished, after the way he was years ago. Some say, revenge. Satisfaction. I don't expect to get any satisfaction out of this. None."

For many people in Boston, the trial was an emotional event, but for Weeks there was an added level of intimacy. For more than a decade, he had spent nearly every day of his life alongside Bulger, listening to his advice about everything under the sun, acting as a surrogate son, beating people up for Whitey, intimidating people in the neighborhood, cleaning up after the gang's many acts of violence and murder. Now he would take the stand, look his former mentor in the eyes, and deliver testimony that presumably would help put him away for the rest of his days. It was a sobering prospect.

THE SECOND DAY of the trial began with a discussion about a couple of charts, though, as in most matters of love and war, the primary topic of discussion was a pretense for something else.

As is standard practice in a RICO case, the prosecutor, Fred Wyshak, sought to enter into evidence organizational charts of crime groups that the defendant was alleged to have been a part of. In Bulger's case, the charts were headlined "Winter Hill Organization Circa 1975 to 1980" and "Winter Hill Organization/South Boston Organized Crime Group 1982" (see Appendices B and C). The motion to submit the charts as evidence brought an objection from the defense, and the person who stood to explain why was Hank Brennan.

For most of the trial up to this point, J. W. Carney had clearly stood front and center as lead counsel, making the majority of the pretrial arguments in court and answering questions from the media at periodic press conferences held on the sidewalk in front of the courthouse. For many who had been following the case, this was the first time they would be hearing Brennan speak.

At age forty-two, Brennan was a former Suffolk County prosecutor. He had a forceful courtroom manner. His black hair was neatly parted on one side, and he had the trim physique of someone who jogged or worked out at the gym on a regular basis. He spoke as if every word mattered, insistent on the logic of his verbal presentation, and in the case of the government's two "highly prejudicial" charts, he had a strong argument to make.

"The charts are not admissible," said Brennan. "They are overview evidence. And there is an inherent danger by allowing the government to introduce both of these exhibits. The first is, I remind the court that Mr. Bulger is charged with a RICO count. In fact, two RICO counts, one being conspiracy. By providing a chart that shows a number of pictures and in order from top to bottom suggests an opinion, it's an inadmissible opinion, and what it suggests to somebody who looks at it, especially a juror, is that the person on top is responsible for the persons underneath him.

"As you can see, on both charts there are lines drawn between the people at the top, notably, for my concern, Mr. Bulger, and people below him. The only implication that can be left or inference that can be drawn is that Mr. Bulger is responsible for the people underneath, as if he is the leader of an organization. The government should have to call witnesses to describe their involvement or known involvement with other people in relation to the person above them, notably Mr. Bulger, before the jury should draw that inference."

Fred Wyshak stood to make the counterargument. With his graying hair and stooped shoulders, Wyshak was the dean of Bulger prosecutors. Earlier in his career, he had served for a time as a federal prosecutor in Brooklyn, and he retained the melodic cadence of a Brooklyn Jew when he spoke, his voice reflecting both distress and weary acceptance in equal measure. No one person had spent more time and energy trying to bring Bulger to justice, and throughout the trial Wyshak would take personally each and every objection from the defense.

A profile of both Wyshak and Kelly in *Boston* magazine once referred to the two of them as the Batman and Robin of federal prosecutors. Both believed they were on a holy crusade, and as the trial progressed it was clear that Wyshak was Batman, the older and more nuanced crime avenger.

Wyshak seemed taken aback by the forcefulness of Brennan's objection to the charts. He counterargued that it was his intention to enter the charts as evidence during the testimony of an upcoming law enforcement witness, someone who would be offered as an expert on the subject of organized crime in Boston. This so-called expert, Brennan responded, had already testified once before in relation to these charts, in the case of *Florida v. Connolly,* and he had been decidedly off the mark. To illustrate his point, Brennan produced a transcript from that trial and read from a section of the testimony.

With Judge Casper interjecting an occasional question to both men, the discussion went back and forth with surprising vigor. The issue itself felt less important than the desire on the part of both combatants to win the trial's first significant point of contention. After twenty minutes, Judge Casper concluded, "I think there may very well be a juncture in this trial where these charts are appropriate based on the evidence that has come in, but it seems to me that at this juncture Mr. Brennan's objection has some legs, so I don't think the charts should come in at this point."

If the trial were a tennis match, the defense had scored the first point with a strong overhand volley.

The trial's first witness was Robert "Bobby" Long, a former Massachusetts state trooper who had taken part in one of the earliest law enforcement attempts to take down Whitey Bulger. Long's direct testimony was elicited by Zachary Hafer, a junior member of the prosecution team. Thirty-seven years old, a Dartmouth graduate, compared to the other two prosecutors Hafer seemed like a kid just out of law school, though he had been with the U.S. attorney's office for six years.

After Hafer led Long through a detailed recitation of his career as a trooper, including twenty-six years with the state police, or "staties," as they are known locally, they got to the meat of why Lieutenant Long was on the stand.

Back in the spring of 1980, Long was part of a law enforcement investigative team that targeted a location that had become known to them as a central meeting place for mobsters from throughout the New England underworld. The Lancaster Street garage, located in the city's West End, was a nondescript former auto body shop situated on a short, one-way street that made it possible for the mobsters to monitor who was coming and going. Trooper Long and the other investigators were able to set up a video surveillance post in a deserted office building across the street from the garage.

From April to June of 1980, a handful of state troopers videotaped comings and going at the garage. The objective was to gather enough footage of known mob figures meeting there so that they would then be able to obtain authorization to plant a wiretap inside the location.

In the courtroom, it was prosecutor Hafer's intention to show snippets of the many surveillance videos that had been compiled, but before he did he asked Long about a particular day, June 21, 1980, when he had been watching the garage from the surveillance post when Arthur "Bucky" Barrett showed up.

From a previous investigation, Long knew Bucky Barrett as a premier safecracker and a "fence," a receiver and seller of stolen goods. At the time, Barrett was a suspect in a daring bank robbery at the Depositors Trust, which had taken place in the nearby town of Medford.

"What was stolen?" Hafer asked Long.

"It was a burglary," he answered, "a break-in where they went through the roof of a vault in the bank. They hacked into seven hundred safe-deposit boxes and reportedly got away with a million and a half in cash, and the rest, about three and a half million, in gold and jewelry."

"Was anyone indicted as part of your investigation?"

"Yes. Six individuals."

"Who specifically?"

"Gerald Clement, former captain on the MDC police; Thomas Doherty, a lieutenant on the Medford Police Department; Joseph Bangs, a sergeant on the Metropolitan Police Department; Arthur Barrett; Kenneth Holmes; and Francis O'Leary."

Seated on the witness stand, Bobby Long, at age seventy-one, projected the same Dudley Do-Right air of rectitude that he had in his many years on the job. He still had the square jaw and full head of black hair, though it was now possibly a dye job. Having retired with honors, he was known to be a good cop. It was logical that a good cop like Long might blanch when describing a major bank robbery pulled off, in part, by a crew of high-ranking police officers. But this was Boston. Bobby Long's reference to the infamous Depositors Trust bank heist, in which cops and professional criminals teamed up to commit a major crime together, was a harbinger of things to come.

Long described how he observed Bucky enter a main office at the garage accompanied by Bulger and Flemmi. They were in there for a long time, with the door closed. For the jury, it was a tiny piece of connecting tissue to the government's opening statement, when prosecutor Kelly related how Barrett ran afoul of Bulger and Flemmi by allegedly withholding proceeds from a major heist. The jury knew how this story ended: with Barrett being chained to a chair, then shot in the head and buried in the basement of the Haunty.

Primarily, Bobby Long had been summoned to the witness stand so that the government could enter into evidence the surveillance videos from the Lancaster Street garage. Without sound, and mostly in black-and-white, clips of assorted videos were shown over the next ninety minutes, a trip back to a time when Whitey Bulger was in his prime.

The videos represented a who's who of Boston-area mobsters from the 1970s and 1980s. As ghostly images from long ago played on a monitor in the courtroom, Long narrated, pointing out the comings and goings of underworld figures such as Georgie Kaufman, the manager of the garage; Vinnie Roberto; Nicky Femia; Larry Zannino; Nick Giso; Bulger; Flemmi; and many others. It was a motley parade of gangsters, many of them slovenly men from the working class seemingly unconcerned about their physical appearance. That is, all except for one person: Bulger.

Forty-nine years old at the time, Whitey was lean and neatly dressed in every video. Mostly, he favored tight-fitting jeans that were pressed with a crease down the front of the legs. He wore tight T-shirts that showed off his physique. While others in the videos were shown talking and gesticulating in the Neapolitan manner, Bulger was contained and controlled. He looked like a prince: a man, touched by vanity, who saw himself as a cut above the rest.

Another notable feature of the videos—uncommented upon by

anyone—was that for thirty-three years they had sat in an evidence vault somewhere in the U.S. attorney's office. Finally, in 2013, here they were being dusted off and used for the first time, the restoration of an investigative narrative that was abruptly aborted in June 1980. As with most of the unseemly corruption-related revelations in the trial, the task of revealing why these surveillance videos were never put to good use would fall on the defense team and take place during cross-examination.

"Good morning, Lieutenant," said Jay Carney, in an overly solicitous tone of voice that, in a court of law, often meant something ruthless was about to take place.

"Good morning, Mr. Carney," said the witness.

With both hands on the podium, Carney launched into a series of questions the answers of which he knew before he asked them, questions about basic law enforcement procedure when launching an operation like the Lancaster Street garage investigation.

The Q&A continued in this vein, Carney speaking slowly and methodically, Long answering as if he were on automatic pilot. They both knew where this was headed. The defense lawyer was leading Long to the moment where his investigative team had enough probable cause to apply for legal authorization to plant a bug. Long got approval from his supervisor, Colonel Jack O'Donovan, a legendary figure in the state police. The next step, before applying to a federal judge, was to obtain the approval of the state's top organized crime prosecutor.

"Now," asked Carney, "in the course of doing this, did you approach Jeremiah O'Sullivan for assistance?"

At the mention of O'Sullivan's name, Hafer stood up: "Objection."

"Grounds, Counsel?" asked Judge Casper.

"Beyond the scope. Relevance."

The judge thought about speaking further on the matter out loud, but instead said, "I'll see counsel at sidebar."

The lawyers huddled off to the side with the judge, away from the jury so they could not be heard.

The sidebar process is a staple of American jurisprudence, an opportunity for both sides to discuss a point with the judge that, by its very nature, might become prejudicial if it were to be discussed in open court. Sidebars can be tedious for a jury and public observers; they interrupt the flow of the proceedings and give the impression that something important is being withheld from the public, which, in this case, was true.

"Where are you going with this?" Judge Casper asked Carney, with the court stenographer nearby recording every word.

The defense lawyer explained how he would question Lieutenant Long about O'Sullivan, chief of the federal New England Organized Crime Strike Force. It was Carney's understanding that, in his request for approval from O'Sullivan, Long told him specifically that he did not want the FBI to know about the bug, telling O'Sullivan that he did not trust them. "And O'Sullivan said, well, the FBI would have to be involved." So Long and his team decided to go around O'Sullivan and instead seek as their cosigner a prosecutor from the Suffolk County District Attorney's Office. They did get approval, and the bug was secretly planted in the garage. Almost immediately, the bug was compromised. Somehow, the gangsters knew about the bug almost before it was planted.

Said Carney to the judge, "I will ask Lieutenant Long if he conveyed knowledge of the bug to many people or rather kept it in a very tight circle. And I expect he'll say he kept the knowledge of the bug to a very select, handpicked group of people that he trusted. I'll ask him if, to his knowledge, John Connolly had any knowledge of the bug. I expect he'll say no. Did he tell John Morris [Connolly's supervisor] any information about the bug? I expect he'll say no. And then I'll ask him, so the only person in federal law enforcement who would have known about the bug was, to his knowledge, Jeremiah O'Sullivan."

"And how is this relevant?" asked the judge.

"Because it suggests that O'Sullivan may have been the person who led to the compromise of the bug."

The prosecutor jumped in: "Anything that O'Sullivan said to Long is hearsay. This entire line is well beyond the scope of direct [examination], and it's not relevant."

The discussion continued, and it was animated. For the defense, it was a major point. In terms of detailing the range of the corrupt conspiracy that had enabled Bulger, it was crucial: Carney was attempting to throw out a broad net, and the biggest fish he hoped to entangle was the late Jeremiah T. O'Sullivan.

Only in recent years had it emerged that O'Sullivan, with his impeccable and imposing reputation as a fierce crime fighter, had quite possibly been the Man Behind the Curtain in the Bulger saga. When he passed away in 2009 at the age of sixty-six, his role in having protected Bulger and Flemmi was not fully known. Though he had been served with a subpoena to appear at the Wolf hearings back in the late 1990s, he was exempted from testifying when he suffered a stroke that allegedly prohibited him from speaking. In later years, he gave no interviews nor ever attempted to fully explain his motives.

In his time with the Strike Force and later as U.S. attorney in Boston, O'Sullivan made some enemies. He could be self-righteous in the manner of New York's Rudolph Giuliani, another crusading federal prosecutor during this same era. Over the years, through hearings and trials and the accounts of participants, it became clear that O'Sullivan was far more central to the DOJ's relationship with Bulger and Flemmi than he had ever been willing to admit publicly.

To the defense, O'Sullivan was the Wizard of Oz, and since he was dead and not around to defend himself, he was a convenient target. Much could be implied about his actions; he served as an attractive receptacle for any conspiracy theory the defense could imagine.

Carney was fully aware of the importance of O'Sullivan to their defense. If, at this early stage in the trial, he were shut down by Judge Casper in this attempt to make O'Sullivan a relevant factor in the case, the prospects for laying out the defense he and his co-counsel had in mind would be severely disabled.

Hafer also seemed to understand the importance of the moment. "I reiterate, this is not relevant, Your Honor," he said forcefully to Casper. "It does not go to this witness's credibility, does not go to any material issue."

"Yes," said Judge Casper, "it's beyond the scope. I'm not going to allow it to go any further."

Carney did not take no for an answer; he continued to argue in favor of establishing O'Sullivan as a primary co-conspirator.

"I made my ruling," said the judge.

Walking back toward the podium to continue his cross-examination of the witness, Carney couldn't help but look defeated. His shoulders were slightly slumped, and, as he resumed his questioning of former state trooper Bobby Long, his voice was meek. His strategy for steering the evidence in a direction that would illuminate the defense he had in mind had been strangled in the crib. It was going to be a long trial.

THOMAS J. FOLEY was another retired statie with a tale of woe to tell. Whereas Bobby Long had seen his three-month-long investigation of the Lancaster Street garage fall prey to sabotage from within Boston's law enforcement fraternity, Foley entered the courtroom with the hope of fulfilling a dream deferred. The dream was to put away James Bulger for the rest of his natural life; the deferral was the consequence of a creeping realization, years ago, that the system to which he had taken an oath of service was riddled with corruption and deceit.

Fred Wyshak, the prosecutor who stood to lead Foley through his direct examination, had an interesting task. As with Trooper Long, Foley had realized over time and with mounting dismay that his attempted investigation of Whitey Bulger was sabotaged by the FBI and the U.S. attorney's office. But Wyshak had nothing to gain by going over this with the witness. Since he worked for the U.S. attorney's office, it was not in Wyshak's interest, or the interest of the case, to wallow in past transgressions of the very office for which he plied his trade. The entire subject was a land mine to be avoided. In many ways, it was a crystallization of the main difficulty that the prosecutors had: how did they convict Bulger without collaterally tarnishing the reputation of the system they represented.

On the witness stand, Foley projected the same aura of integrity for which he had become known in his years as a state trooper. He was Irish American, a redundancy that would become more evident as the trial progressed. There were an unusually high number of Irish American cops and agents in Boston, which sometimes made the trial of Bulger and his mostly Irish American gang seem like a donnybrook between contrasting sides of the Hibernian identity.

Foley had sensitive blue eyes and spoke in a calm, soothing tenor. He had the look and demeanor of a Catholic priest, another profession in which he might have found himself dismayed or disillusioned by the failings of an institution to which he had pledged his undying loyalty. Foley had been, until his retirement in 2004 at the relatively young age of fifty, a devoted officer of the law, but more than that he seemed like a virtuous man forever doomed to smack up against the baser impulses of his own tribe.

"Good morning, Colonel Foley," said Wyshak.

"Good morning," answered the witness.

It was an unusual moment for both men. More than two decades earlier, Foley, along with prosecutors Wyshak and Kelly, had initiated the criminal case against Bulger that brought them all to this courtroom. Now, here they were, paunchier and grayer, like participants in an old-timers' game, still willing to take the field and assume the roles of player and teammate.

The main reason Foley had been called as a witness was to introduce some key pieces of evidence. In 2000, Foley was part of a team that had confiscated a huge cache of weapons that belonged to Bulger and Flemmi's criminal organization. It was Wyshak's intention to initiate the introducing of the weapons into evidence as soon as possible, but first he had a few items he needed to tend to with his witness. One was a recitation of Foley's career in the area of organized crime, so that he could be recognized by the court as an expert witness on the subject. The other thornier item was to put out on the table the fact that Foley had coauthored a book about his pursuit of Bulger, titled *Most Wanted: Pursuing Whitey Bulger, the Murderous Mob Chief the FBI Secretly Protected.*

Like many who had been drawn into Bulger's orbit and later wrote a book about it, Foley had embarked on his venture in publishing at a time when it looked as though Bulger would never resurface. The idea that he would have to explain his book in a court of law was, at the time, likely a distant concern. As with Pat Nee, Kevin Weeks, and others who published Bulger-related memoirs, Foley had taken the opportunity to unleash years of frustration on the page. He was not, apparently, concerned about burning bridges.

Of the FBI, Foley wrote in *Most Wanted*, "I have never known any other organization, or any individuals, where what they said and what they did had so little to do with each other." Foley broadened his critique to include what he called "the feds," a symbiotic partnership between the FBI, the U.S. attorney's office in Boston, and the Justice Department, which seemed determined to shut down local efforts to bring Bulger to justice:

The feds stymied our investigation of Whitey, got *us* investigated on bogus claims, tried to push me off the case, got me banished to distant barracks, phonied up charges against other members of the State Police, lied to reporters, misled Congress, drew in the president of the United States to save themselves, nearly got me and my investigators killed.[2]

Foley had used *Most Wanted* to get things off his chest. In the courtroom Wyshak sought to minimize the book, asking in an offhand manner, "Did you also write a book?"

"Yes, I did," said Foley.

"You didn't write it, right? Somebody else wrote it?"

"I was—I had somebody I collaborated with, yes."

"What's the book about?"

"It's about the investigation into the activities of James Bulger."

"It's fair to say it's a story about your career?"

"Yes."

"How much editorial control did you have over the book?"

"Some editorial control, not total."

"Were there some things in the book that you disagreed about?"

"Yes."

And that was the extent of Wyshak's inquiries about the book. Quickly he moved on to the detailing of Foley's storied career; a series of questions to establish Foley's bona fides as an expert on the subject of organized crime in the Greater Boston area (duly stipulated by the judge); and, most important, his investigative uncovering and acknowledgment in court of the Bulger gang's vast arsenal of weapons.

The handguns, rifles, machine guns, knives, numerous rounds of ammunition, and many other accoutrements of the gangster life had been found in a small guesthouse located directly behind a house occupied by Steve Flemmi's seventy-five-year-old mother. The house was located in South Boston, at 832 Third Street, a half block away from the Haunty.

---

[2]Thomas J. Foley and John Sedgwick, *Most Wanted* (New York: Simon & Schuster, 2013), p. 12.

Colonel Foley pointed out that Flemmi's mother's house, and the stash of weapons that adjoined it, were located directly next to the house of state senate president William Bulger, Whitey's brother.

The fact that various murders, the stashing of guns, and criminal summit meetings had all taken place within a few hundred yards of Senator Billy Bulger's house had been reported in many courtroom accounts, newspaper articles, and books leading up to this current trial. For those who had been following the Bulger saga, it no longer qualified as a shocking revelation. But for the jury listening to the testimony of Trooper Foley, it must have been the beginnings of an understanding of just how insidious was the Bulger gang's nexus of power, with murders, guns, mothers, and powerfully connected political siblings all tied together in a neat little bow on one neat little street in Southie.

And then there was the arsenal itself. Wyshak began by entering into evidence and having the witness describe a series of photos taken inside the guesthouse. The house had been built expressly to serve as a place for criminal summit meetings and the hiding of weapons; there was a secret room behind a wall. Inside that room were row upon row of gun racks; shelves for the storing of ammunition, silencers, knives, brass knuckles, etc.; hooks for the hanging of bulletproof vests, hoods, and masks.

Foley noted that the investigators had expected to find more. They later learned from Flemmi's son and also from Kevin Weeks, both of whom were by then cooperating with the investigators, that months before the raid most of the arsenal had been moved from the guesthouse to another hiding place, in Somerville. So Foley and his team also descended on that location and discovered an even larger arsenal hidden in the cellar of a nondescript working-class house at 62 Dane Street.

Over the next two hours, on a flat-screen monitor in the courtroom, Foley was shown and identified photo after photo of guns and ammunition. "That's an M-1 military rifle. . . . That's a pump-action shotgun with the butt removed. . . . That's a semiautomatic pistol. . . . That's a Thompson submachine gun. . . . That's a derringer. . . . That's a Smith & Wesson revolver. . . . That's a black bag containing multiple clips of ammunition that would be inserted into the automatic weapons. . . ." Along with the guns was a staggering array of criminal supplies: "That's a camouflage mask with a fake beard on it. . . . That's a U.S. Navy gas mask. . . . That's a Boston police officer badge found inside a safe. . . . That's a double-edged military knife. . . . That's a stiletto. . . ."

On and on it went. Either Bulger and his gang had planned on going to war with the U.S. military, or this arsenal was the manifestation of a fevered imagination. More than a collection of items gathered together out of necessity, this accumulation of criminal hardware seemed to be the realization of a fetish. Because the Winter Hill gang was a collection of mobsters, they collected guns, knives, and brass knuckles. If their métier had been sex, their secret hiding places would have been filled with whips, chains, leather masks, and dildos.

HANK BRENNAN HAD been biding his time, waiting patiently to cross-examine Foley. As soon as Wyshak said, "I have no further questions, Your Honor," Brennan was on his feet and at the podium.

"Sir, you wrote a book last year, did you not?"

Foley took a deep breath; he had to know this was coming. "Yes, I did."

"You signed your name to that book?"

"Yes, I did."

"And, sir, when that book was published, you said that that book was the truth?"

"Yes."

"In fact, not only did you say it was the truth, you promoted the book, didn't you?"

"Yes, I did."

Brennan proceeded to list all the Boston-area television shows that the retired trooper had been on to promote the book. "At no time when you were on your speaking tour and you sold your book to members of the public, did you say there were inaccuracies in your book."

"I am unaware of any inaccuracies in the book," said Foley.

Now Brennan was off and running; he noted that Foley had earlier that day, in his direct testimony, said that he had been limited in his efforts to exert editorial control during the writing of the book. "Were you suggesting that there were things that were truthful that you didn't want in the book, or things that were in the book that were inaccurate?"

"There were some things in the book that I was unaware of the information, that it was the other writer who had gone out and did that background on it, and some of the information he came up with I questioned as to where he got it."

Foley was now on a slippery slope, having to defend his book and also disown aspects of it at the same time.

Once Brennan had thoroughly exhausted the book as a topic by which he could make Foley squirm and sweat, he moved on to another subject: Pat Nee.

Already in the trial, Nee's name had come up numerous times. Nee's concern that Bulger's defense lawyers would do their best to drag him into the trial had been confirmed as early as Carney's opening statement, when the lawyer suggested that the case against Bulger had been partially created as a concoction of John Martorano, Flemmi, Weeks, and Pat Nee, all of whom, in the interest of saving their own necks, had "added a little Bulger" to their fictitious retelling of gangland Boston. Both in courtroom testimony and in the books they had written, they were out to pin everything on Whitey.

Foley had never met Pat Nee and was only tangentially aware of his role in the Bulger gang, so Brennan was required to get at Nee by way of Foley's dealings with another Winter Hill mobster—John Martorano.

Back in the 1990s, Foley, along with Wyshak and Kelly, had played a crucial role in negotiating Martorano's cooperation deal with the government. At the time, Martorano, through his lawyer, made it clear that, yes, he would agree to testify against FBI agent Connolly, Bulger, and assorted other targets of the investigators, but he had a list of people that he refused to offer evidence against.

"One of those people was his brother, Jimmy Martorano?" asked Brennan.

"Yes," said Foley.

"And another person was Pat Nee?"

"I had no specific conversation with [Martorano] about Pat Nee."

Brennan was not about to let it drop. He established that Foley, in his interrogations of Martorano, was told about numerous murders involving others, including Nee. He asked, "As a state police officer, you have a right and you also have a duty to pursue charges against people who are alleged to have committed murder in the state of Massachusetts, right?"

"Yes."

"And you had information from John Martorano that Patrick Nee had committed murder, was a murderer, didn't you?"

On this, Foley pushed back, making it clear that he and the investigators were at the time gathering information on the targets of their investigation, people they could actually indict. It was not a "fishing expedition."

"Did you ever encourage the district attorney of Suffolk County to prosecute Pat Nee for the information you had from John Martorano that he was a murderer?"

"We did not have enough information to prosecute Pat Nee at the time."

"John Martorano told you that Pat Nee was involved in murders with him, didn't he?

"Yes, he did."

"And you've based prosecutions on John Martorano's testimony, haven't you?"

To this Wyshak objected, and the judge sustained the objection.

Brennan moved on, but throughout the afternoon he kept coming back to the subject of Nee. It must have seemed odd to the jury and some observers of the trial that so much time was being spent on someone who was not a subject of the trial nor would be called as a witness by the government. Even Foley became annoyed: "We were working on this case, which was taxing us for years, Mr. Brennan. If I sent my people off in every direction we had a lead on, this case would never have been completed. . . . I didn't have information that Pat Nee killed nineteen people. I had information that Stephen Flemmi and James Bulger killed many people, and that's where I was focusing on, because that's where I had to put our resources. I would have loved to have taken out Pat Nee and anyone else he named. But, realistically, Mr. Brennan, it was not going to happen. . . . I took what I could get to get to the bottom of what had been going on here for a long time."

"So when I ask you did you make any efforts to take the information Mr. Martorano gave to you to develop a case against Pat Nee, what is your answer, sir?"

"I've answered it several times."

Again, Wyshak objected, and the judge encouraged Brennan to move on.

LATE THAT AFTERNOON, I spoke with Pat Nee on the phone. "How am I doing?" he asked.

I didn't know how to tell him that his name had been a persistent presence at the trial. "If I tell you," I said, "it may ruin your evening."

"Well, it can't be any worse news than what I already received this morning."

"What's that?" I asked.

"A subpoena," said Nee.

That morning, while Nee was at the L Street Gym in Southie, where he occasionally worked out, a process server walked into the gym and said, "Are you Patrick Nee?" Nee said yes, and the man served him with a notice to appear in court on a date yet to be determined. He was being called as a witness by Bulger's defense lawyers.

"What are you going to do?" I asked.

We both knew that the main issue was going to be an allegation commonly made in Boston, but nowhere in any criminal indictment, that Nee had partaken in at least one double murder with Bulger. This particular killing had not yet come up at the trial, but it would; it was one of the counts with which Bulger had been charged.

"I'll take the Fifth," said Nee. "Only smart thing to do in this situation."

We talked for a bit about the likelihood of whether or not the judge would allow the defense to drag him into court. The only way that was likely to happen was if Bulger did actually take the stand and name Nee as an accomplice in various crimes, including murder.

"Do you think he'll take the stand?" Nee asked.

I reiterated what I had said before: "No, I don't. But who knows? He might. But then the question is, who would believe anything he has to say?"

We went back and forth on the subject for a few minutes. Nee felt the noose tightening around his neck. Officially, he wasn't yet involved with the trial, but, as with so many people caught up in the legacy of the Bulger era, he was being slowly dragged into it by the ghosts of the past.

3

THE O'BRIEN FAMILY BUSINESS

LIKE MANY AMERICAN municipalities, especially those located on the eastern seaboard or those in the Great Lakes region of the Midwest, the city of Boston had a thriving organized crime underworld rooted in the "glory days" of Prohibition. The Bulger era of the 1970s and 1980s was a direct descendant of this period in which criminal rackets first became deeply embedded in the political and social structures of urban life. The era of illegal booze was a boon to bootleggers and gangsters, many of whom made fortunes and, just as important, accumulated power through corrupt relationships with politicians and men in law enforcement. Money generated from Prohibition-era rackets fueled the underground economy, and the alliances that were established helped to create a criminal protocol that remained in place for the next seventy or eighty years.

As a working-class port city with an organized labor force of dockworkers and teamsters, and numerous classic ethnic neighborhoods, Boston was typical of the kind of U.S. city where organized crime found its footing. New York, Cleveland, Philadelphia, Chicago, and other cities had a similar system of criminal rackets. After Prohibition was repealed in 1933, much of the criminal activity transitioned into labor racketeering, loan-sharking, gambling, cargo pilferage, and an assortment of other crimes.

By the postwar years of the 1950s, gangsterism remained pervasive. The Kefauver hearings in 1950 and 1951 had, for the first time, dragged assorted mobsters in front of a committee composed of U.S. senators. Televised live, the hearings were the first time the American public would see gangsters claim their Fifth Amendment privilege to not testify, on the grounds that they would be incriminated. A decade later, the McClellan hearings, chaired by Robert F. Kennedy, shed a harsh light on the Mob's involvement in trade unions such as the International Brotherhood of Teamsters, which had more rank-and-file members in the New England area than anywhere else in the country.

As a mob city, Boston was typical, but it was also unique, at least in one respect. The dominant mafia family in Boston was not based in the city. It was based in Providence, Rhode Island. The Patriarca crime family, led by Raymond Patriarca Sr., held sway over much of New England, with mafia crews and affiliated criminal organizations throughout Massachusetts, Rhode Island, and Connecticut. This left something of a vacuum in Boston. There was a mafia entity in the city, based in the Italian North End, and they were powerful—but no more powerful than various other criminal crews of non-Italian gangsters that existed throughout the city's many neighborhoods and suburbs.

The Boston underworld was decentralized, a series of interconnected suburbs and villages (Somerville, Charlestown, Southie, etc.) each with its own set of local criminal crews. The ethnic makeup of these crews was surprisingly diverse. It was not uncommon for major crimes to be pulled off by crews composed of Italians, Irish, Greeks, Portuguese, etc. One major example of this was the infamous Brinks robbery, which took place on January 17, 1950, and netted $2.7 million in cash and securities. At the time it was the largest heist in U.S. history, and it was conceived of and pulled off by a raffish, mixed-ethnic crew of hoods from around Boston.

It was into this eclectic criminal universe that Jim Bulger arrived on the scene in the mid-1950s.

Born September 3, 1929, Bulger had grown up in the Old Harbor housing projects in South Boston. He was one of six children that included two younger brothers, Jackie and Billy. Bulger's father was a longshoreman whose prospects for work were greatly hindered by the fact that he had lost an arm during an industrial accident. The Bulgers were lower middle class, one step removed from poverty by the fact that they lived in government-subsidized housing. Book authors and amateur psychologists have speculated that Jim Bulger, the oldest son and in many ways the family's provider, was driven to a life of crime by witnessing his father's disability and feelings of inadequacy as the breadwinner of the household.[1] Whatever the reason, Bulger got into crime at a young age. It started with "tailgating," or pilferage off the back of delivery trucks in Southie, and advanced to bank robbery. Bulger would later claim in conversations with his associates that he robbed seventeen banks while in his early twenties. He became part of a crew that was willing to travel if need be to make a score.

In May 1955, Bulger took part in a successful robbery in Pawtucket, Rhode Island. A few months later, he did another, this one in Melrose, a suburb north of Boston. A month after that, in November, he and a partner drove all the way to Hammond, Indiana, where they hit the Hoosier State Bank and netted $12,612.28.

Bulger always brandished a gun in these robberies. In Indiana, after forcing the bank's customers to lie on the floor, he was reported to have announced, "We aren't going to hurt anyone. But we have to make a living. Dillinger did."

Immediately after the robbery, Whitey drove back to Boston. Soon he heard that his partner in the Indiana robbery had gotten pinched and squealed on him. Whitey figured it was a good time to make himself scarce. With his girlfriend at the time, a platinum blonde from Southie, he packed a car and headed out for a long drive that took them to Reno, San Francisco, Salt Lake City, and Chicago. It was a trip similar to those he would make in later decades with two other platinum blondes, Teresa Stanley and Catherine Greig, cross-country jaunts in which the confines of Southie were left behind and Whitey became a speck of dust in the wide-open spaces of the American landscape.

By early 1956, Bulger was back in Boston, but he was still hiding from the law. Because his former bank robbery partner had ratted him out to the FBI, there was a warrant out for his arrest. Eventually, based on a tip from another informant, federal agents caught up with Bulger; he was arrested outside a nightclub in Revere, a city north of Boston.

---

[1] In the lead-up to the Bulger trial, two biographies of the gangster were published with mostly identical biographical information: *Whitey: The Life of America's Most Notorious Mob Boss*, by Dick Lehr and Gerard O'Neill; and *Whitey Bulger: America's Most Wanted Gangster and the Manhunt That Brought Him to Justice*, by Kevin Cullen and Shelley Murphy. All of these writers were at one time reporters for the *Boston Globe* who covered the Bulger story.

The agent who put the cuffs on Bulger was H. Paul Rico, an ambitious young FBI investigator whose primary focus was organized crime. Already, at the age of thirty, Paul Rico was known to have a special talent for cultivating underworld informants. He was exceedingly polite with Bulger, which, in later years, Whitey would remember. Rico would later become a crucial figure in recruiting Bulger as a Top Echelon Informant for the FBI.

With his former partner having already ratted him out, Bulger confessed, he said, so that his girlfriend would not be charged as an accomplice. His understanding was that his confession to a series of bank robberies would also result in a lighter sentence, which did not prove to be the case. The judge sentenced him to twenty years behind bars.

Just twenty-five years old at the time, Bulger was shipped off to a maximum-security federal facility in Atlanta, Georgia, and later transferred to Alcatraz, the legendary prison located on a rock in San Francisco Bay, and eventually to the federal penitentiary in Leavenworth, Kansas.

Bulger's prison years were notable for at least two factors. In Atlanta, he was informed by prison authorities of a highly covert program that was being offered to inmates as a way to cut time off their sentence. The program was called MK-ULTRA and was being administered by the CIA. MK-ULTRA was an experimental project involving lysergic acid diethylamide, or LSD, commonly known as acid. Inmates would take the drug on a regular basis and submit to observation by psychiatric doctors working for the agency. As part of this program, Bulger received injections of LSD once a day for nearly eighteen months. His reactions to the drug were documented.

In later decades, Bulger would claim that he suffered from the aftereffects of this experiment through intense headaches and persistent insomnia.

In the 1980s, during his years of power in the Boston underworld, Bulger told associates Kevin Weeks, Pat Nee, and others that if he were ever arrested, he would use his involvement in this government program and the resulting psychological aftereffects as a defense in court.

The other notable feature of Bulger's years in prison was his use of contacts in "legitimate society" to enhance his position within the criminal justice system.

While in the Atlanta penitentiary, Bulger wrote letters to Father Robert

Drinan, a Boston-area priest who had become friendly with Billy Bulger at Boston College, where they both went to school. A Jesuit scholar, Drinan had vouched for the Bulger family in presentencing reports. Later in the 1960s, Drinan became famous for his activism against the U.S. war in Vietnam, but at the time he was dean at Boston College Law School. "I thank you from the bottom of my heart for all the help you have given me," Bulger wrote to Drinan.

With brother Billy acting as his advocate, Whitey had other friends in high places to lean on. Billy was friendly with the most powerful political figure in Southie, John W. McCormack, a U.S. congressman who would rise from majority leader to Speaker of the House while Whitey was in prison. Bill Bulger implored McCormack to do whatever he could for his brother; McCormack wrote letters and made calls to the director of the Bureau of Prisons in Washington to check on Whitey's status and arrange prison visits for the Bulger family.

There was nothing outwardly untoward in Bulger's utilization of a well-placed priest and a political figure to help out his situation. It was the classic Irish way of doing things: you scratch my back, I scratch yours. In letters from prison, Whitey had promised both of these men that once he was out he would turn his life around and follow a more enlightened, crime-free path. These two pillars of the community may have helped out simply as a favor to Bill Bulger, a fine young man who in 1960, while Whitey was away, was first elected to the state House of Representatives.

Whitey spent nine years in prison. He came out physically the same person—five foot seven inches tall, lean and taut at 178 pounds—but he was, at age thirty-four, a changed man. Hardened by incarceration, with a heightened sense of how to utilize and manipulate enemies and friends alike, he was determined to never return to the penitentiary.

He was released on March 1, 1965. As a condition of his parole he had to have a job, so brother Billy got Whitey a position as a custodian at the Suffolk County Courthouse. Before long, Whitey stopped showing up for work, though he still collected his paycheck. Within a matter of months, he was reestablishing ties with fellow criminals, only now he was no longer interested in being a roving outlaw in the John Dillinger mode and wanted to be more of a mobster with roots in the city's organized crime structure.

THE CRIMINAL LANDSCAPE in Boston had changed since Bulger was sent away. The decentralized nature of the city's underworld, which had once made it possible for criminals of differing ethnicities and localities to work together in relative harmony, had ruptured in a big way. Whitey returned to Boston in the midst of one of the most murderous gang wars ever experienced in the United States.

The war began in the early 1960s with a seemingly endless series of shootings and killings between two criminal factions based primarily in the city's northern neighborhoods. A group of gangsters from Charlestown, led by the McLaughlin brothers (George, Bernie, and Punchy) and the Hughes brothers (Stevie and Con), took on the Winter Hill gang, based in nearby Somerville.

Long before Bulger had any association with the Winter Hill Mob, they existed as a collection of bookies, loan sharks, bank robbers, and hustlers based in an area of Somerville known as Winter Hill. They were led by Buddy McLean, a longshoreman who was a legendary figure in Boston's criminal rackets. Known for his ability to keep the peace and make money for his associates, McLean was drawn into the war with the Charlestown crew against his better judgment. There was no real point to the war, other than a grudge: at a party on Labor Day 1961, George McLaughlin had insulted the wife of a member of the Winter Hill crew, and the war was on.

For nearly a decade, dead bodies turned up all over Boston. Men were stabbed, shot, bludgeoned to death, and mutilated. At the time, few of these killings were seriously investigated by police. They were mob hits carried out by professional hit men, the kind of murders that, if they had been vigorously investigated, would likely only lead to more dead bodies.

In February 1967, *Life* magazine published a six-page spread about the Boston gang wars, focusing on the McLean-McLaughlin feud, which had resulted so far in forty-three mob-related murders in and around the city. Under the headline "The thugs squash each other, one by one," they printed two full pages of mug shots of the victims. By the time the *Life* article appeared in print, Buddy McLean had been murdered, as had the Hughes brothers and all of the McLaughlin brothers, except for George, the man who started it all. In 1965, he was convicted of murder and sentenced to life in prison.

By the time Bulger resettled in Boston, the gang wars had spread and opened a new front in Southie.

By then, Bulger had hooked up with a criminal crew known as the Killeens, after the gang's leader, Donald Killeen, and his two brothers, Kenny and Eddie. Bulger was making money as muscle for the Killeens, who ran a sizable bookmaking and loan-shark operation in the neighborhood. The Killeens became embroiled in a territorial dispute with the Mullen gang, a venerable collection of thieves and wharf rats that had been cofounded by Pat Nee, who in 1967 returned to the neighborhood having served four years in the U.S. Marine Corps, stationed for two of those years in Phu Bai, Vietnam.

Like the McLean-McLaughlin war, the Killeen-Mullen gang war had many casualties. Whitey Bulger, for one, knew that no matter how lucrative his association with the Killeen brothers might become, he would never have control in Southie as long as the Mullen gang was in operation. Together with Billy O'Sullivan, another bodyguard and hit man for the Killeens (and no relation to Jeremiah O'Sullivan), Bulger came up with a takeover scheme. His plan involved the killing of Paul McGonagle, who, along with Pat Nee, was a prominent member of the Mullen gang. Many years later, Kevin Weeks described it in his book:

> One day while the gang war was still going on, Jimmy was driving down Seventh Street in South Boston when he saw Paulie driving toward him. Jimmy pulled up beside him, window-to-window, nose-to-nose, and called his name. As Paulie looked over, Jimmy shot him right between the eyes. Only at that moment, just as he pulled the trigger, Jimmy realized it wasn't Paulie. It was Donald, the most likable of the McGonagle brothers, the only one who wasn't involved in anything. Jimmy drove straight to Billy O'Sullivan's house on Savin Hill Avenue and told Billy O, who was at the stove cooking, "I shot the wrong one. I shot Donald." Billy looked up from the stove and said, "Don't worry about it. He wasn't healthy anyway. He smoked.

He would have gotten lung cancer. How do you want your pork chops?"[2]

Bulger's mistaken-identity killing of Donnie McGonagle had more severe repercussions for O'Sullivan than it did for Bulger. On March 28, 1971, O'Sullivan was gunned down in the street outside his house. The killing of Billy O. was perpetrated by a trio of Mullen gang members, including Paulie McGonagle, who saw it as revenge for his brother's death.

The killings went back and forth. It was during this era that Bulger and Pat Nee became archenemies. As rival gang members from the same neighborhood, they were pitted against one another. One night outside the Mad Hatter, a bar located downtown, they traded gunfire in a wild shootout. Another time, the Vietnam vet had Bulger literally in his sights in an alleyway in Charlestown, but chose not to pull the trigger.

Nee had met Bulger a few times and didn't care for him; he thought Whitey was uptight and pretentious. But he also knew that Bulger was "connected." He had a brother who was a rising political star in Southie. You couldn't kill someone like Bulger without there being repercussions of some kind.

The murder of Billy O. spooked Bulger, who went into hiding for a while out on Cape Cod. By the spring of 1972, he ventured back into South Boston, only to have his world rocked by another high-profile gangland hit. This time it was his boss, Donald Killeen, who was shot multiple times in a car outside his house in suburban Framingham. The murder was carried out by the Mullen gang.

Though it could be argued that by taking out high-ranking members of the Killeen gang, including the top man, the Mullens were winning this war, there were casualties on both sides. As a result, in late 1972, Pat Nee arranged for a major summit meeting between various criminal factions in the city.

The meeting took place at Chandler's, a bar located at the corner of Dartmouth and Chandler streets, in the city's South End. Partly owned by the Martorano brothers, John and Jimmy, Chandler's was not exactly

---

[2]Weeks and Karas, *Brutal,* p. 186.

a dump, but it was raffish, a typical early-1970s saloon for workingmen, hoodlums, and off-duty cops. Present at the meeting was Howie Winter, a highly respected mobster who had taken over as a leader of the Winter Hill gang after Buddy McLean was murdered. Also present was Joe Russo, a Mafioso who represented the Italian North End, with direct links to the all-powerful Patriarca crime family in Providence. Pat Nee represented the Mullen gang. And Bulger was there as a representative of what was left of the Killeen gang, which was now led by Kenny Killeen.

In many ways, the gangsters were doing Bulger a favor by including him in this meeting. With Donald Killeen dead and his gang under siege, Bulger was not dealing from a position of strength. But he did have a card to play.

In the interest of creating an underworld business atmosphere that was more conducive to making money than the endless gang hostilities that benefited no one, the mobsters were looking to establish a power-sharing framework. Kenny Killeen had been making noise that he would never willingly turn over the Killeens' lucrative bookmaking business without a fight. If Bulger could neutralize Kenny Killeen and bring what was left of his organization into the fold, he would be granted an equal spot at the table.

The meeting at Chandler's lasted nearly eight hours. The mobsters ate and drank and worked things out until they reached an agreement. They didn't know it at the time, but this multi-ethnic collection of hoods had just taken part in a gangland summit meeting that would dictate the direction of organized crime in Boston for decades to come.

A few weeks after the meeting at Chandler's, clad in a bathrobe and slippers, Kenny Killeen stepped out onto the patio of his South Boston apartment on Marine Avenue overlooking Dorchester Bay. From somewhere in the distance, a sniper fixed Killeen in his sights. At the moment the sniper fired, Killeen bent down to pick up his morning newspaper. The bullet hit the balcony's wrought-iron railing and splintered into pieces that hit Killeen in the wrist and torso. Killeen went down, but as it turned out, the balcony's wrought-iron railing saved his life.

One week later, Kenny Killeen was limping past a car at City Point when a voice called out, "Hey Kenny." Killeen turned to see the familiar face of Whitey Bulger in the passenger-side window; he was holding a gun. "It's over," said Bulger. "You're out of business. No future warnings." The car drove off.

Having handled what was left of the Killeens put Whitey in good standing with his newfound partners. More and more, they all began hanging out in a garage in Somerville called Marshall Motors, which became the headquarters of the new and improved Winter Hill gang. Bulger was not by any means the leader, but he had survived a gang war and emerged as a member of the underworld's ruling elite.

The bloodshed did not end. Decades later, Pat Nee would look back on the meeting at Chandler's and the alliance with Bulger as a big mistake. Often, when asked if he had any regrets about his life of crime, Nee would say, "Yeah. I wish I killed Whitey Bulger when I had the chance."

IN THE RACKETS, there are the leaders, and then there are the rank and file, the men whose responsibility it is to keep the money flowing via an array of criminal businesses. Throughout the post–World War II years and into the 1970s, among the most solid of moneymaking rackets was bookmaking, a mainstay of the criminal life since at least the late nineteenth century.

Bookmaking was a remnant of the era of the gentleman gangster. As part of a larger organization that backed an individual bookie with money and muscle, the bookmaker was a gangster, but invariably he was not himself a man of violence. Bookies were often guys with personality, people who were popular and well liked. After all, a prospective bettor could place a wager with any number of people; usually, he chose a particular bookie because he had a good personal relationship with that person.

In Boston, the best bookies were often Jewish. The common mythology was that Jews had a head for money, and out of that stereotype began a tradition that lasted for generations.

The profession of bookmaking was on display in day three of the Bulger trial. On this day, Whitey wore a gray Henley, a color that made him look withered and old. From among the various monocolored Henleys that he wore throughout the trial, this was the one that, if he had a stylist, would have been banished from his wardrobe.

The defendant hardly seemed to notice as an unassuming man in his midseventies, wearing a sport coat, was led into the courtroom and put on the witness stand. "Do you swear to tell the truth, the whole truth, and nothing but the truth?" asked the bailiff.

"I do," said the man.

"You may be seated."

Prosecutor Fred Wyshak ambled to the podium. "Good morning, sir. If you can please state your full name and spell your last name for the record."

"James J. Katz. K-A-T-Z."

"You have used another name in the past, have you not?"

"Yes."

"And why is that?"

"The government gave me a new name in the witness protection program."

White-haired and slight of build, Jimmy Katz was clearly not from the strong-arm side of the rackets. He was a bookmaker, a Jew with a head for numbers, and, as such, had once been a valuable cog in the machine.

As with all the former criminals who would take the stand at the Bulger trial, Katz had to first explain how he had come to be a witness. Back in the early 1990s, he had become a target of the original case against Bulger initiated by Wyshak, Kelly, and state trooper Foley, among others. The state police had bugged Heller's Café, a diner in Chelsea that turned out to be a meeting place for some of the most accomplished bookmakers in the Boston area. Katz was caught on tape and approached by the investigators. He refused to cooperate and was later indicted on RICO and conspiracy charges.

In March 1993, when called in front of a grand jury, Katz took the Fifth. He was cited for contempt of court and thrown into jail. While in jail, Katz learned that his rabbi in the bookie business, Chico Krantz, had cut a deal with the government.

Chico Krantz was a legend in the business, the biggest bookmaker in the Boston area. Katz got his start with Chico and had worked for him as a subagent, or street bookie, until 1978, when Chico had a parting of ways with the Winter Hill Mob. Word that Chico was cooperating with a federal investigation and was being held at a secret location—soon to be entered into the witness protection program—was a game changer for Katz.

He hinted that he might be willing to cooperate with investigators.

In January 1994, Katz was once again called in front of a grand jury. All these years later, seated on the witness stand at the Bulger trial, he remembered it as if it were yesterday. Asked Wyshak, "And at that time, in January of 1994, was your testimony truthful?"

"Mostly not," said Katz.

"Were you afraid?" asked Wyshak.

"Yes."

"Why were you afraid?"

"I knew that the people I would testify against, they could even reach me in jail."

"And who were those people you were concerned about?"

"The Bulger group, Stevie and Whitey."

The prosecutor and the witness seemed to share a wry familiarity—and for good reason. It was Wyshak who, twenty years earlier, had sought to elicit Katz's cooperation in front of the grand jury. It wasn't that Katz lied on the stand so much as that he offered very little; his testimony did not meet the legal standard of "substantial assistance." Katz was thrown back in jail and told that the eighteen-month sentence he received on the contempt charge would be added to his four-year sentence on racketeering and conspiracy charges. His home was seized under forfeiture laws and his wife and kids were made to fend for themselves.

Katz stewed in jail for a year, then contacted Fred Wyshak and told him he was ready to spill everything he knew. After consulting with his lawyer, he signed a cooperation agreement with the U.S. government.

It turned out to be a good deal for Katz. He and his family were given new names and identities and relocated to an undisclosed location. In exchange, Katz testified in front of another grand jury—this time, in a manner that was beneficial to the U.S. attorney's case. He named a total of fifty-eight racketeers he did business with as a member of Bulger's organization. Then, in January 1995, Whitey went on the run. Katz never did have to testify in open court. The Bulger case was stillborn. Katz and Wyshak parted ways for twenty years, until now.

Methodically, Wyshak proceeded to do what he had intended to do back in the early 1990s: use Jimmy Katz as a guide through the venerable world of bookmaking. Katz was a suitable guide, his answers short and pithy. Whatever fear he had years ago about taking the stand and testifying against Bulger had dissipated. The passing of the years made Katz nostalgic and relaxed. "I was a bookmaker," he said. "I'd take bets on sporting events," adding with a tinge of pride, "A bookmaker may be able to give a customer credit, so there's no trail for the government to [demand taxes] on winnings and losing."

"When were you a bookmaker?"

"From 1971 to 1993."

"During that period of time, what options did citizens of Massachusetts have to place bets on sporting events?"

"There was none, other than if you lived in Las Vegas."

"So if you wanted to bet on sports, you had to bet through a bookie?"

"That's correct."

As Katz saw it, he was part of a business that provided a public service, a venerable business with a predetermined underworld structure that had been refined over the years through trial and error—which meant beatings, extortion, killings, legal challenges, and other means designed to make bookmaking a profitable venture for all but the inevitable—and necessary—sad sack on a losing streak.

Katz broke it down for the jury: A bettor placed a wager with a bookie, using Vegas odds. The bookie charged a 10 percent commission on the bet. Often, a bookie worked as an agent for a larger bookmaker. The agency covered the bookie's winnings and losings. If a bookie's customer won big, the agency would cover the payment, but the bookie was placed on "makeup," meaning he had to pay that money back out of future proceeds. Often bookies would "lay off" bets with other bookies to protect themselves from taking a big hit.

Mostly, bookies made their money off the vig, or interest, from each bet.

What made the business potentially perilous for the bookie is that there were many ways to cheat; it was a cash business with no records to speak of. A bookie might misrepresent the odds on a game, to his advantage. He might simply underreport his take to "the office." He might engage in "skimming," taking a little off the top. In bookmaking, there were a million ways to get cute. Said Katz, "I mean, in those days, if you wanted to cheat, that was up to you, but if they caught you, you were going to get into trouble one way or another."

"What do you mean by 'trouble'?"

"You could wind up in a hospital, let's put it that way."

Katz explained how, in the late 1970s, there was a seismic shift in the business of "making book" in Boston. After decades of bookmakers acting as free agents, being allowed to align themselves with whomever they wanted, a new mandate was being enforced by the Winter Hill Mob. Whitey Bulger and Steve Flemmi had begun to corral all of the nonaffiliated bookies in town and demand that, if they wanted to stay in operation, from now on they had to pay "rent," or tribute, on a weekly or monthly basis to the Winter Hill Mob.

The bookies didn't like it. It was a thug move by Winter Hill, a strong-arm tactic. If you didn't pay rent, you'd be put out of business. Your family would be threatened. You might be murdered in a most violent manner, so as to serve as an example to others who considered defying the dictates of the Mob.

There were benefits to being aligned with Winter Hill. If a bookie were having a problem with a customer or a fellow bookie, the Winter Hill Mob would take care of it. Since bookies were not normally men of violence, they needed protection. Bulger, Flemmi, and their crew served as the muscle behind the entire operation.

According to Katz, Bulger and Flemmi's blunt demands for rent caused discord and dissension among the bookmakers, though it would not have been wise to voice those concerns too loudly. Chico Krantz, for one—Katz's mentor and benefactor—resented the new arrangement. His dissatisfaction would eventually lead to his becoming a rat and entering into a cooperation agreement with Wyshak and company.

For some, the alliance with Winter Hill was profitable. Katz was able to link up with other bookies, both as an agent and as a partner. His business diversified. He became a loan shark, or shylock, lending money to people at usurious rates. Katz became partners with Joe Yerardi, a Winter Hill guy, who along with being a major bookmaker also controlled the concession on poker and vending machines in bars and diners all around the city. And through the association with Winter Hill, the bookies developed what seemed like a fail-safe way to launder their proceeds, always a problem for bookmakers.

At Heller's Café in Chelsea, a Winter Hill guy named Michael London ran a check-cashing business. If a bookie had a good, solid customer who could only pay by check, he could make out a check to "John Hancock" or "Babe Ruth" and the bookie would bring the check to Heller's.

"And when you brought the check with Babe Ruth's name on it to Michael London," said Wyshak, "wouldn't he say, 'You're not Babe Ruth'?"

"No, he had no qualms about taking the check."

"And how would you endorse that kind of check?"

"I would sign, Babe Ruth."

At this, for the first time since the Bulger trial began, laughter rippled through the courtroom. Even Bulger smiled.

Katz admitted that in his long career as a bookie he had probably laundered millions of dollars through this check-cashing scheme.

It was the plight of the bookmaker to occasionally get arrested and charged with a crime like wire fraud, or violating bank laws, or some other financial offense. In his career, Katz was busted numerous times.

"Have you ever been convicted for any crime other than gaming-related offenses?" asked the prosecutor.

"No," said the witness. "That's been my life."

On cross-examination Katz began to chafe a bit under the questioning. Up until then, his time on the witness stand had mostly been a pleasant trip down memory lane, but the defense counsel had other matters in mind.

"While you were in prison," asked Carney, "did you learn about Federal Rule of Criminal Procedure number thirty-five?"

Katz contended that he had never heard of this rule by name, but, on further questioning, he admitted that he was well aware of the parameters of the statute. Virtually every incarcerated criminal knows about Rule 35. It is the federal statute that provides for a reduction of prison time if a criminal rats on another criminal and provides the feds with "substantial assistance." Said Carney, "The determination about whether you give substantial assistance to the prosecutor is a decision made exclusively by the prosecutor, correct?"

"I was advised of that," answered Katz.

"It's not a decision made by a jury, is it?"

"No, it's not."

"It's not even a decision made by a judge?"

"Right."

"It's made by the prosecutor, correct?"

"Correct."

The implication was clear: prosecutors Wyshak and Kelly had for years had Katz eating out of their hand, telling them what they wanted to hear to get out of prison and stay out.

Carney concluded his cross-examination by getting Katz to admit that in all his years as bookie for the Winter Hill Mob, he met Jim Bulger exactly one time, and that no words were ever spoken between them.

RICHARD "DICKIE" O'BRIEN was another bookie from the old days. But unlike Jimmy Katz, he met Bulger often and considered himself lucky to be alive to talk about it.

Before O'Brien took the stand, Judge Casper was informed by the prosecutors that the witness was nearly eighty-five years old, and that, normally, he was wheelchair-bound and on an oxygen tank. He would be testifying without his tank, it was believed, and everything should be okay, but the judge, in her role as custodian of the courtroom, needed to be informed about these things. It was another reminder that the events of the Bulger years were distant, and that many witnesses at the trial would be in their golden years, using their last remaining breaths to rat out Whitey and exculpate their sins before going to wherever it is that deceased racketeers go when they die.

On the stand, O'Brien was shown surveillance photos from the Lancaster Street garage, the remnants of state trooper Bobby Long's aborted investigation from long ago. O'Brien was shown the photos so that he could identify Bulger and Flemmi, but in one of the photos Flemmi was seen talking with a man in his forties, matinee-idol handsome, with a full head of black hair and impressive posture.

"Who is that man to the right of Mr. Flemmi?" asked the prosecutor.

O'Brien looked at the photo, blinked his eyes, as if he were conjuring memories and images from some faraway place. "That's me," he said.

Thirty-five years later, O'Brien still had the hair, though it was now white. A generation removed from the dangers of the street, he was affable and almost wistful as prosecutor Zach Hafer led him on a journey deep into the hidden corridors and musty closets of his distant past.

He was a graduate of Quincy High School, class of 1947. After joining the army and serving one year in Korea during the war, O'Brien returned to Massachusetts and, utilizing the GI Bill, attended Boston University. That didn't last long. O'Brien dropped out of college and went to work with his father.

"And what did your father do?" asked Hafer.

"He was a bookmaker," said O'Brien.

O'Brien's father had been a bookmaker since the 1930s. Though it was an illegal profession, he never hid the fact that he was a bookie. Cops, politicians, newspapermen, little old ladies—they all placed bets with the neighborhood bookmaker. To Dickie O'Brien, it was the family business, and with his friendly demeanor and old-world sense of honor, it was inevitable that he would follow in his father's footsteps.

By the late 1950s, when Dickie became involved, his father had his own office in Boston's South End. Dickie worked as an agent for his father, who in turn worked under a big-time bookmaker named Bernard McGarry. O'Brien explained his role: "As an agent, you go out on the street and get play. People want to gamble, they'll bet numbers, they'll bet horses, they'll bet sports, and they'll call it into their office, which my father and I ran the office. And you saw to it that if they won, they were paid promptly. . . . Now, the payment arrangements would be if the agent had a winning week with sports and horses, he would receive fifty percent of what he won. The other fifty percent would go to the office. So we would collect what was coming to us, and of course the agent would keep what was coming to them. . . . Now, the office obligation was to pay whatever the agent lost. So say that he lost five thousand for the week. Well, the office paid that five thousand. That five thousand would be set aside, called makeup. Until the agent won that five thousand back and got the office even, he wouldn't receive a commission. So it was an unwritten law that you stayed with an office, the office paid a certain amount of money to keep you in business. You stayed with them, and you tried to work it off."

O'Brien recalled an incident in 1960, after Bernard McGarry was arrested and his father suffered the first in a series of heart attacks that would lead to his retirement. Dickie O'Brien was feeling like a man without a country, or at least a man without a financial benefactor to help sustain the O'Brien family business. That's when a friend of O'Brien said, "Well, I can help you solve that problem."

"How?" asked O'Brien.

"I have a good friend in Providence. Mr. Patriarca."

On the witness stand, O'Brien smiled. He was recapturing the moments of his prime, when the blood pumped vigorously in his veins, the money was good, and he had friends in high places.

Zach Hafer, the prosecutor, was not yet born at the time of these events. "Mr. O'Brien," he asked, "did you go to Providence at some time in the early 1960s?"

"Yes, I did. To meet Mr. Patriarca."

"Who did you understand Raymond Patriarca to be in the early 1960s?"

"A gentleman who was the head of the Mafia in New England."

O'Brien described his meeting with Patriarca in Providence as if it were a high point in his career, akin to having had a sitting with the pope. Apparently, that day Jimmy Hoffa, president of the Teamsters union and a friend of the Mob, had been arrested. "They were all rather up in arms about that," remembered O'Brien. "And so he said to me, Mr. Patriarca"—always "Mister" with O'Brien, never "Raymond"—"Lookit, he said, you go to Boston, it's already been arranged for you to meet with the Angiulo people, which I did."

And so, thanks to the Godfather of New England, O'Brien was assigned as an agent with the Angiulo brothers in the North End. He was officially with the Mafia now.

These were heady days for the O'Brien family business. They lasted for eight years, until late 1968, when Gennaro "Jerry" Angiulo, boss of the Italian North End, was indicted on a murder charge. The main witness against Angiulo was Joe Barboza, scourge of the Boston underworld. Angiulo would eventually beat this case, but in the meantime, the indictment put their bookmaking operations on hold. This meant that Dickie O'Brien was once again without an office to lay off his action. But he was a well-known bookie by now, with friends all over town. He did business with Italians, Irish, African Americans, it didn't matter. O'Brien was able to function as an independent operator and keep his business afloat for the next five years.

And then he received a message from a fellow bookie that there was someone in South Boston who wanted to speak with him.

O'Brien had heard of Whitey Bulger, though they had never met. He was aware that Bulger was affiliated with the Winter Hill Mob, which at the time was headed by Howie Winter. It behooved anyone in the Boston underworld who was engaged in criminal business to know all the players and with whom they were connected. O'Brien was not against the idea of hitching his wagon to a larger organization, always a beneficial arrangement for a bookmaker, because you could lay off bets with the office. So when Dickie was called to a meeting at a bar in Quincy called Kimberly's, he did not hesitate to go.

Asked the prosecutor, "What was the purpose of this meeting at Kimberly's in the early 1970s?"

"Well, the thing was, being independent, the news got out, naturally, it's street talk, that I was independent, and Mr. Bulger wanted to talk to me. . . . He said to me, You're by yourself—in so many words, I don't remember the exact wording, but, in so many words, he said, You're by yourself now. I said, Yes. And he said, Well, I think you should be with us. And I said, Well, I had been with the North End. He said, Forget the North End. If you want to be in business, you're with us. And that was put down by law."

"Did you know who he was associated with?"

"Well, I heard about them, because their reputations always preceded them."

"And what was that reputation?"

"That they were very capable."

"And by 'capable' what do you mean?"

O'Brien explained it as if he were talking with someone who spoke a different language. "Well," he said, "they had somewhat of a gang war in South Boston and people were shot, and Mr. Bulger ended up on top, so you can draw your own conclusions."

This meeting at Kimberly's had taken place not long after the momentous mobster summit meeting at Chandler's, where Pat Nee, Howie Winter,

John Martorano, and others had agreed to an arrangement where Bulger had officially become a member of the Winter Hill Mob. At the time of that meeting, Bulger's gang, led by the Killeen brothers, was in the process of being wiped out. Bulger was at that meeting almost as a favor; the Winter Hill Mob was willing to cut him in partly because he was a guy with an up-and-coming brother in state politics. Somehow, on the street, Bulger had turned this into a story of how he won the gang war. It was an early manifestation of Bulger's talent for burnishing his own legend.

Dickie O'Brien felt as if he had no choice: if he did not go into business with Bulger and his crew, he would be put out of business.

It turned out to be a bad arrangement. Unlike the Mafia, the Winter Hill Mob had no interest in establishing an office so that bookies under their umbrella could lay off bets. The only interest that Winter Hill had was in collecting rent from the bookies, numbers runners, loan sharks, and other racketeers within their domain. "It was like night and day," said O'Brien. "With the Angiulos, they were very businesslike. There was no rent being paid. You gave them your business, layoffs, and they took the opportunity to win or lose. But when it was Stevie and Mr. Bulger, they weren't interested in that. They were interested only in the rent."

O'Brien made payments of two thousand dollars a week to Bulger, usually hand-delivered in a brown paper envelope at Triple O's Lounge or the South Boston Liquor Mart, two locations that served as headquarters for Whitey's criminal operations in Southie.

One thing the Winter Hill Mob was good at was threatening people. From the stand, O'Brien recalled an incident when he had an agent named George Labate who worked for him. "He had run up a considerable amount of makeup. We paid thousands of dollars to keep him in business. For some reason known only to him, he sort of disappeared. He stopped calling, he didn't inquire about doing business, and it was rather—something that's a no-no in the business. You don't get paid from somebody for thousands of dollars and then just throw your hand up and walk away. And we were told he was now with some other office."

When Bulger heard about the problem O'Brien was having with Labate, he arranged for a meeting and told Labate that he better show up.

Asked Hafer, "So what happened at the meeting?"

"Well, we were sitting at the bar having coffee, and Mr. Labate was sitting there next to me, and Mr. Bulger was standing on the side, and John Martorano, I believe, was sitting there. And I think it was Mr. Bulger who said to him, 'Were you treated right by Dickie? You were treated good?' And Labate says, 'Yes, I was.' He said, 'Then what are you doing? You owe him a big amount of money in makeup, but you stopped calling him. He doesn't have a chance to make his money back.' Labate said, 'Oh, I know that isn't right. I will take care of that. But when I do get through with making my makeup, I have my own ideas about what I'm going to do with my business. I'll take care of that and go my own way.' So Mr. Bulger came over to him and said, 'You're going to go your own way?' Labate nodded, and [Bulger] said, 'You know, we have another business besides bookmaking.' Labate says, 'What's that?' Mr. Bulger said, 'Killing assholes like you.'"

The quiet of the courtroom was pierced by the sound of a cackle. It was the defendant, Bulger, amused by the memory.

On cross-examination, Jay Carney picked up on the killing-assholes-like-you story. It was Carney's intention to tactfully posit the suggestion that the incident was a case of Bulger fulfilling the role he had promised O'Brien he would when they became partners. "Didn't [he] tell you, 'You wear the white hat and we wear the black hats'?"

"That's true."

"Did you understand that to mean that you could go about your bookmaking services and deal with customers or agents or others and just be the person who took the bets? That's why you wore the white hat, right?"

"True. Plus the fact that I was brought up by a father being a bookmaker, and he said, Just treat people the way you like to be treated, which I did."

Dickie O'Brien, gentleman bookmaker, was kept on the stand all day—a Friday—and made to return the following Monday. Mostly, his testimony involved fond recollections of the only business he had ever known. Even his memories of being cajoled and extorted into business arrangements with more powerful criminal entities in the city were presented by the witness as the price of doing business. Perhaps they were stories he told his grandkids of skirting the edges of a potentially perilous trade, and living to tell about it.

On Monday, however, near the end of his time on the stand, the testimony veered into an area that was not so pleasant for O'Brien.

In the early 1990s, when the investigation led by Wyshak, Kelly, and Colonel Foley of the state police began to zero in on the bookies, they put the squeeze on O'Brien. Indictments were coming down left and right. O'Brien figured he might be next to be indicted, so he left the state and moved to Florida with his wife and the two youngest of his six children. But he didn't give up his bookmaking business. He left the entire business in the able hands of his oldest daughter, Tara, who had recently graduated from college. Thus bookmaking as the O'Brien family business passed into a third generation. As Dickie explained it, "I had to have somebody I could rely upon and trust. There was a lot of money involved with [the business], you know, and there were certain unsavory characters that you had as agents. It could cost you a lot of money."

In Florida, O'Brien reconnected with John Martorano. It happened purely by chance. Dickie's wife was at a PTA meeting in Florida, and she bumped into Martorano, who had been on the lam since 1979.

O'Brien had always liked John Martorano. He once borrowed one hundred thousand dollars from Martorano to keep afloat the sports betting side of his bookmaking operation. Whereas Whitey was remote and scary, and Steve Flemmi was just plain scary, Martorano struck O'Brien as a fun-loving guy who was in the rackets to have a good time. Of course, O'Brien also knew that Martorano was a stone-cold killer, a professional hit man. To have a friendship with anyone in the underworld—much less someone who was known for settling business disputes by making bodies disappear—involved a certain amount of what psychoanalysts refer to as a "primitive ego defense mechanism." In the rackets, this mechanism—also known as denial—was often the elixir that made friendships possible.

O'Brien kept in regular contact with his daughter back in Boston. Through her, he heard that bookmakers in New England were being rounded up and arrested. He heard that Chico Krantz, the legendary Boston bookmaker, had "flipped" and was cooperating with the federal investigation. Already Tara O'Brien had been approached by someone affiliated with the Winter Hill Mob and told they'd heard a rumor that she and her father were about to "flip." Tara was scared.

At the same time, in Florida, Dickie O'Brien was told by Martorano that Steve Flemmi was coming down to see him. Flemmi needed to be reassured that O'Brien was not going to cooperate with the feds.

Dickie trusted Martorano, but he did not trust Flemmi. So he called his daughter and told her, "I'm going to a meeting with Steve Flemmi. If you don't hear from me in ten hours, I want you to contact the FBI office in Florida."

Tara O'Brien was terrified. She'd heard the rumors that Flemmi was a psycho killer who had murdered at least two women, including Debbie Davis, one of his ex-girlfriends.

O'Brien had his meeting with Flemmi. He reassured the mobster that neither he nor his daughter would be cooperating with the feds.

The O'Briens survived that meeting with Flemmi, but afterward, things got worse. A few months later, both Dickie O'Brien and his daughter were indicted. They were charged with various crimes, including RICO violations. Tara was facing eighteen to twenty-four months in prison under mandatory sentencing guidelines. As a result, she suffered a nervous breakdown and was hospitalized in a mental institution.

From the witness stand, O'Brien's guilt was palpable. "I was the cause of that," he said. "I took her to the hospital, and every day I went to visit her."

"You were a loving father," noted Carney.

"I always tried to be."

Back in 1994, the investigators—Wyshak and Kelly—put pressure on O'Brien. They used the fact that his daughter, now hospitalized, would be sent away to prison for two years unless he cooperated with them.

The O'Brien family business had become the O'Brien family nightmare. To spare his daughter prison time, O'Brien cut a deal with the feds and became the very thing that Steve Flemmi had feared he would become: a rat.

AFTER DICKIE O'BRIEN finished with his testimony, the trial was adjourned for the day. I closed up my laptop computer, gathered up my belongings, and headed down to the cafeteria for a cup of java. There I ran into Steve Davis.

Steve, age fifty-five, was the brother of Debra Davis, who, according to the indictment, had been strangled to death by Bulger, her body later disposed of by Bulger and Flemmi. Just fifteen months apart from Debra in age, Steve had been close to his sister. He had tried to warn her about Flemmi, who was twenty-six years her senior and a man notorious for his womanizing and violent tendencies.

I first met Steve Davis nearly a year earlier, when I interviewed him for an article I wrote for *Newsweek* leading up to the trial. In the wake of Bulger's capture, Davis had been a ubiquitous figure on the news and in the local media. The reporters liked Steve because he was voluble and emotional; he wore his hatred for Whitey on his sleeve. And he was always good for a punchy quote. When I first interviewed Davis in the lobby of Boston's Seaport Hotel in June 2011, he did not disappoint, saying of Bulger, "I'm an eye-for-eye kind of guy; I'd do to him what he did to my sister. . . . They talk about closure. Fuck closure. Give me fifteen minutes with Bulger and I'll give him closure. I'll shoot him in the fuckin' head."

In subsequent interviews at pretrial court proceedings and in phone conversations, I got to know Steve better. I noticed that after the initial jolt of Bulger's arrest and the raw emotional viscera it had unleashed, Steve calmed down somewhat. Not that his desire to see Bulger punished had diminished; it had not. But Davis became savvier about how to present himself in the public domain. He wore designer glasses and, on occasion, a silk suit, his hair styled and his snow-white goatee neatly trimmed.

In the courthouse cafeteria, I asked Steve how he was doing. "It's emotional," he said. "I never thought I would see this day. Just hoping to get through it and that it goes the way we want it to go."

I knew from previous conversations with Steve that what drove him to follow through on his commitment to maintain a presence at each and every stage of Bulger's legal demise was the memory of his mother, Olga Davis, who died in 2008 at the age of seventy-eight. Way back in the early 1980s, when Debra Davis first disappeared, Steve Flemmi, the co-perpetrator, had come to Olga Davis in tears, saying that he had no idea what had happened to her. At first, Mrs. Davis didn't know what to believe. She reached out to the FBI, which proved to be a mistake, since the FBI at that time was protecting both Flemmi and Bulger. When they told her to forget Debra, that she now had nine other children to worry about, she took it as a threat and cut off contact with the FBI.

I asked Steve if it was bittersweet facing the prospect of finally getting justice in his sister's murder with his mother not here to see the day.

"She would have been here every day of the trial," said Steve, his eyes moistening.

Back in 2003, the Davis family, along with the families of Deborah Hussey and Louis Latif, two other murder victims of Bulger and Flemmi, filed a joint lawsuit against the FBI and DOJ on the theory that the government had aided and abetted Bulger and Flemmi in the murders of their loved ones. The family of murder victim John McIntyre filed a similar suit. Later, more wrongful death lawsuits were filed, this time by the families of additional murder victims Brian Halloran and Michael Donahue. The fact that the government vociferously contested these cases rather than reach settlements with the families had done much to create a feeling of ill will in Boston toward the DOJ.

In the case of Debra Davis, the government had even argued that the family did not deserve to receive damages because she had bedded down with a known criminal, a claim that federal district judge William G. Young ruled to be "unfounded and baseless . . . a meritless defense with the sole purpose of embarrassing" the Davis family.

In 2005, the McIntyre family received a favorable judgment of $2.3 million, the money to be paid by U.S. taxpayers. The Halloran and Donahue families won their cases and were awarded, collectively, $4 million in damages, but the rulings were overturned on appeal, on the grounds that the families had filed their suit after the statute of limitations had expired. The Davis family, along with the families of Hussey and Latif, won their case. They received judgments ranging from $335,000 to $1.3 million. Again, the government appealed the ruling, but in 2012 the financial judgment was upheld.

The millions of dollars did not bring back the murder victims of Whitey Bulger. Steve Davis lost his sister in the most brutal manner imaginable, and then the murder was partially covered up for years by the FBI. Bulger and Flemmi went on to kill others, including Deborah Hussey, Flemmi's twenty-six-year-old stepdaughter.

"You think the government would be ashamed of its behavior in this case," said Steve, "but there are things they are still covering up to this day."

As Steve and I continued to chat about new details that might come to light during the trial, we were approached by someone I knew to be a producer from CNN. "Sorry to interrupt," said the producer. "Steve, we need to get you on camera."

The CNN crew had been highly visible since the proceedings began. Producer and director Joe Berlinger, an award-winning filmmaker, was shooting a documentary on the trial for the network and had been interviewing many of the family members of Bulger's victims, including Steve Davis.

"Sorry, I gotta run," said Davis. "We'll talk later." I watched Steve hustle off with the producer, his life now a series of interviews and business propositions that included a book deal and a movie deal about his life in the shadow of Bulger and Flemmi.

Later, I exited the courthouse and came upon what had become the usual media constellation outside the front entrance. Steve was off to one side being "miked up" by the CNN crew. A gaggle of one hundred or so media people were assembled behind a rope, with handheld cameras and boom microphones extended toward three standing microphones. At one of the mics was Tommy Donahue, who, like Steve Davis, had become a familiar representative of the victims' families. Donahue's father, Michael Donahue, was killed by Bulger when he offered a ride home to a man Bulger had targeted for death. Michael Donahue had been collateral damage. Young Tommy was four years old at the time of his father's death. Standing alongside Tommy Donahue was his mother, Patricia, age sixty-five, who had been waiting more than thirty years for closure in the death of her husband.

Next to the Donahues, waiting for an opportunity to speak, was Stephen Rakes, another familiar member of the Bulger survivors' club. Back in the 1980s, Rakes had been extorted by Bulger, who took over his South Boston Liquor Mart by threatening to have him killed. Rakes had also filed a civil lawsuit, given dozens of interviews to the media over the years, and become something of a local celebrity in Boston due to his past associations with the Bulger story.

Many of these people had been waiting decades for some form of justice against the notorious gangster who, at one time, had been so powerful that you couldn't speak ill of him in public without fear of retribution. Now they were almost tripping over one another to get before the cameras and have their say.

As the boom mics swung into position and the cameramen jostled with reporters to get a better view, Steve Davis and the others willingly played their role. Many of the media people knew them by name. They were asked questions about arcane matters of the law of which they knew nothing, but they attempted to answer, because that was expected.

Certainly these folks deserved to be heard, but I couldn't help thinking that the obsessive focusing on the families was becoming, like so much of the trial thus far, a compelling diversion from the big picture. The media needed the pathos of Steve Davis, Patricia Donahue, and the others because it put a human face on what was otherwise a dark tale about events that had happened long ago. There were few good guys in the Whitey Bulger story, and so the family members of Bulger's victims provided the human interest angle that made viable the media's coverage of a complex story.

It was telling that among the throng of reporters and filmmakers covering the trial, none had thought to seek out and interview someone like Joe Salvati. The argument could be made that Salvati—though he had been framed for a crime he did not commit, served thirty years in prison, and was the victim of a massive injustice—was not a victim of any crimes committed by Bulger. Factually, this was true. But within this argument were the seeds of what was becoming, in relation to the Bulger trial, a source of frustration.

In the courtroom, the prosecutors and the judge were engaged in an effort to protect the system from "outrageous allegations" on the part of the defense. At its worst, this represented a process of obfuscation, an attempt to keep the Bulger trial from becoming associated with the history that had helped to create Whitey. The activities outside the courtroom, with the media obsessively soliciting commentary from the family members of victims, had become part of that same diversion. Certainly, the family members had emotional stories to tell, but none of them were in a position to shed light on the historical circumstances that had sustained the likes of Barboza and Bulger and, ultimately, led to the deaths of their lived ones.

The narrative that was being buried inside the courtroom was being left equally unexamined outside the courtroom. Each day of the trial, with the concurrent layers of physical evidence and witness testimony, the likelihood that the full conspiracy would or could be revealed diminished with each banging of the gavel signaling the trial's adjournment for the day.

The anguish of the family members had become one more excuse for diverting attention from the full horror of the Bulger era.

4

DEMON SEED

IN THE CASE against Whitey Bulger, history was on trial. There were those aspects of history that had been cobbled together to form the RICO charges against Bulger, acts of crime both depraved and voluminous. But there was also the history that was being omitted; history that the jury would never hear about because the prosecutors and the court—meaning the judge—would do everything in their power to make sure it did not become a significant factor in the trial.

So far, this history had been successfully kept at bay. The witnesses, mostly elderly men with dwindling or selective memories, were there, ostensibly, to reclaim history, but it was history preordained by the DOJ. It was the desire of Wyshak, Kelly, and others in the U.S. attorney's office that had spent decades formulating the case that their version of history would appear so overwhelming and irrefutable that it would render irrelevant any larger picture of the Bulger saga. This was a strategy that, with the help of a compliant judge, seemed likely to rule the day.

For those who had followed the Bulger story for years, however, the unspoken history haunted courtroom number eleven at the Moakley federal courthouse.

The name Barboza had not yet been mentioned at all by the prosecution, and if Wyshak and Kelly had any say in the matter, it would stay that way.

Back in the mid-1960s, when Whitey Bulger was still a federal prisoner on Alcatraz Island in San Francisco Bay, Joe Barboza was in the process of turning himself into a criminal legend as notorious as Bulger would become decades later. Like Bulger, Joe the Animal was a product of his times. He maneuvered himself into a position of strength in the underworld through a mutually compromising covert relationship with the upperworld. The more nefarious this alliance became, the better it was for Barboza, because his handlers in the upperworld had a vested interest in making sure the true dimensions of this relationship were never known to the public at large.

With Barboza, as with Bulger, this relationship was highly beneficial for an extended period of time, until it wasn't.

Barboza was born June 20, 1932, in New Bedford, Massachusetts, the son of Portuguese immigrants originally from the city of Lisbon. Barboza's father was a middleweight boxer and his mother a seamstress. His life of crime began early, with robberies and assaults, and he was first imprisoned in 1950, at the age of eighteen. At the Massachusetts Correctional Institution in Concord, he met a number of underworld figures affiliated with the Patriarca crime family. Upon his release from prison in 1955, Barboza went to work for the Mafia as a bodyguard and thug while at the same time pursuing a career in boxing as a light-heavyweight contender. Fighting under the nickname "the Baron," he had twelve professional fights, winning eight, five of those by knockout.

Around New England, Barboza was known as a vicious thug. He was stocky and muscular, with a thick neck and an angular skull shaped like a watermelon. With less than an eighth-grade education, he was barely literate, though he liked to draw and would later show true talent as a sketch artist.

The Mafia in New England wasn't interested in his abilities as an artist, unless those skills could be applied to the art of murder.

Barboza was willing to kill people for money, and, while still in his twenties, he became known as a proficient contract killer for the Mafia. Because he was not Italian, he would never be a made member, though it was Barboza's dream, expressed to many of his associates in the underworld, that for him the Honored Society would make an exception and he would become the first non-Italian to be inducted. His Sicilian friends slapped him on the back and said, "Hey, you never know. Keep trying." Behind his back, his mafia friends referred to him as "the nigger."

His nickname "Animal" came about because he once bit a chunk of flesh out of a person's cheek during a bar fight. In later years, he admitted to having committed seven murders for the Mob, but he was believed to have killed many more, perhaps as many as twenty-six people.[1]

In the mid-1960s, Barboza found himself in the middle of the Boston gang wars. Although he officially worked for the Italians, he was also aligned with the Winter Hill Mob, which at that time was still led by Buddy McLean. Barboza is believed to have taken part in some of the era's most notorious killings, including the murders of Punchy McLaughlin and the two Hughes brothers, Stevie and Con.

The Boston underworld was a weird intersection of alliances born out of necessity, relationships that were a manifestation of the Machiavellian philosophy that the enemy of my enemy is my friend. Many of Barboza's closest associates during this period would later resurface as key players in the Bulger saga, including John Martorano, Steve Flemmi, and Flemmi's younger brother Vincent "Jimmy the Bear" Flemmi.

In March 1965—the same month that Whitey Bulger was released from prison and returned to Boston—Barboza, Jimmy the Bear, and others had decided to add another body to their ever-growing hit list. The target they had in mind was a low-level hood named Teddy Deegan.

For a hustler in the Boston underworld, the odds of stepping on somebody's toes were great. Deegan had murdered a hood named Anthony Sacramone, who was affiliated with the Winter Hill gang. Deegan was associated with the McLaughlin brothers in Charlestown, a competing faction. In the ongoing tit-for-tat of the Boston gang wars, Deegan having killed Sacramone meant that someone would be looking for revenge. Someone, in this case, was Barboza and Jimmy Flemmi.

Deegan also owed Jimmy Flemmi three hundred dollars, which, by the dictates of gangster logic, was further justification to use him as an example.

At the time, there had been many killings in the Boston underworld—so many that Barboza and Flemmi decided that, in the interest of protocol and self-preservation, they would first get approval for the Deegan hit from the North End mafia boss Jerry Angiulo.

---

[1] The book *Barboza*, by Joseph Barboza with Hank Messick (New York: Dell, 1975), is an entertaining though highly specious account of Barboza's career as a gangster. A more credible depiction of Barboza is to be found in *Animal*, by Casey Sherman (Boston: Northeastern University Press, 2013).

The Italians wanted nothing to do with the crazy war going on between the Winter Hill Mob and the Charlestown crew. At a meeting in the North End, Angiulo told Flemmi and Barboza, "You can't kill someone just because you had an argument with him." The boss told the two hoods that he would only sanction the hit if *capo di tutti capi* Raymond Patriarca gave his approval.

A meeting was set up for Barboza and Flemmi to convene with "the Office" in Providence. Barboza was excited; it would be his first face-to-face meeting with Patriarca, a big moment for someone who harbored dreams of becoming a made man.

They met the Godfather at Badway's Garage in the Federal Hill section of Providence. Raymond Patriarca showed up looking like exactly what he was: mafia royalty. He wore a lavish, tailored suit and had a diamond pinky ring that caught the light and sparkled.

The sit-down lasted forty-five minutes. Jimmy Flemmi made the case for killing Deegan. "He's a sneak, and I don't fuckin' trust him," he told Patriarca.

Later, the results of this meeting would remain in dispute. Patriarca insisted that he never authorized the Deegan hit but simply told the two killers that if they received approval from Jerry Angiulo, then they would have his approval. Flemmi and Barboza took this as a yes and began planning the hit.

After the meeting, Flemmi said to Barboza, "You didn't have much to say in there. What were you thinking?"

Said Barboza, "I was thinking how I could bite his finger and get that diamond ring."

What none of the men at the meeting in Providence realized was that the location where they met to discuss the killing of Deegan was bugged by the FBI's organized crime division. It was an illegal wire, known as a "gypsy wire," unauthorized by any court of law but fully sanctioned by Director J. Edgar Hoover.

There are multiple FBI memos, never revealed until many decades later, that show the FBI knew what was coming next. They sat back and let it happen.

It was a complicated hit for such an insignificant hood. On the night of March 12, 1965, Barboza, Flemmi, and four other gangsters traveled to Chelsea, where it was known Deegan and two others were to take part in the robbery of a finance company located inside the Lincoln National Bank. One of Deegan's partners was Roy French. Unbeknownst to Deegan, French was a traitor working in cahoots with Barboza and Flemmi.

The robbery was an inside job: a contact at the bank was going to leave an alleyway door open for Deegan and French to enter, where a couple bags of cash would be waiting for them to snatch. It was Barboza and Flemmi's plan to murder Deegan as he was in the midst of the heist.

Jimmy Flemmi was in the getaway car, with Barboza and two others acting as gunmen. The idea was for Roy French to shoot Deegan, but the killers were leaving nothing to chance.

Deegan was gunned down in the alleyway. The autopsy revealed that he had been hit with six bullets from three different guns.

On the night of the murder, the one Deegan accomplice who was not in on the killing was able to escape. Barboza and Jimmy the Bear heard that he was currently in the custody of police. Barboza was worried that this man would rat them out. He told the Bear that they might have to go on the run.

Jimmy the Bear smiled. It was then that he told Barboza not to worry, he had it covered. The Bear explained that for months he had secretly been meeting with an FBI agent named H. Paul Rico. The Bear was facing charges on another murder he'd done with Barboza, and Paul Rico had suggested to Flemmi that he could make those charges go away if he was willing to become an informant. Jimmy Flemmi had officially signed on as a Top Echelon Informant on March 12, the exact day that he and Barboza murdered Teddy Deegan.

The FBI was fully aware of what they were getting into with Jimmy Flemmi. On March 9, following Flemmi and Barboza's secretly recorded meeting with Patriarca in Providence, a memo was sent from the special agent in charge (SAC) of the Boston field office to Director Hoover. The memo stated, "[Jimmy] Flemmi is suspected of a number of gangland murders and has told [the informant] of his plans to be recognized as the No. One 'hit man' in this area as a contract killer. . . . Flemmi told the informant that all he wants to do now is kill people, and that it is better than hitting banks. . . . Informant said, Flemmi said he can now be the best hit man in the area and intends to be."

The memo further stated, "[Flemmi] is going to continue to commit murder, but informant's potential outweighs the risk involved."

Hoover authorized Jimmy Flemmi's role as a Top Echelon Informant knowing that he was a homicidal maniac whose stated goal was to become the biggest hit man in Boston.[2]

IN AN AUTOBIOGRAPHY published in 1975, allegedly written by Barboza with the aid of crime writer Hank Messick, the Animal claimed that he was stunned to hear that Flemmi was an informant. Being a rat for the feds was a violation of the underworld code, a betrayal punishable by death. At least, that's what the gangsters told each other. In truth, informants were common.

In the days of the Boston gang wars, paranoia was running high. Gangsters were constantly looking for an edge, and one way to be "in the know" was to have contacts in law enforcement, an exchange of information that could possibly save your life. You scratch my back, I scratch yours, was a philosophy steeped in treachery, because it meant the criminals were also leaking information to the lawmen, though no one in the underworld was supposed to know.

According to Barboza, Jimmy Flemmi suggested to the Animal that he too should become an FBI informant. It was the smart thing to do.

Barboza later learned that Flemmi's brother Stevie had also signed on with Paul Rico as a Top Echelon Informant.

Barboza was reluctant. He met Paul Rico but did not yet know the agent well enough to feel he could be trusted. The Animal needed reassurance, which he was to receive a few months later, in October 1965.

For many months, Barboza and his gangster affiliates had been looking to kill members of the Charlestown faction, most notably the McLaughlin

---

[2]The circumstances surrounding the murder of Teddy Deegan and details of the FBI's culpability in the matter remained largely unknown until 2001, when the U.S. House Committee on Oversight and Government Reform sought to access documents as part of a congressional investigation into the FBI's use of criminal informants. That investigation resulted in a report titled "Everything Secret Degenerates," which is the most complete picture that exists of the bureaucratic corruption surrounding the use of Barboza and the Flemmi brothers as informants.

brothers. Bernie McLaughlin had already been whacked, and a hit team that included Barboza, Steve Flemmi, and Cadillac Frank Salemme, who was Flemmi's partner, had been hunting for Punchy McLaughlin. On one occasion, they had come close to nailing Punchy. In August 1964, in the parking lot of Beth Israel Hospital, Steve Flemmi and Salemme, disguised as Hasidic rabbis, snuck up on McLaughlin and opened fire with a sawed-off shotgun. Punchy was hit in the side of the face with buckshot, but before the two hit men could finish the job a potential witness stumbled upon the scene; Flemmi and Salemme were forced to flee. McLaughlin survived the hit.

On another occasion, the hit team of Flemmi and Salemme ambushed McLaughlin while he was driving on a rural roadway near Dedham, Massachusetts. Flemmi and his crew pulled up alongside Punchy and opened fire. They blew off part of McLaughlin's hand, which later had to be amputated. Spewing blood, Punchy veered his car onto the wrong side of the road and escaped, then went into hiding.

Ever since, the hit men had been looking for yet another opportunity to take out Punchy, but he was nowhere to be found.

Special Agent Rico had become conversant with the Flemmi brothers, Salemme, and assorted other Boston hoodlums. In his quest to recruit new informants, he occasionally socialized and drank at known mobster locations and became entangled with various players.

Rico had a personal beef with the McLaughlins, especially George, Punchy's brother, who had been picked up on an FBI gypsy wire calling him a "fag." George drunkenly alleged that Rico had been involved in three-way sex with FBI director J. Edgar Hoover and his close associate Clyde Tolson, who was rumored to be Hoover's lover. It was an absurd accusation, but Rico, a family man with four kids, took umbrage. When Rico received information about where George McLaughlin was hiding out (many Boston gangsters seemed to be on the lam or in hiding during this period), he took matters into his own hands.

According to Steve Flemmi—who had at the time only recently signed on as a Top Echelon Informant—Rico and his FBI partner, Special Agent Dennis Condon, came to him one day with an extraordinary request. Decades later, Flemmi revealed the nature of this request to federal investigators Wyshak and Kelly. The information was recorded in Flemmi's confidential file, known as a DEA-6:

> RICO asked FLEMMI for a throwdown handgun. He explained that the agents were about to arrest George MCLAUGHLIN, who had been an FBI Ten Most Wanted fugitive since March 1964. RICO added that the arresting agents were planning on shooting MCLAUGHLIN as they took him into custody. The agents were going to plant the gun on a dresser next to MCLAUGHLIN and claim that [he] had reached for the weapon. The agents were planning on shooting MCLAUGHLIN and claiming self-defense. FLEMMI told RICO and CONDON to return a short while later, at which time he supplied them with a .38 caliber handgun. After MCLAUGHLIN's uneventful arrest, RICO explained to FLEMMI that there were five agents involved in the arrest, but that while four were in agreement to kill MCLAUGHLIN, the group was uncertain about a fifth agent on the arrest team, and the plan was dropped. FLEMMI added that RICO never returned the firearm to him.

Rico was aware that Barboza, Flemmi, and Salemme had been hunting for George McLaughlin's brother, Punchy, with no luck. As an agent who was constantly on the lookout for ways to cultivate potential informants, Rico saw an opportunity. Again, from Flemmi's file:

> FLEMMI stated that he was standing on the sidewalk on Dudley Street, when H. Paul RICO walked up to him. . . . RICO told FLEMMI that Punchy MCLAUGHLIN could no longer drive since his hand had been amputated. So he had begun taking the bus every morning from the Spring Street, West Roxbury T station, in Pemberton Square. Rico said that prior to this, MCLAUGHLIN's girlfriend had driven Punchy directly to the courthouse. RICO then said he wouldn't be working the following day and was going golfing. FLEMMI recalled that RICO then took a make-believe golf swing.

Flemmi took the hint; Rico was telling him that tomorrow, while he was out of the office, would be a good day for Flemmi and his team to take out McLaughlin.

On the morning of October 20, 1965, Punchy McLaughlin stood with a handful of commuters waiting for the bus at the exact spot identified by Rico. He held in his hand a brown paper bag that contained a gun.

The team of hit men used two cars, one for the shooters and the other a "crash car" driven by Joe Barboza.

Wearing wigs and fake beards, Steve Flemmi and Frank Salemme jumped out of the lead car and opened fire at McLaughlin. They hit him five times, once in the heart, lung, liver, and spleen. The last shot, as he lay on the pavement, was fired directly into his groin. The hit men fled. Punchy was found dead at the scene.

To Barboza, Paul Rico had revealed himself to be a valuable co-conspirator by providing crucial information that led to the murder of Punchy. But the Animal still played coy and refused to sign on as an official FBI snitch.

More than ever, Rico needed Barboza. In the fall of 1965, he lost Jimmy the Bear Flemmi as an informant when Flemmi shot a man and was identified by the victim as the shooter. The Bear went on the run and hid out in Vermont.

"In view of the fact that informant Jimmy Flemmi is presently a local fugitive, any contacts with him might prove to be difficult and embarrassing," Rico wrote in a memo to his FBI superiors. "In view of the above, this case is closed."

Over the next year, as the Boston gang wars continued to yield a staggering body count, Rico continued his pursuit of the man who had become his grand obsession. Eventually, surmised the master recruiter of street informants, he and Barboza's needs would converge, which is exactly what happened in October 1966.

In Boston's notorious vice district known as the Combat Zone (which no longer exists today), Barboza was arrested on gun possession charges while cruising in his car. Over the following months, as the Animal stewed at Walpole prison, several of his crew were killed by the Mafia. Barboza was feeling vulnerable and paranoid, but still he was refusing to meet with Rico and Condon. So the FBI agents enlisted the help of their newest Top Echelon Informant, Steve Flemmi.

Director Hoover approved Flemmi as an informant especially for this assignment. The date was February 14, 1967, Valentine's Day. The arrangement would prove to be a toxic love connection between mutual deceivers.

Many years before Flemmi ever formed his partnership with Whitey Bulger, he was hooked in with the FBI. This is a crucial fact often overlooked by people who seek to portray Bulger as the central figure in Boston's narrative of corruption. It was Flemmi who first established the key link between various spheres of corruption on both sides of the law, an inheritance he would later share with Bulger.

Flemmi's initial task as an informant was an important one: he was sent by Rico and Condon to visit Barboza at Walpole prison. The purpose of the visit was immortalized in a memo from Special Agent John J. Kehoe Jr., supervisor of the Boston division's organized crime squad, to the division's Special Agent in Charge (SAC) James L. Handley, who initialed the memo and sent it on to Director Hoover. Kehoe and Handley put special emphasis on the contributions of the division's two star agents, whom they were recommending for a "Quality Salary Increase":

Realizing the potential that [redacted name] might one day be victim of a homicide, SAs Condon and Rico have continued vigorous attempts to obtain additional high quality LCN [La Cosa Nostra] sources. Accordingly, BS 955 C-TE [Steve Flemmi] was developed by these agents and via imaginative direction and professional ingenuity utilized said source in connections with interviews of JOSEPH BARBOZA, a professional assassin responsible for numerous homicides and acknowledged by all professional law enforcement representatives in this area to be the most dangerous individual known. SAs Rico and Condon contacted Barboza in an effort to convince him he should testify against the LCN. Barboza initially declined to testify but through utilization of [Flemmi], the agents were able to convey to Barboza that his present incarceration and potential for continued incarceration for the rest of his life, was wholly attributable to LCN efforts directed by Gennaro J. Angiulo, LCN Boston head. As a result of this information received by Barboza from [Flemmi], said individual said he would testify against LCN members.[3]

Steve Flemmi had delivered. Barboza saw the writing on the prison wall; he signed a deal with Rico and Condon to become a "cooperating subject."

A cooperating subject was different from a Top Echelon Informant in that they were not being asked to circulate on the street and surreptitiously provide criminal intel. Rather, they were being asked to testify in court, a far more visible and direct form of underworld betrayal.

News of Barboza's cooperation rocked the Boston underworld. The Animal was moved to a compound on Thacher Island, a rugged, fifty-acre pile of rock about a mile off the coast of Rockport, Massachusetts, and kept under twenty-four-hour guard by armed U.S. marshals. Among his only visitors were Rico and Condon, who began the process of interviewing and prepping Barboza in anticipation of making a case against the target of their dreams, the top man in the New England Mafia, Raymond Patriarca.

FOR A LONG time, J. Edgar Hoover had denied there was such a thing as the Mafia operating in the United States. Throughout much of the postwar years, the primary focus of the FBI was what it called "subversives"—alleged communists, labor organizers, and civil rights activists. In the 1950s, a major focus of the bureau was bank robbers, who, because they often crossed state lines while fleeing a robbery, had been a primary target of the FBI since the days of John Dillinger and Pretty Boy Floyd. But in November 1957 an event that took place in upstate New York changed all that.

The conference in Apalachin, about fifteen miles west of Binghamton,

---

[3]In keeping with his vaunted reputation as a "hands on" overseer, J. Edgar Hoover signed off on this memo and all others related to the handling of the Flemmi brothers and Barboza.

In occasional directives to the bureau's various SACs, Hoover made clear that the use of criminal informants was a high-priority initiative, and he was diligent bordering on obsessive in his monitoring of the program. The repucussions of Hoover's complicity in the Barboza era and beyond are detailed in an extraordinary 2007 report issued by U.S. District Court Judge Nancy Gertner, in response to *Peter J. Limone, et al. v. United States of America*, the lawsuit filed by Joe Salvati and others after it was revealed they had been framed for the Teddy Deegan murder.

was a seminal event not so much in the history of the Mob, but in the history of federal law enforcement's understanding of the Mob. When a local police officer in rural Tioga County stumbled upon a large-scale summit meeting of Mafiosi from all around the United States, the estimated eighty gangsters scattered into the woods. Some had outstanding warrants, and many were rounded up and detained. For those, like Hoover, who had been dismissive of the idea that there existed a ruling body of mobsters that met on a regular or semiregular basis, it was a dramatic public rebuke.

This revelation was further underscored several years later when mobster Joseph Valachi testified in front of a senatorial committee in Washington, D.C. A low-level mafia soldier from New York City, Valachi testified live on television. With his gravelly Bronx accent and colorful detailing of mob jargon and underworld folklore, his testimony captured the public imagination.

Valachi's cooperation was a major coup for Attorney General Robert Kennedy, who presented the Mafioso's testimony to the public, and an embarrassment to Hoover. When it came to the Mafia in America, it looked as though the FBI was years behind the curve. Hoover and his boys had some catching up to do.

In April 1961, Hoover dictated and sent out a memo to each of the SACs of various field offices around the country emphasizing the importance of intelligence gathering in the field of organized crime. The memo stated that it was "urgently necessary to develop particularly qualified, live sources within the upper echelon of the organized hoodlum element who will be capable of furnishing the quality information required."

Thus, the Top Echelon Informant Program was born.

Paul Rico was in an excellent position to benefit from the FBI's newly energized mandate. Already, in his first decade as an agent, he had distinguished himself as a cultivator of informants. It was an informant that had tipped him off as to the whereabouts of James J. Bulger back in 1957, leading to the young bank robber's arrest and imprisonment. Rico had been polite and deferential during the arrest, on the outside chance that the kid might be a viable informant somewhere down the line.

Getting criminals to trust you and pass along usable information is a unique and highly valued skill in law enforcement. Especially in the FBI, which had been designed by Hoover as an elite division of law enforcement, with agents chosen to give the impression of propriety, someone who could operate at the street level with real hoodlums was a rare item. Rico had the gift.

Born into a lower-middle-class household of Portuguese, Italian, and Irish ancestry, he was a microcosm of the New England criminal class. He would be described in later years as Runyonesque, like a character out of *Guys and Dolls*. Even Barboza, the Flemmi brothers, and some of the most hardened gangsters in Boston thought of him as one of their own.

One of Rico's weaknesses as an agent was that he could be sloppy with paperwork and bureau protocol. He had been censured early in his career for minor infractions such as administrative errors, inadequate filling out of reports, and, on one occasions, failure to report that he had misplaced his weapon. It was not uncommon for an agent who was good at the important things like developing informants and solving big cases to be weak when dealing with administrative details required by the system. It was the job of a special agent in charge, or SAC, to pair up an agent with someone who complemented his skill set, which is how Rico wound up with Dennis Condon as his partner.

Condon was from Charlestown, an upright Catholic who regularly attended Mass and never swore in public. He did not have Rico's street skills, but he was good at paperwork and expert at handling the bureaucracy. Together, they were a dynamic duo.

With Barboza, Rico and Condon had landed a big fish. Barboza was the most infamous mob turncoat in history, and would remain so until Sammy "the Bull" Gravano was used to take down mafia boss John Gotti in the early 1990s. Before he was finished, Barboza would be used as a witness in multiple trials, but the one where he was given an opportunity to truly prove his worth commenced in June 1967, when Assistant U.S. Attorney Edward "Ted" Harrington announced the indictment of Raymond Patriarca Sr. and two others on the charge of murder.

With Barboza as the lead witness, it was a strong case, and Patriarca knew it. Through an underling, he communicated to Barboza's lawyer that "the Office," as mafia headquarters in Providence was known, would be willing to make a fifty-thousand-dollar payoff to Barboza to keep his mouth shut. When told of this offer, Barboza responded, "Tell Raymond to go fuck his mother in the mouth."

Predictably, the Mafia devised a counterresponse. The man enlisted to lead the charge was Barboza's own friend, Steve Flemmi.

No one in the Mob knew that Flemmi was a Top Echelon Informant, or that he had secretly met with Barboza at Walpole and talked him into testifying against the Mafia. All they knew was that he was a local gangster on the rise who would likely jump at the chance to prove his value to the Office. And so, Flemmi, playing both sides of the fence, took on the assignment from the Mafia of planting a bomb in the car of John E. Fitzgerald Jr., Barboza's lawyer. Flemmi undertook the job with his partner, Frank Salemme, who did not know that Flemmi was a covert informant for the FBI.

On the night of January 30, 1968, Barboza's lawyer left his office in Everett, Massachusetts, got in his car, and turned the key in the ignition, which ignited an explosive device. The car went up in a ball of flames. Fitzgerald crawled from the vehicle. Among his many injuries, Fitzgerald's right leg was severed at the knee, but he survived the attack.

The bombing had been devised to intimidate Barboza and make him change his mind about testifying, but it had the opposite effect. More determined than ever, Barboza took the stand and testified against Raymond Patriarca, helping to bring about what was, at the time, the most significant conviction of a high-ranking mafia figure since Hoover became director.

It was a huge victory for the bureau, and a major validation of Hoover's creation of a Top Echelon Informant Program. In this case, federal prosecutors had been able to take down the Godfather from within, something that had never been done before.

To call the conviction a feather in the caps of Rico and Condon would be an understatement. U.S. attorney general Ramsey Clarke wrote a personal letter to J. Edgar Hoover stating, "The recent conviction of New England Cosa Nostra leader Raymond Patriarca and two of his cohorts is one of the major accomplishments in the Organized Crime Drive Program. Without the outstanding work performed by Special Agents Dennis Condon and H. Paul Rico these convictions could not have been obtained." Rico was given an immediate salary increase, and Condon received a $150 incentive award

for "skillfully handling an important government witness whose cooperation was vital to the conviction of Patriarca and two associates."

The two agents did not have much time to bask in the glory of the Patriarca conviction. One month after the trial, it was announced that Barboza's
services as a witness would be utilized once again in what would become
known as "the Deegan murder case."

Two years had passed since small-time hood Teddy Deegan was murdered in an alleyway outside the Lincoln National Bank in Chelsea. What
had initially seemed like a minor case had grown in stature now that the
main witness was Barboza, the man who took down the Mafia.

The FBI and many local police officers had a good idea who was behind the Deegan murder. There was the secret gypsy wire transcript of
Barboza and Jimmy the Bear Flemmi visiting Raymond Patriarca in Providence seeking authorization for the murder. Through street scuttlebutt and
underworld intel, a composite picture had come into focus. One Chelsea
cop had even come upon the getaway car that night and caught a glimpse,
from behind, of the driver, whom he described as being partially bald. That
was Jimmy Flemmi, a victim of male-pattern baldness from an early age.
Through other witnesses, it was possible to establish that a total of six men
had been involved, though none of the witnesses had seen the faces of the
assailants.

From the beginning of his cooperation, Barboza admitted to Rico and
Condon that he had been an accomplice in the Deegan murder. He gave
them an accurate account, including the fact that Jimmy Flemmi had initiated and been in on the planning of the murder and served as the getaway
driver. Barboza also made it clear that, as a condition of his cooperation
agreement, he would not testify against Jimmy Flemmi. Not only did Rico
and Condon accept this condition, but they set about creating a version of
the murder that would minimize Barboza's involvement and leave Jimmy
Flemmi out of it.

The plan: Barboza would plead guilty to having played a role in the planning of the hit. Two men he identified as having been involved—Ronald
Cassesso and Roy French—actually were participants in the murder. That
left four others. Rico and Condon saw it as an opportunity to implicate two
known mafia figures they had been trying to indict for years—Peter Lim-

one and Enrico "Henry" Tameleo. These two men had nothing to do with the Deegan murder, but in the eyes of Rico and Condon they were probably guilty of other crimes and therefore fair game.

That left two more accomplices to be named. They left that up to Barboza, who implicated two completely innocent men who just happened to be on his shit list: Louis Greco, a former boxer and bar owner who had once punched out an associate of his, and Joe Salvati, who owed Barboza four hundred dollars.

With Salvati, the investigators had a problem. After creating their story of what had taken place that night and identifying Salvati as the getaway driver, they learned that there was an eyewitness identification from a Chelsea police officer: he had seen the getaway driver from behind, and the man was bald. Joe Salvati, of Sicilian extraction, had a full head of black hair. So a detail was added to Barboza's confession that Salvati that night had worn a bald wig.

All six of the men named by Barboza were arrested and indicted for the murder of Teddy Deegan.

Pulling it off would not be easy. The case was being prosecuted in Suffolk County, not in federal court. They would not have Assistant U.S. Attorney Ted Harrington to help them stage manage Barboza's testimony, as they had during the Patriarca trial. Ensuring that Barboza would be able to maintain such a complicated conspiracy would require due diligence from Rico and Condon.

In later years, the two FBI agents would claim that they had little involvement in the Deegan prosecution, since it was not a federal case. Condon even took the stand as a witness at the trial and testified that he had not met with Barboza in the weeks and months leading up to the trial. This was a lie. Decades later, in FBI memos uncovered via court order, it was revealed that the agents had met with Barboza on twenty-one different occasions in the month before the trial. Getting Barboza to digest and remember the details of a false story that involved so many moving parts took a concentrated effort by the agents.

And they weren't the only ones: FBI memos also showed that supervisors, deputy directors, and Hoover himself were kept abreast of every stage of this government conspiracy to frame four innocent men.

In May 1968, the Deegan murder trial got under way. Already, the feds had suppressed exculpatory evidence and suborned perjury. Barboza took the stand, and at first his testimony was wobbly; then Rico, Condon, and other FBI agents showed up in court.

Joe Salvati, seated at the defendants' table, looked around with a mounting sense of horror. "You think a third-base coach has hand signals," he noted, decades later. "You should have seen those agents giving hand signals to Barboza when he was on the witness stand."

Special Agent Condon, who came across as more professional than Rico, the street agent, testified on behalf of Barboza as a character witness. He reminded the jury how valuable Barboza's testimony had been in the FBI's ongoing war against the Mafia.

Based on the testimony of Barboza, the six defendants were all found guilty. Four were given the death penalty; two others—including Joe Salvati—were given life in prison.

On the heels of the Patriarca case, the FBI received international acclaim for yet another significant victory against the evils of organized crime. Both Rico and Condon received personal letters of acknowledgment from Hoover. But the agents realized they might have a problem. Nearly everyone in the Boston underworld knew that Barboza's testimony was fraudulent and that innocent people had been framed. The Deegan case was a Pyrrhic victory, because keeping the truth hidden and maintaining the lie would involve more diligence for many years to come.

SHORTLY AFTER THE Deegan murder trial, Special Agents Rico and Condon visited Steve Flemmi and his partner Frank Salemme at Salemme's auto garage in Boston's Roxbury section. Condon made a lighthearted reference to the convictions of the innocent men, and Salemme responded with anger, saying, "[Joe Salvati and the others] weren't even there, and you know it." Salemme's father was a member of the Knights of Columbus; he knew that Condon was also a member of the Catholic fraternal organization. "You're a fourth-degree knight. One of the commandments is 'Thou shalt not bear false witness.' How do you expect to get through the pearly gates with St. Peter after you put that slob up there to tell his lies?"

The vitriol that Rico and Condon received presented a sobering reality. The Big Lie was known or at least suspected by many in the criminal underworld. It put the agents in a defensive posture. Sure, the arrangement of cooperating with the government was wonderful for the informants, like Barboza, but what about those who were on the receiving end of such an outrageous injustice? These were the very kinds of people that Rico and Condon were always on the lookout to recruit. How could the system be trusted when agents and prosecutors were willing to engage in a level of treachery that put even innocent people at risk?

It was now incumbent upon Rico and Condon to show that the informant arrangement was a two-way street, that they would be willing to reciprocate and protect criminals who cooperated with the government, secretly or otherwise.

Two months after the confrontation with Cadillac Frank Salemme at the Roxbury garage, the agents learned that Flemmi, their Top Echelon Informant, and Salemme were about to be indicted for their role in the bombing of lawyer Fitzgerald's car. Flemmi was also soon to be indicted for the murder of Edward "Wimpy" Bennett, a rival gangster. Here was an opportunity for Rico and Condon to show that they knew how to protect their informants.

Flemmi was in bed one morning when he received a call from Paul Rico: "You and your partner are about to be arrested and indicted. You better get out of town as soon as you can."

Flemmi thanked Rico for the info, and then he and Salemme fled.

This tip-off had consequences for the agents. Because Steve Flemmi was now designated as a fugitive from the law, he was automatically closed as a Top Echelon Informant.

Flemmi went to Nevada and then Montreal and was not seen in Boston for five years. Salemme also went to Nevada, then branched off on his own and hid out in New York City.

While on the run, Flemmi kept in touch with Paul Rico. Occasionally, he called Rico at the FBI office, usually via pay phone from some far-flung location. To the secretary, Flemmi identified himself as "Jack from South Boston." It was not uncommon for agents to receive unusual calls, tips from informants or others who did not want to offer many details about why they were calling. Eventually, Jack from South Boston became a familiar caller. Rico would sit in his office, maybe chewing on a sandwich, while he chatted with a fugitive from the law who was wanted by his own FBI.

Meanwhile, Joe Barboza's partnership with the U.S. criminal justice system continued. He testified at another big case, a murder trial that involved Jerry Angiulo and two others. The case ended in an acquittal for Angiulo. Barboza's role as a witness had been tarnished somewhat, but the government was already deeply entangled with the Animal. The degree to which agents and prosecutors were willing to go to protect Barboza was extreme, and it would become instrumental in understanding later events that shaped the era of Whitey Bulger.

In 1969, Barboza became the first person initiated into the newfangled federal witness protection program. Along with his wife and three kids, he was relocated to Santa Rosa, California, under the name of Joseph Bentley. He was there for one year before he returned to Boston, in violation of the terms of the program.

In May 1970, he met secretly with an associate of Raymond Patriarca and indicated that, for a price of five hundred thousand dollars, he would recant his trial testimony. He also contacted the famous criminal defense attorney F. Lee Bailey. He told Bailey that he was ready to sign an affidavit declaring that he had committed perjury at the Deegan murder trial, and that four of the men convicted were innocent, and that FBI agents Rico and Condon had assisted him in his fabricated testimony.

Barboza had become—to put it mildly—a loose cannon.

And then, suddenly, on the night of July 17, while driving in his hometown of New Bedford, he got pulled over by a local police officer and was found to have guns and marijuana in his car. He was arrested and thrown in Walpole state prison.

Of the many people who had become concerned by Barboza's increasingly unpredictable behavior, first in line were members of the New England Organized Crime Strike Force. Even more so than Rico and Condon, the Strike Force, headed by Assistant U.S. Attorney Ted Harrington, had much to lose if the Deegan murder convictions were ever thrown out. Among other things, it could possibly lead to the overturning of the conviction of Raymond Patriarca, which stood as the single greatest achievement of federal prosecutors in New England. Careers had been made off that prosecution, and to think that it could fall apart or be discredited in any way required damage control at the highest levels.

On August 28, Harrington met with Barboza at Walpole prison, and later, in a memo to FBI Director Hoover, he wrote:

> [Barboza] stated that it was his original intention to inveigle members of the underworld into giving him money on the pretext that he would recant his testimony given in previous trials and that, when he received the money, he would leave the area without recanting.

Within weeks of this memo, the charges against Barboza were dropped. But before Barboza was released from custody, his benefactors had an even more serious problem on their hands. In California, where Barboza had lived under a false identity for a year before returning to Boston, he had murdered someone. In Sonoma County, Barboza was indicted and, in February 1971, he was extradited to California to face trial on a first-degree murder charge.

A reasonable person might ask: why didn't the FBI and prosecutors with the U.S. attorney's office in Massachusetts wash their hands of Joe "the Animal" Barboza? Obviously, he was a dangerous recidivist criminal.

The answer is that the agents and lawyers were wedded to Barboza. In the Deegan case, they had knowingly been party to a grave injustice, and as long as Barboza was disgruntled, or in a jam, there was the potential that he would expose their entire conspiracy of deception.

In California, the case against Barboza was strong. The local prosecutor had an eyewitness to the murder, in which Barboza killed a man in a dispute over stolen security bonds. Barboza's defense was that he didn't do the shooting; the entire scenario was a mafia setup to get revenge for his having testified against Patriarca back in Boston.

On March 25, Harrington flew to California and visited Barboza in jail. The Animal told Harrington that he did shoot the person but that it was in self-defense. Harrington did not believe him. What Harrington did next, spelled out in a memo to his supervisor, is extraordinary:

[I] will do nothing to attempt to dissuade the prosecution from bringing its case but will alert them of the possibility that the murder is a mafia frame. The fulfillment of this obligation is also in the practical interest of the government as [Barboza] may otherwise determine that the government has failed him in his time of need and, it is my judgment, that he will then retaliate against the government by submitting false affidavits to the effect that his testimony in the Patriarca and Deegan cases was in fact false, and thus tarnish those most significant prosecutions.

The wording of the memo is accurate except for the word *false*. Based on their involvement with Barboza thus far, it seems reasonable to conclude that the government was not concerned that Barboza would submit false affidavits; more likely they were worried that he might finally tell the truth.

The government went even further: Harrington notified Barboza's defense lawyer that he and FBI agents Rico and Condon would be available to testify on behalf of his defense. On the stand, they would detail Barboza's cooperation in cases against the Mafia, and verify that the Mafia both in Massachusetts and California had threatened his life.

And so they did, to the shock of the local prosecutor in the case. Years later, the prosecutor would admit, "We thought we had a pretty good capital murder case. . . . And we got to the end and we're having FBI agents suddenly appear as almost character witnesses. . . . [T]hey had damaged our case to the point we didn't think the jury was going to convict on a first-degree murder case." So worried was the prosecutor that he immediately halted the trial and offered Barboza a plea deal. They would reduce the charge to second-degree murder, and the defendant would get off with a sentence of five years.

Joe Barboza took the deal and did his five years. When released from prison, he settled in San Francisco. Shortly thereafter, on the night of February 11, 1976, he was murdered, gunned down in the street by a professional hit man who was believed to have been sent from Boston.

IN THE EARLY 1970s, Paul Rico was transferred to a field office in Miami. He maintained contact with his old partner, Dennis Condon, who was more active than ever in the FBI's ongoing battle against organized crime. As a stomping ground for racketeers who had an unyielding tendency to kill each other, Boston was still the place to be. What had started out as the McLean-McLaughlin gang war in the mid and late 1960s shifted to the Killeen-Mullen gang war of the early 1970s. Condon, along with Rico, had served as handler for a variety of informants from Charlestown and Somerville, including Barboza and the Flemmi brothers, but Condon did not have a single major informant in South Boston. That is where Whitey Bulger came into the picture.

Ever since Bulger's return to the neighborhood from prison, Rico and Condon had had their sights on the Killeen gang's bodyguard, who seemed to be slightly more intelligent than the average hood. He spoke reasonably well and read books. He was a physical fitness buff who seemed to have a personal sense of discipline that was sometimes the province of men who had served time behind bars. He was the kind of person smart enough to see the value in forging a covert relationship with the criminal justice system.

In May 1971, Condon met with Bulger. That same month, he opened a confidential informant file on the gangster. After a few secret meetings between the two, Condon became frustrated and, in an internal FBI memo dated July 7, 1971, he wrote:

> Contact with this informant on this occasion was not overly productive and it is felt that he still has some inhibitions about furnishing information. Additional contacts will be had with him and if his productivity does not increase, consideration will be given to closing him out.

Subsequent meetings between Condon and Bulger were no more fruitful for the FBI, and in August, after only three months, Bulger was officially closed as an informant.

Put simply, Condon did not have Rico's skills for developing and manipulating street-level informants. If the FBI field office in Boston hoped to maintain its standard as the most heralded in the bureau, they needed to come up with the next generation's H. Paul Rico. There was one potential candidate—a young agent who had been born and raised in the same housing project as Bulger. His name was John Connolly.

Connolly was close to the Bulger family. A former English teacher at South Boston High School, he had joined the FBI in 1968, partly on the advice of Billy Bulger, a childhood friend. In order to expedite his confirmation as an agent, Billy Bulger had helped Connolly secure a letter of recommendation from Speaker of the House John McCormack, the same politician who had written letters to federal prison authorities on behalf of Whitey Bulger. Connolly had worked on Billy Bulger's initial campaign for state representative and remained a vocal supporter of Southie's new rising star.

With an air of confidence bordering on cockiness, and a feel for the rhythms of the street, Connolly was cut from the same cloth as Rico. He even dressed in the same flashy style. Since 1970, Connolly had been assigned to an organized crime squad in New York City, but his real dream was to be assigned to his hometown office.

Rico and Condon had conversations with Connolly; they knew he was trying to get back to Boston. This dovetailed nicely with their own belief that the young agent was the right man to continue what they had started in the organized crime division of the Boston office. But Connolly was a junior agent. He did not have the juice within the bureau's rigid bureaucracy to choose his own assignment.

In 1972, Rico got a hot tip via "Jack from Boston," that is, Steve Flemmi. While on the lam, Flemmi had had a falling-out with Frank Salemme. It was a hazard of the profession: two hoodlums entangled together, cooped up in motel rooms and on long drives—the opportunities for discord are many. Plus, they had committed a murder together while on the run, in the Nevada desert. Their partnership took a bad turn. Flemmi headed to Montreal; Flemmi hunkered down with contacts in New York City.

Frank Salemme was a Ten Most Wanted fugitive. When Flemmi told Rico that Cadillac Frank was in New York, where John Connolly just happened to be stationed with the FBI organized crime squad, Rico seized on the opportunity.

The FBI agents devised a scheme so that Connolly could apprehend Salemme, but it had to look good. It could not be an arrest based on Connolly receiving information via someone else; it had to appear as if Connolly apprehended Salemme based solely on his own initiative.

The official story would become that, on a snowy day in December 1972, Connolly was walking down a street in midtown Manhattan and happened to spot Frank Salemme. He chased down the Ten Most Wanted fugitive on the street, cuffed him, and placed him under arrest.

With such a daring apprehension of a high-ranking criminal, as a reward Connolly was allowed to select a posting of his choice. He chose Boston, and, in 1973, was assigned to what was known as the C-3 Unit, Paul Rico's old organized crime unit.

Having Connolly in town was crucial to Rico, Condon, and others who had become custodians of the criminal justice system's dirty little secrets in Boston.

Now that John Connolly was securely ensconced in Boston, he undertook the heady task of following in the footprints of a legend, H. Paul Rico. He would do so by fulfilling his potential as the one man capable of bringing gangster Jim Bulger into the fold.

The legend is that Connolly approached Bulger and that, seated together in a car at Quincy's Wollaston Beach, they chatted about how a mutual arrangement would work to both of their advantages. This story, first made public in the book *Black Mass* by former *Boston Globe* reporters Dick Lehr and Gerard O'Neill, is clear in its suggestion that Connolly alone is the man who convinced Bulger that he should go to work for the DOJ.

There was, however, another factor that may have been crucial in Bulger's decision to enter into a relationship with the U.S. government.

By this time, Bulger had formed a partnership with Steve Flemmi. As a former Top Echelon Informant (TE) who was the brother of another TE, few knew the benefits of being a government rat as much as Stevie. He knew that the government had allowed Joe Barboza to lie to protect his brother, and he knew that the government had been willing to go to extraordinary lengths to protect Barboza. Not only that, Flemmi had himself received tremendous benefits from his role as a TE. He had been tipped off about pending indictments that made it possible for him to stay a few steps ahead of the law. And more recently, in 1974, he had been told by Paul Rico that it was safe to return to Boston.

Flemmi had been somewhat suspicious about that; he was afraid it might be a trap. But Rico told Flemmi that the Wimpy Bennett murder charge would be dismissed, as would be the charges against Flemmi for the bombing of the lawyer Fitzgerald's car.

It was almost too good to believe. Flemmi knew that, given the nature of his alliance with the FBI, he would be expected to deliver something in return.

Could it be possible that what they expected in return was for Steve Flemmi to help Rico, Condon, and now Connolly secure the cooperation of Jim Bulger as an FBI informant?

Within months of his return to Boston, Flemmi met Bulger at a bar in Somerville. They had met once before, briefly, in the late 1960s. They were both known on the street as "capable," the preferred word in the local underworld for someone who was willing and able to kill, if necessary. Each had attributes that the other did not: Flemmi had connections in the Mafia, which was a potential source of work assignments and revenue. Bulger had a level of intelligence and managerial skill that Flemmi would never have. They formed a partnership and soon became affiliated with the Winter Hill Mob.

According to Flemmi, at the gang's Marshall Motors headquarters in Somerville, Bulger informed the crew that he had been approached by John Connolly at Wollaston Beach. He was hesitant to take Connolly up on his offer.

Flemmi knew the benefits of the agent-gangster relationship in a way the others did not. He knew all the advantages. But there was also something more.

Flemmi knew that, in New England, becoming a federal informant meant you were being asked to keep hidden the seeds of corruption first planted by J. Edgar Hoover, Paul Rico, Condon, and others who had decided long ago that the best way to take down gangsters was to become like them. Part of this meant becoming an inheritor of the Big Lie, the secret history of the framing of Joe Salvati and others. Making sure that this diabolical history remained hidden had become a partnership between the upperworld and underworld in Boston.

If you were willing to sign on as a player in this ongoing conspiracy, you could not be touched. Because if someone within the conspiracy sought to take you down, they risked exposing their own involvement in the conspiracy. Therefore, fellow members in the conspiracy had an interest in protecting each other, doing favors for each other, and generally covering each other's ass; it was in their own self-interest to do so.

Because of this, to become an FBI informant in Boston was cosmic in nature. It was mind-blowing. You would be protected by the system at every turn. You would become invulnerable in ways that outsiders would not be able to comprehend. You would become God.

It was this arrangement—how it came into being and how it was protected and advanced during the Bulger era—that the defense lawyers, Carney and Brennan, at Bulger's insistence, were hoping to put on the public record. Their client, it seemed, was determined that if he were to go down, the entire system would go down with him. He would rip the scab off the wound, and the entire festering infection would be exposed.

The prosecutors had other ideas. Using a scalpel, and with great precision, their plan was to separate Bulger from the larger organism, to leave little or no trace of Barboza and how his legacy had helped to foster the Bulger era.

So far, in the first week of the trial, their strategy was working. But it was about to get its first real test with the calling to the stand of someone who was steeped in Boston's underworld history, a man who had known Barboza and had benefited greatly from the city's unusual bonds of corruption: John Martorano.

JUDAS UNBOUND

IN THE SECOND week of the Bulger trial, John Martorano strolled into the courtroom like a man without a care in the world. Which is not easy to do when you weigh close to three hundred pounds and are about to take the stand to testify against a man you once considered among your closest friends. There was no sweat on Martorano's brow. Dressed in a dark blue silk suit, light blue shirt, with a polka-dot tie and hanky in the breast pocket, he lumbered onto the witness stand and took a seat.

On this day, Bulger was dressed in a white, long-sleeved dress shirt with an open collar. It was odd seeing the defendant adopt this sartorial style. In all the surveillance photos and videos of Whitey over the years, he is invariably wearing a tight T-shirt. The possibility that this more formal look might be in deference to the importance of Martorano as a witness was undercut by Bulger's demeanor. As Johnny walked past the defense table and took the stand, Whitey glanced up only briefly, without any trace of emotion.

A seasoned witness who had testified at all Bulger-related trials to date, including, in 2008, the Miami murder trial of John Connolly, Martorano was aware of the physiological side effects. Knowing that the salivary glands easily become parched during moments of stress, he reached for a nearby decanter of water and poured himself a drink. He sipped the water and settled in before Fred Wyshak had asked his first question.

"Good morning, Mr. Martorano," said Wyshak.

"Good morning," said the witness, in a gravelly monotone.

"Could you please state your full name and spell your last name?"

"John Martorano. M-A-R-T-O-R-A-N-O."

"How old are you, sir?"

"Seventy-two."

"And where were you born?"

"Cambridge, Mass."

"Can you describe your educational background?"

"High school."

"Are you married?"

"No. Divorced."

"Do you have any children?"

"Yes."

"How many?"

"Five."

"Are you currently employed?"

"No."

"How do you make a living?"

"Social Security."

"Are you testifying here today pursuant to a plea agreement with the United States?"

"Correct."

Martorano's answers reflected his seasoning as a witness: give as little as possible, say no more than what is asked, betray no emotion. As with all witnesses, the introductory questions elicited mundane facts of life. They were polite, with answers that reflected a shared commonality with the human experience. There were no indications of the horrors that lay just around the corner.

The prosecutors' number-one priority in presenting Martorano to the jury was to delve into the murders of Roger Wheeler and John Callahan. These two murders, one of which took place in Tulsa, Oklahoma, and the other in South Florida, had represented something new for the Winter Hill Mob. Neither of the victims was a gangster but rather they were legitimate businessmen who had become entangled with the gang. And the fact that both these killings had taken place far from Boston was unprecedented. The investigation of these two murders—both of which were committed by Martorano, allegedly at the behest of Bulger and Flemmi—were what would eventually bring down the entire mob underworld in Boston.

Before Fred Wyshak could get to these crimes, he had a lot of work to do with his witness. There were eighteen other murders committed by Martorano. And also, more immediately, Wyshak had to put forth to the jury an explanation of how it was that the most murderous gangster in Boston history was now on the stand as a free man.

"Your Honor," said Wyshak, addressing Judge Casper, "at this time I'd like to show the witness what's been marked government exhibit eleven fifty-nine for identification."

"You may approach," responded Casper.

Wyshak walked over to Martorano and handed him a piece of paper. The witness removed reading glasses from his breast pocket and looked over the document.

Said Wyshak, "Showing you what's been marked government exhibit eleven fifty-nine for identification, do you recognize that?"

"Yes," said Martorano.

"What is it?"

"It's my plea agreement."

Wyshak and Martorano spent the better part of the next hour attempting to put the plea agreement in context, though the explanation would be as noteworthy for what was left out as for what was explained.

John Martorano received one of the best plea deals in the history of gangland prosecutions. In 1997, after agreeing to cooperate with the government and admitting to twenty murders, he received a sentence of fourteen years. He was released after serving eight, a sentence of roughly seven months for each of his twenty murders.

The man who negotiated the mob hit man's deal was attorney Martin "Marty" Weinberg, whom Martorano invariably referred to on the stand as "a great lawyer" or "the best." Indeed, Marty Weinberg had, back in the late 1990s, proven to be a legal magician; by engineering Martorano's cooperation, he was in many ways the man who paved the way for the Bulger prosecution.

In 1995, Martorano was a gangster in exile living in Delray Beach, Florida. He had been on the lam since 1979, when an indictment on charges of fixing horse races in various northeastern states had resulted in the arrest and conviction of more than forty crime figures in New England. Johnny and his girlfriend at the time took off. He lived under various assumed names—

Richard Aucoin, Peter Connolly, and Vincent Mancourt, to name a few. Throughout the 1980s and into the 1990s, he regularly received money from Bulger and Flemmi, who still considered him part of their organization. He communicated regularly with Flemmi but rarely with Bulger, who considered it too much of a risk to talk on the phone. Martorano continued to function as a criminal, running a modest bookmaking business in Florida and, of course, the committing of two murders—Wheeler and Callahan—in consort with his Boston partners.

In 1995, in the wake of Bulger's indictment and disappearance on the lam, Martorano was apprehended outside his home in Delray Beach. He was brought back to the District of Massachusetts to face the music, including his old indictment from 1979, which carried a twenty-year sentence. This is where Marty Weinberg came into the picture.

The two men—lawyer and indicted felon—were seeking to cut a deal with the government, but their position was weak. Then, a neutron bomb hit Boston: Steve Flemmi and Whitey Bulger were outed as longtime FBI informants. The Wolf hearings began to unfold. Flemmi was attempting to escape prosecution by claiming he'd been given immunity by his FBI handlers. Weinberg and Martorano realized they had better act fast. If Flemmi were to strike first by copping a plea and cutting a deal with the feds, there would be no deal left for Martorano to cut.

It was Weinberg who devised the strategy. He posed the question: who was it the feds wanted most? Answer: Bulger. But Bulger was in the wind, to perhaps never be seen again. Question: who was the next-highest target? Answer: John Connolly. If the feds could prosecute Connolly, they could contain the toxic spill that was the FBI-gangster arrangement in Boston, stopping all further investigations from potentially spreading and implicating the entire criminal justice system in New England.

Weinberg approached the feds and said, My client can give you John Connolly, and, by extension, Bulger, if he should ever be apprehended. In exchange, you will give him a reduced sentence on the race-fixing charges, to which he will plead guilty. Martorano had one other condition: he would not testify against his brother or against Howie Winter, who had been arrested and incarcerated back in 1979 on the same horse-race-fixing indictment that had forced Martorano to go on the lam.

The government was interested. They showed Martorano a list of seven people they were proposing that he would likely be called on to testify against. Four of the names on the list were people he hardly knew. The others—Bulger, Connolly, and Flemmi—were the exact names Martorano had expected to see on that list. He agreed that he would testify against all three.

To the feds: so far, so good. But there was more: Wyshak and Kelly had a list of ten murders they believed Martorano was involved in. To strike a deal, he would have to be willing to plead guilty to them.

Through Weinberg, Martorano gave notice that, yes, he would be willing to plead guilty to the murders, but once he signed an agreement and began to be debriefed by investigators, he would have to have immunity from any and all other crimes that he might reveal he had committed.

The feds thought it over: Well, he's admitting to ten murders. How much more could there be? The prosecutors agreed to Martorano's terms. The deal was signed in April 1999.

That deal had taken more than a year to negotiate. Martorano's lawyer had taken a hard line. His client was content to waste away in the infamous La Tuna federal prison, where he was being held, near El Paso, Texas, along the U.S. border with Mexico. Once the two sides had reached a deal, and Martorano signed a plea agreement, the feds were in for their biggest surprise.

Now that Martorano had a sweet deal by which he could not be prosecuted for any other crimes he might admit to, he let the floodgates open, admitting to ten additional murders he had committed back in the 1970s.

One of the investigators who interrogated Martorano was state police colonel Tom Foley. Decades later, in his memoir, *Most Wanted,* Foley described how hearing about all the murders almost made him physically ill:

> At a certain point . . . all the killing got to me. Not the killing itself, but the way [Martorano] talked about it, so flat and factual. As if the victims weren't people to him. Somebody lives, somebody dies. It was no big deal which was which. It was as if he was describing the best

route to Providence, Interstate 95 or Route 24. You could go either way.[1]

By the time of the Bulger trial, Martorano had gone over the murders numerous times. They had been stripped of all emotional content. Wyshak had to run through each and every murder. To get to the killings that implicated Bulger, he had no choice but to reveal the numerous other killings on which Martorano built his reputation as one of Boston's most proficient executioners.

There was Bobby Palladino, Johnny's first body, in 1964. That came about after a waitress at Luigi's, an after-hours club owned by the Martorano brothers, was killed on the premises during a dispute with a customer. The Martoranos did not commit the murder, but they helped hide the body in an upstairs attic. They heard that two fellows—Bobby Palladino and John Jackson—were cooperating with the police in an investigation of the murder. So Johnny and Jimmy went and found Bobby Palladino. "He was playing cards in an after-hours joint," remembered Johnny.

Their intention was to talk some sense into Palladino. "Hey, what's the matter with you? We don't cooperate with police." They would negotiate a deal, make it worth his while to keep his mouth shut. Said Martorano, "[Palladino] came downstairs with me and my brother and got in the car. We went to talk to him, and he pulled a gun."

"What did you do?" asked Wyshak.

"He got off a shot, and then I shot him."

"What did you do with the body?"

"We dumped it down at North Station."

Martorano then explained how, years later, he went and found the other guy, John Jackson, and shot him dead also.

Then there was Tony Veranis, a professional boxer from Southie. Veranis had borrowed money from a loan shark associated with the Martoranos, and he hadn't paid them back. So Jim Martorano and an associate had gone to see Veranis at a club in Southie. Not only would Veranis not pay his debt, but the professional pugilist roughed up Jimmy Martorano.

---

[1]Foley and Sedgwick, *Most Wanted*, p. 210.

When Johnny Martorano heard what happened, he went looking for Veranis. He found him in an after-hours club in Roxbury. "Veranis came over with some girls . . . and started mouthing off about he just gave my brother a beating, some stuff like that, and 'F' him, 'F' you, and went to pull a gun. So I shot him."

"Were there people in the bar at the time?"

"Yes."

"How many?"

"Thirty or forty."

"Were you ever charged with that crime?"

"No."

With hardly enough time to digest that Martorano was talking about the actual killings of actual human beings, Wyshak was on to the next atrocity. "I would like to direct your attention to January of 1968. Did you know a man named Herbert Smith?"

Here was a slaughter worth noting, because it was a trifecta. Martorano killed three people in one fell swoop.

On this night, Johnny was approached by Stevie Flemmi. The two had become associates, of sorts. Martorano knew that Flemmi had connections with the Mafia, which provided potential business opportunities. This was the late 1960s, before the Martoranos, Flemmi, and Bulger officially became partners and began to coalesce as the Winter Hill Mob, but Johnny and Steve Flemmi did already consider themselves partners. So Johnny was concerned when Flemmi told him that, on the previous night, he had gone to a club called Basin Street to look for Martorano. There he ran into Herbert Smith, who was a bouncer at the club. Smith and two other bouncers gave Flemmi a beating.

"As a result of learning this from Stephen Flemmi," asked Wyshak, "what did you do?"

"I went down to see what happened. . . . I had a conversation with Herbert Smith."

"What did he say to you and what did you say to him?"

"He started laughing about giving Stevie a beating. And that was it."

"When you say 'that was it,' what does that mean?"

"That's when I decided to shoot him."

By now, Martorano had learned that you don't shoot somebody dead in a crowded club, with multiple witnesses present. Martorano showed no anger. In fact, he became friendly with Smith. They agreed to meet later at an after-hours gambling club in Roxbury, near where Martorano was living at the time. "I told him, 'I will meet you at the corner near the place, and we'll go in. I got to stop and pick up some money to play with.'"

"What did you pick up?"

"A .38."

There was a raging snowstorm that early morning in Roxbury. Martorano arrived at the location on foot. He saw Smith sitting in his car near the corner where they had agreed to meet. As Martorano approached the car, he noticed that there were two other people inside it with Smith. "I saw the shadows of three silhouettes, three people in the car." Alarm bells went off in Johnny's head: this was some kind of setup. He would have to act fast.

"What did you do?" asked Wyshak.

"Well," said Martorano, "he was supposed to be there alone to meet me. But he was with two other people. So I thought they might have the same idea of doing to me [as I had with Smith]. So when I got in the car, I just shot three times."

"You killed three people."

"Yes."

Martorano then stumbled out of the car. He had arranged for an associate to serve as a getaway driver, but the person never showed. "I had to walk out of there in the snow and wash up in the snow."

"Did you later learn that one of the people in the car was a female?"

"Yes, I did."

"And the other person was a teenager?"

"Yes."

"How did you feel after you learned that?"

"I felt terrible. My first initial—I wanted to shoot myself. But you can't change it."

Wyshak whizzed through the other murders, a cavalcade of shootings, stabbings, dead bodies rolled up in tarps, postmortem cleanups of blood and brain matter. The testimony was like a montage from a crime movie, the implications of each and every act too horrid to dwell on in detail, too overwhelming, so that they must be presented as one big bloodstained blur.

Wyshak asked the witness about his relationship with Bulger and Flemmi.

"They were my partners in crime. They were my best friends. They were my children's godfathers."

"And what motivated you to cooperate against them?"

"Well, after I heard they were informants, it sort of broke my heart. They broke all trust that we had, all loyalties, and I was just beside myself with it."

On this point, Martorano's testimony was especially pungent: he may have had in mind the famous line from *The Godfather: Part II:* "I know it was you, Fredo. You broke my heart." In a fantasy universe, this was the point where Johnny would have given Whitey the Sicilian kiss of death. Instead, he cut a deal with the government and became a federal witness. Thanks to Marty Weinberg ("the best"), it was a good deal: eight short years and Johnny was back out on the golf course.

Then there was the money: since being released from prison in 2007, how had Martorano lived? Turns out that upon his release, as part of his agreement he received a payment of $20,000 from the U.S. government. There was also the memoir he published, cowritten by noted *Boston Herald* columnist and local radio personality Howie Carr. Martorano and Carr split an advance payment from Forge Books, the publisher, of $110,000—that was $55,000 for the hit man. Since the book's release, Martorano had received another $20,000 in royalties. And then came the big payday: Johnny had sold the rights to his life story to a movie company for $250,000, with much more to come if a movie actually gets made.

In the six years since his release, Martorano had done well for himself.

I HAD MET John Martorano one year earlier, over dinner at Abe & Louie's, an upscale steak house on Boylston Street in Boston's Back Bay. The meeting was arranged through a mutual acquaintance who had known Martorano for many years.

A couple of years earlier, via Pat Nee, I had also met John Martorano's younger brother, James, known to friends as Jimmy. The two Martoranos had been among the earliest members of the Winter Hill Mob, going back to the early 1960s. The children of an immigrant father from Riesi, Sicily, and a partly Irish American mother, the Martoranos were eleven months apart in age. They had both gone to the Mount St. Charles Academy in Woonsocket, Rhode Island, a private middle school, and then graduated from Milton High School in 1959. Both were star athletes on the football team, where they played alongside a kid named Ed Bradley, who in later years would go on to become the first African American co-anchor on the popular TV newsmagazine *60 Minutes*.

Both Martoranos were offered athletic scholarships to attend college. Jimmy accepted an offer from Boston College and eventually received a bachelor of arts degree. Brother Johnny went on to become one of the most proficient killers in the history of the Boston underworld.

When I was first introduced to Jimmy Martorano in 2004, I had a hard time picturing him as an underworld figure. By then I had met and interviewed many gangsters of differing ethnicities, and by any standard Jimmy Martorano did not fit the mold. With his wire-rimmed glasses and gentlemanly manner, he had the demeanor of a kindly Italian uncle—friendly, solicitous, and affectionate. He was an intelligent man, astute and thoughtful in ways I did not associate with the typical street mentality. He was manly without being macho. Brother John had a nickname for Jimmy, "the Cardinal," which seemed to fit. Jimmy was the kind of guy who liked to settle disputes; he listened to all sides and dispensed judgments from on high.

On the back porch of a classic triple-decker in Southie, I sat with Jim Martorano and Pat Nee listening as they related old war stories from the Boston underworld. At the time, John Martorano was still in prison serving his sentence as part of his plea deal with the government, and Whitey was on the run.

Jimmy had read my book *The Westies,* or at least knew of it. He was complimentary about how, as he put it, the book had captured the organized crime lifestyle without attempting "to get moralistic about it." Technically, I was not interviewing Martorano or, on that occasion, Pat Nee, so both men were forthcoming with stories and opinions they might have been more cautious about had it been for publication. As with other conversations I've had with professional criminals in Boston, these two former gangsters—decades removed from their lives "on the street"—seemed compelled to explain what the criminal underworld in Boston was all about. Since the details of Whitey Bulger and Steve Flemmi's reign had been catapulted into the media, in their view the Boston rackets had been given a bad name. Despite what I might have heard, they wanted me to know that there could be such a thing as honor among thieves.

Eight years later, I met Johnny Martorano at Abe & Louie's. I had been told about Johnny by Pat Nee, who had great affection for Martorano. To Nee and others who circulated in the Boston underworld, Martorano was Dr. Feelgood, the kind of guy who made being a gangster seem like an entertaining pursuit. According to Pat, "Johnny would pull up in a black Cadillac, tinted windows, with a driver. He'd be in the back. The door would swing open and, first thing, a cloud of marijuana smoke would come wafting out. Then Johnny would appear, with a black babe on one arm and a beautiful Asian woman on the other. That was Johnny. He was always looking for a good time."

At Abe & Louie's restaurant, I caught glimpses of this Johnny Martorano, though he was now decades past his prime. He wasn't yet as hulking and obese as he would appear at the Bulger trial, but he was definitely overweight, a man of large appetites who did not hesitate to indulge those appetites whenever the opportunity presented itself.

I had not yet read *Hitman: The Untold Story of John Martorano, Whitey Bulger's Enforcer and the Most Feared Gangster in the Underworld,* by Howie Carr. Martorano had cooperated in the writing of the book, which was published in April 2011. Carr, well-known for his animus toward the Bulgers, both Whitey and Billy, had been handpicked by Martorano as his collaborator.

My knowledge of the totality of Martorano's murders was vague, which was just as well, because had I known the full extent of his many killings, I would have had a hard time reconciling those crimes with the person I was having dinner with.

Having written about criminals of Martorano's vintage for more than two decades, I had adopted a loose philosophical creed. Generally, I come into the relationship out of a sense of professional curiosity. I am attempting to write about their world—to the extent that I can—from the inside out. This requires that I not bring with me the baggage of moral judgment. It is essential that the person who is talking to me feels as though I am at least attempting to see the world from their point of view—assuming that what they are telling me is sincere and not a pack of lies. In an interviewer/interviewee situation, this can sometime become a dance, as they are in a process of assessing your motives, and vice versa. As an interviewer, it is a basic premise that you are more likely to get candor and honesty from someone if they feel comfortable that you are not motivated by a hidden agenda.

At Abe & Louie's, I was not interviewing John Martorano. He had agreed to meet based on respect he had for a book that I had written, and—more important—on the fact that Nee and his brother Jimmy had given me the "okay" as someone who could be trusted.

At the restaurant, it seemed as though John Martorano was known by everyone—the maître d', the waiters, even one of the owners came over to our table to say hello. Johnny was a different personality type than his brother Jimmy—more fun loving, less bookish. He was dressed in a nice silk suit with an open collar and had what I suspected was a perpetual suntan. Clearly, Johnny reveled in the sensual pleasures of life. At our table, he ordered the wine and took charge of placing the food orders—the shrimp and lobster appetizer, a meal in itself; porterhouse steak, however you liked it; a dessert sampler of cheesecake, cannolis, etc.; and cognac as an after-dinner drink.

During the meal, Johnny told stories. He was a great raconteur, with an eye for color and detail. He was also a good listener. Both of the Martoranos were "people persons"; their involvement in the criminal life was, in many ways, an extension of their innate sociability. They had started out in the bar and nightclub businesses not only as financiers, but as management, people who valued interaction with the differing characters who populated their mostly working-class community.

Martorano was especially interested in Cuba. Since I had recently published a book about the years of the Mob in Havana in the 1950s, Johnny wanted to compare notes. In 1960, as a nineteen-year-old gangster's apprentice, he had lived for six months in Havana.

Following his first-ever arrest on a gun possession charge, he'd gone on the lam for the first time. It was while staying in Miami with an uncle that it was suggested he hide out for a while in Cuba, a well-worn path for U.S. mobsters on the lam. Only now, with the fall of Mafia-friendly President Fulgencio Batista and the rise of Fidel Castro, things weren't so friendly anymore.

It was all hazy to Martorano now, but what he did remember vividly was the revolutionary police, soldiers not much older than he was at the time, with beards and a victor's swagger. Martorano was barely there long enough to have a mojito and a cigar. Back in the States, his mob benefactors had made the gun charge go away, and he was free to return to Beantown.

At Abe & Louie's, Martorano insisted on picking up the check, which I'm guessing topped out at somewhere around five hundred dollars. As we were saying our goodbyes, he introduced me to a woman Pat Nee had told me was Johnny's girlfriend, though he introduced her as a business associate. A Chinese American in her midforties, she was starting her own business, and Johnny was helping her out. While Johnny went to the men's room and retrieved his coat, I spoke briefly with the woman, who was intelligent and well spoken. She was not a bimbo. I asked her if she was aware of Johnny's reputation. She said that she was but it didn't concern her. The Johnny Martorano of legend, a notorious hit man for the Mob, was not the man she knew.

As with many people who have spent social time with Martorano, I came away from that dinner charmed and beguiled. So I rewatched an interview that I had seen with Martorano on *60 Minutes,* originally broadcast on January 6, 2008, and also read Howie Carr's book.

The level of murder and mayhem perpetrated by Martorano in the 1960s, '70s, and '80s was staggering. He had stabbed people, shot people, and spent an inordinate amount of time in his life cleaning up after murders and figuring out ways to dispose of a dead body. Though the majority of the twenty murders he admitted to having carried out were professional hits—planned murders that had been thought out and executed with calm precision, as opposed to spontaneous crimes of passion—it was hard to imagine that he was not haunted in some way. My own impression was that for a person whose life was steeped in such bloodshed and horrific violence, there would be psychological consequences. A man would find himself tormented, if not by pangs of guilt or remorse, then at least by disturbing imagery—bad dreams—from a lifetime of bad deeds.

I asked Pat Nee about it: "You think Johnny is haunted in any way by all the killings and dead bodies from over the years?"

Pat chuckled at the question. It was not a frivolous laugh. He had undoubtedly been asked this question before; it is the obvious question someone would ask after meeting Martorano, who seems so unaffected by his crimes.

"You know," answered Pat, "I've known Johnny a long time, and I don't think he's lost a minute's sleep over the murders. I don't think it bothers him one bit."

That was Johnny. The original title he had wanted to use for his book with Howie Carr was *What We Did*. The world according to Johnny, in unvarnished detail. What happened happened, and there ain't nothing you can do about it now, so why lose sleep over it?

The most disconcerting thing about Johnny Martorano was that, after a lifetime of mayhem and killing, he didn't seem the least bit disconcerted at all.

HANK BRENNAN HAD been waiting his entire professional life for an opportunity like this. One of the most notorious gangsters in the city's history was sitting on the witness stand with no gun, knife, or gangland protection of any kind. He was defenseless. And Brennan had been entrusted with the power of cross-examination. He stood at the podium and, with the directness of a firm overhand right to the nose, delivered his first question: "Mr. Martorano, you are a mass murderer, are you not?"

Martorano did not flinch. "I don't think so," he said.

Before he got to the details of Martorano's crimes, Brennan was determined to explore the mind-set of a mass murderer. If he could get Martorano to talk about himself beyond the clipped and unrevealing answers of a professional witness, he could get him to discredit himself in the eyes of the jury. "You don't like the term 'hit man,' do you, Mr. Martorano?"

"Not especially."

"You don't like the term 'hit man' because you think it undermines your credibility, sir?"

"No, I wouldn't accept money to kill somebody."

"So there's a difference between what you did and someone who's a hit man?"

"I would think so."

The fact that Martorano had cooperated in the writing of a book about his life did not need to be restated; it was a fact already on the table. The book was called *Hitman,* and Martorano had profited from its publication.

"Were you a serial killer?" Brennan asked.

"No."

"You don't like that word?"

"Serial killers kill until they get caught or stopped. I wasn't a serial killer. I could stop to confess my problems."

Brennan had the witness on his heels, leaning back against the ropes. "You went on *60 Minutes* and you didn't like that term 'serial killer,' either, did you?"

"No."

"Well, what is a serial killer to you?"

"I don't know what you would think a serial killer is. A serial murderer kills for fun. They like it. I don't like it. I never did like it."

"The twenty murders you admitted to, you didn't like any of them, sir?"

"No, I didn't like doing any of it. I don't like risking my life, either."

"Well, put aside risking your life for right now. Let's talk about the joy that you had."

"I never had any joy. I never had any joy at all."

For the next hour, Brennan picked at the scab. There was much to cover with Martorano, but the defense lawyer was determined that there be a full airing of Martorano's character, that he be made to wallow in the dubious self-justifications for his actions that he'd been peddling in TV interviews, a book, and in previous trials. "Did you just wake up learning how to kill somebody when you were a kid? Is it something you learned?"

"Nobody taught me. It just happened."

"You just woke up one day and started killing people?"

"No. I was always taught to take care of my family and my friends. The first situation that I had was somebody was going to hurt my brother, and I defended it. . . . Family and friends come first."

"Who told you that if it comes down to family and friends, you can murder somebody?"

"I don't know who told me that. I told myself that."

"So you had your own code?"

"My family, my father always taught me that. The priests and the nuns that I grew up with taught me that."

Brennan's eyes lit up, and he cocked his head. "The priests and nuns taught you that?"

Martorano squirmed a bit; he was being made to put forth a personal theology to a greater degree than he would have liked. "They always talked about Judas and stuff like that. And I always believed that—that Judas is the worst person in the world."

With a quizzical look, Brennan asked, "So with [these early murders— Palladino, Jackson]—did Judas come to you and tell you to do these things?"

"Did Judas come to me? I just thought of Judas. [They] represented Judas to me."

"I see. So when you saw these people, before you took their lives, you looked at them and you saw Judas?"

"I saw my family in trouble and a guy trying to hurt them."

Brennan smiled. He seemed to be enjoying himself. He noted that in Martorano's highly touted interview on *60 Minutes,* the word he had chosen to describe himself was "vigilante." "What does 'vigilante' mean to you?" Brennan asked the witness.

"It's somebody that would hurt somebody who is doing wrong."

"Okay. So what you're saying is that all the murders were because you hurt somebody who was doing something wrong to somebody else. . . . And that makes you a vigilante like Batman, sir?"

There were titters in the spectators' gallery. Even Martorano seemed amused. "I don't know about Batman," he answered.

Brennan could have gone on with this all day. Listening to Martorano delineate the differences between a hit man, mass murderer, serial killer, and vigilante was like a Boston underworld version of *Tuesdays with Morrie.* But the defense had much work to do with Martorano on the stand, a lifetime of bloodshed to go over. Of particular interest were seven murders that

Martorano claimed he committed in cahoots with Bulger. And of those seven, five were killings aided and abetted from deep within the criminal justice system:

Richie Castucci—In the late 1960s, Castucci was a loan shark and occasional bookmaker affiliated with the Patriarca family. He owned a popular bar overlooking Revere Beach, the Ebb Tide, which had become a mobster clubhouse where many infamous criminal schemes were hatched, including, in 1965, the murder of Teddy Deegan by Barboza and company. Castucci also owned numerous strip clubs and was rumored to have killed a "made man" he believed was having an affair with his wife.

By 1970, Castucci was up to his neck in debt and in need of protection for having killed a made man without authorization. And so he became a secret FBI informant. Initially, his handler as a Top Echelon Informant was Special Agent Thomas J. Daly, but later John Connolly took over.

Castucci functioned as a rat for six years, until 1976. That year, two key Winter Hill mobsters—Joseph "Joe Mac" McDonald and Jimmy Sims—were forced to go into hiding after being indicted for the theft of a million-dollar rare stamp collection. Joe Mac and Sims were among the founding fathers of the Winter Hill gang, close associates of Howie Winter, and beneficiaries of everything the gang had to offer. At the Marshall Motors headquarters, Bulger, Martorano, and the others helped devise a scheme for their two associates to go on the lam. Martorano went to New York City and found an apartment in Greenwich Village. He paid one year's rent—fourteen thousand dollars—in advance, and gave Joe Mac the address and keys to the apartment.

Castucci was a regular at Marshall Motors, where he dropped off and picked up cash for his loan-shark business, which was partially bankrolled by the Winter Hill Mob. Castucci heard about McDonald and Sims's secret hideout in New York and passed the information on to his new FBI handler, John Connolly. Connolly went to Bulger and Flemmi and told them they had a snitch in their midst: Richie Castucci.

On a night in December 1976, Castucci showed up at Marshall Motors feeling chipper. He was there to collect a sizable wad of cash, his stake in the gang's sports betting operation. From the stand, Martorano explained: "I told him I didn't have all the money together. I gave him a bag of money and said, Go down to the apartment we had down the street, count this up, and I'll give you the difference when I get there. . . . I told Whitey to take him down there. . . . I waited for them to get down there and start counting the money. Then I walked down there. . . . [Castucci] was sitting at the kitchen table counting the money with Whitey. I walked around to the side of Castucci and shot him . . . in the temple, here." Martorano put a finger to his right temple.

In his book, *Hitman,* Martorano described the messy cleanup. Richie bled all over the money, the table, and the floor. They put his body in a sleeping bag, rolled it up, dragged it downstairs, and stuffed it in the trunk of Richie's Cadillac Deville. With Whitey following, Johnny drove the Cadillac over to Revere, Richie's home turf, and, with Castucci's dead body in the trunk, left it behind an apartment building in the middle of a snowstorm. Martorano and Whitey drove back to Somerville.

After that, all the gang members were greatly impressed with John Connolly, who had functioned as if he were a member of the gang.

Bulger told Martorano that Connolly had a wedding anniversary coming up, a good opportunity to show their appreciation. So Johnny kicked in a two-carat diamond. After that, more money was pooled to pay Connolly on a semiregular basis.

Roger Wheeler—In the early 1980s, while Martorano was living on the lam in Florida, the Winter Hill gang became embroiled with World Jai Lai, a professional sports league. Jai lai is a sport of Spanish origin, played on an indoor court called a fronton, with a rubber ball that is hurled off a wall with a scoop-shaped racket. The sport is especially popular among Portuguese and Spanish immigrants living in the United States, and was at the time a major source of betting among gamblers on the East Coast.

The president of World Jai Lai was a businessman named John Callahan, who also happened to be a good buddy of the Martorano brothers. Callahan was what was known in the underworld as a "wannabe gangster," or, as Martorano put it, "He was a high-priced accountant during the day and put on a leather jacket and wanted to hang out with rogues at night." Callahan had a problem: he had recently been forcibly removed as president of World Jai Lai by the company's CEO, Roger Wheeler. Callahan came to the conclusion that if he could make Roger Wheeler disappear, he could talk Wheeler's widow into allowing him to reassume his position as president.

In Boston, there was a series of meetings between Callahan and Bulger and Flemmi. Callahan was asking them to authorize a hit on Wheeler. He noted that there was immediate money to be made through the parking and vending machine concessions at World Jai Lai events, to the tune of ten thousand dollars per week, and untold millions to be made if he were reinstalled as president. Callahan even had a hit man in mind, whom he brought along to two of his meetings with Bulger and Flemmi.

Brian Halloran was a midlevel cog in the Winter Hill Mob's gangster machinery, known for being not too bright but willing to do hits for money. The Wheeler hit had an added logic in that a key player in the hit would be none other than H. Paul Rico, long since retired from the FBI. Since the late 1970s, Rico had been working as head of security for World Jai Lai, based out of their corporate headquarters in Miami. The Wheeler hit would be like a Winter Hill Mob family reunion, with veteran players from the gang's beginnings going back in the mid-1960s.

Bulger and Flemmi were open to the idea of a hit on Wheeler, but they didn't want Brian Halloran as the triggerman. They felt Halloran was unreliable, and so they booted him from the plan. Instead they turned to Johnny Martorano, living in South Florida, to carry out the hit. Martorano chose as his accomplice another old-time Winter Hill associate—"Joe Mac" McDonald—who was also hiding out in Florida at the time.

The problem for the two hit men was that their target didn't live in Florida or in Boston; he lived in Tulsa, Oklahoma. This meant that Martorano and McDonald would have to travel to Tulsa, track down Roger Wheeler, kill him, and get out of town. It was a surgical reconnaissance mission that required more than just blowing a guy away in a bar filled with witnesses, or whacking somebody in the friendly confines of the Marshall Motors garage. Considerable advance planning was required, starting with input from Paul Rico, who gave to the two hit men a detailed physical description of Wheeler and also addresses for work, home, and socializing locations in Tulsa where they might track down their target. Without Rico's input, the hit never could have happened.

Martorano and Joe Mac flew to Oklahoma City, rented a car at the airport, and drove to Tulsa. Their first stop was a Greyhound bus station, where they picked up a suitcase that had been sent to them by Steve Flemmi. Inside the suitcase were a machine gun, a carbine, a couple of pistols, and masks and wigs. The two hit men checked into a hotel and, over the next five days, tracked Roger Wheeler. They decided that the best place to take him out was at the Southern Hills Country Club, where Wheeler routinely played golf.

First, Martorano and McDonald needed to steal a car, a "boiler," which they could use to do the hit and discard immediately. That taken care of, on the afternoon of May 27, 1981, they drove to the country club and found a Cadillac they knew to be Wheeler's, with a license plate number that matched. They sat in the parking lot and waited until they spotted Wheeler walking toward his car. As Martorano explained during his direct testimony: "I saw a guy come over the hill, carrying a briefcase, and it looked like his description. And he was heading towards his car. So I headed towards the car, also."

Martorano was wearing a disguise of a fake beard, sunglasses, and a baseball cap. He waited until Wheeler unlocked the front door of his car, then he snuck up from behind. "I pulled open the door and shot him."

"Where did you shoot him?" Martorano was asked.

"Between the eyes."

Martorano explained how the gun virtually exploded in his hands after he opened fire. McDonald was waiting for him in the boiler. They drove to a parking lot, ditched the boiler, and retrieved their rental car. They drove back to their motel. Martorano stripped off his clothes and cut everything into pieces, to be discarded. They then loaded their guns back in the suitcase.

"What did you do with the [suitcase] that Mr. Flemmi had sent you?"

"Bus."

"Put it back on a bus?"

"Hm-hmm."

"And then what did you do?"

"Got out of Oklahoma."

"How?"

"We flew."

"Flew back to Florida."

"Yes."

For a while, the Wheeler murder looked like a clean hit. But, in fact, it set off a chain reaction of events that would bring about the end of the Winter Hill Mob.

Brian Halloran and **Michael Donahue**—John Martorano did not have any direct involvement in the killings of these two men, but it was a hit that would serve as a bridge between the Wheeler murder and another that Martorano would do a year later.

Once Wheeler was killed, Bulger and Flemmi began to worry that Brian Halloran knew too much. Halloran had become a disaster in the making. He was believed to have committed a cold-blooded murder in Boston's Chinatown, and the heat from that crime, the gangsters believed, made Halloran a likely candidate to cut a deal with investigators to save his own neck. Which is exactly what happened: Halloran reached out to and began cooperating with two FBI agents from the Boston field office. Unbeknownst to those agents, behind their back John Connolly passed the information along to Bulger and Flemmi that Halloran was an active snitch.

The two agents who were handling Halloran knew he was not safe out on the street. They tried to get Halloran into the witness protection program, but they were rebuffed by Jeremiah O'Sullivan, chief of the New England Organized Crime Strike Force. Halloran was determined by O'Sullivan to be an unreliable source—a drunk, drug user, and all-around desperate man—who was not worth the budgetary expenditures it would require to provide government-sponsored witness protection. In making this call, O'Sullivan, in essence, signed Halloran's death warrant.

Early on the evening of May 11, 1982, Halloran was spotted at a bar on Pier 61, near where the Moakley Courthouse now stands in Boston. Word got back to Bulger, who took matters into his own hands. With a second unidentified gunman, Bulger put on a curly blond wig, and the two men drove over to Pier 61.

That evening, Halloran hitched a ride home with a longtime friend named Michael Donahue, a laborer who was married with four kids. It was a devastating choice by Michael Donahue. As he and the doomed Brian Halloran drove out of the parking lot at Pier 61, in another car Whitey

Bulger and a masked gunman drove up and opened fire with a machine gun. Both Halloran and Donahue were killed.

John Callahan—John Martorano first heard about the killings of Halloran and Donahue directly from Bulger and Flemmi. Not long after the Halloran murder, he was called to meet his two Winter Hill associates at the Marriott hotel in New York City near LaGuardia Airport. It was an unusual meeting. Martorano had seen Flemmi a few times since moving to Florida, but he had not seen Bulger since he first went on the lam in 1979. They all arrived in New York on separate flights and checked into a room that had been booked for the occasion by Martorano, under the alias Richard Aucoin.

In his direct testimony, Martorano detailed how Bulger told him at the Marriott that they'd had to kill Halloran. The reason, said Whitey, was that he had gone to the FBI and told them that he, Martorano, had killed Roger Wheeler.

"What else did [Bulger] tell you?" Martorano was asked.

"He said that because of that, you know, there would be a big investigation and they're going to call Callahan in. I guess Callahan was already out of the country, he's hiding. But Whitey said they're going to put so much pressure on Callahan. He said that Zip [Bulger's nickname for John Connolly] told him that Callahan is going to get so much pressure on him, he's going to fold, in their opinion. And if he does fold, we're all going to jail for the rest of our life."

"What else did he tell you?"

"That they wanted to take him out. I objected. You know, Callahan was a friend of mine, and you know, I just killed a guy for him, risked my life. I didn't want to kill Callahan. So they're saying, Well, he ratted on you by telling Brian Halloran that you killed Wheeler. Can I guarantee that he's not going to fold? I said, I can't guarantee he's not going to fold. He said, Well then, we're going to all go away [to prison]. So, eventually, they convinced me. Okay, if that's the case, it was two against one. . . . I agreed. If it has to be done, it has to be done."

They all agreed that the murder would take place in Florida, away from Boston. Martorano wasn't crazy about that, either, but he agreed.

There was discussion about how they would try to pin the murder on some Cubans in Miami. Already, they had told Connolly, their FBI partner, to plant information in the FBI files that Callahan was rumored to be in business with drug dealers in Miami. Callahan owned a condo in Miami and lived there part of the year. If they dumped his dead body in Little Havana, Miami's Cuban neighborhood, the conjecture in law enforcement would be that he got into trouble with some Cuban *narcotraficantes*.

The meeting at the airport Marriott in New York lasted one hour. "How did you feel after that?" Martorano was asked.

"I felt lousy, but, you know, these were my partners. It was sort of dictated to me. We were up to our necks in murders already. This is what they wanted, I have to do it."

On cross-examination, Hank Brennan spent lots of time on the Callahan murder, because it represented a diabolical level of personal treachery. It had been established that Callahan was Martorano's close friend. Martorano often stayed at Callahan's condo in Miami when Callahan was out of town. The Boston businessman let him use his Cadillac. Not only that: Callahan took care of Martorano. After the Wheeler murder, Callahan was so pleased with the result that he paid Martorano and McDonald fifty thousand dollars for the hit. Martorano characterized this money not as a payment, but as a gift—a gratuity—for a job well done. The two hit men split the money with Bulger, Flemmi, and H. Paul Rico.

So Martorano called John Callahan and told him he needed to see him in Florida. They needed to discuss the latest developments, and it wasn't safe to do it over the phone. Callahan trusted Martorano. He got on a plane and flew to the airport in Fort Lauderdale, near Miami. Martorano would meet Callahan at the airport, with Joe Mac secretly waiting in the wings to help carry out the murder.

Perhaps John Callahan might have given some thought to the fact that he was in trouble with the Winter Hill Mob. But the successful businessman was guileless. He was a Harvard graduate with an MBA and an impressive resume, though he also had a secret life where he hung out with gangsters and ordered hits. In his mind, he was a member of the gang.

Brennan asked Martorano, "When [your friend] got off the plane, you went and took his luggage for him, didn't you?"

"I grabbed his bag and said hi."

The defense lawyer paused; he was going to milk this series of questions for all it was worth. The witness had been claiming that he was some kind of noble avenger, a man with a code who killed people on behalf of his friends and family. But here he was methodically lying to and luring a good friend to his death. "When you said hi to your friend before you murdered him, did you look him in the eye?"

"Yes, I did."

"And then you walked him to the car where you were going to kill him?"

"Yes."

"And when you put him in the car, you had him take the front seat, sir?"

"Yes."

"So where you were going to murder your friend, you wanted to do it from behind, didn't you?"

"Well, I'd put the gun in the backseat, so that's how I arranged it."

The car was Martorano's Dodge Ram conversion van, with bucket seats. Brennan had the witness explain how he'd covered the front seat with plastic and towels so that his best friend, after being shot, would not spill all over the interior of the car. Callahan, apparently, did not notice the seat coverings.

Said Brennan, "You were going to keep the car after you murdered your best friend in it, so you wanted it to be clean, didn't you?"

"Well," said Martorano, "I didn't want it to cause an arrest." That was the old-school hit man schooling the prosecutor on the practicalities of a hit.

As Martorano described it, he was loading Callahan's suitcase in the backseat when he grabbed the gun and shot his friend in the back of the head.

"Did you shoot him once or twice in the back of the head?" asked Brennan.

"I believe it was once."

The shooting occurred around midnight. With Joe Mac following in his car, Johnny drove the van to a garage in Miami, where they had parked Callahan's Cadillac. The idea was to take the body from the van and stuff it in the trunk of Callahan's Caddy, then abandon the car somewhere in Little Havana. But when Martorano and Joe Mac arrived at the garage, they discovered that it did not open up until seven in the morning. Martorano and Joe Mac had five hours to wait and a dead body on their hands.

"We went for a coffee to kill some time," said Martorano.

At 7 A.M., they finally prepared to move the body from the van to the trunk of the Cadillac. Joe Mac thought he heard a groaning sound coming from Callahan, and so he fired a couple more shots into the body.

Said Brennan, "Before Joe shot him a couple more times, when you heard your friend groan, when you were moving him from the van to the trunk of his car, did you have any second thoughts that maybe you could take him out of the wrapper and try to help your friend?"

"I didn't think he was alive."

"Did you hear the groan?"

"Yeah, but I didn't think he was alive."

"Was there anybody else in the trunk other than Mr. Callahan?"

"No, but bodies can make noise and be dead."

Brennan seemed ready to make a comment but left it at that. If dead bodies make noises after they are dead, Martorano would know. He was the expert.

The hit man's cross-examination continued to the end of that day and well into the next, followed by re-direct testimony presented by Wyshak, and re-cross by Brennan. By the time John Martorano was off the stand, the Bulger trial seemed to have entered a new realm of savagery and depravity. But it had not yet reached its nadir, its true heart of darkness.

6

BROTHERHOOD OF THE CLADDAGH

JUROR NUMBER TWELVE, Janet Uhlar, had begun to leave the courtroom each day with a sinking feeling in her gut. Her mood started to shift somewhere around day seven, after the Martorano testimony was finally complete.

Martorano's three days on the stand had been stomach churning, to say the least. For a woman who had little interest in the world of organized crime or serial killers or the differences between a hit man and a vigilante, it was a master's course in Boston gangland psychopathology. Martorano talked about his various murders as if they were akin to swatting a mosquito on his forearm. The lack of emotion, or remorse, was chilling.

But that was not what had begun Janet Uhlar's downward spiral. That began with the witness that followed the hit man, an unassuming sixty-three-year-old woman named Diane Sussman de Tennen. The woman had been subpoenaed to take the stand at the Bulger trial because, forty years earlier, on a fateful night in March 1973, she found herself in the middle of a shooting that had nothing to do with her but changed the direction of her life.

Uhlar and the other jurors had heard about the shooting already, during Martorano's direct testimony and again on cross-examination. The hit man had described a series of gangland shootings and killings intended to eliminate a renegade gangster named Al "Indian Al" Notarangeli.

It all started back in late 1972, not long after Bulger, Howie Winter, Pat Nee, and others had their mobster summit meeting at Chandler's bar in the South End. That was the meeting that ended the gang wars that had been raging since the mid-1960s and brought together Bulger and the Winter Hill Mob under one umbrella. One of the first initiatives of this new confederation of gangsters was to hunt down and take out Indian Al.

According to Martorano, he, Howie Winter, Bulger, and others took on this task as an assignment from Jerry Angiulo, the mafia boss of Boston. Al Notarangeli and his crew had made it known that they were going to take over the Angiulos' sports betting book. They had already murdered one of Angiulo's bookmakers, a Mafioso named Paulie Folino. Afterward, Jerry Angiulo had a meeting with John Martorano and Howie Winter. Angiulo explained that Indian Al was out of control, and his war on the Italians was going to lead to death and destruction throughout the Boston underworld. The Winter Hill crew took the hint. They offered to take out Indian Al.

A Winter Hill crew led by Howie Winter, Martorano, Jimmy Sims, and Whitey Bulger began hunting for the doomed gangster. Since none of them were close to Notarangeli, they first had to develop information on his daily routine—what he looked like, where he lived, and what kind of car he drove. They learned that Indian Al drove a brown Mercedes and often frequented a bar called Mother's Cafe, located near Boston Garden, where the Bruins played hockey and the Celtics had won a string of basketball championships.

On the night of March 8, the Winter Hill crew received word that Notarangeli was at Mother's drinking with friends. Martorano, Bulger, and the others swung into action. They arrived in two cars, with Winter, Martorano, and Sims in a boiler car, one of a dozen stolen vehicles that Howie Winter kept in garages all around Somerville. In this car were two machine guns. In a backup car was Bulger—a crash car but also a radio car. Bulger had a police scanner so that he could track police whereabouts in the area. Also, all of the gangsters had walkie-talkies and were in communication. They even had a lookout inside Mother's to notify them when Indian Al was leaving the premises.

They received that message around two in the morning. The person identified as Al Notarangeli, their target, exited the bar with a couple of friends—a woman and another male. The target got into the brown Mercedes, in the front seat behind the wheel, with the woman in the front passenger seat and the other guy in the back. The Winter Hill hit team followed. A couple of blocks away, the car with Martorano and Winter inside drove up alongside the Mercedes. "We gave it what you'd call a broadside," Martorano explained. Two machine guns blasting away. Later, after the assault, Bulger told Martorano that from where he was in the crash car, it looked as though the entire Mercedes had exploded.

It was an outrageous gangland "drive-by." The problem was that it was not Al Notarangeli in the car. Their spotter had identified the wrong person. The gangsters had killed a kid named Michael Milano, a bartender at Mother's, a completely innocent twenty-three-year-old with no criminal affiliations.

Since the Milano murder was one of twenty that Martorano testified about, many jurors—including Janet Uhlar—remembered the crime in the swirl of testimony surrounding the attempted murder of Indian Al. There were other cases of mistaken identity killings. The mobsters wound up killing four separate men—including Notarangeli's brother—before they got their man. The jurors could be forgiven for having a blurred remembrance of the killing of Michael Milano. But then Diane Sussman de Tennen took the stand.

In 1973, she was in Boston serving an internship as a dietitian at Beth Israel Hospital. She was twenty-three years old and had met and fallen in love with a young man named Louis Lapiana. Louis had recently started working as a bartender at Mother's Cafe, where Michael Milano, his good friend and fellow bartender, had helped him land the job.

Early on the morning of March 8, Diane Sussman de Tennen waited as Michael and Louis closed up the bar. Afterward, they headed outside to Michael's Mercedes. Milano had offered to give both Louis and Diane a ride home.

Milano was very proud of his new car. It was identical to a brown Mercedes owned by Indian Al Notarangeli. At Mother's, it was well known that Michael Milano worshipped Al Notarangeli. He admired his look and his tough-guy swagger. Though Notarangeli was fifteen years older, Milano slightly resembled Indian Al, a fact that he heightened by wearing his hair like the notorious hoodlum. He'd bought a leather coat that was identical to one owned by Notarangeli. The pièce d' résistance was when he bought the brown Mercedes. Milano had no way of knowing it, but it was his copycat fascination with Indian Al—and especially his buying an identical car— that would lead to his death that night.

Diane Sussman de Tennen recalled the night as if it were a sense memory, deeply embedded in her soul: "I got the honor of sitting in the front passenger side, getting to play with all the newness of the car. . . . Michael was driving; Louis was in the back. They played chess together, and they were giving each other a hard time about who was going to win the next game and, you know, egging each other on."

With some witnesses, prosecutor Brian Kelly had a tendency to rush through the direct examination, but not with Diane Sussman de Tennen. He took his time and let the jury ruminate upon her evident decency and goodness, thankful, perhaps, that here was a noncriminal witness—an average person—during a trial overstocked with depraved and cynical denizens of the criminal class.

"Now," said Kelly, "after a while with this drive, did something highly unusual happen?"

"Yes. Close to the apartment, we were at a stoplight, and all of a sudden there was this noise, a continuous stream of noise of, you know, gunfire, and it was just nonstop. There were dozens and dozens of rounds, or whatever. In retrospect, it was a machine gun, but whatever I heard was going on and on. The car was hit with machine gun bullets. . . . When I heard the sound, I ducked. I don't know why or what, but I will tell you I come from California, and we have earthquakes. You grow up knowing certain survival skills. Not that you duck in an earthquake, but the minute you hear any rattling or something unusual, there's a procedure. And I think out of training, I ducked. That's probably the only reason I'm here today.

"After the shooting stopped, I got up. Michael was forward on the steering wheel. I looked at him and asked if he was okay, and I got no response.

"I turned around to ask Louis how he was, and he was slumped forward, his eyes were glazed, and he barely shook his head. I heard a very low noise of, 'No.' Having been trained in a hospital, I knew I couldn't do anything. So I put my hand on the horn and just figured someone would hear it."

Sirens sounded, and cop cars and medical vehicles arrived. Diane realized that she also had been hit. She was covered in shards of glass. She took off her coat; her arm was drenched in blood. But she did not want to leave her boyfriend. "I remember fighting with the police because they wouldn't let me get in the ambulance with Louis. I didn't want to be separated from him. I didn't know his status, and I was afraid to leave him."

At the hospital, Diane was treated for a gunshot wound to the arm. Later, she was informed that Michael Milano had died.

They wouldn't let Diane see Louis the first day, but at some time on the second or third day she was allowed into his room. "When I finally saw him, he could not speak. They had to shave his head because he had bullet wounds all over him. They saved his mustache, and that was, like, the only recognizable thing about Louis at that point. He could not move, and he was on a breathing apparatus."

"So he was paralyzed?"

"He was paralyzed."

Up to this point, Sussman de Tennen's testimony was riveting enough, but then she described the aftermath. "I had a fellowship [in Seattle], and I was supposed to leave Boston in two weeks. I really didn't want to leave not knowing the status of Louis. I had friends who offered me a place to stay. But at that point the police told me that they were concerned for my safety, because they thought I might be a target because the people who machine-gunned down the car probably did not want me as a witness. I wasn't concerned for myself, but they said whoever I stayed with I was putting in jeopardy, and so I left Boston."

Diane Sussman de Tennen moved to Seattle and went on with her life, but she did not forget Louis Lapiana. "It was a real long recovery. For twenty-eight years he was a quadriplegic on a respirator. But the first eight to twelve months were very difficult. He couldn't speak at all. The nurses were really nice; they got used to my calls. They would put the phone by Louis's head. I could talk to Louis. Since he couldn't talk, it was a one-way stream. But the nurses helped out by saying he's smiling or [responding] in some way."

After her internship was complete, Diane returned to Boston for two years. She saw Louis almost every day. Eventually he got to a point where he could sit up and talk through a respirator. He was as good as someone could be under the circumstances. Eventually, Diane and Louis had a heart-to-heart conversation. He told her that she was not responsible for his life and that she needed to move on. Diane moved back to the state of her upbringing: California. She married and had three children.

"Did you stay in touch with [Louis]?" asked Kelly.

"Louis was part of my life for the next twenty-eight years. He moved to Long Beach VA hospital. I lived in Los Angeles. My children grew up from infancy with Louis. Louis's parents were like a second set of grandparents to my children. I was to this day emotionally connected to Louis. And, yes, I was married and my children are not Louis's, but part of the deal was Louis would always be part of my life, and we did things together. We would go out, have lunch, have dinner, in the wheelchair. I was trained how to suction him on the respirator, how to handle the wheelchair, what to do if the batteries went low. And so, you know, I developed with him over the twenty-eight years [we had together]."

"Did he eventually pass away?"

"Yeah, he passed away in 2001."

By the time Sussman de Tennen was finished, there was hardly a dry eye in the courtroom or the media overflow room. The testimony touched trial observers who had been numbed by Martorano's litany of murders so devoid of emotion. Here was someone speaking from the other side—a victim of a horrible crime whose life had been changed forever.

Like many on the jury, Janet Uhlar choked up, and she noticed one of the other female jurors with her head lowered in tears.

The emotion that Janet felt toward this witness started out as empathy, but as the day went on, with other witnesses taking the stand, she felt her emotions transitioning into something else. What Janet began to feel was anger. Initially, that anger was focused on the man who had first described the killing of Michael Milano and the shooting of Louis Lapiana as if it meant nothing to him: John Martorano. Clearly, the man was a monster. But as Janet processed her feelings of repulsion toward Martorano, a question arose:

How the hell can this man be out on the street today? What kind of justice system makes a deal with a person who has killed twenty people—some of them completely innocent—a man with no feeling or remorse?

Martorano's deal with the government shocked Janet Uhlar, and for the first time she found herself questioning the government's case.

And it didn't end there.

Throughout most of the trial, Uhlar had been staying at her mother's house in Quincy.

On train rides to and from the courthouse, her head brimming with images and details from the trial, there were other imponderables: *Why Whitey Bulger? What was it about Bulger that made the government feel they needed to make unconscionable deals with men who were as bad—or worse—than he was?*

As the trial headed into its third week of testimony, juror number twelve developed the earliest inklings of a troubling realization: she was leaving and arriving at the courtroom each day with more questions than answers.

RALPH DEMASI WAS a character. He took the stand on a Friday morning, a stooped old man in his seventies. He did not want to be there. That morning, he had refused to talk with the prosecutors in the hallway. He had been given full immunity to testify; nothing he said in court could be used against him. But Ralph, a former hoodlum and ex-con, was not the kind of guy who talked openly about criminal matters to anyone, much less during a public proceeding.

At a sidebar between the lawyers and the judge, it was revealed that Ralph had written a letter to Bulger's lawyer, Jay Carney. In the letter, De-Masi made it clear that he was not testifying under his own volition; he had been forced by a federal order of compulsion. Carney, of course, knew this, and he realized that the letter was really meant for his client, Jim Bulger, so that he could see that Ralph DeMasi was not doing this on his own. Even then, DeMasi refused to take the stand, claiming that he would invoke his Fifth Amendment privilege unless the prosecutor and the judge made it clear in open court that he was only there because the government had forced him to be there by federal decree. The prosecutor and the judge agreed to do that, since it was common procedure anyway.

Given DeMasi's reluctance, when he finally got on the stand, he was surprisingly verbose. His testimony was not crucial. He had been along during the shooting death of William "Billy" O'Brien, a Southie hood who had fallen afoul of the Winter Hill Mob. The killing of O'Brien had been described in considerable detail by Martorano. DeMasi was there in the same capacity as Diane Sussman de Tennen, to give survivor testimony.

Unlike Martorano, DeMasi was not a seasoned witness. He had only recently been released after serving twenty-one years in prison on an armed robbery conviction. He'd never before testified in a courtroom. Apparently, he had not been prepped on how to give short, pithy answers and instead delivered his testimony as a monologue.

After describing in detail how he wound up in a car with Billy O'Brien on the night in question, he moved on to the shooting: "I got in the car with Billy and we pulled out on Morrissey Boulevard [in the Dorchester section of Boston]. I said, 'Billy, keep your eye on the rearview mirror, the side mirror. If a car comes up fast, hit the gas.' He started laughing. 'Ah, Ralph you're—ain't nobody gonna hurt us, blah, blah, blah.' I said, 'Billy, pay attention, I got bad vibrations. Watch your mirrors. If a car comes up fast, hit the gas.' He keeps laughing.

"All of a sudden, a car pulls up and people start shooting at us. . . . Billy O'Brien said, 'What the fuck,' hit the gas, hit the brake, the car started fishtailing. . . . He must have died instantly. As soon as he said 'What the fuck' we started fishtailing. . . . I got hit and thrown forward, and just instinct made me go down as low as I could near the floorboards. I got shot eight times. I read somewhere it said three times. I had eight bullets in me.

"The car hit the guardrail. Boom.

"My adrenaline was going. I didn't have a gun, but I had a stiletto. Pulled the stiletto out, opened the door, jumped out of the car. The cars that were shooting at us stopped about thirty yards ahead. The two shooters were getting out. I ran towards them, hoping I could stab one of them and get a gun from him. When they saw me coming, one of them yelled, 'Here he comes,' and they jumped back in the car and burned rubber. My adrenaline is going. I start running after them—"

"Now, wait a minute," interjected prosecutor Kelly. "You were shot eight times and you were running [after two armed] guys with a knife?"

"Right. I got shot here, here, my shoulder, and in my back a number of times."

"I take it, given your presence here today, you survived that shooting?"

"It's pretty obvious."

"Did you go to the hospital?"

"Let me finish the story." DeMasi ignored the prosecutor and continued. "All right, so after I realize I'm a nitwit running after a car that's burning rubber, I stop. My whole side was paralyzed. I walked back to the car. I'm looking in. I yell, 'Billy, Billy.' Looked in, got close, but it was dark. The whole side of his face was blood. It's obvious he was dead.

"I started walking down Morrissey Boulevard to try to get away from the area. Probably within five minutes a cop car pulled up. A cop jumped out. 'Holy shit, you've got blood all over.' I said, 'Yeah. What happened?' He said, 'You got shot.' I said, 'What did you shoot me for?' I was disoriented a little bit.

"He said, 'I didn't shoot you. Get in the car.'

" 'No, I ain't getting in the car. So you can shoot me again?' He goes, 'Come on, get in the car.' He grabbed me, put me in the car, took me to the hospital. I'm in the hospital two or three days, checked out, went to Billy O'Brien's funeral."

"In fact, when you went to Mr. O'Brien's funeral, what happened to you there?"

"Got arrested coming out of the church—for getting shot."

"Yes, but didn't you also have a gun with you?"

"They didn't know that at the time."

"All right, but you got arrested on gun charges coming out of Mr. O'Brien's funeral, right?"

"No, no, that isn't why I got arrested. I got arrested for parole violations for getting shot."

"The bottom line is, sir, you don't know who actually shot you, do you?"

"No, I do not."

"IF RALPH DEMASI thinks he was an innocent bystander that night, he's got it wrong," said Pat Nee. "They were trying to hit DeMasi, not O'Brien."

I met Pat Nee after the DeMasi testimony and relayed the version that had been detailed in court. It was DeMasi's contention that he had been an innocent bystander that night. His friend, Billy O'Brien, whom he knew from prison (O'Brien did a stint in Walpole for killing another man named O'Brien in a Southie tavern), must have been the target, figured DeMasi. But what DeMasi never mentioned on the witness stand was that he was in Southie that night to buy guns. Unbeknownst to him, because of his association with Indian Al Notarangeli and his crew, he was on a Winter Hill gang hit list. It was Martorano and Jimmy Sims who shot up the car, with Whitey Bulger following in a backup car.

Hearing Nee's version that DeMasi was the target reminded me that just because a witness takes an oath and testifies in court, it doesn't mean they know what they're talking about.

I did not reach out to Nee to talk about Ralph DeMasi. I reached out, rather, to talk about a different series of murders that his friend John Martorano had testified about. These murders, engineered and perpetrated by Bulger, had changed the criminal landscape in South Boston and left Pat Nee in an especially vulnerable position. Sensing that these killings were key to understanding how Whitey had come to rule the neighborhood, I wanted to know more.

When talking about local gangland lore and, more specifically, murders that were still open cases that had never been solved, Nee and I had some unofficial ground rules. Sometimes, if I asked about a specific killing, Nee might say "no comment," or, "I can't talk about that." That could mean that he didn't want to implicate someone he knew who was still alive. It could also mean that maybe he had been involved in some way.

It was no secret that Nee had been involved in aspects of the Killeen-Mullen gang war of the late 1960s and early 1970s. He had revealed some of the details of this gang war in his book, *A Criminal and an Irishman*. In the past, he had described to me the attempted sniper shooting of Eddie Killeen on an apartment balcony overlooking Dorchester Bay, with such detail that it made me think Pat himself may have been the shooter. There were other notorious crimes. I had been told by a knowledgeable source that Pat Nee was one of the shooters in the killing of Billy O'Sullivan, a Killeen bodyguard who was a close partner of Whitey Bulger. The rumor was that Nee did the killing along with Paulie McGonagle, a fellow Mullen gang member whose brother was murdered by Bulger.

Another crime Nee was alleged by some to have participated in was a double killing that figured prominently in the Bulger trial—the murder of Brian Halloran and Michael Donahue. Halloran was riddled with gunfire for being an FBI rat, with Donahue merely an unlucky victim who had offered him a ride home.

Everyone in Boston seemed to believe that Pat Nee was the mystery man in the backseat. Tommy Donahue, Michael Donahue's son, was out in front of the Moakley Courthouse almost daily speaking to the media, accusing Pat Nee of having murdered his father.

Pat had never openly denied the accusations, and so the rumors persisted. As to the Halloran-Donahue hit, he told me "no comment," though he did have an opinion about the Donahues. "They know where I am," he said. "If they wanted to say something to me or do something, they know where to find me." The implication was: That's how we do things in Southie. If need be, we take matters into our own hands.

Certain crimes were buried deep in the molten foundations of the neighborhood. That's what I wanted to ask Pat about.

In the mid-1970s, not long after the mob summit meeting at Chandler's, Whitey Bulger began to systematically remove some of his most fearsome rivals in South Boston. Bulger, now affiliated with the Winter Hill Mob, was meeting on a daily basis in Somerville at the Marshall Motors garage. But Whitey knew that he needed to have his own base of operation. He also knew that in Southie he would never be viewed as the top guy as long as various members of the Mullen gang were still around.

I had interviewed Pat Nee before about the founding of the Mullen gang in the late 1950s and how they had emerged, during a time of greasers and early rock and roll, as the most feared street gang in South Boston. Named after John Joseph Mullen, a decorated war veteran who had a neighborhood intersection at East Second and O streets named in his honor, the gang was mostly a collection of "wharf rats"—burglars, thieves, and tailgaters known for pilfering goods along the Boston waterfront. The Mullens were not an organized crime unit—that is, until they hooked up with the Winter Hill Mob and became more involved in high-level criminal rackets in the city.

Pat Nee had been responsible for bringing the Mullen gang into the realm of organized crime, and not everyone in the gang was in accordance with the move. By 1974, dissention among what was left of the gang created a situation that was problematic for the Winter Hill Mob, which had essentially absorbed the Mullen gang into its structure. Whitey Bulger began to complain to fellow leaders of the Winter Hill Mob—namely Howie Winter, Steve Flemmi, John Martorano, and others—that some of the former Mullen gang members were more trouble than they were worth.

If any one criminal entity truly represented the hoodlum heart and soul of Southie, it was the Mullen gang. While Bulger had been away in prison, submitting to LSD tests under the watchful eye of the CIA, the Mullens had established themselves as the toughest street fighters in town. Many of the original founders of the gang were ex-military, and others, like Pat Nee, had gone on to fight in Vietnam. In a strange and perhaps perverted way, the dedication and sense of loyalty that these men had known in the service became the foundation of their bond as criminals on the street.

And then, of course, there was the sense of ethnic solidarity. The Mullens were Irish American to the core, with rambunctious, brawling temperaments to prove it. As a further show of solidarity, many of the gang's members wore a claddagh ring. In Celtic tradition, the claddagh is a symbol of friendship, love, and loyalty. Two hands holding a heart with a crown on top is adorned in the ring's setting, along with various jewels. The claddagh has its origins in Galway, the county of Pat Nee's birth and also the county most highly represented among the Irish immigrants and second- and third-generation Irish Americans of South Boston.

As Whitey Bulger surveyed the criminal landscape in Boston, he knew he had a problem. Though he was now affiliated with the Winter Hill Mob and therefore had access to big-money rackets that were beyond the reach of the Mullen gang, he would never rule the great ancestral homeland of South Boston as long as remnants of the Mullen gang were still around.

As with most things, Bulger moved strategically, without anyone fully realizing what his maneuvers were about as they took place.

Over a period of twelve months, from November 1974 to November 1975, Bulger, along with Martorano, Flemmi, and others, murdered three members of the Mullen gang. By the time Bulger was done, he had effectively cut off the legs of what remained of the gang and eliminated the biggest threat to his power in Southie. Once these three bodies had been buried underground, Whitey could, for the first time, legitimately refer to himself as the mob boss of South Boston.

Pat Nee had been there for all of it; he was a reluctant participant in this brutal transfer of power.

I knew from previous interviews I had done with Nee that this was a difficult subject for him to talk about. All these decades later, Nee could now see things about this era that he did not fully recognize at the time. He had slowly come to realize that quite possibly he had been played by Whitey Bulger and made to take part in the elimination of men who were among his closest cohorts in the neighborhood.

Pat agreed to speak with me, but we had to do the interview while he ran a few errands around town. It was Friday afternoon, and Nee was leaving later that evening on an Amtrak Acela train to New York City, where he and a lady friend had tickets to see the Broadway show *Jersey Boys*. They planned on staying in New York through the weekend.

"I want to ask you about those killings of the Mullen gang members back in '74 and '75," I said to Pat.

"Oh boy," he said. "Not a pleasant topic. But go ahead, what do you want to know?"

In November 1974, Bulger murdered Paulie McGonagle, who was a close associate of Pat. Nee and McGonagle were among the most prominent members of the Mullen gang; they had pulled off many capers together. Bulger, on the other hand, had a hostile relationship with the McGonagle family. An earlier attempt by Bulger to kill Paulie had resulted in him accidentally murdering the twin brother, Donnie McGonagle. Bulger knew that for the rest of his life he would probably have McGonagles wanting to seek revenge against him. And so he murdered Paulie.

It was done in typical Bulger fashion—devious and effective. On the day before McGonagle's death, Bulger went to the bank and withdrew cash—all fresh, crisp bills, enough to fill a briefcase. He showed the money to McGonagle, claiming that they were counterfeit bills. McGonagle was impressed. Bulger and McGonagle made an arrangement to meet the following day; McGonagle wanted to purchase some of the counterfeit bills.

The next day Bulger and McGonagle met. Seated in Bulger's car, Whitey opened the briefcase, supposedly to show Paulie the bills. Instead, he pulled out a gun and shot McGonagle in the face.

The next Mullen that Bulger killed was Tommy King, another prominent member of the gang. At the time, King believed that he was in a partnership with Bulger, which is why when Whitey told him that he needed his assistance in tracking down and killing a criminal rival named Alan "Suitcase" Fidler, King was game. He met with Bulger, Howie Winter, and Johnny Martorano. They were all seated in Bulger's car, with Steve Flemmi behind them in a crash car. Flemmi had handed out guns to everyone. What King didn't know was that the chamber of the gun he'd been handed was filled with blanks.

Seated in the backseat behind Tommy King was Martorano. As Johnny explained it, "We were supposed to drive over and shoot Fidler, and on the way, pretty much after we pulled out, I shot Tommy."

"Where did you shoot him?"

"In the head."

Two down, one to go. On the very same night that King was killed, Bulger sought out a third Mullen member, Francis "Buddy" Leonard. Bulger had a beef with Leonard mostly because of his drunken behavior in the neighborhood. Bulger was not a big drinker and never used drugs of any kind. Part of his plan for taking over as boss of the neighborhood was attempting to instill a more rigorous code of personal behavior among Southie gangsters. Buddy did not go along with the program. That night, a few hours after killing King, Bulger found Buddy Leonard and shot him in the head. He then took Leonard's body and put it in King's car, to make it appear as if King had killed Leonard.

Pat Nee did not have anything to do with these murders, but he was alleged to have played a role in the disposal of two of the bodies.

Said Nee, "The killing of Paulie [McGonagle] was a shock to all of us. We knew Whitey had engineered it, but now that we were all affiliated together with Winter Hill, it wasn't like you could go murder Whitey. To do that would mean taking on the entire organization. Paulie was collateral damage."

We were driving in Pat's Jeep across the Tobin Memorial Bridge, over the Mystic River, on our way into the city of Chelsea. Pat had to drop off a gift for a friend, and as we slowed down in afternoon traffic on the bridge, Nee was determined to make sense of it all.

We were not far from the actual location of the Teddy Deegan murder, in a part of the city that hadn't changed much in the last thirty years. The bridge descended into an area of deserted warehouses and crumbling sidewalks. As we talked about events from the 1970s, a time of hard men, secret deals, and dead bodies left in the trunks of cars, it was not hard to conjure the ghosts of the past.

I had interviewed enough gangsters to know that it was sometimes difficult for a professional criminal to explain the ways of the underworld to a "civilian," even someone like myself who had heard many stories. The truth was, in the criminal rackets it was not uncommon to have a partner who was someone you did not completely trust. Strange alliances were born out of the overweening desire to make money. Nee had entered into a partnership with Bulger, but he'd never dealt with someone whose ambitions were so devious and corrupt.

Not only had Bulger killed Paulie McGonagle, but he spread the word among other Mullen members that Tommy King had played a role in the murder. That put Tommy on the outs with Pat and other remaining members of the Mullens, so that a year after the McGonagle murder—when Bulger made his move on King—Tommy had few defenders left in the gang.

Nee did not know that Bulger, just a couple of months before killing King, had entered into a partnership with FBI agent John Connolly. This would prove to be crucial; immediately following the dual killings of King and Leonard, Bulger had Connolly input disinformation into FBI 302s (confidential intelligence files) that King had murdered Buddy Leonard, left him in the car, and skedaddled. It was the beginning of a sneaky pattern of misdirection orchestrated by Bulger and his corrupt enablers in law enforcement. As an informant, he fed them information that helped cover up his murders, and his G-men enablers willingly memorialized his lies via law enforcement files.

Another fact that Nee did not know was that Bulger had gone over his head to get authorization for the murders of King and Leonard from the Winter Hill Mob's ruling board.

I explained to Pat how, during his testimony, John Martorano described Bulger coming to the leadership at Marshall Motors seeking approval for the murders. According to Martorano, "I guess [Bulger] and Tommy couldn't get along; they were always butting heads together. Whitey said, 'Tommy's uncontrollable and he's going to kill some police detective.' . . . So he wanted to kill Tommy, take him out."

According to Martorano, there was disagreement among the group about killing King. But Whitey's argument was convincing: the detective whom King was threatening to kill was Eddie Walsh, a Boston police legend (Eddie was not related to Frank Walsh, the cop who arrested Joe Salvati). Walsh was practically a member of the underworld, a cop whom the gangsters routinely fed information for their own purposes—information that made Walsh look like a rainmaker, with sources in the underworld that were the envy of others in law enforcement. Killing Detective Eddie Walsh would open a can of worms and bring about a level of scrutiny that would be harmful to everyone.

Nee listened carefully as I described how his partners in the Winter Hill Mob made the decision to take out his former associate in the Mullen gang. "The bit about Tommy wanting to kill Eddie Walsh is bullshit," he said. "Tommy was a drinker and a loud-mouth. He might have said something like that—boasting—but he never would have done it." Unlike the Paulie McGonagle killing, which was done surreptitiously, the killing of Tommy King had been planned and approved by the Winter Hill gang braintrust. Nee was alleged to have helped dig King's grave.

The digging of graves and burying of bodies would become a Southie underworld ritual during the Bulger era. Before that, during the gang wars, bodies had been dumped in alleyways or left in car trunks, but Whitey was far too finicky and thorough to leave behind such obvious loose ends.

To be a member of the underworld's inner circle in Southie meant you sometimes got roped into burial duty, whether you liked it or not.

Nee supposedly had been called on to help bury Paulie McGonagle in a grave at Tenean Beach, in Dorchester. Alongside him that night digging the hole, according to court testimony, was Tommy King.

Given the statute of limitations, Nee could not be chargd for his role in this or other burials, but as with most allegations stemming from the Bulger years, he neither confirms nor denies the particulars.

Even so, the details are revealing, because a year later Nee is alleged to have been at a nearby location, this time helping to bury King.

If true, the irony was instructive, with a succession of burials that had to feel ominous for anyone holding the shovel. Being a gangster in Southie had become like the children's rhyme, "Ring Around the Rosie." You thought everyone was working in unison, but before you knew you it, you had a pocketful of posies and were digging your own grave.

IN THE EARLY weeks of the Bulger trial, I sometimes found myself asking, What's so special about Whitey Bulger? In the Boston underworld of the late 1960s and early 1970s, he was a gangster without portfolio. He had gained some stature through his role in the Killeen organization but that was on the wane as the Killeens were wiped out by the Mullen gang. He rebounded nicely by latching on with the Winter Hill Mob, but even there he was part of a ruling board; he was not the sole leader. He had shown a willingness to kill, which was a prized skill in the underworld, but when it came to killing people he was no Joe Barboza, or John Martorano, or Steve Flemmi. In many ways, in the mid 1970s, he was a garden-variety Boston gangster.

Beginning in 1973, from the time he became part of the Winter Hill Mob, Bulger began a systematic rise in the underworld that distinguished him as a man of near-psychotic ambition. And he was able to rise above the fray because of one single factor that put him in a category by himself: his connections.

It started with his brother, the politician, who served as kind of an un-spoken safety net. More than once, I asked Pat Nee, "Why didn't you kill Whitey Bulger? He was whacking out former partners of yours left and right. You'd begun to feel like maybe you were next on his hit list. Why didn't you kill him before he killed you?" Pat's answer was always the same: Billy.

To kill the brother of the most powerful political figure in the com-munity, a rising star in state politics, would have brought about a level of heat that would have—at least temporarily—wiped out the city's criminal rackets. Billy Bulger's standing in the city protected Whitey Bulger from retribution.

The other factor was John Connolly—or, to be more precise, the inroads that Connolly provided Bulger into a vast universe of corruption within the criminal justice system.

Having a cop in your pocket was nothing new. Before Connolly, the

Winter Hill Mob had David Schneiderhan, a state trooper who, from 1968 to 1978, worked for the state attorney general's organized crime unit. Schneiderhan grew up with the Flemmi brothers, Jimmy the Bear and Stevie, and had been selling information to Steve Flemmi since the late 1960s. As a criminal gang in Boston, you weren't worth much unless you had multiple agents, troopers, or local cops on the payroll.

Even so, Connolly was a gold-plated connection, and the benefits of this alliance were apparent almost immediately. The agent intervened in a dispute that had flared up between a vending company called Melotone and the team of Bulger and Flemmi. The two gangsters had started their own vending company and had been going all over town threatening bar owners who installed Melotone vending machines. The company approached the FBI to see if there was a criminal case to be made against Bulger and Flemmi. Connolly handled the overture, assuring Melotone lawyers that it would not be in their interest to pursue legal action. He had, in other words, acted as a front man for the gang, protecting their financial interests.

On another occasion, Connolly gave Bulger information that allowed the Winter Hill Mob to eliminate an informant in their midst—Richie Castucci. As John Martorano mentioned in his testimony, the gangsters were especially impressed by this because, in giving up Castucci—a registered Top Echelon Informant—Connolly signaled that his loyalty to the gang overrode fidelity to his own FBI.

In 1977, Connolly introduced Jim Bulger to his new supervisor at the organized crime squad, which was also known as C-3. John Morris was from the Midwest, with a personality that was the opposite of Connolly, who was highly personable and tried to give the impression of being street-smart. Morris was soft-spoken, plain, and couldn't have passed for street-wise even if he tried. Mostly, he didn't try, choosing instead to emphasize his strengths as a team player and consummate company man who seemingly followed orders to the letter. His paperwork was impeccable. He had arrived in Boston from the Miami field office and brought with him a reputation as one of the best supervisors in the FBI.

Most confidential informants are reluctant to meet anyone within law enforcement except for their direct handler, for obvious reasons. The fewer people who know about a person's role as an informant the better it is for the informant. But Bulger and Connolly had entered into a relationship that was not your typical gangster-handler arrangement. They were more like associates, two men who each saw the other as an opportunity to enhance his standing within his chosen careers.

In the Irish Mob, connections were everything. Irish gangsters did not function within a structured hierarchy like the Mafia. With Cosa Nostra—literally, "Our Thing"—the reputation of the organization itself was enough to facilitate business and keep people in line. The Mafia was a tradition larger than any one individual. In the Irish Mob, there seemed to be an aversion to structure. An Irish gangster was only as powerful or successful as the connections he was able to make both in the underworld and in the legitimate worlds of business and law enforcement. The history of the Irish Mob going back to the years of Prohibition and before was littered with illicit alliances between gangsters, lawmen, and politicos.

Bulger seemed to have an intuitive awareness of this history. In his early years as a criminal, he'd envisioned himself an outlaw in the manner of Dillinger, roaming from state to state committing robberies. But if he expected to operate within the universe of organized crime as an Irish American gangster, he knew that he needed to have a base of operation, or turf, of his own. In the old country, turf was something you burned for heat, but it also represented home and hearth, the foundation of all civilization. Southie fit the bill; it was an insular Irish American community with a strong code of loyalty where, it just so happened, Whitey was one step removed from a ruling overlord: his brother.

But the statehouse was not the street, and so Bulger still had to take over Southie's underworld the old-fashioned way—by killing people. He moved on from conquering the Mullen gang to compromising law enforcement, starting with Connolly, a fellow son of Southie who also understood the empirical power of having the right connections. The two men were side by side. Whitey's code name for Connolly was Zip, because they lived in the same zip code. Through Zip, Bulger got to know nearly every agent in the FBI's organized crime unit, including Morris, the supervisor. But he did not stop there.

In 2012, when I interviewed John Connolly, he told me about the time he introduced Bulger to Jeremiah O'Sullivan. The meeting took place in

December 1978, and it had a sense of urgency. A few months earlier, Bulger had been abruptly dropped as a Top Echelon Informant when it was announced to the FBI that he was the target of a federal investigation. Being the target of a criminal probe disqualified someone from being an informant.

In Bulger's case, he and his partner Flemmi were part of a massive investigation involving the fixing of horse races at tracks throughout the Northeast. Spearheaded by a consortium of prosecutors from different jurisdictions, the investigation had been ongoing for years. A sprawling web of criminals, led by Howie Winter, had bought off jockeys and had been fixing races at eight different tracks in five states. Investigators in New Jersey had initiated the case revolving around an informant named Anthony "Fat Tony" Ciulla, a Boston Mafiosi who, along with Winter, had devised the scam. For nearly four years the gangsters had been fixing horse races at tracks in New Jersey, Massachusetts, New York, Rhode Island, and elsewhere. It was estimated that, from 1974 to 1978, they had netted more than $8 million.

In the fall of 1978, Ciulla testified in front of a grand jury in New Jersey. Now the case was spreading to the District of Massachusetts, and federal indictments seemed imminent.

Agents John Connolly and John Morris were concerned that they were about to lose their prize informants, Bulger and Flemmi. So they met with Jeremiah O'Sullivan, lead prosecutor in the case.

It went against FBI informant-handling regulations for the agents to reveal the identity of an active informant to anyone, including a federal prosecutor. But these were special circumstances. Bulger and Flemmi represented the FBI's best chance for making a major case against Jerry Angiulo and the Mafia, which had became the number-one priority in the Boston field office. The agents explained all this to O'Sullivan, who shared their dream of a major case targeting the Angiulo brothers. O'Sullivan told the agents he would look into it and get back to them.

According to Connolly, he later heard from O'Sullivan, who wanted to meet Bulger. "I asked him, 'Are you sure? You don't have to.'" It was highly unusual for an assistant U.S. attorney to meet face-to-face with someone like Bulger. But O'Sullivan insisted. Connolly set up a meeting between the city's rising mobster and its top organized crime prosecutor in a hotel room on a rainy afternoon around Christmas. "I was there," Connolly told me. "Jimmy met Jerry. As I remember it, they were both quite impressed with one another."

After this meeting, in January 1979, O'Sullivan agreed to drop Bulger and Flemmi from the indictment. They were free and clear.

On February 3, 1979, the indictments were announced. It was as if an atomic bomb had been dropped on the New England underworld. Twenty-one gangsters were arrested in a series of high-profile raids throughout the region. Thanks to Connolly, John Martorano had learned about the indictment and gone on the run. Howie Winter was not tipped off and had been arrested; he was facing a twenty-year sentence.

Bulger was reinstated as a Top Echelon Informant. In addition, Steve Flemmi was officially reopened as a TE in February 1980, with Special Agent John Connolly as his handler.

The circle of continuity was complete: as Flemmi's handler, Connolly officially assumed the role of H. Paul Rico, an agent he still referred to many years later, from prison, as "a great man."

The race-fixing case was a turning point on many levels. It virtually wiped out the Winter Hill Mob: along with Howie Winter, Jim Martorano was also arrested. Brother Johnny was forced to go on the lam. "Joe Mac" McDonald, who was already on the lam, was forced to stay. A host of other affiliated criminals were either arrested or forced into hiding and out of the rackets.

Already, Whitey had eliminated the Mullen gang. Now, with the help of the FBI and the most powerful federal prosecutor in New England, he had been a party to the elimination of the Winter Hill Mob. The gang that had been founded by Buddy McLean, then expanded upon by Howie Winter, Joe Mac, Jimmy Sims, and the Martorano brothers, was now under the sole control of Bulger and Flemmi.

Whitey didn't have to make trips over to the Marshall Motors garage in Somerville anymore. The Winter Hill Mob was dead. It was all Whitey and Stevie now, with South Boston as their exclusive base of operation.

The FBI agents made the introductions, but O'Sullivan had pulled the trigger. Bulger's connections had now expanded beyond Connolly and

Morris into a new and more exalted realm of the criminal justice system. The pieces were in place for Bulger to become boss of the entire Boston underworld. Only one thing stood in his way: the Mafia.

AT THE BULGER trial, prosecutors Wyshak and Kelly had little to gain by shedding light on this narrative of alliances between the underworld and the upperworld in Boston. They were more concerned with establishing a link between Bulger and the victims of his crimes. The links to O'Sullivan were especially problematic for the prosecutors. After O'Sullivan left the Organized Crime Strike Force in 1987, he became U.S. attorney, a predecessor to the person currently holding the job, Carmen Ortiz. To ponder the irony that O'Sullivan, a key component in Bulger's rise to power, was once in control of the very office that now sought to prosecute the mob boss was something the prosecutors needed to stifle at every turn. Instead, the jury was treated to a more plebeian narrative, some of it punctuated with low humor.

When Frank Capizzi took the stand, courtroom spectators might have guessed they were in for a show. Capizzi was seventy-nine years old, with his white hair in a ponytail. He wore an out-of-date sport coat, and had a voice out of central casting. He spoke in the gravelly tones of the late actor Michael V. Gazzo, who played the character Frank Pantangeli in *The Godfather: Part II*—a voice so redolent of the streets that for generations after that movie was released, young Mafiosi who thought they sounded tough were merely doing an imitation of Michael Gazzo.

Capizzi, on the other hand, was an original. His time in the underworld predated both *Godfather* movies.

He took the stand with a wild-eyed look, as if taking the stand in a criminal court preceding was something he had feared his entire life. He glanced in the direction of Bulger but seemed disoriented, as if everything about the environment he was in suggested that he had arrived prematurely at his own conception of hell on earth.

The prosecutor, Zach Hafer, sensed the witness's discomfort and sought to put him at ease. "Sir," he said, "before we get to the substance of your testimony, I want to ask you a few questions about your medical condition, if I could. Do you have a condition, sir, that causes something referred to as audio interruption?"

"Yes, absolutely," said Capizzi.

"Could you explain that?"

"After I had encephalitis meningitis, I got a condition. When I hear you speak, I have to stop and think about what you're saying, because what you're saying to me comes over in the Sicilian language. Some words are English, some words are Sicilian, and I have to decipher."

Oh boy: audio interruption. Did such a thing exist? There were titters in the courtroom among the jury and the spectators. It sounded like the beginnings of a comedy routine. Said Hafer, "If you need me to repeat anything or slow down, just let me know."

Capizzi was there to serve the same function as Diane Sussman de Tennen, Ralph DeMasi, and others who had survived Winter Hill gangland mayhem from the time of the gang wars and could now provide sinew and flesh to crimes that might otherwise be perceived as remote or outdated.

Back in 1973, like a lot of gangsters in Boston, Capizzi found himself caught up in the Winter Hill Mob's murderous hunt for Indian Al Notarangeli. In Capizzi's case, he was in a car one night with a couple of members of Notarangeli's crew, Al "Bud" Plummer and Hugh "Sonny" Shields. They had just pulled up to a stoplight at the intersection of Commercial and Hanover streets, in the heart of the city's North End.

Capizzi felt safe on Hanover Street. He'd been born and raised in a cold-water flat at 452 Hanover Street, on the exact corner where he now sat in the backseat of Al Plummer's car. This was his neighborhood. His parents had come here from the same town in Sicily, only they didn't know that until they met on Hanover Street. They both found work in the garment industry. But Capizzi's father, who was a tailor, died suddenly when Frank was in his late teens, and his mother passed away a year later. Frank was on his own. In 1952, he joined the U.S. Coast Guard, and for a time was stationed at a Coast Guard facility located, of all places, at the corner of Commercial and Hanover streets. After leaving the Coast Guard, young Frank Capizzi became a numbers runner and a gambler and, according to law enforcement, a made member of La Cosa Nostra.

Before he was sitting in the backseat of Al Plummer's car, at an intersection near where much of his life seemed to have taken place, Capizzi was at a bar having a drink. He decided to go see his Sicilian grandmother. "She still lived in the North End, and thinking about this, I knew she never slept. So it was ten o'clock at night, and I was going to pay her a good-night visit. She was about eighty-five, I think, or eighty-eight at the time. And she still lived on Hanover Street." So he was on his way to give his grandmother a good-night kiss on the cheek, and he'd enlisted Al Plummer to give him a ride.

Asked Hafer, "What happened after you got into the car with Plummer and Shields on March 19, 1973?"

Capizzi paused; the prosecutor's words seemed to be bouncing around inside his head. "Excuse me. I was just deciphering what you were saying."

"No problem. Take your time. After you were in the car driving towards Hanover Street, did something unusual happen?"

"Unusual?" The witness seemed insulted by the word's inadequacy. "A firing squad hit us," he proclaimed. "For maybe two and a half minutes, about a hundred slugs hit the automobile, and it imploded."

"Could you tell from the noise how many guns were firing at you?"

"I'll speculate. It sounded and felt like maybe two automatic weapons and maybe a couple of rifles or pistols."

The jury had heard about this event from one of the men on the other side of the guns—Martorano—who testified that he and Howie Winter did the shooting from one car, with Bulger and others providing backup in another.

"What did you do when the shooting stopped?" asked Hafer.

"Unbelievably, although I had been hit in the head and could feel warm blood running down my neck and excruciating pain in my back, I said, 'Let's get the fuck out of this car. Bud, come on.' And I put my hand into his neck where his head should have been." Plummer's head had been obliterated by the fusillade of bullets.

Capizzi's testimony was dramatic, and as he explained being rushed to the hospital and undergoing emergency surgery—which saved his life—he warmed to the idea of having a captive audience. Capizzi told the jury and everyone in the courtroom that after that fateful day in 1973, which resulted in the death of Al Plummer, he left the city of his birth and never returned.

On cross-examination, the witness became feisty, as if he were once again a gangster back on the streets. When defense attorney Carney asked if Jerry Angiulo was the head of a criminal group in the North End, he answered, "That's what the papers say."

"Do you know that yourself?" asked Carney.

"You know, ask me a more specific question. Did I know that? The question should be, Who doesn't know that?"

The courtroom erupted in laughter. Capizzi smiled; he was getting the hang of this. But then Carney started asking about specific criminal activities, and Capizzi's audio interruption kicked in. "Say that again?" he responded to a question about illegal gambling, which he theoretically heard half in Sicilian and half in English. And to another question, "Would you repeat that again—slowly? I wanna get every word," to which jurors and spectators again burst into laughter.

When Carney asked Capizzi about whether Al Notarangeli made his living from bookmaking forty years ago, he responded, "Forty years ago? Who remembers a lot of what we did forty years ago? He probably gambled like the rest of us."

Then Carney got specific: "Were you involved in any way in illegal bookmaking?"

Capizzi gave the lawyer a hard stare, the kind he may have given to late-paying gambling clients back in the day. He turned to the judge. "Your Honor, I'm going to invoke my right under the Fifth Amendment."

The judge tried to explain to Capizzi that he already had immunity to testify; he didn't need to claim the Fifth. He could not be prosecuted for anything he might say. But Capizzi wasn't buying it. He asked to see a court-appointed lawyer. So he was removed from the stand until a lawyer could be found to explain the situation. Meanwhile, other minor witnesses were brought to the stand to give testimony.

After a few hours, Capizzi was brought back to the witness stand. He was ready to resume. But, in the intervening time, defense lawyer Carney had apparently decided that this witness, with his audio interruption and selective memory, was more trouble than he was worth. Capizzi took the stand, and Carney said, "Your Honor, I have no further questions."

"Mr. Capizzi," said Judge Casper. "You don't have to get comfortable. Examination is completed. You're excused."

Capizzi seemed positively thrilled. "Thank you, Your Honor."

"No problem, sir."

As the aging Mafiosi stood up, there were chuckles of appreciation in the courtroom. He looked out at the people, as if a standing ovation might be in order. "Thank you, everyone," he announced. "I appreciate it. It's been an experience."

And then he left, a minor though memorable player in the trial of Whitey Bulger.

7

THE BIG SLEAZE

WAS THE DEFENDANT a Top Echelon Informant, or was he not?

If the defense had their way, this question should have dominated the trial. Weeks earlier, in his opening statement, Jay Carney had planted the seed, hoping that it might produce a tuber or a spore all on its own, since precious little had been done so far to nurture its growth. Through witness testimony and legal posturing among the competing sides, Whitey's status with the FBI had been little more than a stalking horse—derided by some witnesses, speculated upon by others, or accepted as a given fact.

The man who would serve as the catalyst for bringing Whitey's informant status to the forefront was James Marra, a most unassuming bureaucrat. Marra worked for the DOJ's Office of the Inspector General. Before that he worked at the U.S. Office of Social Security; the Labor Department; and the Treasury Department, all as a special agent with the Inspector General's Office.

A little-known federal agency that is empowered to investigate accusations of corruption, fraud, and waste within agencies of the federal government, the Inspector General's Office proudly flies below the radar. Their agents do not carry guns or do stakeouts or make arrests. Marra had been with the Inspector General's Office for twenty-nine years. Since he is a man in his late forties, it's fair to say that he was weaned at the bosom of the federal law enforcement bureaucracy.

In 2004, Marra was assigned to investigate matters of internal corruption surrounding Bulger's relationship with the FBI. Over a nine-year period, he had become an expert on all government documentation pertaining to the relationship between the FBI and Bulger. Marra testified at Connolly's 2008 murder trial in Florida, and even before he took the stand at the current Bulger trial, he was in the courtroom nearly every day monitoring the proceedings. Very little happened in regards to the prosecution of Bulger that was not duly noted and recorded by Marra, who then reported to his supervisors in Washington, D.C.

Like a character out of a John le Carré novel, he was an anonymous figure buried deep within the machine, until the day arrived that he was called upon to step forward into the light. Day eight of testimony in the Bulger trial was that moment for John Marra. He was the vehicle by which the prosecution would enter into evidence the informant file for BS-1544, otherwise known as James Joseph Bulger Jr.

On a large screen, the prosecution projected the image of government exhibit No. 354, which Marra identified as Bulger's informant index card. On the card were the date Bulger was first enlisted as an informant—September 1975—and the name of his "contacting agent," John Connolly. This information was highly confidential, noted Marra. "The identity of individuals who are cooperating with the federal government, their names would not be disclosed in most reports. This would be on a strict need-to-know who that person was. It would be limited usually to the people that are working the informant, supervisors, and agents that are working the case."

About Bulger, Marra said, "During the approximately fifteen years that the file existed on him, at different times he was considered an Organized Crime Informant, was elevated to Top Echelon Informant, then he was closed. He was reopened as an Organized Crime Informant, but again he's elevated to Top Echelon Informant based upon the information he's providing to the FBI."

Prosecutor Wyshak swiftly immersed the witness into what would become known colloquially as Bulger's "rat file." Again, on the screen were projected facsimiles of reports known as 209s or 302s, internal memos, most of them filed by Special Agent Connolly.

Wyshak would instruct Marra to read from a portion of the file, which he did with little or no inflection. It was an instructive process. The Bulger files contained seven hundred pages and read like a who's who of the Boston underworld. The official story had always been that Bulger was enlisted by Connolly to rat on the Mafia, but even a cursory sampling of the files revealed information on Bulger's own partners:

Joseph "Joe Mac" McDonald—*On 1/16/83, BS 1544-OC advised that the weapons that Joe McDonald was carrying were two converted Ingram .380 semiautomatic weapons which had been converted to fully automatic weapons. McDonald also had home made silencers with him. Source advised that Mc-Donald was transporting the weapons to Queens, New York City, and they were going to a first cousin who is active in raising money for the IRA.*

The Winter Hill Mob—*On 8/15/80, BS 1544-TE advised that Joe Mc-Donald is supposed to be drinking heavily and the word is that Johnny Marto-rano is spending time with him to straighten him out. Source advised that the Hill people will back away from McDonald if he cannot control his drinking. Source considers McDonald to be an extremely dangerous and volatile individ-ual. . . . NOTE: Same source in past insert advised that Martorano was in the Miami, Florida area.*

On 1/26/83, BS 1499-OC advised that Joe McDonald and/or Jimmy Sims are attempting to be assigned to Leavenworth Penitentiary to get with Howie Winters. Source advised that one or both may try to pull some strings politically to wind up in the same penitentiary as Winters.

The Joe Murray Crew from Charlestown—*On 2/8/82, BS 1544-OC advised that Joe Murray, who owns Murray Towing Company in Charlestown, is the biggest importer and distributor of marijuana on the East Coast and possibly the whole country. Source advised that Murray is a "real sleeper" and is probably "the best kept secret in organized crime." . . . Source emphasized that Murray has high level Coast Guard personnel on the "pad."*

On 4/20/88, BS 1544-TE advised that the conventional wisdom in the underworld is that the Liberty Bank burglary score was taken down by the Joe Murray crew from Charlestown. Source advised that Michael Murray, an ac-knowledged alarm expert, handled that end of it with Gigi Eatherton, Jimmy Murray, and John McCormack also participating.

Depositors Trust robbery—*On 6/25/80, BS 1544-TE advised that the word on the street is that two police officers, a Medford sergeant named Doherty and an MDC police captain named Jerry Clement were "in" on the Depositors Trust score. The set-up guy is supposed to be Bucky Barrett who, in turn, is supposed to have brought in other unknown help. The talk is that Barrett has control over the majority of the gold and diamonds. There is supposed to be over 80 pounds of gold.*

Tommy King—*On 12/31/75, source stated that the word is out that Tommy King has been taken out. Source stated that various rumors are flying about as to whether or not he is actually dead and the reason for it. Source heard that King had gone "kill crazy" and was putting people's lives in jeopardy in that he was talking crazy about killing various people including police officers. Source stated that King gave them no alternative but to make a move on him.*

From the lips of Jim Marra came what had once been viewed as an unprecedented treasure trove: names, dates, and references to criminal activities of which Whitey Bulger had privileged, inside information. There were sheets of paper, now being projected onto a computer screen in the courtroom, filled with underworld intelligence and gossip. Some of this information had contributed to the securing of warrants and court-authorized wiretaps and other investigative techniques that could and did, on occasion, lead to indictments and arrests—though Bulger's name was never linked to any of these actions.

Marra had taken the stand on a Friday, and on Monday his direct testimony continued with little contention until Wyshak asked a question for which he'd spent numerous hours laying the foundation: "Mr. Marra, based on your review of these particular files, is there any doubt in your mind that Mr. Bulger was an informant for the FBI?"

"Objection, Your Honor," interjected Hank Brennan.

The entire proceeding had reached a cul-de-sac, one that had been inevitable ever since the defense first claimed in open court that the defendant, contrary to public legend, never was an FBI informant. Up until now, everyone had been able to ignore this claim, but the time had arrived to confront the beast.

Judge Casper dismissed the jury and the witness.

The lawyers and spectators stood as the jurors filed out of the courtroom. Once the jurors were gone, Casper said, "Everyone can be seated. Counsel, I know there was an objection. I'll hear Mr. Wyshak."

The prosecutor stood before the court. "Your Honor, I understand that for whatever reasons, whether it's the ego of the defendant or attempting to preserve his reputation, he does not want to be called an informant. But I am not going to tailor my questions in a manner that preserves that ridiculous contention." Normally, Wyshak spoke with the common sense of a corner druggist, but here his voice had an unusual tone, a trace of exasperation—some might say a whine—in reference to Bulger.

"It's not as though we have one report or two reports. We have fifteen years of reports from Mr. Bulger. As a matter of fact, the exercise that I'm currently going to undertake is to demonstrate that not only did Mr. Bulger report to Mr. Connolly, but he reported to Mr. Morris, he reported to Mr. [James] Ring, he had meetings with the Special Agent in Charge of the FBI in 1980. He reported to another special agent, Nick Gianturco.

"So unless it is Mr. Bulger's contention that all of these agents got together to fabricate this file for some reason, his contention that he was not an FBI informant is simply absurd. And I don't think the government should be required in the face of all this evidence to tailor its questions in a manner which preserves this contention."

The judge raised an eyebrow. "Mr. Brennan, I'll hear you."

Brennan took a breath. For the defense, this was an issue that, they believed, defined their case. "Your Honor, the Department of Justice has historically engaged in inappropriate relationships with organized crime figures. There are documented histories of relationships with organized crime figures who are serial murderers, not limited to this case. There is an extraordinary history that when the Department of Justice employees can benefit their objectives, they'll allow organized crime figures to engage in whatever conduct they want. . . . That is the historical backdrop to this case. It goes through Barboza, it goes through this case. . . .

"Furthermore, there is a long-standing history of the Department of Justice, FBI Washington, Strike Force employees overlooking the relationship between Mr. Connolly and Mr. Bulger. There is a long-standing history of them choosing not to indict or charge Mr. Bulger with any crimes. The DOJ had an obligation on a quarterly or yearly basis to look into these files, to consider whether or not they were viable. They didn't do that, or if they did, they didn't do a very thorough job. There is missing information suggesting that there isn't any authenticity to these files. There is no pink sheet, which is a piece of paper [with personal information] about the intake a person must go through in order to sign up to be an informant. That is absent here.

"Certainly the DOJ needs to protect the fact that they let somebody they believe is a killer run loose, kill people throughout the Boston area, and never charge him. If they were now to come in and admit the truth, that there was a special relationship and nobody cared about it because they were pursuing the LCN, then they would have a problem.

"So to come in now and say that somehow this person, Mr. Marra, who's never had a conversation with Mr. Bulger, to give an opinion that he was an informant . . . There is absolutely no basis for it."

Wyshak seemed miffed by the sweeping, roundhouse nature of Brennan's objection. "Your Honor, all of that information—whatever happened with Barboza and those relationships [from long ago] has nothing to do with the fact of whether or not Mr. Bulger was an informant. He was an informant who corrupted his handler, and, you know, the Justice Department, the FBI, shares some responsibility for continuing to operate Mr. Bulger as an informant over the years. The government doesn't dispute that, but one does not follow the other. It doesn't mean that Mr. Bulger was not an informant."

The discussion continued for the better part of an hour. Brennan was objecting on a number of different grounds to a number of different issues, though he kept trying to bring the argument back to his contention that the central fallacy of the government's case was that Whitey Bulger was an informant.

It was a circular argument, and the more Brennan spoke, with occasional injections of support from his co-counsel Carney, the farther the defense team drifted from shore.

The leakiness of their position was obvious: From before the trial began, they had been arguing that Bulger's position was that he had been given immunity from prosecution by Jeremiah O'Sullivan. Few specific details about that arrangement were put forth. There was no mention of a meeting in a hotel room around Christmas of 1978, with John Connolly present. The defense team preferred to leave it as vague as possible. All they would say is that a meeting or meetings had taken place. Consequently, Bulger promised something to O'Sullivan, and O'Sullivan, in return, offered immunity to one of the most notorious gangsters within his jurisdiction.

Assuming that this exchange did take place, and that some sort of mutual arrangement was discussed, the most credible conclusion would be that Bulger was offering to help O'Sullivan take down the Mafia by serving as

THE BIG SLEAZE   187

an informant, and in exchange the top crime prosecutor promised that he would cover Bulger's back. But the defense wasn't making that argument. Instead, they were asking the jury—and the public—to make a leap of faith and accept, for the sake of argument, that Bulger never was an informant.

Which begged the question: if Bulger wasn't an informant, why would O'Sullivan offer him immunity?

Throughout pretrial hearings, and now well into the presentation of evidence, the defense lawyers had not answered this question, except to say that their client, Jim Bulger, would take the stand and tell all. Their frequent provocative claims that Bulger would testify on his own behalf had galvanized the media and brought great attention to their case, but in the absence of any further explanation of what Bulger's arrangement with O'Sullivan had been, they were making an argument without adequate foundation. The entire discussion was a red herring. Bulger was not charged with being an informant; it wasn't one of the counts in the indictment. By spending so much time and energy on this point, the defense lawyers were obscuring what should have been their primary argument: that Bulger's relationship with Connolly, Morris, O'Sullivan, et al. was a historical continuation of the Barboza years. Jim Bulger was merely a player in a dirty and corrupt game that had been ongoing in Boston for close to half a century.

Both Brennan and Carney had alluded to this position, and, beginning with Carney's opening statement, had attempted to establish it as part of the defense narrative. But every time they sought to claim that Bulger had never been an informant, it muddied the waters and diluted their defense.

In his cross-examination of Marra, Brennan did score some points. He made it clear that Bulger's informant file had many peculiarities. When a special agent enlists an informant, he's supposed to have him read and sign a "pink sheet," which includes a set of guidelines. The agent is supposed to take fingerprints of the informant, and also to supply a current photo, ideally one taken by the agent himself.

Bulger's file did have a pink sheet, but it contained none of the above. There was no signature from Bulger acknowledging that he had entered into an informant relationship with the FBI. No fingerprints. And the only photo in his file was an ancient arrest photo from 1959, taken when Bulger was twenty-one years old.

Brennan spent much of Marra's time on the stand seeking to establish that Bulger's informant file, in its totality, was a work of fiction. He projected onto a screen many of the same memoranda first entered into evidence by Wyshak: reports, signed by Connolly, purporting to be "insert files" of information provided to the agent by Bulger.

"Mr. Marra," asked the defense attorney about one insert file, "when you say you saw this in the file that Mr. Connolly had for Mr. Bulger, did you make any other determination about whether Bulger actually gave this information to Connolly or got it from somewhere else?"

Marra was asked a version of this question nearly a dozen times in relation to a dozen different memos and insert files, and he rarely gave a straightforward answer. When finally pinned down, he was forced to say, "No. I did no independent investigation on that." It was in the Bulger informant file, as created by Connolly, and therefore assumed by Marra and everyone else in the FBI to be what it was purported to be.

Brennan asked Marra about "the rotor," a circular, rotating file cabinet inside the FBI office that contained files pertaining to all criminal matters under the purview of the office, including, in some cases, open informant files. The rotor would become a running theme throughout the trial. Both the defense team and prosecution acknowledged that the rotor was likely plundered by John Connolly, who stole information from other files and put it in Bulger's file, as if it originally came from BS-1544.

Though Marra was curiously unwilling to concede the point, it was clear to any discerning observer that Connolly had engaged in a system of puffery; he had ginned up Bulger's informant file with information stolen from other files, or garnered from other informants and attributed to Bulger. In some cases, the information in Bulger's informant file was identical to information in Stephen Flemmi's file, as the defense lawyers illustrated by projecting the file memos side by side in open court.

Bulger's rat file began to emerge as a talisman that, when split open and examined, became a portal into a world of bureaucratic deception, chicanery, and lies. Connolly needed to pad and puff up Bulger's file because he needed him to be designated a Top Echelon Informant, which was the cream of the crop. In general, informants were seedy little vermin who hid in dark alleyways and traded information for a pat on the head by their law enforcement masters, but a TE was at the top of the pyramid, a high-ranking mobster who was privy to policy-making decisions by an underworld board of directors. Special agents who handled TEs were royalty within the bureau. They received commendations and monetary prizes and incentives. Among other agents, they were the cock of the walk.

An agent would go to great lengths to protect their golden goose, and they were enabled in their efforts to do so from within the system. In this regard, the FBI was in a league by itself.

The National Crime Information Center (NCIC) system is a central database of criminal information available to all U.S. law enforcement. Whenever any agency of law enforcement, federal or local, ran a search on someone who was designated as an FBI informant, like, say, James J. "Whitey" Bulger, the bureau was immediately notified. No other branch of law enforcement was accorded this privilege. As Marra put it from the stand, "The end result is Mr. Connolly would be aware of any law enforcement agency who conducted a criminal inquiry on Mr. Bulger. He would get a notice that this was the agency that ran the query and the purpose for that query, which usually is criminal or investigative, and he would be aware that someone's looking or at least running criminal histories on his informant."

The witness had no problems with designating Connolly and the FBI as the primary culprits in the cultivation and protection of Bulger. In fact, that's why Marra was on the stand. Whenever he was asked if he pursued other avenues of questionable contacts with Bulger above and beyond the FBI, Marra retreated to what would become a mantra: he had been assigned to investigate whether Agent Connolly had supplied information to Bulger that led to the murders of Castucci, Wheeler, Halloran, Donahue, and Callahan. Nothing more.

Marra was a veteran employee of the DOJ. He had been assigned to monitor the Bulger prosecutions and, it could be argued, make sure that damage did not spread beyond the Boston office of the FBI. He was the Little Dutch Boy with his finger in the dike, and as such, he undertook his duties with extreme prejudice.

CORRUPTION IN LAW enforcement is nothing new. The emphasis on the ceremonial aspects of policing—the pride that comes from pledging allegiance to a military-style organization based on dedication and loyalty—seems to exist partly as a counterbalance to the reality that there will always be officers who choose personal aggrandizement over ethics. In the public domain, there is a yearning to present cops and agents as heroic figures, with a job that requires a level of stress and danger that no mere mortal could ever understand. Yet cops and agents are themselves drawn from the ranks of mere mortals, susceptible to the same temptations and lapses in judgment as the average schnook.

The type of lawman most likely to become entangled in corruption is one on the front lines, a cop or agent who comes into direct contact with criminals or criminal activity. The most obvious lures are money and power. John Connolly took money from Bulger and Flemmi, cash payments totaling $250,000 over roughly a ten-year period. By most accounts, he reveled in the financial largesse—he wore expensive jewelry and suits that were beyond the means of the average FBI agent. Along with his home in Boston, he acquired a house on the Cape—the de rigueur status symbol for upwardly mobile New Englanders—and he purchased a boat to go with it.

In retrospect, money was likely not the primary motivator for Connolly. What he seemed to value most in his relationship with Bulger and Flemmi was the status and stature it accorded him within the ranks of federal law enforcement. For an insecure person—or someone whose reputation for confidence is based primarily on external measures—the pursuit of this kind of stature represents its own kind of corruption. To be respected or revered or feared—to have that kind of power—is, in the pantheon of human motivators, as much a manifestation of corruption as taking an illegal cash payoff under the table.

A far more nuanced form of corruption is that which is rooted in the system. This type of corruption is often predicated on the performance and policies of an institution. To enhance the institution's reputation, or to safeguard a history of impropriety within the institution, individual officers or agents are encouraged to do what needs to be done on behalf of it. If they do it well, they are rewarded with commendations, promotions, and plum assignments; they will be accorded esteem within their universe of influence. In return it is understood that if they are exposed in any way, they will fall on their sword; they will take the hit on behalf of the organization.

In this regard, Paul Rico and Dennis Condon had never been tested.

Anything untoward they might have done, such as suppressing evidence and suborning perjury, or criminal, such as acting as an accessory to a murder, they had gotten away with it. By the mid-1970s it was time for a new generation to do the dirty work.

When John Morris first came to the Boston office of the FBI, he was, as he himself has noted, a hayseed from Kansas City. Just two years out of the academy, Morris was assigned to the unit known as Squad-5, the organized crime (OC) unit that would later change its designation to C-3. The Boston division's OC squad was famous within law enforcement for having convicted Raymond Patriarca, who was at that time the highest-ranking member of Cosa Nostra ever prosecuted in federal court.

Morris was lucky. The star of the squad was Dennis Condon, who had played a vital role in the Patriarca case. Condon's partner, Paul Rico, had moved on to the FBI's Miami office and would soon retire, but Condon was still in Boston basking in the glow of earlier successes. Having been a crucial player during the Barboza years, Condon had an unparalleled reputation as a handler of informants, not so much through his personal connections with criminals out on the street, but rather from his ability to finesse those relationships within the bureaucracy and maintain credible informant files. By the time Morris arrived, Condon had even been given a special designation as "supervisor of informants."

To those within the system who had been a party to the framing of innocent men during the Teddy Deegan murder trial, Condon—along with Rico and prosecutor Ted Harrington—was something of a local legend. The Barboza years and the Deegan case had created a potential sinkhole that could have engulfed the entire Boston division of the FBI, and somehow Condon, Rico, and Harrington had not only emerged unscathed, they had safeguarded the Patriarca conviction and burnished the reputation of the criminal justice system in Boston.

Morris and Condon lived in the same neighborhood of Lexington, the leafy Boston suburb that was at the center of much local Revolutionary War history. Not long after Morris arrived in Boston, he and Condon began carpooling to work every morning. On these drives, Morris learned about the years of the Boston gang wars, Joe Barboza, and the Patriarca convictions. He was schooled on how FBI business was handled in Boston.

Morris and Condon were far apart in age, but they had some similarities. Neither was particularly street-savvy; they did not have the types of personalities that would make it easy for them to talk or circulate among gangsters, à la Paul Rico. Condon communicated to Morris that for an agent like him to rise in the organization, he needed to find his own Paul Rico, his own swaggering doppelganger who could function as yin to his yang.

Within a year of Morris's arrival in Boston, John Connolly would be transferred from the New York office, after his dramatic arrest of Most Wanted fugitive Frank Salemme on a street in Manhattan. All three men—Morris, Condon, and Connolly—were now part of the same unit. The pieces were in place for a passing of the baton from the Barboza years to whatever was to come next.

WHITEY BULGER HARDLY looked up from the notepad he was doodling on when John Morris entered the courtroom. Unlike with some of the witnesses so far, where Bulger's disinterest seemed genuine, in this case the defendant's body language spoke volumes. Bulger seemed to be pissed-off about something. His mood was also reflected in his attire. Today, his Hensley was a dark blue bordering on black.

On the other hand, the witness, as he was sworn in and took the stand, was the picture of harmlessness. Since his years in the FBI, Morris had gone soft, his face jowly and complexion rosy from his retirement job as a "wine educator," which, no doubt, included some sampling of the product. Morris wore a suit not unlike the type he might have worn back in his days as supervisor of the C-3 squad, a suit without distinction, moderately priced, designed to project conformity and functionality over style.

These two men had not seen each other in decades. They had not spoken since late 1995, in a fateful phone conversation that almost ended Morris's life.

Back then, Morris was working at the FBI's training center in Quantico, Virginia, serving out the latter months of a seemingly distinguished career as chief of training and administration. A year earlier, Whitey Bulger had disappeared on the run and become a Ten Most Wanted fugitive. The

Bulger-Flemmi indictment was causing Morris great consternation. For more than a decade he and Connolly had engaged in a felonious relationship with Bulger and Flemmi, and now, with Bulger on the lam and Flemmi facing charges, it all had the potential to blow wide open.

Chief Morris was in his office one afternoon when his secretary told him there was a Mr. White on the phone. Morris took the call and immediately recognized a voice he hadn't heard in a long time: it was Bulger.

Bulger threatened Morris, telling him that he better "use his Machiavellian ways" to get a hold of the *Boston Globe* and clear up allegations that he was an FBI informant—an allegation that had originated with a leak from Morris. Bulger reminded Morris that he, Morris, had taken money from him on numerous occasions. Bulger's tone was aggressive and terrifying. Morris was getting a full blast of the Whitey Bulger from the streets—the mob boss—not the nice guy with whom he had shared pasta and wine in the years he had cosponsored Bulger as a prize informant for the bureau. Bulger told Morris, "If I go to prison, you're going with me."

When the phone conversation ended, Morris was shaken. He reported the encounter to his supervisor and was instructed to fill out a report, which he did, leaving out details of the conversation that would be self-incriminating. FBI technicians tried to put a trace on the origins of the call from Bulger, but it was too late. The location of the call would remain unknown.

After leaving work that day, Morris began to feel a pain in his chest. He checked himself into a medical clinic, where he proceeded to go into cardiac arrest. Had it not happened when he was already at the clinic, Morris likely would have died from a heart attack that was precipitated by his phone call from Bulger.

Morris recovered. He retired from the FBI on December 31, 1995. Two years later, when he received a call from someone representing the FBI's Office of Professional Responsibility, Morris knew the jig was up. He cut a deal with Fred Wyshak, who was putting together a case against John Connolly. In exchange for telling all that he knew, Morris was given immunity. He testified over eight days at the Wolf hearings, which began a seemingly never-ending series of depositions, hearings, and trial testimony that was now culminating with the Bulger trial.

"Good morning, Mr. Morris," said Wyshak.

"Good morning," said the witness.

Morris had the unenviable position of representing the face of corruption at the trial. Connolly had been rendered useless as a witness in the eyes of both the prosecution and the defense. For more than three weeks, jurors and spectators had been listening to a steady diet of stories about Connolly that portrayed him as being at the heart of a duplicitous and criminal relationship with Bulger and Flemmi. Now here was Connolly's supervisor, the man who helped implement that strategy.

After having Morris take the jury through a distillation of his career in law enforcement, Wyshak got to the heart of the matter. "Now, all right, did you come to know a man named James Bulger?"

"Yes," answered Morris.

"Do you see him sitting in the courtroom today?"

"Yes, I do."

"Would you point him out."

"Right there," said Morris, pointing toward the defendant.

Bulger continued to disdainfully ignore the witness.

"Indicating the defendant, Your Honor," said the prosecutor.

"The record may so reflect," noted Judge Casper.

Morris was asked to describe his very first meeting with Bulger. It was 1978, and he had just taken over as supervisor of the C-3 squad. Back in the early 1970s, he'd been a rank-and-file member of the squad, along with John Connolly, with whom he had developed a close friendship. Now that he had taken over as supervisor, Morris and Connolly rekindled their relationship and began to chart out a plan for making a major case against the Mafia in Boston. The linchpin, as Connolly described it, involved bringing Bulger into the fold.

"Where did you meet with Mr. Bulger?" Morris was asked.

"My home in Lexington."

"Why did you choose that location?"

"John [Connolly], in discussing where we could possibly meet, and describing the type of relationship that he was trying to develop with Mr. Bulger, he wanted it to be pleasant surroundings, not the type of surroundings that you would ordinarily meet an informant, in an automobile, possibly in a hotel room, and so forth. He wanted Mr. Bulger to be comfortable, and essentially, he wanted him handled in a manner in which informants typically aren't handled."

Thus, from the beginning, Bulger was coddled by his FBI handlers. The relationship was obsequious and adoring. Morris and Connolly kissed Bulger's ass, and before long the entire supervisory structure of the bureau would also be kissing the ass of Whitey Bulger.

After that first meeting, Morris's descent into corruption seemed preordained. There were at least two other meetings at his home in Lexington involving Bulger and, later on, Steve Flemmi. The gangsters brought bottles of wine for their host, and Morris cooked pasta for his guests, as if he were a paramour courting a new lover. When John Connolly told Morris, "Hey, these guys really like you," Morris beamed. He was a quasi-nerd from the Midwest, and he was liked by two of the most powerful street hoodlums in Boston. This meant a lot to Morris.

Throughout his direct examination, the former FBI supervisor detailed his acts of corruption in a mostly matter-of-fact manner. He was aided in his attempts to demystify his lack of ethics and criminal inclinations by Wyshak, whose questioning allowed Morris to persistently shift the blame to John Connolly. In Morris's telling of events, Connolly was the engine behind the FBI's relationship with Bulger and Flemmi. This was the prosecution's narrative: Bulger corrupted Connolly, and then Connolly seduced Morris. The corruption spread throughout the C-3 squad, and there it ended.

With his diffident manner on the stand, which occasionally gave way to awkward moments of false humility and regret, Morris was slippery and disingenuous. He made a show of his willingness to accept responsibility for his own actions and express sorrow but at the same time consistently portrayed Connolly as the instigator of his criminal actions. It was as if he were merely along for the ride.

At one point, Wyshak asked the retired special agent if he ever had a conversation with Bulger and Flemmi about what they wanted in exchange for providing information to the FBI.

"I did not," answered Morris.

"Did you ever have a conversation with anybody about that?"

"I asked John Connolly. . . . I don't recall which meeting it was. I think it was at my home, and John and I were in the kitchen. And I asked, What is it that these guys want from us? And he told me, A head start."

"What does that mean, 'a head start'?"

"If they were going to be indicted, charged, arrested, to tip them off and let them flee."

Wyshak then asked if the term "fair game" had come up in his conversation with Connolly about Bulger and Flemmi.

"Yes," said Morris. "I remember Connolly using that term. I think it may have come up in connection with the circumstances surrounding the race-fix case. . . . And I remember, I'm pretty sure it was John, neither Mr. Bulger nor Mr. Flemmi, who said that they realize they are fair game. . . . If it ever came to the point that they were charged, and if one of the alternatives was to go to the judge and make their cooperation known, they did not want that."

"So what did you understand that the term 'fair game' meant?"

"Well, that meant that they knew they're engaged in criminal activity and that at some point they might get charged, and in the event that happened, they did not want their identity disclosed, and, specifically, they did not want it disclosed to a judge."

Wyshak did not ask the obvious follow-up questions: *Did you, Mr. Morris, object to the arrangement that was being suggested by Connolly and Bulger and Flemmi? Did you, as John Connolly's supervisor, say that the FBI could never agree to such an arrangement?*

In truth, if Morris had ever once said no to the various corrupt and criminal schemes that were suggested to him by his subordinate co-agent, the entire Bulger era might never have happened.

On the first day of Morris's testimony, the court adjourned for a twenty-minute midmorning break. As the jury was led out of the courtroom, it was clear that prosecutor Brian Kelly was peeved about something. Judge Casper told the witness that he could "step down." Morris was led out of the courtroom by a U.S. marshal.

"Everyone can be seated," said the judge. "Counsel, before we break, Mr. Kelly, did you want to be heard on anything first?"

"I do, Your Honor," Kelly answered, standing to address the court. "Obviously, Mr. Bulger has got a Sixth Amendment right to confront his accusers, but he doesn't have the right to sit at the defense table and say to the witness, 'You're a fuckin' liar' when the witness testifies. Which is what he did earlier in Mr. Morris's testimony when Morris was talking. . . . Now, I know he spent his whole life trying to intimidate people, including fifteen-year-old boys in South Boston, but he should not be able to do that here in federal court in the midst of trial." Kelly's voice crackled with emotion. He asked that Judge Casper admonish Bulger to "keep his little remarks to himself."

Bulger had mostly been a nonpresence during the proceedings so far, but he now throbbed with an anger that seemed ready to boil over. Few people had heard Bulger's aside during Morris's testimony—though neither Bulger nor his counsel denied that he had said it—but his reaction to Kelly's tirade was clear for all to see. He would have strangled Kelly with his bare hands were he the Whitey Bulger of old.

As Jay Carney rose to his feet and the spectators in the courtroom rustled and buzzed in reaction, the judge interrupted. "Counsel, I did not observe that, but, Mr. Carney, do you want to be heard?"

"Your Honor," said Carney, "I'll speak to Mr. Bulger at break and convey the sentiments that I know your honor would want me to."

Sensing that her effectiveness as a jurist in the case might be evaluated by this dramatic interlude, Casper quickly added, "And just for the record, Mr. Bulger, so it's clear, you're well served by both counsel in this case, and they are to speak for you in this courtroom at the present time. Do you understand that, sir?"

Bulger answered, "Yes, Your Honor. Yes."

Court adjourned for recess. Bulger was led from the courtroom, and the media rushed to file their reports on the trial's first genuinely confrontational moment.

THE DIRECT TESTIMONY of John Morris took up the better part of two full days that spanned over a weekend. The following week, on cross-examination, Hank Brennan was not about to let Morris get away with presenting himself as a dedicated civil servant who had regretfully allowed himself to be "compromised" by a junior partner. Carney set out to show that Morris was not only the person most responsible for his own demise, but that at the same time he was involved in one of the most corrupt relationships ever devised between FBI agents and an underworld figure, he was being heralded within the law enforcement bureaucracy as, according to one internal FBI evaluation, a "consistently excellent, highly motivated and capable supervisor"; and in another, "A very effective leader . . . Among the supervisory staff Morris is seen as a leader, and other supervisors rely on his leadership"; and in still another, "In the area of informant development and direction he has been directly involved in the development of one of the most valuable top echelon informants" in the bureau's history.

While being lauded internally as an ideal FBI supervisory agent, Morris took payments of cash stuffed in envelopes from Bulger, on one occasion five thousand dollars; he received gratuities of a fancy silver wine bucket and cases of wine, slipped to him in a parking garage at the John F. Kennedy Federal Building, so that the transaction would not be seen. Once, when Morris was in Glencoe, Georgia, for a law enforcement training conference, he arranged for Bulger and Connolly to purchase an airplane ticket for his secretary, Janet Noseworthy—who was also his mistress—so she could be flown down to Florida, where Morris and his paramour were put up in a condominium owned by another underworld figure.

Being bought off by gangsters was the least problematic aspect of Morris's alternate existence as a fraudulent "exemplary agent." In January 1980, the C-3 squad was successful in planting a Title III wiretap, an act of audio surveillance authorized by a federal warrant. A bug was planted in the headquarters of Jerry Angiulo. Known as "the Dog Pound," Angiulo's modest headquarters at 98 Prince Street in the North End was thought to be at the center of all decision making in the Boston Mafia. It had been a dream of the FBI since at least the fall of Raymond Patriarca, back in the early 1970s, to plant a bug at 98 Prince Street.

From the witness stand, Morris continued to peddle the fiction that Whitey Bulger had played a key role in giving the FBI information that helped make it possible to plant the bug. "Substantial assistance" was the term Morris used, though it had long ago been revealed that the placement of the bug had been aided by a hand-drawn schematic of the interior of the Angiulo headquarters that was provided not by Bulger, but by Steve Flemmi. Connolly lied, deliberately placing the information in Bulger's file and later insisting that Bulger's confidential informant number be added to the affidavit requesting Title III authorization to plant the bug. Morris reviewed and signed off on these fabrications.

To Connolly and Morris, the fiction was needed: Jeremiah O'Sullivan had earlier dropped Bulger from the race-fix indictment, upon request from the two agents, on the grounds that Bulger and Flemmi were necessary to take down the Mafia. Here was the "proof."

The bug at 98 Prince remained in place for more than a year. As supervisor of the C-3 squad, Morris received regular audio surveillance reports and transcripts of the recordings. On one occasion, Morris was so impressed with the recordings that he arranged to meet Bulger and Flemmi at the Colonnade hotel in Boston. He brought along actual tapes and played them for the gangsters in the hotel room. Morris and Connolly, Bulger and Flemmi all drank wine and slapped each other on the back and listened to a tape in which Mafioso Nicky Giso talked about his girlfriend.

The impropriety of this meeting was breathtaking: the supervisor and a lead agent in the FBI's organized crime squad playing a confidential Title III recording to two of the city's most notorious mobsters. Morris got so drunk that Flemmi had to drive him home. Later, in a state of panic, he realized that in his drunken state he had left the 98 Prince Street tape in the room at the Colonnade. He had to rush back to the hotel and retrieve the tape.

The extent of Morris's corruption seemed to know no bounds. In 1981, he was temporarily transferred from the C-3 squad to oversee an investigation concerning—of all things—officers of the Boston Police Department taking gratuities from known criminals. This was a subject of which Morris had become something of an expert, since he'd been taking gifts and money from two of the biggest gangsters in the city. Eventually, Morris's investigation of the Boston police would lead to nearly a dozen officers pleading guilty to charges, with some being sent away to prison.

"You saw to it that these men inevitably lost their jobs for what they did," said Brennan to Morris on the stand. Brennan was commenting on the damage that Morris had wrought, destroying people's careers for doing the same things that he was doing.

"Yeah, it made me sick," said Morris

"It made you sick, but you didn't stop, did you?"

"Objection," said Fred Wyshak. "Badgering the witness, Your Honor."

"Overruled," said the judge. Brennan was allowed the question.

Morris answered with a long, tortured explanation about when exactly he started to feel bad about what he was doing. "I changed my image of myself a long time ago," he said.

By early 1982, Morris's moral gauge hit empty: he was not only corrupt but also desperate to conceal his corruption. Sometime in April, he was approached by two agents from the labor racketeering squad, Gerald Montanari and Leo Brunnick. They explained to Morris that they had begun to cultivate Brian Halloran, the Southie hoodlum, as a potential informant. The two agents had come to Morris to ask him what he thought of Halloran's suitability as a CI (confidential informant). In the course of this debriefing, Montanari and Brunnick also revealed to Morris that Halloran was claiming that he had been offered the contract to murder Roger Wheeler, owner of World Jai Lai, by Bulger and Flemmi, and that he had turned it down.

Mention of the Wheeler murder jangled Morris's nerves. Wheeler had been gunned down in Tulsa, and local and state police in Oklahoma had already traced a link to Boston. The investigator in charge—an aggressive Oklahoma state policeman named Mike Huff—had contacted Boston FBI with questions about Bulger, Flemmi, et al. As the FBI's liaison with the Oklahoma investigation, Morris had assigned John Connolly. It was Connolly's job to protect the FBI's prize informants.

In his conversation with the two agents, Morris was further alarmed to hear that it was their intention to wire up Brian Halloran and have him meet with John Callahan, the former president of World Jai Lai. Morris was aware that Callahan had quite possibly initiated the murder of Roger Wheeler. Any conversation between Halloran and Callahan, memorialized on a secret recording device, would be devastating to Bulger and Flemmi.

Not long after his conversation with Montanari and Brunnick, Morris was in his office when John Connolly entered. Connolly had been away from the office taking a master's course in public administration at Harvard University. Although Morris's conversation with Montanari and Brunnick had been confidential, Morris blurted out "spontaneously" to Connolly that

Halloran was being cultivated as a CI. Morris noted that Halloran was spilling the beans about the Wheeler murder and would imminently be used to gather potentially devastating evidence against Bulger and Flemmi via a wired-up conversation with Callahan.

Special Agent Connolly didn't need to be told more than once; he got the message. Within a matter of days, Connolly went directly to Bulger and told him that he had a potential problem he needed to take care of: Brian Halloran.

On the witness stand, Morris looked stricken. The deviousness of his former self was an unpleasant memory, like looking in the mirror and seeing something ugly, not the person you perceive yourself to be. Morris squirmed in his seat. He had testified in court about these facts many times over the last sixteen years, but that didn't make it any easier. Of all his many crimes, this may have been one that Morris, a Catholic, knew could result in the eternal damnation of his soul.

Asked Hank Brennan, "After you told Mr. Connolly about Mr. Halloran, you had another conversation with him, didn't you?"

Morris spoke quietly now, his voice barely a whisper. "Yes. He came back to me."

"And during that conversation, you inferred that he had told members of organized crime about your little secret."

"I inferred from what he told me that he had talked to them. Whether they had the information already or whether he told them, I don't know, but he, obviously, had been in contact with them."

Four weeks later—on May 11, 1982—Morris came in to work at the federal building one day and learned that Brian Halloran had been gunned down on the Boston waterfront, along with Michael Donahue, an innocent victim who had been giving Halloran a ride home.

Morris knew that he had provided information to Connolly that had likely led to the murders of Halloran and Donahue.

From the stand, Morris wanted the jury and everyone else in the courtroom to know how bad he felt. It was part of his performance as a man racked by guilt. His decision to divulge confidential information to Connolly had led to the murder of two men. What a terrible burden for John Morris. His brow furrowed in contemplation; his eyes moistened.

Hank Brennan wasn't buying it: "After you learned that Halloran and Donahue were murdered following your tip [to Connolly], did you then do something to try to uncover the truth, Mr. Morris?"

"No, I did not."

"Did you tell any of your superiors about the information so they could do a proper investigation?"

"No, I did not."

Not only did Morris keep his knowledge of Bulger's possible connection to the murders under wraps; he also set out, along with Connolly, to create a false investigative narrative, as he and Connolly had done on other occasions.

"Your Honor," said Brennan, "with your permission I'd like to publish Exhibit 282 into evidence."

"You may," said the judge.

Brennan handed to the witness an FBI memorandum that was also projected onto a screen for the jury to see. The defense lawyer noted that the memo was a report, filed by John Connolly, in which Bulger placed the blame for the Halloran-Donahue murder on "a group from Charlestown." Said Brennan, "Let's look at the second paragraph, Mr. Morris. Would you read that, please?"

Morris cleared his throat. "Source advised that the story being put out by the state police is that the FBI got Halloran killed, but source advised that the people from Charlestown say it was the state police who let the cat out of the bag and in fact the Charlestown crew had information that Halloran was talking to Colonel O'Donovan and Trooper Fralick."

After Morris finished, Brennan let the silence linger. The memo encapsulated the Morris-Connolly conspiracy: not only had they provided Whitey Bulger with information that led to the murder of two men, but they were now attempting to shift responsibility onto the Massachusetts State Police, and in particular, Colonel Jack O'Donovan, a man who had for years been trying to sound alarm bells within law enforcement about the FBI's unseemly relationship with Bulger.

"Two days after you received that memo from Special Agent Connolly," said Brennan, "you endorsed it, didn't you?"

"I reviewed it and initialed it," said Morris.

"When Mr. Connolly gave that to you and you read that, you knew it was untrue, didn't you?"

Morris's mood seemed to shift. Over a series of defensive equivocations, he ducked the substance of Brennan's inquiries and would not give straight answers. His voice hardened. For a while on the stand, he had been wallowing in self-pity but, now, whatever shield of denial he had constructed for himself, whatever he needed to do so that he could sleep at night, led him to forcefully defend himself. He sat upright, with renewed energy. The need to assert his theology of self-deception had reinforced his spine like an injection of B_{12}.

All these years later, he was still seeking to protect his reputation. He was still pretending.

BY THE TIME John Morris neared the end of his testimony, defense attorney Jay Carney appeared to be exhausted. Although Hank Brennan was the one handling the cross-examination of Morris, Carney had been handling many of the legal arguments related to Morris, and there were many. The defense team was frequently frustrated in their efforts to enter a piece of evidence or pursue a line of questioning, due to objections from the prosecution. In some cases, the jury was removed from the courtroom and the witness asked to step down. The two sides would stand before the judge and make their case. As lead counsel, Carney argued with vigor and passion, but given the defense strategy he was frequently left spinning his wheels.

The insistence that Bulger was not an informant was the rock upon which Carney and Brennan often found themselves stranded far from the shore. In their cross-examination of both James Marra and Morris, they had contested nearly every FBI airtel (exclusive correspondence) and teletype that was placed into evidence. In support of this strategy, Carney explained to the judge, "What if Mr. Connolly fabricated the entire informant file? What if not a single item in that informant file was based on a statement by James Bulger? . . . And the evidence today that we've heard through Mr. Morris gave some insight into that, to what we've been saying since my opening statement, which is, Mr. Bulger was not providing information as an informant to Connolly, he was providing money to these FBI agents so that he could get tipped off about wiretaps, search warrants, indictments being issued."

"But isn't there a view of the evidence," countered Judge Casper, "that he was also getting tipped off about people cooperating? I guess what I'm saying is, why can't both be true?"

For a moment, Carney appeared stumped, his arms dangled at his side, and then he said, "It's possible that both can be true—theoretically—but the defendant's position is that only one is true."

It was telling that Carney said "the defendant's position" and not "the position of the defense." It was becoming apparent that the insistence on the canard of whether or not Bulger was an informant was a position devised by Whitey Bulger. During these arguments, Bulger listened attentively. To him, this is what the trial was all about: an attempt to salvage his reputation as an "honorable racketeer" who could never be a snitch. But for the defense lawyers, it was a road to nowhere.

Carney's exasperation was based partly on his inability to get any love from the judge on this issue, but it was also likely founded on the reality that the entire debate had sidetracked the defense from exploring the more prescient point, also laid out in Carney's opening statement, that the Bulger era was one chapter in a long, dark history of law enforcement corruption in New England. Morris had been their best chance so far to probe the continuity of sleaze between the Barboza era and the Bulger era. That opportunity had come and gone without the defense making the necessary connections.

A telling moment in this regard had taken place when Brennan asked Morris about "the Limone matter."

Peter Limone had been the lead defendant in the Teddy Deegan murder trial back in 1967. When it was finally exposed that Limone, along with Joe Salvati and two others, had been wrongfully convicted and spent thirty years in prison, the aggrieved parties filed a lawsuit. The government contested the lawsuit, leading, in 2006, to hearings in federal court before Judge Nancy Gertner. Many witnesses were called; the hearings became the most full and complete rendering of the manner in which the four men were framed, and how the lie had been maintained by the DOJ over the years.

Among the witnesses before Judge Gertner was a man named Michael Albano, who in the early 1980s was a member of the Massachusetts State Parole Board. Albano spoke in court, and later with the media, about how, in 1983, he was approached by FBI special agents John Morris and John Connolly.

At the time, Peter Limone was being considered for commutation of his sentence. He'd been in prison for eighteen years on the Deegan murder conviction. There had always been rumors that the conviction of Limone, Salvati, and the others was tainted, but the criminal justice system always fought back against these rumors. On this day in 1983, the guardians of the system were Morris and Connolly.

According to Albano, he was visited in his office and verbally bullied by the two agents, who told him if he voted for commutation of Limone's sentence his career in public life would be over. Albano considered the attempt to influence his decision by the two agents to be a flagrant effort by the FBI to intimidate him. He voted for commutation anyway. Years later, after Limone's sentence was commuted, Albano went on to become the mayor of Springfield, Massachusetts. In 1995, he was the subject of a suspicious FBI investigation into wrongdoing in his administration. Albano believed the investigation was an act of revenge by the FBI for his vote on the Limone matter. The FBI's probe of Mayor Albano was eventually thrown out of court.

Now, all these years later, during the cross-examination of John Morris, the issue resurfaced at the Bulger trial. The mere mention of "the Limone matter" brought an objection from Wyshak: "Your Honor, this is the second time that [the defense] has tried to insert the Limone case, which was a prosecution in the sixties and has absolutely nothing to do with Bulger in this case. Obviously, the reason they are trying to insert it into this case is because it's, you know, I think they believe it's a black eye for the government. What the relevance is of questioning this witness who had nothing to do with that case, it escapes me."

Since Brennan was the one cross-examining Morris, he responded. For the next ten minutes he detailed how Morris had testified in five previous legal proceedings on the subject, and when confronted about his and Connolly's efforts to bully Albano, he always answered with some version of "I don't remember the details of that meeting." His partner, John Connolly, publicly denied ever having met with Albano. That position was discredited by Albano having produced records to show that he was paid a visit by the two agents, and by Morris, who admitted that the meeting took place but was unable or unwilling to shed light on the details.

"Mr. Albano currently works for the Governor's Council," said Brennan to the judge. "We have him listed on our witness list, and I expect that we'll call him. . . . And so I'm going to ask [Morris] about his earlier denials, and then I'm going to impeach him when I call Mr. Albano as a witness. Because I suspect that he's going to continue to deny it, and then it will be an issue of credibility for the jury. Do they believe Mr. Morris and his pattern of misconduct or do they believe a gentleman from the Governor's Council, Mr. Albano? There could be no more central role of credibility than this example. It goes to the heart of the defense."

Wyshak stood to respond. "You know, if, yes, [Morris] made efforts to oppose [the Limone commutation] and he's denying it now, I think, you know, that's a basis for impeachment. . . . But I think what [the defense] is trying to do is to hang this whole misconduct by the FBI on this witness, who had absolutely nothing to do with it, and make it appear as though the reason that Mr. Morris opposed the commutation was some effort to cover up the misconduct. I think, you know, as they do with many other topics, they go far afield."

Wyshak's comment was a rebuttal to an argument that Brennan had not yet made. Wyshak's need to counteract any link between the Bulger case and the dirty little secrets of the Barboza era was a knee-jerk reaction, and it roused Brennan to make the argument he should have made in the first place.

"If I could just add, Your Honor. There's one fact I left out that's important. Not only the fact of the manner in which [Morris] bullied Mr. Albano, but also the fact that this was a case where the impropriety was on behalf of other FBI agents, including Mr. Condon and Mr. Rico, who handled [the Limone] case. It's no coincidence that Mr. Condon is Mr. Morris's friend. It's no coincidence that Mr. Condon shows up at private social gatherings at Mr. Morris's house years later with Mr. Bulger. There is a link between Condon, Rico, and Morris. . . . There is an inference based on the evidence that [Morris] is acting upon—the baton has been passed from Rico and Condon to Mr. Morris."

This argument should have been at the center of the defense case, instead of tacked on only after Wyshak inadvertently put it out on the table. But it was too late. Judge Casper had been given an option, one that allowed her to appear judicious and accommodating by offering a bone to both sides. "Counsel," said Casper, the monotone of her voice designed to reflect the evenness of her judgment, "I'm going to allow you to ask to the extent that you're trying to show that [Morris] has been untruthful in regards to these efforts, but to the fact that you're attempting to go into the whole Limone matter, I'm not going to allow you to go that far."

It was a legal smackdown, couched in the niceties of modern jurisprudence.

AT THE END of his final day on the stand, John Morris was dismissed; he stepped out of the witness box and walked from the courtroom.

Bulger eyeballed his former accomplice on the way out.

In the hallway, Morris shook hands with John Marra; they practically fell into each other's arms. Both men had been called to testify at least partly as a bulwark against broader accountability, and against history. Marra, the company man still operating from deep within the machine, and Morris, the disgraced supervisory agent, whose only remaining move was to fall on his sword and thus, hopefully, contain the damage. It seemed to have worked. The two G-men left the courthouse with smiles on their faces. And the prosecutors—Wyshak and Kelly—strutted from the courtroom with a look of satisfaction.

The prosecution of Whitey Bulger was on course.

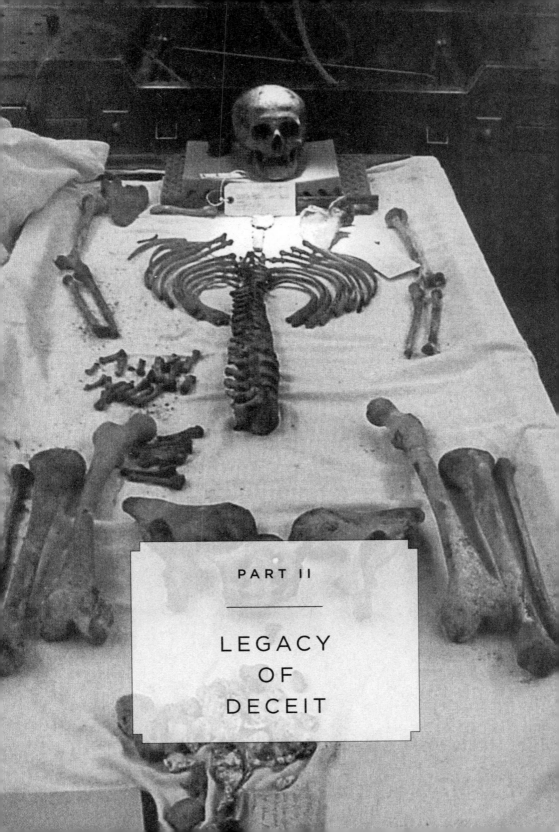

PART II

LEGACY
OF
DECEIT

8

WHITEY AND COCAINE

EACH DAY AT the completion of testimony in the Bulger trial, the media gathered behind a rope on the sidewalk outside the main entrance to the courthouse. With microphones and cameras at the ready, they shouted questions at anyone connected to the trial that happened to walk out the door. It was mostly an empty exercise. With a gag order in place, the legal representatives offered nothing of substance. Occasionally, the defense lawyers stopped at the microphones. Following the testimony of John Morris, Jay Carney, with co-counsel Hank Brennan at his side, stopped to say, "Today was one of the most dramatic and poignant days we've ever spent in a courtroom." He would say no more than that.

Tommy Donahue, whose father had been killed partly as a result of Morris's criminal negligence, had a different interpretation of the day's event. "The whole thing disgusts me," he said.

In the larger universe of media coverage, the trial had fallen into a predictable pattern. The prosecution solicited testimony on the horrible acts of Whitey Bulger, and the press reported on these acts with little cognizance or understanding of the historical context. On the stand, Morris had been slippery and hollow, and his testimony was interpreted by the media as the sad story of yet one more sleazy character who had been corrupted by Bulger. Even locally, where reporters had for decades been covering various aspects of the moral quagmire surrounding the case, there was little clamoring for a more complete picture. All roads led back to Bulger, and the local media seemed to be okay with that.

In some ways, this myopia was a continuation and culmination of the ways the Bulger story had been shaped from the beginning.

By the time of the trial, the Bulger saga had become a national phenomenon, but for a long time the local press in Boston had the story all to themselves. The details had been reported on and presented by a handful of influential journalists and commentators in town, some of whom made a career off the case. Occasionally, the reporting was extraordinary, even groundbreaking, but much of what appeared in the press about Whitey Bulger was the result of leaks from government sources—prosecutors and people in law enforcement. Later, the accounts of cooperating witnesses and Bulger's enemies on the street were added to the mix. Consequently, a certain narrative, or point of view, of the Bulger story unfolded over the years that dovetailed nicely with the prosecution's theory of the case, that is, Bulger was a master manipulator who had corrupted the system, Connolly and Morris were his enablers, and it didn't extend much further than that.

It had taken congressional hearings generated in Washington, D.C., and lawsuits in federal court to expose the larger horrors of the Bulger conspiracy. Among institutions of government in Boston, there had been no clamoring to dig deeper into the scandal. In many ways, the local media reflected this ambivalence. As state trooper Colonel Tom Foley once told me when I asked why there had never been a comprehensive investigation or demand locally to fully explore the Bulger fiasco, "Nobody around here has any stomach for that."

Back in the early and mid-1980s, the name of James J. Bulger was mostly a no-show in the Boston media. Even though Bulger had by then risen to become a top player in the city's criminal underworld by eliminating rivals and associates in South Boston and among the Winter Hill Mob; even though he had forged a relationship with the FBI that had been used to secure warrants and federal authorization to install electronic surveillance devices; even though his brother, Senator William Bulger, was one of the most powerful political figures in the commonwealth, James Bulger's name had never once appeared in a news article in the *Boston Globe*.

One name that did appear often in the *Globe* and elsewhere in the Boston media was that of Jerry Angiulo. Especially in the early and mid-1980s, as the FBI and federal New England Organized Crime Strike Force under Jeremiah O'Sullivan were building a major case against Angiulo and his brothers, Michele (Mikey), Donato (Danny), and Vittori Nicoli (Nick), articles on the Mafia frequently appeared in the front of the *Globe*'s metro section. These articles were based almost exclusively on law enforcement sources—cops, FBI agents, and prosecutors—who leaked information to the press with the understanding that their names would not appear in print.

It later years, it would become known that Special Agents John Morris and John Connolly were among those unnamed sources.

It is not unusual for big-city reporters to get their tips from off-the-record sources within law enforcement and the prosecutor's office; it is generally how the game is played. In Boston, where gangsters and cops had grown up in similar working-class neighborhoods, many of the city's best reporters were also from those same neighborhoods. Newsmen and lawmen meeting quietly for a drink in an out-of-the-way saloon was part of the city's daily discourse. Information could be exchanged that served the purposes of both sides. The reporter gets "exclusive" inside information, and the lawmen get to generate and, to an extent, control the parameters of how the story will be presented to the public.

In Boston in the early 1980s, the only organized crime stories to make it into the pages of the *Globe* and other media outlets were frequent exposés on the criminal activities of the Angiulo brothers and the local Mafia. This was a tremendous benefit to Whitey Bulger, whose relationship with Connolly, Morris, and Strike Force prosecutor Jeremiah O'Sullivan was, by that point, based entirely on his willingness and ability to help them take down the Mafia in Boston.

All of that changed in 1988, when the *Globe* ran an explosive four-part series of articles under the heading "The Bulger Mystique." The series, put together by a group of four reporters designated the Spotlight Team, was as much about Senator Billy Bulger as it was about his alleged gangster brother. The articles delved into what became known as "the 75 State Street investigation," a proposed federal probe into a real estate deal in which Senator Bulger had received a suspicious $250,000 payment that might have been an illegal transaction. Senator Bulger claimed the payment had been a loan; the money was returned to the person who made the payment. The transaction had nothing to do with Whitey Bulger. The investigation of the senator had been terminated and no charges were ever filed against Billy Bulger.

In the *Globe* series, the most explosive nugget to appear in print was the revelation that Whitey Bulger had what the paper called "a special relationship" with the FBI. At the time, the *Globe's* reporters and editors knew what the general public would not learn for years, that the unnamed source of that information was John Morris. On the stand at the Bulger trial, Morris claimed that he had leaked the information to the *Globe* to bring an end to the FBI's relationship with Whitey, so that other agents would not be compromised as he had been in his dealings with Bulger and Flemmi. Whitey Bulger believed that Morris had leaked it to the press in an effort to get him killed by underworld rivals.

The Spotlight Team's reporting did not suggest that the FBI was engaged in criminal activity. It did quote unnamed sources in the Massachusetts State Police who complained that the FBI was possibly protecting Bulger from investigation by other agencies. But there was no suggestion of overt corruption. Anyone who read the series might even have concluded that the use of Bulger as an informant was simply an ingenious tactic on the part of the lawmen, a successful and mutually beneficial ploy to crush the Mafia. Although Bulger's career as a racketeer, including a number of early gangland murders, was detailed in the *Globe* series, there was no mention of the FBI leaking information to Bulger so that he could murder potential informants or rivals, no mention of his possible role in the disappearances of Debra Davis, Deborah Hussey, and many others.

The Spotlight series was unprecedented in its public exposure of the Brothers Bulger. Not long after that series appeared in print, a member of the Spotlight Team—Gerard O'Neill—and another *Globe* reporter—Dick Lehr—went on to publish a book titled *The Underboss*. Originally published by St. Martin's Press in January 1989, the book was subtitled *The Rise and Fall of a Mafia Family*. The primary narrative of the book was the investigation of the local Mafia as conceived by the FBI's C-3 Squad, led by John Morris, and the prosecution of Jerry Angiulo, led by Jeremiah O'Sullivan. The book bordered on hagiography of a group of agents and prosecutors some of whom, at the time, were involved in an insidiously corrupt relationship with Bulger and Flemmi.

Years later, in 2000, Lehr and O'Neill published a corrective, of sorts, titled *Black Mass*. By then, through public testimony under oath, the Wolf

hearings had spewed forth a staggering litany of corruption, some of it perpetrated by the same people the writers had lionized a decade earlier in *The
Underboss*. Through the testimony of dozens of witnesses, it was learned
that Bulger and Flemmi were far more homicidal and depraved than anyone
had imagined, and that the criminal enabling of Bulger by the FBI was vast
and scurrilous. Consequently, the tone of *Black Mass* was one of shock and
revulsion—a point of view brought about, perhaps, by the fact that these
same reporters had previously been played by their "friendly" FBI sources.

In the wake of the Wolf hearings and the Bulger indictment, which
evolved as more and more informants came forward, a new narrative
emerged in the media. The FBI's organized crime squad, and particularly
John Connolly, now took center stage. With Bulger on the lam, Connolly
became the primary target of Wyshak and Kelly, who became the driving
force not only in how the various Bulger-related prosecutions would unfold,
but also in how the story was to be shaped in the press.[1] Following the
double-whammy prosecutions of Connolly in 2001 (Massachusetts) and
2007 (Florida), Wyshak and Kelly were profiled by writer Dick Lehr, who
since the publication of *Black Mass*—a number-one bestseller in Boston—
had retired from the *Globe* and become a full-time author. In the pages of
Boston magazine, Lehr wrote about Wyshak and Kelly in a manner similar
to the way he and Gerard O'Neill had written about FBI agents Ed Quinn,
John Morris, and others in *The Underboss*—that is to say, glowingly.

While Bulger was on the run, he became a figure of national promi-
nence. As the legend grew, the chance that the popular media might be
willing or able to look beyond Bulger, the man, to an examination of the
universe that had created Bulger became less likely. The story became all
about Whitey.

This was especially relevant to the Bulger trial, which, legally speaking,
was likely to be the final chance for those public servants who had enabled

---

[1] *The Underboss* was reissued in 2002, with a new introduction by co-author Dick Lehr. As
with previous publications of the book, there were no footnotes nor even a cursory explanation
of sources, though it is reasonable to assume that the book is based on law enforcement sources
deep inside the Angiulo investigation. Lehr refers to *The Underboss* and *Black Mass* as "companion pieces," with the former "still standing as a story of a remarkable bugging operation,"
and the latter as "a larger history of a band of FBI agents in Boston who lost their way and, in
effect, became gangsters themselves."

Bulger to be called to task for their actions. But this was not to be; the local media representatives best equipped to hold the government's feet to the fire and make sure that the trial was probative and transparent had, thus far in the proceedings, preferred that the trial be about Whitey "the monster" and little else.

Howie Carr had built a mini-career around his journalism and radio commentary about Bulger and also through the writing of numerous books, most notably *The Brothers Bulger,* a bestseller, and *Hitman.* His knowledge of the Boston underworld is vast and expansive, and through the popularity of his daytime radio talk show on WRKO radio, he had cultivated sources of information on many subjects, including crime and politics, that are second to none. But Carr had long since turned his analysis of the Bulger story into a personalized vendetta against Whitey—perhaps understandably so.

In 2005, in an interview that Kevin Weeks did with the CBS News program *60 Minutes,* it was revealed that Bulger and Weeks had considered killing Howie Carr because of his incessant lampooning of Senator Billy Bulger in print and on his radio show. Weeks had even gone so far as to stalk Carr to his summer vacation home, where he staked out the location with the intention of shooting the famed columnist when he came out his front door. When Carr emerged with his young daughter, the hit was called off.

During the trial, in his column in the *Boston Herald,* and on his radio show, Carr preferred to speculate endlessly about Bulger's sexual preferences, portraying the gangster as a covert gay hustler who liked young boys. Often irreverent, occasionally juvenile, and frequently entertaining in his on-air presentation, Carr seemed to have little interest in interpreting the trial as an occasion to examine the world that had created Bulger.

Kevin Cullen was another prominent journalistic voice in the city who had written about Bulger frequently over the years, as a reporter and prominent columnist for the *Globe.* In February 2013, on the brink of the Bulger trial, Cullen and Shelley Murphy, another veteran *Globe* reporter who had covered aspects of the Bulger story for decades, published a bestselling biography of Bulger titled *Whitey Bulger: America's Most Wanted Gangster and the Manhunt that Brought Him to Justice.* The book was unprecedented in many respects, informed by sources the two writers had cultivated over an extended period. Their portrait of Bulger was both horrifying and human-izing, as they sought to puncture the mythology that had developed around Whitey and bring him down to size.

Cullen's nuanced analysis of Bulger in his and Shelley Murphy's book was nowhere to be seen in his columns in the *Globe,* which were devoted almost exclusively to the trial during its duration. Cullen seemed to feel as though he needed to play the role of Bulger's primary tormentor, the one person who could make Bulger pay for his many years as a bully and psychopath who terrorized people in Southie, where Cullen had lived while working as a young reporter.

As with Carr, the writer chose to personalize his approach, adding a tone of self-righteous indignation that sometimes bordered on hysteria. Again, like Carr, Cullen had his reasons.

Back in 1988, Cullen had been part of the Spotlight Team that first learned that Whitey had "a special relationship" with the FBI. On the brink of that series first appearing in the pages of the *Globe,* Cullen received a phone call from Special Agent Tom Daly, who was a member of the C-3 squad and also a fellow Southie native. Daly had heard that the *Globe* was about to run their explosive series, and he was calling Cullen in an attempt to intimidate him into canceling "The Bulger Mystique." The agent told the reporter that Bulger "wasn't going to like it" and implied that because Cullen was a resident of Southie, his life could be in danger. Cullen re-ported the call from the FBI agent to his publishers at the *Globe;* they per-ceived the call to be a threat and took it seriously enough to temporarily relocate Cullen and his family out of the city.

The role the media had played in creating and cultivating the myth of Whitey Bulger was complex and personal. Boston is a media town, with a history of top-notch reporters and columnists. Particularly in the wake of the Wolf hearings of 1997, local reporters had done superlative work in unearthing aspects of the Bulger conspiracy. Some had turned their work into bestselling books that found a readership far beyond the city of Boston. But as the prosecution of Bulger—as shaped by Wyshak and Kelly—had begun to dominate and misconstrue many important questions about who ultimately was responsible for the Bulger fiasco, you could argue that the local media engaged in coverage that bordered on dereliction of duty.

There were exceptions. David Boeri, a writer for the *Boston Phoenix* and other publications, as well as for radio and television news, had consistently sought to set the Bulger story against the larger context of institutional corruption in New England. In the overall flow of trial coverage, which was voluminous, there were insights by Boeri and others that occasionally went beyond whether or not Whitey was a bad man, or speculation on just how bad a man he truly was.

Nonetheless, among the most powerful and influential media outlets in the city, the coverage bordered on cheerleading for the prosecutors and the U.S. attorney's office. Some reporters, in private conversations, used the defense that other aspects of the Bulger story had been covered over the years and didn't need to be rehashed. This, coincidentally, was the view of the prosecutors.

The trial was exhaustively covered, but not with much depth. The best journalists in town were more interested in settling old scores with Whitey than probing the parameters of a skewed prosecution. The hidden horrors of the Bulger trial seemed destined to remain so.

AS A FULL and penetrating accounting of the era, the Bulger trial had begun to show signs of being a well-oiled cover-up, but in some areas it tread new ground. On the subject of illegal narcotics, the proceedings addressed for the first time in public a topic that was central to the Bulger mythology.

During the mobster's heyday as the boss of Southie, a large part of his legend was based on the belief that he kept drugs out of the neighborhood. People who advocated on Bulger's behalf used this "fact" to sustain the myth that Bulger may have been a gangster, but he was also Southie's pre-eminent protector. Mostly composed of socially conservative Catholics, Southie was a working-class enclave, highly family oriented. The concept of drug use, be it hard drugs like heroin or cocaine, or more benign drugs like marijuana, was not tolerated as it might be in a ghetto neighborhood like Roxbury. In the 1970s, the desire to keep drugs out of the neighborhood had been used as a primary explanation for violent resistance to school busing, on the theory that bringing blacks into Southie was tantamount to despoiling the town with drugs.

The myth of a drug-free Southie and the role Whitey Bulger played in keeping it that way was perpetrated by, among others, John Connolly and Senator Billy Bulger. In his off-the-record chats with people in the Boston media and in the community, Connolly extolled the virtues of Jim Bulger, the primary virtue being that he kept Southie free from "bad elements" like street drug dealers, who by then were a common phenomenon on the urban landscape throughout the United States, especially in poor and working-class neighborhoods.

Billy Bulger promulgated this myth to an even greater extent, though he did so without ever publicly mentioning his brother by name.

A major part of Billy Bulger's pitch to the electorate in campaign after campaign had been how South Boston was the model of a close-knit, upright, righteous community where parents kept tabs on their kids, made them stay in school, and took pride in the fact that Southie residents insisted on not allowing dope to denigrate their community.

Billy Bulger did not invent the concept of "Southie pride," but he certainly knew how to make it a central component of his career in public life. The fact that he had a brother who was known to be a gangster boss did not detract from his skill at capitalizing on the community's sense of pride; in fact, it was quite the opposite. The idea that Jim Bulger was "our gangster" in a world of dope peddlers, Mafiosi, "crazy niggers," and liberal apologists had somehow, in the inverted morality that the Bulger brothers seemed to represent, become a subterranean though undeniable aspect of Southie pride.

Nowhere was this proclivity more in evidence than at the annual St. Patrick's Day breakfast held in Southie, presided over by Senator Billy Bulger. As the president of the Massachusetts Senate, Bulger had risen above his earliest beginnings as the representative from Southie to being among the most powerful lawmakers in the state. The annual breakfast had become a manifestation of his standing in the city. Politicians running for office routinely stopped by the breakfast and submitted themselves to sometimes not so gentle ribbing from Senator Bulger and others, who welcomed the opportunity to make them squirm. U.S. senator Ted Kennedy; Massachusetts governor and later presidential candidate Michael Dukakis; Speaker of the U.S. House Thomas P. "Tip" O'Neill Jr.; and presidential candidate Ronald Reagan were among the many luminaries who spoke at the breakfast.

John Morris, from the witness stand, had described how impressed he was to attend the event as a guest of John Connolly. Morris described the breakfast as "probably the single-most spectacular political event of the year . . . hosted by the Senate president and attended by a who's who in politics." FBI agents, both retired and currently on the job, were given special treatment at the breakfast, with a table up near the dais. Connolly was so well connected with Billy Bulger that he didn't even have to wait in line at the main entrance. With Morris at his side, Connolly entered the hall through a private back entrance. Seated at their table was Special Agent Dennis Condon, who maintained a prized spot at the breakfast even after his retirement from the bureau in 1980. Also in attendance, in varying years, were numerous SACs and ASACs (assistant special agents in charge) from the Boston office of the FBI.

Extolling the virtues of Southie through anecdotes and song was often an aspect of the breakfast. Occasionally, there were offhand references to Senator Bulger's notorious brother, always in a jocular manner and never by name. One year, William Weld made a notable appearance. Weld served as a U.S. attorney in Boston, where he was known for pursuing political corruption cases with great vigor. He went on to become head of the U.S. Justice Department's Criminal Division and eventually was elected governor of Massachusetts. At Billy Bulger's St. Patrick's Day breakfast, from the podium Weld sang a little ditty, the punch line of which was a reference to Billy Bulger becoming rich courtesy of his brother's criminal activities. Senator Bulger and everyone else burst out laughing.

Political and some community leaders could react with good-natured laughter at the Whitey references because they operated under the myth that Bulger was a Robin Hood type who kept drugs out of the neighborhood. In truth, beginning in the early 1980s, Bulger implemented a hostile takeover of the neighborhood's drug trade. Within a year, he would become the largest peddler of illegal narcotics in the history of Southie.

At the trial, the unlikely narrator of Bulger's foray into the cocaine and marijuana business was Joe Tower, a man who had thus far avoided scrutiny in all the many legal proceedings and books on the Bulger era. At fifty-nine years of age, he was the youngest witness so far with direct involvement in Bulger's criminal gang to take the stand.

With his deep suntan, full head of silver hair, and casual sport coat, Tower seemed like a man who had long ago removed himself from the grittier aspects of his hometown of Boston. But then he spoke. His cadence and manner of speech could only have come from one place: Southie.

In August 2000, Tower was living peacefully in Port St. Lucie, Florida, working as a luthier, someone who constructs and repairs custom guitars. It was then that Tower was served with a federal subpoena to testify before a grand jury back in Boston about his years as a cocaine dealer for Whitey Bulger. Tower had not been charged with a crime, but the implication was that he could be if he didn't cooperate. He had followed news about the ongoing Bulger-related prosecutions ever since Whitey disappeared on the lam back in 1995. Through an attorney, Tower negotiated an immunity deal: he would agree to testify as long as nothing he said could be used against him in court.

Brian Kelly stood before Joe Tower and got things rolling: "Let me direct your attention to the 1970s. What were you doing at that time?"

"In the 1970s I was a musician in a band. I played music."

"What kind of band?"

"It was disco, rock and roll, blues."

"What sort of places did you play at?"

"We played at local establishments in the area. Local bars."

"Did you ever play at a place called Triple O's?"

"Yes, I did."

Kelly stepped forward with a photo in his hand; at the same time the photo was projected onto the monitor in the courtroom. "I'd like to show you what I've marked for identification purposes as exhibit eighty-one. Do you recognize that photo, sir?"

"Yes, I do. This is Triple O's in South Boston."

The introduction of Triple O's into the trial's narrative was no small matter. By the 1980s, with Bulger no longer making trips into Somerville to convene with confederates in the Winter Hill Mob (which was now moribund), or trips to the Lancaster Street garage, which was closed down after it became known that the place was bugged by state police, Triple O's became the official headquarters of the Bulger organization. In a previous incarnation it was known as the Transit Café, meeting place for the Southie branch of the Killeen brothers gang, for whom Whitey got his start as a debt collector and leg breaker.

Named after the three O'Neill brothers, Southie natives who were co-owners, the bar was located on West Broadway, a main thoroughfare. The façade was classic 1970s working class, with a hand-painted sign with the bar's name—Triple O's Lounge—that also advertised Coors and Rolling Rock. Anyone who entered the place knew they were entering a domain of the neighborhood's rough-and-tumble gangster element, a bloody chain of succession that had brought Southie under the control of a man known as Whitey, though no one dared call him that to his face.

In the late 1970s and into the 1980s, Joe Tower and his band played at Triple O's on Friday and Saturday nights. Everyone liked Joe. He played a passable guitar solo and was a vigorous talker, but more than that he was at the head of a modest drug operation that provided cocaine to the neighborhood.

Like most American cities in the 1980s, Boston was on the receiving end of a veritable blizzard of cocaine, causing the street-level purchase price to tumble. What had once been the drug of the rich and famous, used only at exclusive nightclubs among the celebrity elite, had now become a working-class drug common among construction workers, housewives, off-duty cops—you name it.

Prosecutor Kelly asked Tower, "Did there come a time in approximately 1980 when you developed a problem with respect to your drug dealing?"

"Yes."

"What was the problem?"

"Well, I had a pretty big-sized organization on my behalf, and there was problems in the town at the time. There was a fellow named Tommy Nee [no relation to Pat Nee] going around—I guess this fellow might have just gotten out of jail. . . . I didn't know him well, but I knew of him. . . . I guess there were threats going around. They were chasing people that were involved in drugs and shaking them down."

"What was your understanding of Thomas Nee's reputation?"

"I understood Thomas Nee was a very bad person, a murderer, and if you crossed him, you would be in serious trouble."

"So he had a fearsome reputation?"

"Yes."

"And you heard he was shaking down drug dealers in South Boston?"

"That's correct."

"So what did you do about it?"

What followed from Tower was a torrent of verbiage and splintered syntax, a roundabout description of how he approached Kevin O'Neill, a proprietor of Triple O's, and explained his predicament. From the stand, Tower sounded as if he were presently coked up, though he swore he had not touched the white powder in more than a decade. Those years were behind him. His current state was apparently a combination of his innate gregariousness and nervousness about being on the stand. He twitched and moved around in his seat a lot; it was easy to see how he had once been not only a boss but also the primary sampler of his organization. The old adage "don't get high on your own supply" had fallen on deaf ears with Joe.

Said Kelly, "Sir, I am going to have to ask you to slow down a bit."

The courtroom roiled with laughter; everyone was aware that Tower had been prattling like a South Boston version of Joe Pesci, the motormouth actor of *Goodfellas* fame.

"I'm sorry," said Tower, sheepishly.

"Our court reporter, his fingers are flying. Slow it down. The jury wants to understand it."

Joe was smiling now. "Sorry. It just happens to be the way I am."

The laughter in the courtroom seemed to lessen the anxiety for Tower, and from then on he regaled the jury and spectators with a street-level discourse on how Bulger became the cocaine boss of Southie.

It was Kevin O'Neill who had suggested to Tower that, given his problems with the renegade gangster Tommy Nee disrupting his organization, maybe he needed to have a talk with Jim Bulger.

Joe Tower was a musician and a cocaine and marijuana dealer; he was not a gangster. But he knew who Jim Bulger was; everyone knew. Joe had said hello a few times to Bulger at Triple O's. He knew that Bulger was the neighborhood mob boss. He knew that entering into any kind of arrangement with Bulger would be taking his drug business into another realm, but he didn't know what else to do. Tommy Nee was ruining his business.

"You know," Tower said to Kevin O'Neill, "that sounds like something I would be interested in. Set up a meeting."

To a rapt jury, Tower described his first meeting with Whitey, the blue Malibu with wire-rimmed wheels and a vinyl top that everyone in the neighborhood knew to be Bulger's, pulling up in front of his home on L and Seventh streets in South Boston. Tower sat in front, with Whitey in the driver's seat and Kevin O'Neill riding shotgun. After a few moments of neighborhood small talk, Whitey got to the point: "You know, Joe, I understand Kevin says you have a problem you're concerned about." Tower explained the situation. To which Whitey said, "Yeah, you do have a problem. But, you know what? Maybe this problem can be rectified."

Bulger asked Joe to give a detailed accounting of his business—how many "customers," meaning dealers working for him; weekly expenditures; weekly profits; where he got his product; where he stored his product. By the time he was done, Bulger said, "I can help you. I would like you to hook up with a friend of mine. His name is Billy Shea."

"Okay," said Tower.

"If you do this, there will be no more problems. No one will bother you. You will be free to do what you do with Billy Shea. You take him in, explain what this business is all about, show him the ropes, and you will not be bothered."

From then on, Tower met nearly every day with Billy Shea. They went around to every known cocaine and marijuana dealer in Southie and surrounding environs and told them that from now on, they did business with one entity and one entity only. It was made clear that entity was Jim Bulger. The Tommy Nee problem disappeared. Everyone fell in line. Said Tower, "I told my customers there was no longer going to be any problems. They weren't going to get any intimidation from anybody. Nobody was going to approach them, because I had taken care of the situation."

Tower explained how, with Billy Shea as his new partner, they purchased what amounted to a weekly intake of anywhere between forty and seventy ounces, at least a kilo (2.2 pounds), which they always referred to as "pizzas," just in case anyone was listening. A kilo could cost anywhere from $28,000 to $34,000. "We would cut that," said Tower, "using special solvents. If I remember correctly, things like mannitol, inositol. There was different ingredients that could be bought and double-boiled and made into a particular formula the same color as cocaine. It could be mixed undetected and, in doing so, it gained weight. And weight was money."

Tower estimated that he and Shea were eventually taking in $100,000 a week from sales. As for his relationship with Shea, Tower said, "He had a way of doing things. It was always the tough-guy approach. And I always said, 'That isn't how you run a business. These people aren't going to work with you like that.'" Nonetheless, generally things ran smoothly, and everyone got rich together. When things didn't run smoothly, that's where Bulger came into the picture.

To illustrate Bulger's role, the prosecutor elicited from Tower a story the likes of which a person might have heard over a beer at Triple O's a long time ago.

As Joe remembered it, there was that one time when his brother, who was an active part of the operation, ran into a problem. "What it was all about," said Tower, "is that a particular customer up in Wakefield—and he was a good customer. He pretty much had an open run up there. Whatever he needed, we would give him. And in so doing, he incurred quite a large bill with us. And it turned out that he informed me that he couldn't pay. I asked him why he couldn't pay, and he said he had given it to a friend of his, a so-called customer of his, and that he wasn't going to pay him or me. I said, Well, why is that? And he said, The bottom line is that his uncle's some kind of big wheel, and he said you best not pursue this and forget about the money. And I said to him, Well that ain't going to happen. So I said to my buddy up there I was dealing with, I said, You should tell your friend to give me a call, and let's discuss this and see if we can work it out."

"So what happened next?" asked Brian Kelly.

"Next I got a call, probably that afternoon, from the actual individual up there. And he said to me to call this number and talk to the girl, which would be the wife of the person who owed us money. So I said, Well, what's this? I'm talking to his wife? So I give her a call. She tells me that I have a problem, that we're not getting nothing. That her uncle, if anything, will create serious problems for me and anybody who tried to come up looking for the money."

"So what did you do?"

"So I told her, I said, Listen. It's just the opposite. You have a serious problem, and, you know, we need to rectify this right now. And so with that in mind, I said, You think about it. And have your husband call me.

So I got a call back from her. She said, Listen, I spoke to my uncle. He got the money for you. And I says, Fine. That's great. She says, Yeah, go ahead up and see my uncle at the Roadhouse in Lynn. . . . I picked up the phone and called my brother, Thomas. I informed him that he could go up to the Roadhouse in Lynn, and the man would be there to pay him the money. . . . So off he goes. I get a phone call an hour later from somebody on the phone telling me, Hey, Joe, guess what. We got the money *and* your brother. I says, Who's this? He says, Never mind who's this. You got some serious problems and your brother's got some serious problems. I says, again, You got it wrong. I don't think you know who you're dealing with here. I said, I think what you should do is let my brother go and pay him the money. He insists, emphatically, No, we're going to kill your brother."

The guy put Tower's brother on the phone. "My brother says, Joe, these guys are serious. One of them's definitely a triggerman. They got a gun on me. They're talking about making plans how to get rid of me. . . . I says, You put him on the phone again. He puts him back on the phone. I told that gentleman that he is a piece of shit and that if he touched my brother, he was going to be a dead man, and you know, he's going to be getting a phone call. And I hung up on him."

Tower immediately called Billy Shea. "Billy says to me, I'm making a call now to Jimmy. Sit tight."

From that point on things were handled without Joe knowing about it, as if the game had been kicked up to a higher level. Billy Shea called and told Tower to get in his car and drive to Rotary Variety in Southie, another Bulger headquarters. Tower drove over there and parked across the street, in front of a machine repair shop. He saw Bulger, Billy Shea, and a couple of key Bulger associates—Steve Flemmi and Kevin Weeks. Occasionally one of them would disappear into the Rotary Variety store and then reappear. Eventually, Jim Bulger looked over at Tower and waved a hand, a gesture that seemed to indicate everything was okay. "Then Billy Shea comes over to me and he says the same thing. Your brother Tom is on his way home. It's taken care of. It's all over."

Tower was relieved, but not so relieved that he'd forgotten about the money he was owed. He asked Billy Shea about that. "He says, We won't be seeing anybody in Wakefield no more. We won't be worrying about the money or the Roadhouse in Lynn. It's out of our hands."

"So," said prosecutor Kelly, "you didn't get your money back but you got your brother back?"

"Correct."

"And that's the sort of protection you wanted by being aligned with Mr. Bulger?"

"Absolutely."

Shortly after that incident, in September 1983, Tower took a pinch. He pleaded guilty to a misdemeanor narcotics charge and served less than a year at Concord prison. In that time, in accordance with the unwritten rules of the gang, his wife was taken care of. She received a payment of one thousand dollars a month.

When Tower was released from prison and returned to Southie, it seemed as though things had changed. The Bulger organization was no longer getting their cocaine from his source, a group of Colombians based in Florida. They were getting it from somewhere else. Tower had little involvement, though he was still paid a weekly stipend of one thousand dollars.

One day, Joe got a call from Patrick Linskey, a member of Bulger's gang. "Mr. Linskey told me that I was no longer to be involved with any customers, any money, any part of the business, and I would no longer be receiving any thousand dollars a week."

Tower wasn't happy about it. He complained to Kevin O'Neill, owner of Triple O's, who had first connected him to Bulger. "Mr. O'Neill pulled me aside and said, Listen, you don't want to do that. This was orders from the Other Guy. The Other Guy said it was over."

"Who did you understand 'the Other Guy' to be?"

"Mr. Bulger."

"Did you ever consider starting your own individual drug business in South Boston?"

Tower winced at the thought. "No. . . . If I had done any of that—I was too well known in South Boston, from all the customers, from all the players. Everybody knew me. If there was any way, shape, or form that anybody within the organization found out that I was doing something—they don't fool around. You'd get a pass, once, if you were lucky, but you would get hurt."

That was it. Case closed. Joe Tower was out.

IN A RICO trial, with multiple counts and witnesses testifying out of chronological order, the proceedings can be like a jigsaw puzzle, with evidence being presented in a confusing jumble. As with a movie production, the jury is expected to assemble a rough cut in their heads during the testimony phase, then reconstruct the evidence in sequential order during deliberations. With the Bulger case, the prosecution made an effort to put witnesses on the stand who would allow the narrative to unfold chronologically. Along with making it easier for jurors to keep track of the evidence—events, names, and specific criminal counts in the indictment in the order they occurred—it illuminated details of the testimony in remarkable ways.

On the same day that Joe Tower finished his testimony, a subsequent witness was Billy Shea. As a key player in the Bulger organization's drug operations, Shea had figured prominently in Tower's testimony. The story Tower told about having his cocaine customers terrorized by the renegade gangster Tommy Nee, forcing Tower to turn to the Bulger crew for assistance, was still fresh in the jury's mind. Because of that incident, Tower and Shea had become partners, driving around town together nearly every day checking up on their drug connections, making payments and picking up cash.

Back in the late 1970s and 1980s, Billy Shea had been a tough little Irish hoodlum, quick with his fists and even quicker with a gun. He had done seven years in Walpole state prison on an armed robbery conviction. When he returned in November 1977, Jimmy Bulger put him to work as a loan shark and a debt collector.

The passage of years had not been especially kind to Billy Shea. At the age of seventy-four, he was gnomelike, with wrinkles, a wispy comb-over, and missing teeth. To envision the Billy Shea of old, a cocky gangster with the requisite Southie swagger, required an active imagination. At one point, when prosecutor Brian Kelly asked Shea to pull the microphone closer and speak up, the witness explained, "I have a little cold, so my voice sounds like Kermit the Frog right now."

It was a Freudian slip: Shea didn't sound like Kermit the Frog, but he did look like him, or at least like Kermit the Frog's aging Irish uncle.

In a soothing voice, slightly raspy but soft, Shea described how, with Bulger's permission, he opened an after-hours card room for high rollers.

Many of the clientele at the card room represented something that had not existed when Shea went off to prison a decade earlier: they were drug dealers with money to burn. Said Shea, "I couldn't help notice that there was many individuals walking around with rolls of one-hundred-dollar bills large enough to choke a horse. But it appeared to me they had no protection. It appeared to me that they were not organized."

"So what did you do?" asked the prosecutor.

"I visited Jim and made that fact known to him and explained that it could be very lucrative, that I could put them in line. . . . In other words, they're not mavericks anymore, the day of being a maverick is over, that I'm going to absorb them."

"They'd have to pay you?"

"Well, yeah, that was the basic idea, originally."

As Billy remembered it, Bulger liked the idea, but he had a concern. "He did not want his image involved in drugs. He didn't want his name attached to it."

And so, Billy Shea, Whitey, and his crew had to come up with a plan to force the neighborhood drug dealers into the fold without it appearing as if Bulger were the puppet master. Thus they hired Tommy Nee to do the dirty work. "He was viewed as very dangerous in the neighborhood," said Billy. "I would be playing the part of a diplomat."

The Tommy Nee renegade gangster strategy had worked so well that thirty-three years later, when Joe Tower took the stand and testified, he still believed that it was legitimate. He had no idea that it had all been a ploy put in motion by Bulger and Billy Shea to take over the drug trade in Southie. Tower was forced to turn to them for protection, which is exactly how they planned it.

In the early days, there had been some hiccups. For one thing, Bulger was not a drug user of any kind. He didn't know much about the product or the business. Early on, for instance, the organization was forcing dealers to take inferior marijuana, which became known in Southie as "gangster weed." Shea realized that they needed a new supplier. "I went to Jim and explained that we had a problem with supply. I mentioned that this so-called gangster weed was getting even worse."

Whitey didn't know weed, but he knew business. That's how he saw himself, as a businessman. Even though he did not want it known that the drug trade in Southie was within his domain, everybody knew. And Whitey knew that everybody knew. If anyone in the town were ever caught mentioning Bulger's name in relation to marijuana or cocaine, they might very well "take a beating." But, in truth, everybody knew. And they were expected to keep their mouths shut.

As for a new weed supply, Bulger took matters into his own hands. He introduced Shea to a guy who had a schooner down in the marina and made regular trips south of the border. The guy was an offloader of goods on the docks in Southie. Shea wasn't sure; he didn't know the guy, but both Bulger and Steve Flemmi said the guy was a major player. Said Shea, "We made arrangements and started buying some very, very good Colombian gold. They came in fifty-pound bales. Our grass problem was over."

Bales of incoming grass were picked up on the waterfront and transferred to a location the gang referred to as the Vault. "Because marijuana comes in bales," said Shea, "it's bulky. You need a place to store it and distribute it. I owned a triple-decker at 252 E Street. I turned the first floor into what appeared to be a living space, made it look like somebody was living there, furnished, with timers on the lights. Nobody lived there. In the closet of the apartment was a trapdoor. At first you wouldn't see it, clothes, shoes, carpet. But pick up the carpet, you had a trapdoor. That would drop down into a cellar that was partly walled off. Anyone coming into that cellar, it would appear to be a complete cellar. It wasn't. It was blocked off with the same brick as the foundation of the building. This is where the Vault was created."

Cocaine was also a major local commodity, now that Bulger's organization was in charge. They ran into a similar problem with supply as they had with weed. The people Joe Tower had been getting his coke from—a group of Colombians associated with the Medellín Cartel—had come under investigative scrutiny. Tower and Shea had been making regular trips down to Florida to purchase the product, but in 1985 the Colombians abruptly closed up shop.

Shea was concerned, but Bulger told him not to worry. Again, Whitey had someone he wanted Billy to meet. That person turned out to be Joe Murray, whom Shea first met one evening in M Street Park, across from some of the neighborhood's most fashionable brownstones.

Originally from Charlestown, the city's other rambunctious Irish American enclave, on the other side of town from Southie, Joe Murray was a legendary trafficker of various illegal goods, including cocaine, marijuana, and guns.

What Billy Shea didn't know, of course, was that at the same time Bulger was initiating business with Joe Murray, he was "ratting" on him to John Connolly and the FBI. Thanks to Bulger, the feds were compiling a file on Murray, which meant that anyone who did business with him could one day be a target. Bulger was protected; he had a special relationship with the FBI. But Billy Shea did not.

With high-grade product provided by master smuggler Joe Murray, Southie was awash in cocaine in the 1980s. There were rumors that the organization was also smuggling heroin, but Kevin Weeks, Pat Nee, and others who eventually turned against Bulger deny this was ever true. If it was known that smack was being sold in Southie, members of the Bulger organization would track them down and give them a beating—which happened one time when the crew found out that the Sullivan brothers, a notorious family in the neighborhood that often engaged in renegade criminal activity, was selling dope. Kevin Weeks, as Bulger's primary enforcer, put together a crew of thugs and boxers, sought out the brothers, and gave them a beating in the street. Heroin and prostitution in Southie were forbidden under the Bulger regime.

Bulger's drug operation became a smooth-running machine, and Billy Shea was an important player. "My responsibilities primarily, after the initial creation of the enterprise, was collections, making sure collections were on time and then chopping up the pie. . . . One of the things I did learn from Jim, he schooled me pretty good in the beginning, was to create buffers. I basically was his buffer to the endeavor, and, of course, I created buffers with trusted associates so they would take the heat before I did. And I learned to stay away from the product. I was never there with the product."

Prosecutor Kelly had elicited from the witness a detailed description of the organization's structure and distribution process. Now he asked, "Describe for us how much sales you were making from cocaine."

"I would say close to a hundred thousand or more every week, at its height." From the witness box, Shea smiled sheepishly and glanced toward the defendant. "I'm thinking Jim is looking at me and saying, You son of a bitch. You made that kind of money and I got my lousy end."

Bulger let loose with a genuine, good-natured chuckle. He seemed to be enjoying Shea's testimony. Billy was a great storyteller with an eye for detail, and he told his tales in a mood of nostalgia. For the gangsters in Southie, these had been the good old days.

Said Kelly, "So, if it's one hundred grand a week, you're talking over five million dollars a year, gross."

"Yes. That sounds about right."

Shea and Bulger became tight during those years. Bulger would stop by Shea's home at least once and sometimes twice a week.

"How long did these meetings last?" asked Kelly.

"It varied, depending on, I guess, Jim's mood. Sometimes he would sit there quite a while. He appeared to generally like my family, and he would sit and chat and talk with my wife and blah, blah. And he liked animals. I had a couple of dogs, he liked that. He would stay awhile. Sometimes he would not. Sometimes, if he was busy, bing, bing, and he was out, got his chop and was gone."

This note of kitchen table camaraderie between the witness and the defendant from long ago reminded Kelly that he had not yet done his due diligence. "By the way," he said, "could you, for the record—do you see Mr. Bulger anywhere in the courtroom? Can you identify him, please?"

"Sure, I can identify him. He's the young fella there with the green shirt."

Billy pointed at Whitey, who smiled. It was a smile tinged with acceptance and regret. He seemed to harbor no hard feelings toward Billy Shea.

IT WAS CLEAR from Billy Shea's testimony that he liked Jim Bulger. He spoke of the neighborhood gang boss with affection. Shea was impressed with Bulger's intelligence and his leadership abilities. As Billy put it, "I was always able to reason with Jim. If we had a difference of opinion all those years, we would work it out, you know. I didn't always win the argument, but we could always reason it out. There was never no violence or hint of violence towards me."

But there came a time, in early 1986, when Billy Shea began to grow tired of the drug business. For six straight years it had been an everyday thing; the money they made was phenomenal. But Shea was worried that it was only a matter of time before he would wind up on "the screen," his term for the radar screen, the focus of a law enforcement investigation. Involvement in the narcotics business is supposed to be temporary, a way to make quick cash and move on to other things. Because eventually some human cog in the operation will get jammed up, maybe for something that has nothing to do with their involvement in the drug trade, and that person will cut a deal to save their hide. It is as certain as the rising and setting of the sun that it will happen one day. Better to get out now before the law comes knocking, and people start getting killed to prevent them from becoming a snitch.

Said Shea, "It's early 1986. I decided I'm going to talk to Jim and tell him I want out." Billy felt it was a good time to make his pitch. The pie was huge, money rolling in. It was Shea's intention to make a clean break and therefore leave his "chop" behind. His getting out would be a windfall for Bulger. "I assured him I could step away, and I told him I'm not looking for a pension plan, because there is none in this type of business. And I said, Do what you want with my share.

"He said no. At that time, he said it's running smooth as a sewing machine. You're important. You need to stay."

"So what happened?" asked the prosecutor

Shea furrowed his brow. All these years later, the memory was still fragrant. "Okay. That ended that conversation. I made up my mind that the argument he presented to me—which was, 'It wouldn't run without you, Bill, it would fall apart'—well, I'll just show him. I'll show him that it can run, that I don't need to be here. Okay. So. I go down to Florida. And I stayed there, I don't know, a month, maybe longer. I was trying to demonstrate to Jim that this could run, I could pull away. I had put people in place, people he knew and trusted. I wasn't needed."

Shea received a call from Bulger, which was highly unusual. Bulger didn't like to talk on the phone. "He says to me, 'It's all falling apart, ba-be, ba-be, ba-be. It's falling apart. I told you it would. You can't just go off to Florida like that and think you're retired.' He did not threaten me at that point. Up to this point, we had a good working relationship.

"Okay. So now I'm back [in Southie]. I listen to the riot act [from Jim]. I stay maybe three weeks, make sure all the little fires are put out, everything is running smooth again, and I leave. That was very stupid. That angered Jim. . . . I can't speak for him, but I believe that angered him."

Again, Shea received a call from Bulger while down in Florida. "He said, 'If you don't come back up, I'll come down there.' I didn't take that as a threat, just his patience running out."

Prosecutor Kelly was incredulous. "Well, did you think he was coming down there to vacation with you?"

"No. But he didn't say it in a threatening way. I took it as he was just blowing off some hot air. . . . Anyway, I did come back.

"Okay. I'm back. I was probably back only a day, and I got a message that he wanted to see me. Usually, if I seen him, it would be at my home. But he wanted to see me at Triple O's."

Nobody wanted to be called to a meeting with Bulger at the Triple O's Lounge. It was a bad omen. But Billy knew he had to go. One of Bulger's sidekicks, Patrick Linskey, came by and picked him up. They drove to the bar. Jim Bulger was waiting. "So we sat down. I knew he was very angry. I said, 'Look, Jim'—I tried to reason, the same story. And his reply this time, first time ever, he threatened me. He said, quote—I'm sure he remembers it because I remember it real clear, the first time he ever threatened me—he says, 'You remember what happened to Bucky Barrett.'

"Now, you know, I wasn't even upset he said that. What was more upsetting, he embarrassed me in front of Patrick."

"What did you understand that to mean?"

"I understood that to be what it meant. 'Do you remember what happened to Bucky Barrett?' Hey, I took it as Bucky Barrett is among the missing. You know. I took it as a threat, and it was the first time he ever did that. It changed my perception of Jim just like that.

"I got up. I'm feeling embarrassed. I'm looking at a guy that I thought I knew for many years, and he's threatening me, like, you know, You'll do as I say or I'll whack you, basically.

"I told him, I said, 'Are you threatening me, Jim?' He didn't answer. I said, 'Because I don't respond good with threats.' I didn't mean I was going to do something to him. I meant, I don't fucking—threats is—I don't respond well to them. I'll do the opposite. I do that most of my life when people threaten me. I'll do the opposite.

"So, I left Triple O's. I go home, clean up some old business, tie up some loose ends. . . . I proceed right to Florida again. That's what I did. . . . I was down there about three weeks, maybe more, and I came back. I didn't get no phone call this time. I thought, Hey, hopefully he's starting to realize that I'm breaking away."

Billy Shea was home one day when his front door buzzer sounded. It was Bulger. Shea came outside and was surprised to see not only Bulger but two others, his partner Steve Flemmi and his bodyguard, Kevin Weeks. "He said he needed to talk to me. Well, I found that odd. Whenever we talked, all those years, he didn't want anybody around. So now he wants to talk with two other individuals, one of them, Flemmi, being a very, very dangerous person, just as dangerous as Jim.

"So I said, 'Okay, just a minute.' I went upstairs, and for the first time ever—I never carried a gun around Jim, ever—I armed myself.

"I come out, I got in the car. Best I can remember, I was in the back with Stevie, and Jim and Kevin was in the front. Okay. We're in the car. I know the car routine. So we drive down not too far from where I live on the Seventh Street side of the D Street housing project. It just so happened it was being remodeled. The courtyards are deserted, there's nobody living in those apartments; plywood on some of the windows. Yeah, okay. Not as comfortable as my house, or even as comfortable as the Triple O's. So, Jim gets out. We're going in there. I believe Stevie said something to me to the effect of, I wish you would reconsider. I got some of it, because by now my antenna is up, I'm focused. I'm paying attention.

"There is no one around there for me. The only people there was us four.

"Jim and I walked into the courtyard. The courtyard, as I said, was abandoned. Deserted . . . I think we're going to stop, there's some wash yards there, there's a doorway there, there's four or five doorways. No, he doesn't want to talk there. He wants to talk down on the cellar steps.

"Now, I don't know how many people are familiar with housing projects. But in housing projects, the cellar steps are like a coffin. As you walk down the cellar steps, deeper and deeper, to get to the cellar door, there's concrete reinforcement that is built around those stairs. So by the time you hit the bottom of the stairs, you're in a well-enclosed area. That's what really got me very paranoid. Very paranoid."

"What happened? What did you do?"

"We come down the stairs. I think Jim was in front of me. I'm trying to the best of my ability to remember this. It should be burnt in my memory. I think he was in front, I was in back. I wanted to get down the stairs before him, because at the bottom, basically, there's four feet of concrete all around you. I tried to get in front of him, and I succeeded. Very quickly, I got in front of him and turned so my back was at the cement wall, so there would be nobody coming from my back side.

"So we talked. And I didn't see any tells that he was aggravated. What I was doing was watching his hands. . . . He didn't normally carry a gun. He normally carries a knife, and it's down here. . . ." Billy tapped his ankle, where Bulger kept a knife in his cowboy-style leather boots. "I was looking at his hands to make sure they didn't move anywhere, and I was looking over his shoulder at the top of the stairs to make sure I didn't see Stevie's head show up."

"What was discussed?"

"Again, my getting out of the business. The same argument I presented many times. I'm adamant. But I'm thinking that he took me down there to either frighten me or whack me, either one."

"By 'whack' you, what does that mean?"

"Well, I don't come out of the cellar. If I come up, I'm gone.

"So, this is the first time—I've always feared him a little bit, because I know he's smart and clever—but this is the first time I really focused on him, like if he makes a move, you're going with me. That's basically the state of my mind at the time. Jim, you make a move on me, you're gone. And, of course, I know I'm gone if Stevie shows up at the stairs."

"So how did the conversation conclude?"

"He surprised me. We talked back and forth. He mentioned something—trust. That's what I remember. Don't forget, I'm down there, you know, my heart's beating a little bit. I'm focusing on him, but I'm very nervous. I know there's other people with him. I know that if it went bad, I'd be gone. I'd be left there.

"So, he mentioned trust. I couldn't think right away what he meant by trust. Is he thinking I'll be a loose end? Is that what he's worried about? Because there's no other reason. He's not greedy. I pointed out that he would be getting a big piece of the pie. So it isn't greed. If it was greed, he'd say, 'See you later, Bill.' So it had to be trust."

"Trust as to what?"

"A loose end. Maybe I knew too much. You know, the knowledge of the years in the business. I don't know, I can't speak for him. Only he can speak for himself."

"So what happened?"

"All of a sudden, he relaxed. The tension came out of his face. . . . He turned and he said, 'Let's get the hell out of here.' And we walked up the steps."

"Did he invite you back to his car?"

"You know, as a matter of fact, he did. It was over then. I was relieved. I was very nervous, but then we were talking and walking back out to the car, where Kevin and Stevie was, and he asked if I wanted a ride. I said, 'No, I can walk.'"

After that, Billy Shea was out of the drug business. Bulger never bothered him. It was years before he ever saw the mob boss again, and that was a random encounter with Bulger one day near the Old Colony housing project. Billy was with his son, who was four years old at the time.

"Did you ever see him again after that?" asked the prosecutor.

"No. Not until today."

Kelly told Judge Casper that he had no more questions.

Defense attorney Carney stood and announced that they had no cross-examination of the witness.

Billy Shea was dismissed.

The entire inhabitants of the courtroom, including the jury, the lawyers, the judge, the guards, and the spectators, had been lost in a near-mystical state of fascination. The intimacy of Billy's testimony, the emotional and physical details, the softness of his delivery: it was as if Shea had cast a spell over his listeners.

9

SURROGATE SON

ON THE AFTERNOON of July 2, after Billy Shea completed his testimony, it was time for the trial to adjourn for the Fourth of July holiday. Before releasing the jury for the long weekend, the judge called the legal representatives from both sides over to the bench for a sidebar. She asked Wyshak and Kelly for an assessment of how many more witnesses the government would call to the stand, and how much longer their case would take.

"We continue to make great progress with our schedule," Brian Kelly informed the judge. "We anticipate being done with our case by the end of July."

Jay Carney tried to throw water on the notion that the end was near. He reiterated to the judge that the defense had a substantial list of witnesses they wanted to call to the stand. "Our plan now, based on our witness list, is to go into September."

Unsurprisingly, the two sides were at cross purposes, with different versions of reality.

Judge Casper first gave the eighteen people seated in the jury box an assessment, based on what she'd just been told by the lawyers, of how much longer the trial was likely to continue. Then she gave them the standard admonition: "As you leave for the weekend, please keep all of my cautionary instructions in mind. . . . Don't discuss the case with anyone. Don't let anyone discuss it with you. Avoid any media coverage of the case. Don't do any research of any kind on your own about the case. Have a great afternoon, and a great holiday. Thank you."

The jury was dismissed.

Janet Uhlar had been planning on spending the Fourth of July weekend with her mother in Quincy. But she felt so overloaded by the trial—the sheer volume of evidence and also the unseemly nature of much of the testimony—that she decided to stay at her place in Cape Cod. One thing about living on the Cape: you don't need to go anywhere for a vacation. The summer weather is nice and the beach is inviting. On the Fourth of July weekend, tourists traditionally flood into the area from around New England, the United States, and even the world. In July and August, the population of the Cape doubles in size, making it difficult to get around due to traffic. Mostly, throughout the long mini-vacation, Janet stayed indoors and away from the throngs of people.

It should have been a time for Uhlar to forget about the trial and return to normal life, but she couldn't. The testimony of John Morris had been a kind of tipping point. Morris was creepy, for sure, and obsequious in his corruption, but what she found more disturbing was the fact that he not only functioned but flourished within the law enforcement bureaucracy. Each year, he received the highest possible commendations from his superiors. As long as he played the good company man, dotting his *i*'s and crossing his *t*'s, the system seemed incapable of recognizing this con man in its midst.

Morris was depraved, but that wasn't what bothered Uhlar most of all. What really had her shaking her head was that, as with John Martorano, Morris had parlayed his career as a corrupt federal agent into the deal of a lifetime. Here was a man who could and should have been in prison for the rest of his life, and he was still free and collecting a government pension for his years of "service."

Why?

Because the government wanted Whitey Bulger, that's why. And they had made unconscionable deals with men as bad as Bulger—or worse—in the interest of "justice."

For Uhlar, who had spent much of her adult life studying the Revolutionary War, justice as defined in the U.S. Constitution was something she took seriously. Both of the historical novels she had written were a consequence of this fascination. One of those books told the story of Joseph Warren, one of the original Sons of Liberty who united the First Continental Congress. Another of her novels delved into the life of Nathanael Greene, the Revolutionary War commander who first petitioned Congress for a Declaration of Independence. These were men who devoted their lives to the concept that personal liberty had to be protected under the U.S. Constitution. They had fought in battle partly to help pave the way for a system of justice that was fair and above reproach. Central to that ideal was the notion of due process, a fundamental principle of fairness in all matters of law, criminal and civil.

The universal guarantee of due process is in the Fifth Amendment to the Constitution, which provides, "No person shall . . . be deprived of life, liberty, or property without due process of law." Inherent in that edict is the requirement that the law be applied fairly, without manipulation, selective prosecution, perjury, the withholding of evidence, and many other legal tactics that can lead to the overturning of verdicts and censure by judges representing the appellate court system.

Through her research as a writer and historian, and through her personal belief system, Janet Uhlar believed that the concept of due process, as spelled out in the Constitution, was sacrosanct. She believed that even a man who had committed as many reprehensible acts as James Bulger, who had begun his trial by admitting to many of the acts in the indictment, was deserving of due process.

In the Bulger trial, Uhlar was developing a nagging feeling that due process was being trampled upon. Part of this, she would admit, had to do with her own lack of awareness of criminal procedures, especially those relating to organized crime prosecutions. She was not a mob aficionado. Most people who do follow mob prosecutions know that cases against mobsters are frequently constructed on evidence provided by informants and testimony put forth by "rats" or "snitches," criminals who have often engaged in activities as bad as anything for which the defendant has been charged. When it comes to mob prosecutions, making sweetheart deals with hardened criminals is the name of the game.

Call it naïveté, perhaps, but Uhlar was shocked by what she had seen so far. It was bad enough that the justice system was willing to use people like Joe Barboza, Steve Flemmi, and Bulger as informants and witnesses, to make cases by manipulating criminals while they were out on the street. But to then have men like John Martorano and John

Morris, after they have been caught, walking free because they were able to bargain with federal authorities—it was like *Let's Make a Deal,* with the notion of justice merely the result of whoever could best pull one over on the system.

Throughout the entire long weekend, Uhlar did very little. Normally she would have been celebrating with family, but she felt mildly depressed. She felt as though she were in mourning. She made a point of avoiding the holiday revelers, families with young children communing together in honor of the birth of a nation. Most days before noon, she was alone in the garden, watering plants, pulling weeds. In the afternoons, she caught up on her reading. None of this made it any easier for her to stop thinking about the trial.

Most evenings, after preparing and eating a light meal, she wrote in her journal, as she did on the evening of the Fourth:

> Independence day—a day I truly cherish. A day for grateful reflection, celebration, and patriotic display. Quite different this year. Sorrow overwhelms me. Can't bring myself to celebrate the birth of a nation. The men who determinedly purchased for us what they considered a sacred judicial system, which protected the accused and properly and swiftly punished the guilty, has been replaced with one that now views the accused as guilty until proven innocent, and sets free the most vile if they can be used as means to an end. If our judicial system is gone, the nation is gone. Liberty is an illusion. The price paid by the men who fought for the right to a fair trial was to offer their lives. Today is not a day to celebrate—it's a day to mourn.

For juror number twelve, the Bulger trial had become a personal crisis. She wanted it to be over. But she knew that before it was over, she and her fellow jurors would have to reach a verdict.

It should have been simple. Bulger was a bad man; he had admitted to a life of crime. But the men who were being used to make the case against him were worse, and the manner in which the government was using these men was sleazy, and it undermined her faith in the case. Uhlar was beginning to wonder how she would ever be able to reach a verdict.

I HADN'T SEEN Kevin Weeks in a while. Not since the beginning of the trial, at Mirisola's restaurant in Southie. Since then, Kevin's name had become a mainstay at the trial, with references to his being involved in, among other things, extortions and body disposals with Bulger. I knew there was much more to come. Unlike with many of the other witnesses at the trial, Weeks's relationship with Bulger had been singular. As Whitey's right-hand man, Kevin had stories to tell that no one else could tell, because much of his time with the mob boss was spent one-on-one.

Weeks was scheduled to take the stand as soon as the trial resumed on Monday, July 8. The day before, on Sunday afternoon, I saw Weeks at a backyard barbecue in Malden, a suburban town twenty miles outside Boston. I was invited to the gathering by Pat Nee.

The barbecue was held at the house of a Southie expatriate who had moved there with his wife and kids. Though the setting was suburban, miles removed from the city, it was most definitely a Southie gathering composed of people from the "old neighborhood," some of whom had driven out for the occasion.

Even with all the demographic changes that have taken place in Southie, the spirit of the neighborhood remained strong among those who stay connected, either because they still live there or because once you have Southie in your bloodstream it never goes away, whether you want it to or not.

Both Weeks and Nee still live in Southie. Both had been sent away to do time in prison and returned to the neighborhood, because, even with all the bad memories and water under the bridge, Southie is where they felt they belonged.

On this particular post–Fourth of July afternoon, Southie had been transplanted to a bucolic suburban backyard miles from the city.

Weeks looked better than when I last saw him, when he had only recently suffered a shoulder injury and undergone surgery. He had lost weight, and his girlfriend had freshly dyed his hair in anticipation of all the public exposure he would receive when he showed up at court to testify. His time on the stand was expected to stretch over at least two full days.

I reached out to shake Kevin's hand, and I could see that he had not yet regained mobility in his right shoulder and arm. "It's better," he said when

I asked how his recovery was progressing. "Physical therapy three times a week. The pain is gone, but I have a long ways to go before I'll be anywhere near one hundred percent."

As with most gatherings of Southie folk, it was a social occasion: there was plenty of beer and barbecued meat and lively conversation. Some people brought their children; kids of varying ages ran around the yard, tossing a football and incessantly asking questions of the adults.

I sat off to one side with Weeks and, in anticipation of his testimony, peppered him with questions.

I knew from experience that over the years, since Kevin had been released from prison in 2006, he'd grown wary of commentary and queries about the Bulger years from outsiders. It seemed that everyone had an opinion based primarily on what they had read or seen on a TV report. Over a twelve-year period, Weeks spent nearly every day of his life in the company of Bulger; other than Steve Flemmi, there was no more central player in the Bulger organization. To listen to journalists and pundits pontificate about the Bulger years was, for Kevin, annoying at best and, at worst, downright nauseating.

Contrary to what I'd been told about Kevin's quick temper, my personal experience was that he listened carefully and thoughtfully to what I had to say. Which was good, because I had a theory I wanted to run by him that was a bit contrary to the accepted wisdom.

I had gotten my hands on a copy of Steve Flemmi's federal debriefing file, which contained dozens of DEA-6s, concise reports of information Flemmi had given to the authorities after he first began cooperating with Wyshak and Kelly in 1999. I was startled to see how involved Flemmi had been, back in the mid-1960s, with Special Agents Rico and Condon, aided primarily by the fact that his brother Vincent "the Bear" Flemmi was a Top Echelon Informant. It was because of the Bear that Steve Flemmi had been recruited and signed on as an informant, with Condon as his handler. Steve Flemmi established this relationship with the Boston FBI before he ever knew James Bulger. It was an alliance that made it possible for Stevie to commit murders and get away with it.

"Hear me out," I said to Weeks. "What if Steve Flemmi was the key link between the Rico and Condon era and the Connolly and Morris era. What if he was the one who convinced Jim Bulger that becoming an informant was the way to go, that it would be a virtual license to commit crimes. And Flemmi was acting, in part, at the behest of his contacts in the FBI. They used Flemmi as a way to bring Bulger into the fold. Sure, Connolly made the overture, but it was Flemmi who convinced Bulger by citing his own personal experience as an example of how advantageous it could be."

Weeks said nothing; by his silence he was saying, Go ahead, I'm listening.

"Furthermore," I continued, "by establishing this relationship with the FBI, Flemmi and Bulger solidified their partnership. Because up until then they were simply co-members of the Winter Hill Mob. But once they both signed on with John Connolly, they became a team. And this is crucial for Bulger. Because his arrangement with Connolly and the FBI is based on his ability to deliver the Italians to them. Bulger can't do that on his own; he knows that. He doesn't have the access. He needs Stevie Flemmi for that. Flemmi is his link to the Mafia."

Weeks sipped his beer and mulled over what I'd been saying. "You know," he said, "Jim Bulger used to always say about Stevie—if left to his own devices, he would self-destruct."

It was a cryptic remark. But I understood what Kevin was saying. "Right," I said. "I'm not saying that Flemmi was the guy pulling the strings in all this. I'm saying that the FBI used Flemmi to help facilitate the recruitment of Bulger. And then once the partnership was formed, Bulger used Flemmi for his own needs, to help the feds nail the Italians, with him getting equal credit for it."

"It's not a bad theory," said Weeks. In the past, he'd told me that most of what he knew about the era of the Boston gang wars and the involvement of Rico, Condon, and other key players had come from Bulger, or Flemmi, who used to regale him with stories about the good old days. They were fascinating remembrances, but, of course, they tended to be self-serving. Ever since Weeks learned that Bugler and Flemmi had been informants for nearly a decade before he came along, filling the FBI rotor file with intel about many fellow criminals with whom Weeks had been doing business, everything he'd been told by those two was cast in a different light.

Pat Nee pulled up a chair and sat down. "Hey," he said to Weeks, "did you tell him about the time Whitey ordered you to kill me?"

Kevin chuckled. There were a lot of things that Weeks and Nee were able to laugh about now that weren't so funny at the time.

Back in the early 1980s, at the same time Weeks was in the process of becoming Bulger's full-time pit bull, he also became friendly with Nee. They shared some things in common, one of them being an interest in martial arts, a skill that Nee had picked up during his years in the Marine Corps. In early 1981, they entered a tournament together and fought as partners, with matches in various karate clubs around New England. Pat is thirteen years older than Kevin, so there were plenty of jokes from their opponents about Kevin's "geriatric" partner. Their time together during that tournament would form the basis of a friendship that exists to this day.

Nee's uneasy partnership with Bulger is well documented in his book; I had interviewed him about it numerous times. Less well known was Bulger's animosity toward Pat.

"Bulger called him Cement Head," said Kevin. "He felt Pat didn't listen to him."

In the early 1980s, Nee began spending more and more time in Charlestown. The ostensible reason was that Nee had begun to explore a secret, transatlantic connection with the IRA. Charlestown's Irish American gangsters had a preexisting relationship with the IRA, in particular master smuggler Joe Murray. Ever since "the Troubles" in Northern Ireland exploded in the late 1960s, with British troops and the Royal Ulster Constabulary implementing repressive tactics to quell the minority Catholic population, it had been a dream of Pat's—and others in Boston's Irish American community—to ship guns to the IRA.

Bulger became involved in preparations for the IRA gunrunning scheme, though according to Nee, "He never had any real knowledge or sympathy for what was happening in Northern Ireland." Bulger became interested after Joe Murray linked the planned outgoing shipment of weapons to Ireland to an incoming shipment of marijuana, organized and overseen by the same crew of smugglers and gangsters.

"Jim didn't trust Pat," said Kevin. "He knew he was off meeting regularly with the Charlestown people and the IRA. Jimmy has to be in control at all times. He didn't know for sure what Pat was up to, and it made him nervous."

The tension between Nee and Bulger came to a head one night when the two had words. "It was about the IRA," said Pat. "Whitey wanted to pull out of the gun-smuggling operation. He kept saying, 'It's costing us money and we're getting nothing in return.'" Bulger was a gangster and a businessman, not a revolutionary. Where was the profit in sending weapons to a guerrilla army on the other side of the ocean, a costly operation with no profit margin?

The exchange of words between the two old rivals was like having salt rubbed in a wound that had never really healed. Bulger knew that his prized bodyguard Kevin Weeks was making trips into Charlestown with Nee, and he didn't like it. Feelings of jealousy that Bulger had harbored ever since the two became karate partners left a bad taste in his mouth.

One day, Bulger and Weeks were making the rounds in Whitey's Chevy Malibu. Whitey asked, "When you're with Pat, what do you guys do?"

Kevin described to Bulger how, on those occasions when he met Nee at his house on I Street, they often sat in the kitchen and had tea.

"Does he ever turn his back on you?" asked his boss.

"Yeah, when he's at the stove making tea, his back is to me."

Bulger thought about it and said, "Well, next time he turns his back on you, put two in his head."

Sitting in the backyard in Malden at a Fourth of July barbecue, Weeks's story seemed incongruous, even lighthearted, but he wasn't joking. "That's when I realized how cheap life is," he said.

"He came to me and told me about it the next day," said Pat. "He said, 'Hey, you better watch your back. Whitey's looking to do away with you.'"

This touched off a line of discussion I'd had on other occasions with Nee: did you consider taking Bulger out before he got you? The same response as always: not as easy as it sounded. Bulger was connected on so many levels: his brother, the FBI, business partners in the underworld. Killing Whitey would have brought down a load of shit; it would have been an act of suicide.

"But after that I never met him unless I was strapped," said Nee. "And I never met him alone, one-on-one. It always had to be in a semipublic setting, with other people around. I didn't trust the cocksucker."

I asked Kevin why he had warned Pat, which could be viewed as an act of insubordination. "I was in tight with Jim. I gave him complete loyalty on most things. But that didn't mean I was going to start killing my own friends for no reason. Because then you start to worry, Gee, maybe I'm next."

As we spoke, one of the kids kicked a ball that hit the picnic table and knocked over some plates of food. "Hey," said Kevin, "be careful"—more an observation than a command—"somebody might get hurt."

THE FOLLOWING DAY, on Monday, July 8, Kevin Weeks showed up to testify at the Moakley Courthouse. There was a media frenzy in front of the building as he was escorted by a couple of U.S. marshals through the front door. The entourage of onlookers surrounding Weeks grew in size as he passed through security, entered an elevator, and disembarked on the fifth floor. By the time he'd been led into the courtroom and seated on the stand, interested spectators and media people had hunkered down, both in the courtroom and in the media room two floors below, in expectation of what promised to be one of the trial's most significant encounters.

On the stand, Weeks still looked formidable and relatively youthful, a reminder that thirty years earlier, when he first started working for the neighborhood mob boss, he was a young man in his early twenties. At the time, he had a day job with the Massachusetts Bay Transportation Authority (MBTA), Boston's transit system, as a trackman. At night he worked as a bouncer at a bar on Commonwealth Avenue called Flix. In 1980, Weeks was hired by the O'Neill brothers to work as a bouncer at Triple O's, a job that would change the course of not only his career, but his life.

It is a common dictum in the underworld that as a mob boss gets older, he becomes vulnerable. Southie, in particular, was ruled by the belief that you distinguished yourself as a leader in the streets with your fists. Bulger was revered and feared by some because he was known to be a guy who would not hesitate to do what needed to be done: if someone crossed him, that person would be killed. Bulger was a master at physical intimidation. But he was not known to be a fighter, and by the time he brought Weeks into the fold, he was in his fifties. Yes, he was a physical fitness buff; he looked fit and was menacing. But the laws of the jungle dictated that someone who was younger, faster, and stronger might seek to challenge Bulger. And so having someone like Weeks became a necessity.

Kevin was athletic, and he seemed to enjoy punching people. Bulger tested him out right away; he had Weeks beat up not only people who had crossed him in areas of criminal business, but also those who had violated the neighborhood's code of ethics. Someone who disrespected a woman, or someone who had received complaints for playing their music loud and still continued to do so, or someone who was generally drunk and disorderly might find themselves on the receiving end of a beating by Weeks, as ordered by Bulger. Occasionally these beatings took place in the upstairs function room at Triple O's.

On the stand, Weeks delved into his early years with Whitey with an easy familiarity. This was the fifth legal proceeding at which he had been called to testify since he began cooperating in 1999.

Brian Kelly handled the presentation of Weeks's direct testimony. As he had with other witnesses, he delivered his questions in a hurry, as if he had a train to catch.

"Initially, what did working for James Bulger involve?" asked Kelly.

"Basically, we just rode around. Sometimes I beat somebody up. Or picked up some envelopes from bookmakers."

"When you say 'envelopes,' what would be in the envelopes? Mail?"

Weeks smiled at that and answered, "Money."

"Did you have any sort of routine about your association with Bulger?"

"Well, in the beginning, when I was working for the MBTA, I'd leave work, I'd meet Jim at the furniture store in the afternoon around four. We'd ride around South Boston doing various things, and then I'd meet him later on at night. Eventually, I quit the MBTA and I was with him all the time. But Jim would usually come out between three or three thirty in the afternoon. We'd go around, take care of business, whatever was up for the day, and go to dinner. And then I'd meet him later that night."

"Did you have any rules about where you could talk about crime?"

"We never talked in enclosed areas, houses, cars, never talked on the phone. We were afraid of being intercepted by wiretaps, bugs."

"So you would go outside and walk on occasion to avoid detection?"

"Well, Jim liked to walk for fresh air and the exercise, and, yeah, we could talk about what we had to talk about for the day. . . . Usually we went down to Castle Island; sometimes we'd walk through the projects."

At this point, Kelly entered into evidence a series of law enforcement surveillance photos that showed Bulger and Weeks on their many strolls, Bulger wearing a Boston Red Sox baseball cap and Kevin with his bulging muscles. The photos were familiar to anyone who had followed the Bulger story over the years; they had been used on television programs like *America's Most Wanted* and *Unsolved Mysteries,* and by the FBI in its official media campaign in search of Bulger the fugitive.

After having Weeks identify each of the photos and give a brief narration of where they were taken, Kelly asked, "Now, sir, do you see James Bulger anywhere in the courtroom today?"

"Yes," said Kevin.

"Would you please point to him and identify him?"

"He's right in front of me," said the witness, pointing a finger at the defendant. Whitey gave the appearance that he was jotting notes on a legal pad and paid no attention to his former right-hand man.

Weeks was on the stand to detail his involvement in a number of activities crucial to the daily running of the Bulger organization. He had been a guardian of the gang's arsenal of weapons, which were, over the years, moved around to various locations in the neighborhood until they found a home at the "screen house," the cabana or shed that had been built behind the home of Steve Flemmi's mother. Weeks was also a player in the organization's loan-sharking, gambling, and drug operations. These rackets were crucial ongoing moneymakers, the financial backbone of the enterprise, and Kevin was given the task of organizing the many bookies and drug dealers who worked under the umbrella of the Bulger gang. He picked up payments and kept tabs on who was or was not up to speed. If some form of punishment was necessary for those who did not fulfill their obligations or stepped out of line, that decision was made by Bulger, but Kevin Weeks was often the administrator of "street justice."

Shakedowns and extortions were another crucial aspect of the gang's income stream. Whitey alone was often enough to strike fear in the hearts of anyone the gang was seeking to bleed dry, but having young Weeks standing behind the boss, a hulking presence with a wicked gleam in his eye, was an added motivator that inevitably helped seal the deal.

The irony was that unlike Bulger, Flemmi, Martorano, or even Pat Nee—men who had become professional desperados and gangsters early in their lives—Kevin Weeks never set out to be in the Mob. He had two older brothers who graduated from Harvard University. Kevin had himself been a decent student. He attended college for one year before dropping out to pursue an interest in boxing. He had been a Golden Gloves champion. Kevin was a tough guy, but he was not a killer. He had grown up hard, but he hadn't grown up interacting with people who killed other human beings for a living. Even after he became Bulger's attack dog, a dispenser of threats and beatings, he remained a bridesmaid and never a bride when it came to stabbing people to death, strangling them with your bare hands, or shooting them in the head.

Nonetheless, in the eyes of the law, a bridesmaid is most definitely guilty by association, and so Weeks was currently seated across from his former boss to explain his role as accomplice in no less than five murders perpetrated by the organization.

The first was the double killing of Brian Halloran and the hapless Michael Donahue.

By now, the jury was familiar with the saga of Halloran, after having heard testimony from Martorano, Morris, and others on how the Southie gangster's ongoing role as FBI snitch had become the worst-kept secret in all of Boston. Specifically, Halloran had been titillating his FBI handlers with information about the murders of Roger Wheeler in Oklahoma and John Callahan in Miami, two far-flung hits that had allegedly been put in motion by Bulger and Flemmi and carried out by Martorano.

After leading the witness through a quick overview of who Halloran was and how he had run afoul of the gang, prosecutor Kelly got right to the actual day of the killing—May 11, 1982. "Tell us how it happened," he said to Weeks.

Kevin took a deep breath. "Well, I came home from work, the MBTA. I went to the furniture store on West Broadway. I was there talking with Jim, and John Hurley came in. . . . Hurley was an old Winter Hill member. He's from Charlestown. He came in and told Jim that he'd just spotted Brian Halloran down the waterfront on a pay phone."

The entire South Boston underworld had been looking for Halloran.

Supposedly, the FBI had him at a safe house out on the Cape. Nobody could find him. But now here he was like a nice fat chicken nestled in his coop, just a few miles away, ready to be plucked.

"So Jim turned to me and said, 'I'll meet you down at the club,' meaning the Mullens' club down at O and Third streets." The old hangout of the Mullens gang, which had been vanquished by Bulger, survived as a no-frills, nondescript meeting location for neighborhood gangsters. In the days before cell phones and text messaging, it was necessary to have a regular meeting place. "I drove down there. He drove down there. He was looking for people—Steve Flemmi, Pat Nee, anyone that was around. Nothing. There was no one there." Bulger had Weeks drive him over to the house he shared with Teresa Stanley and drop him off. He told Weeks to go back to the Mullens' club and wait there for instructions, which his underling did without questions.

"Fifteen, twenty minutes later, Jim Bulger showed up back at the club. He was in the tow truck. That was a boiler hit car that we had. We used to use the code name 'tow truck,' so if anyone heard us talking about it, they'd just think it was a tow truck. . . . It was a '75 Malibu. It was all souped up, equipped with a smoke screen, an oil slick we could lay down. You could drive it at night with the rear lights out. It was a hit car."

The first thing Weeks noticed when Bulger drove up was that he was wearing a disguise—a sandy-blond, curly-haired wig and a floppy mustache.

Bulger told Weeks to drive down to Jimmy's Harborside bar, near where Brian Halloran had been spotted, and wait for him there. Weeks did as he was told. It was a short ten-minute drive down to the waterfront. Kevin backed his car into a parking space in the lot outside Jimmy's Harborside, which was located near Anthony's Pier 4 restaurant, a popular seafood place at the end of the pier. A few minutes later, Bulger pulled into the parking lot in the familiar Chevy Malibu. He eased into the parking space next to Weeks.

"Was he still alone?" prosecutor Kelly asked the witness.

"No. There was a person in the backseat with a ski mask on. He was kind of lying down. He leaned up and waved at me."

"Did you have any idea who it was?"

"No. I thought it was, you know, Steve Flemmi at first. Thought it might be Pat Nee."

Bulger got out of the car and handed Weeks a police-issue walkie-talkie, a type the gang frequently used in the commission of a crime. Bulger told Weeks, "Our target is sitting in the Pier restaurant. Go down there and watch him. Let me know when he's coming out." The code name they used to identify Brian Halloran was "Balloon Head."

Asked Brain Kelly, "Why was he nicknamed Balloon Head?"

The witness shrugged. "Because he had a big head."

Weeks drove closer to Anthony's Pier 4 and parked. Using a set of binoculars, he scanned the large plate-glass windows that were so big they revealed nearly the entire interior of the restaurant. Weeks didn't have to scan very long, because Brian Halloran was sitting in a booth right by the window. Not long after Weeks had spotted their target, Halloran got up to leave. Kevin raised the walkie-talkie and said, "The balloon is rising." As soon as Halloran was outside he said, "The balloon is in the air."

Halloran was not alone. He was with a friend, Michael Donahue. By chance, they had run into each other at the restaurant, and Donahue offered to give Halloran a ride to wherever he was headed. The two men climbed into Donahue's pale blue Datsun, with Halloran in the front passenger seat.

By now, Bulger and the other gunman had driven up to Anthony's Pier 4 and put themselves in a position to intercept the Datsun on its way out of the lot.

Weeks had a ringside seat. He watched the entire episode unfold before his eyes. The Malibu pulled up alongside the Datsun, which was moving slowly toward the parking lot exit. Bulger leaned out the window and called out, "Brian!" Halloran looked over, and Whitey cut loose with a volley of machine-gun fire.

"What did you see happening when he started shooting?"

"Well, there was a lot of people there. They were diving [for cover] and running around. People were screaming. Eventually, the car that Michael Donahue was driving just drifted across the road and bumped into a restaurant, I think it was called the Port of Call, or something. It's now the Whiskey Priest. Jim Bulger made a U-turn, came back around. Brian Halloran had exited the vehicle. He was still alive [though he had been hit]. He walked toward the rear of the vehicle; he actually walked right towards where Jim Bulger was parked in the street. And Jim Bulger just started shooting right at him. Brian Halloran went down, and Bulger kept shooting. [Halloran's] body was bouncing off the ground. . . . Then Jim drove away in the car. . . . I waited a minute or two, then I pulled away from where I was parked. Drove by. As I was leaving, the cops were pulling up. I could see the bodies."

"Then where did you go?"

Weeks said that Bulger had told him to meet afterward at Capital Market, on Morrissey Boulevard in Dorchester. Kevin drove over there and was surprised that Bulger was nowhere to be seen. He beeped him, giving the number of a public phone outside the market. Bulger called back and said, "Where are you?"

Kevin answered, "Capital Market, like you said."

"Oh," said Bulger. "I'm at Teresa's having something to eat. Go get yourself some dinner. I'll catch up with you later."

The gangland slaying of Halloran and Donahue was all over the news. It had been a highly public killing, just as Bulger had intended it to be. It was what is known in the trade as a "message killing." Halloran was a rat. He had been used as an example to show what happens to rats.

For Weeks, it was an initiation, of sorts, his first homicide on behalf of the organization. There would be others, as he described in vivid detail from his perch on the witness stand.

"In August of 1983," said the prosecutor, "did you know a man named Arthur 'Bucky' Barrett?"

The spectators in the courtroom squirmed a bit in their seats. The name of Bucky Barrett, which had come up during Kelly's opening statement and also elsewhere during the proceedings, meant that Weeks's testimony was now going to take us to the house on Third Street—the Haunty—a chamber of horrors that had come to represent the dark core of Southie violence.

The circumstances of Barrett's murder may have been previously touched upon, but Kevin added firsthand details that brought the incident alive in the courtroom, starting with the fact that the horrific murder had begun with a chance encounter.

"Jim Bulger and myself were over in Dorchester by the Puritan Mall, which is next to Lambert's. Jim was going to a travel agency to make plans to go away on a vacation. As we were going up the stairs, Bucky Barrett came walking down the stairs. Jim saw him. He said, 'Hey, Bucky, what are you doing over here?' He said, 'I got to see my PO.' His probation officer, I guess, was in the same building. A quick conversation. Then we continued up the stairs and Jim went in the travel agency. After that, Jim got interested in Bucky again."

Bucky Barrett had done well for himself as a freelance criminal. Everyone knew that he had been a party to the Depositors Trust bank robbery, which had netted millions. Bulger and Flemmi had already tried to shake down Barrett, insisting that they deserved a cut of the heist simply because they were in charge now, and any major score that occurred in the greater Boston area was within their domain. Not only had Barrett resisted the shakedown, but he went to Frankie Salemme, Steve Flemmi's old partner from the time of the Boston gang wars in the 1960s. As Weeks explained it, "Frankie basically said that [Bucky] was with him, he was an earner, so [Bulger and Flemmi] backed away."

Bulger let it slide, but he never forgot how Bucky had finagled his way out of the shakedown. It was now a number of years later, and Whitey had ascended in the underworld; he had gone from being a hustler to being a predator. With his powerful political brother, and his secret relationship with the FBI, Bulger believed he was untouchable. And so part of his modus operandi became feeding off other criminals in the area, luring them into scams and extortions, knowing that, unlike him, they had nowhere to turn.

Said Weeks, "A plan was devised to suck Bucky in, to shake him down. . . . There was a fellow who had a lot of hot diamonds. The plan was that Bucky was going to meet this fellow and buy diamonds off him."

"Who was this fellow?" asked the prosecutor.

"Well, it was myself."

Barrett was brought to the house on Third Street to meet the diamond dealer. He was brought by Jim Martorano, Johnny's brother. Bucky had known Jimmy Martorano for years; he trusted him.

"Bucky came in the house. . . . We shook hands, and I grabbed him by the hand and held him. Jim Bulger stepped out of the kitchen with a Mac-10 nine-millimeter, and he said, 'Bucky Barrett, freeze!' He then took possession of him. . . . Barrett was taken to the kitchen and chained and manacled, you know, handcuffed to a chair. . . . Jim told Jimmy Martorano to take off, which he did immediately. It was now Steve Flemmi, myself, and Jim Bulger."

The interrogation of Bucky Barrett lasted nearly all day. With him chained to a chair, a machine gun pointed at his chest, Bulger and Flemmi grilled Bucky about all the money they believed he had hidden away from his many successful scores. Eventually Barrett began to wear down; he admitted that he had money hidden in his house. The gangsters made Barrett call home to his wife. The conversation was on speakerphone, so they could hear everything that was said. Barrett told his wife to leave the house. She was worried and wanted to know what was going on. Bucky told her to do as she was told, not to worry, everything would be okay.

The plan was for Bulger and Flemmi to go over to the house and take the money.

At some point, Pat Nee came by the house. His brother Michael, the proprietor of the house, was on vacation in Florida. Pat had allowed Bulger and Flemmi access to the house. They wanted to use it because it was conveniently located a half block away from the home of Steve Flemmi's mother and also the screen house where the gang stored its arsenal of weapons.

While Bulger and Flemmi headed over to the home of Bucky Barrett, Weeks and Nee were assigned the task of keeping an eye on Bucky. He remained strapped to a kitchen chair. At one point, Bucky took out a wallet-size photo of his newborn daughter and began to pray.

Bulger and Flemmi returned with forty-seven thousand dollars in cash they had retrieved from Barrett's house. But that wasn't enough. Bulger told Bucky they wanted more. Bucky told them that he had ten thousand dollars over at Rascal's, a popular bar and restaurant located at Faneuil Hall, the city's famous historic site and tourist mall. Weeks was told to drive over there and pick up the money, which he did. Then he returned to the house. By the time he returned, Pat Nee was no longer there.

They had now extorted $57,000 out of Bucky, but they wanted more. They came up with a plan for Bucky to call Joe Murray in Charlestown. They knew that Bucky had made money as a partner of Murray in the cocaine and marijuana business. They told him to call Murray and inform him that he was leaving town and wanted to cash out his end of the cocaine business. If Murray didn't go along with it, Bucky was to tell him he would rat out everybody.

By now, Bucky Barrett was a beaten man. He was bartering to save his life and was willing to do whatever Bulger and Flemmi ordered him to do. He called Murray and made his demands, according to the script. Over the speakerphone, Murray cursed at Bucky and said, "You always were a rat. Fuck off!" Then Joe Murray hung up.

Well, it had been a long day, and they had apparently squeezed all they could out of Bucky Barrett. So Bucky, still manacled and in chains, was led down towards the basement, where Whitey Bulger shot him in the back of the head.

Said Weeks, "Bucky tumbled down to the bottom of the stairs, where Stevie grabbed his body and dragged him over to the side. . . . Stevie had me go get a plastic container with water. He wanted cold water. He explained to me that the cold water helps congeal the blood; it's easier for the cleanup. He was talking to me, kind of teaching as he went. We cleaned up all the blood and everything, and then [Stevie] went over and proceeded to take out Bucky's teeth."

"What were you doing?"

"I was down there with him. I started digging the hole."

"Who helped you digging the hole?"

"Originally, [it was me], then Pat Nee came back. He came downstairs. He was a little upset because it was his brother's house. It was supposed to be a shakedown; we weren't supposed to be killing anybody. So he was mad that [Bucky] got murdered in his brother's house. Then we were digging the hole, he didn't like it. He said, 'I feel like I'm digging my own hole.' I said, 'What do you want to do?' He said, 'There's nothing we can do. They got the guns.' So we continued digging the hole. Stevie prepared the body; we took it over, put it in the hole, put lime on it, and covered it over."

For Kevin Weeks, the murder and burial of Bucky Barrett was a disorienting initiation into the more macabre aspects of the Bulger organization, but he had made his commitment to the gang. In for a penny, in for a pound. He left the house on Third Street that night hoping that nothing like that ever happened again. Which made it all the more unnerving when, just fifteen months later, he found himself in the midst of a similar situation.

This time the victim was John McIntyre. An experienced sailor and a boat mechanic, McIntyre, in his early thirties, had played a key role in the shipping of weapons to the IRA aboard a schooner named the *Valhalla*. The shipment was intercepted at sea by Irish authorities. The fact that the guns were seized and the mission apparently sabotaged by an informant was bad enough, but even worse was the fact the Bulger gang's follow-up shipment of marijuana, on a ship called the *Ramsland,* was also busted.

The gang learned from John Connolly, their man in the FBI, that they had an informant in their midst. They suspected McIntyre.

This time it was Pat Nee who brought the unsuspecting victim over to the house on Third Street. In interviews I'd done with Nee, he told me that it had been discussed and agreed that McIntyre would not be killed. He would be interrogated and have the fear of God put in him, then he would be moved out of the country and relocated in South America, through contacts of Joe Murray; there he would be out of the reach of any grand jury subpoena.

Nee brought McIntyre to the house under the false pretense that there was another drug shipment deal to discuss. He and McIntyre brought a couple of six-packs of beer. Once Kevin Weeks wrapped his arms around McIntyre, and Whitey stepped out of the shadows with his Mac-10 machine gun, Nee left to go to the Mullens' club.

What followed next, according to Weeks, was the same routine as with Bucky. McIntyre was strapped to a chair in the kitchen and interrogated over the course of many hours. Eventually, he confessed to ratting out the *Ramsland* and cooperating with law enforcement. "I'm sorry," said McIntyre. "I was weak." McIntyre began to unravel, as though he suspected he would be killed.

Said Weeks, "Jim Bulger told him to calm down. He said, 'Don't worry, we'll figure this out.'" Bulger reassured McIntyre that his only punishment would be that he would be forced to leave the country. "McIntyre started to relax. He felt a little better, I guess. And Jim started asking him questions about Joe Murray's business again, you know, how many boats he brought in, the offloading procedure, who was with him, how much money they made, things like that."

Asked prosecutor Kelly, "What was the point of asking him so many questions?"

"Looking for the next score," said Kevin, "the next person that we were going to rob, shake down."

When they were done questioning McIntyre, he was taken downstairs and first strangled and then shot in the head by Bulger. As soon as the body hit the floor, Steve Flemmi bent down and put his ear to McIntyre's chest. "He's still alive," said Flemmi. Bulger stepped forward and fired five or six shots directly into McIntyre's face. "He's dead now," said Whitey.

McIntyre was stripped down and buried in a hole next to the body of Bucky Barrett.

"How long did this process take?" asked Kelly.

"Maybe an hour," Weeks answered.

"And where was Bulger while you were digging the hole."

"Upstairs. Lying on the couch."

The third and final killing at 799 Third Street occurred only a few months later.

"Jim picked me up and brought me to the house. We went inside. He told me Stevie was bringing Debbie by, he was out buying her a coat." Kevin knew that Debbie was Deborah Hussey, Flemmi's stepdaughter, just twenty-six years old. Weeks had never met Deborah Hussey, but he knew that Bulger and Flemmi were having problems with her; she was a drug user and part-time prostitute who had been publicly bad-mouthing her stepfather, making them look bad, as though they couldn't control the people in their orbit. Weeks knew all this, but he was still relieved to hear that Flemmi was bringing the young lady by the house.

"Why were you relieved?" asked Kelly.

"It was a girl. She wasn't a criminal. She wasn't involved with us or anything I knew of, in any crimes. So I didn't think anything was going to come of it."

Weeks described what happened next: Flemmi arrived at the house with Deborah. Weeks went upstairs to use the bathroom. While he was there, he heard a loud thud. He zipped up and came downstairs to discover Deborah on the floor with Bulger straddling her, his hands wrapped around her neck. Her eyes rolled up in her head and her lips were turning blue. It took a good three or four minutes, but eventually Bulger had strangled her to death.

They dragged the body down to the basement. Again, Steve Flemmi determined that she was not yet dead. He wrapped a rope around her neck, put a wood stick through it, and twisted the stick until she was good and dead. Flemmi extracted the teeth; Whitey went upstairs and lay down on the sofa, as you might after having vigorous sex. A hole was dug and she was buried in the same general area as the other two.

The murder of Deborah Hussey bothered Kevin Weeks. He could justify the other two as a logical consequence of the gangster life—a dead fellow criminal and a dead informant. But Deborah Hussey was a female, and she was not a criminal. What he heard was that Flemmi had been having a sexual relationship with his stepdaughter since she was a teenager, and she was threatening to call him out. To murder her for that reason had nothing to do with business.

As violent and jarring as these three murders had been, they were, to Weeks, not the most disturbing event to take place at the Haunty. That occurred on Halloween 1985, when it was decided the bodies had to be moved.

Pat Nee's brother had made it known that he was going to sell the house. Said Weeks, "Originally, Jim wanted to buy the house off Pat's brother. But then Stevie figured it would be easier to move the bodies. It would be cheaper, too."

They arrived at five in the morning—Flemmi, Weeks, and Nee—with picks and shovels, trowels, gloves, surgical masks, cleaning fluids, and body bags.

"Where did you get the body bags?" asked Kelly.

"Steve Flemmi had a connection with some funeral home."

As usual, Kelly rushed through Weeks's testimony; the exhumation of the bodies was not a criminal charge in the indictment, so perhaps he felt it did not merit going into great detail.

In interviews, both Weeks and Nee had described this event for me, as it was for them a low point in their association with Bulger and Flemmi.

Apparently, when the bodies were first buried, they had used the wrong kind of lime. In the case of Bucky Barrett, instead of using a lime that speeds up decomposition, they had used a fertilizer lime that had partly mummified the body. As they attempted to lift Barrett's body, the skull snapped off. Nee tossed the head to Weeks and said, "Bucky ain't looking so good." The other two bodies had been mostly liquefied except for the bones. As Kevin sought to raise the remains of Deborah Hussey from the hole, his shovel caught under the clavicle and her entire insides spilled out. The stench was overwhelming. Kevin stumbled into a nearby bathroom and vomited.

Both Weeks and Nee noticed how easy the process was for Flemmi, who took a special fascination with various body parts and aspects of decomposition. They knew now why Bulger referred to Stevie as "Dr. Mengele," the notorious Nazi officer who oversaw unscientific and often deadly human experiments on prisoners at the Auschwitz concentration camp.

It took all day, but they finally fully exhumed and bagged up the remains. Then they sifted through the dirt floor of the basement for small bones or bone fragments, anything that might serve as a clue that this basement had once been an unceremonious grave for three murdered Bostonians.

After all the heavy lifting was done, Bulger showed up in an old family-style station wagon that opened in the back, with seats that folded down. Under cover of darkness, the body bags were to be taken to a previously chosen location. Pat Nee did not go along. Nee told me that he refused to take part in any more burials. In court, when asked why Nee did not go with the other three to dispose of the bodies, Kevin had a different explanation. "Jimmy never really trusted Pat. I don't think he wanted him to know where the bodies were buried."

Bulger, Flemmi, and Weeks drove over to Dorchester, near Florian Hall, a catering hall where firemen, cops, and other civil servants frequently held retirement parties and work-related functions. Across Hallet Street from Florian Hall was a parking lot, and behind the parking lot, a gully that was dense with trees and overgrowth. The three men unloaded the bags from the station wagon and took them down in the gully. Weeks and Flemmi dug the grave, while Bulger stood guard with a machine gun. At one point, Bulger came over and let Weeks go stand guard for a while. While Kevin stood at the edge of the gully hidden by shrubbery, someone drove up in a car. With the engine still running, a young male in his twenties got out and, unaware that Weeks was nearby, urinated in the bushes, then got back in his car and drove off.

Immediately, Bulger came over to Kevin. "Dammit, you let him get too close," said Whitey. "You should have shot him. There's plenty of room in the hole."

Bulger was annoyed. He snatched the machine gun from Kevin and said, "I'll stand guard. You go back there and finish digging the hole."

IN HIS BOOK, *Brutal,* Weeks made it clear that while he was working for the Bulger organization, he held his boss in high regard. Jim, as Weeks called him—never Whitey—was a stern taskmaster, but he was fair. Wrote Weeks:

> Jimmy had his own sense of morality. Even though he spent much of his life involved in violent crime, he still believed that certain crimes could not be committed, certainly not on his turf, anyhow. And he never hesitated to help someone that he felt needed help. . . . Ninety-eight percent of his life was business, while two percent was pleasure. While other guys might be out drinking, he'd be thinking. While other people would be going to sleep at night, he'd be up planning. He was disciplined and lived and breathed the life of crime.[1]

Kevin didn't like it when the media described Bulger as his "father figure" or when he was referred to as Whitey's surrogate son. Bulger himself had used that term to describe his relationship with Kevin. But Weeks wasn't buying it. He already had a father. In fact, his course in life as a fighter and a tough guy had been set in motion by his father, John Weeks, a former boxer who was often physically abusive with his sons. Bill Weeks, Kevin's older brother, wrote about their upbringing in the introduction to *Brutal*:

> The streets of Southie were tough. But not as tough as the apartment at 8 Pilsudski Way. There violence reigned supreme. What do you do when the streets are safer than your own home? It was better to go out and take

---

[1]Weeks and Karas, *Brutal,* p. 186.

a beating (though mostly you were inflicting one) than face the consequences of failing. And you could win and still fail—you didn't win by enough, the other person wasn't bloodied enough or got up too soon after the punishment was inflicted. Do nothing, and you got a beating. There was malevolence that permeated the air we breathed.[2]

John Weeks originally hailed from Brooklyn. He married a girl from Southie and changed tires for a living. He beat one or more of his kids nearly every day while at the same time instilling in them a near-psychotic desire for achievement. Billy and the other brother, Johnny, chose the conventional route: academic achievement at Harvard and careers in politics and civic administration.

Ironically, the son the father most admired for his choices was Kevin. He was the one who settled problems with his fists and developed a reputation as someone both respected and feared, but mostly feared. When John Weeks learned that his son was serving as a protégé of the notorious Whitey Bulger, he put a hand on his shoulder and told him, "Listen and learn."

Kevin did not need to be told twice; he listened and he learned. His loyalty to Bulger was such that he was willing to kill without question; he was willing to die for Jim Bulger if it came to that.

It was this deep sense of loyalty to Bulger that Jay Carney sought to mine as he stood to cross-examine Kevin Weeks.

During direct testimony, Weeks had spoken in mostly a dispassionate tone of voice. He seemed removed from the events of the past, even the murders he described, as if he had long ago come to terms with whatever emotional discomfort might be unearthed by these memories. But Carney was going for a different kind of emotional turmoil, the kind that comes from the rupture of a deep bond.

"Jim Bulger is approximately twenty-seven years older than you," said the defense lawyer.

"Correct," said Weeks.

"And during that time you were working with him, it's fair to say that at times he played the role of teacher to you, right?"

---

[2]Weeks and Karas, *Brutal*, pp. xi–xii.

"Oh, yeah, everything was a learning experience."

"He was your mentor, isn't that fair to say?"

"Correct."

"He was basically teaching you, I guess, all things criminal."

"No, not all things criminal. . . . Also, how to act. To look formidable. If you look formidable, you're less likely to have trouble with people. He also wanted me to stay out of bars so I didn't get in fights and get in trouble."

"Don't get drunk because you're vulnerable if you're drunk?"

"No. Don't get drunk because I had a bad temper. I was going to hurt somebody."

"Did he treat you well, Mr. Bulger?"

"He treated me great."

As Carney burrowed deeper into the nature of the relationship between Bulger and his young acolyte, Kevin's voice rose an octave with each answer. Carney was touching a nerve, softening up the witness, a tried-and-true technique of skilled trial attorneys. When Kevin mentioned the subject of his own temper, it seemed to be the verbal cue that Carney had been listening for. He moved on from the subject of Jim Bulger to another that was certain to raise the ire of the witness, that of Stephen "Stippo" Rakes.

In his direct testimony, Weeks had detailed the circumstances of events surrounding Act of Racketeering No. 21, the extortion of Stippo Rakes. In 1984, Rakes, a well-known businessman in Southie, had approached Bulger and Weeks with an offer to buy his liquor store, which was strategically located between the Old Colony and Old Harbor housing projects, on West Broadway. Bulger and Weeks immediately recognized that the liquor store was the perfect opportunity for them to launder their proceeds from gambling, loan-sharking, narcotics, extortion, and other criminal rackets.

Weeks knew Stippo well; they were close in age and had grown up together in Southie. Furthermore, Stippo's sister Mary was a dealer in the Bulger organization's drug business. She was the one who had first approached Bulger and Weeks with the proposition that they purchase Stippo's store.

Weeks did not like Stippo Rakes. He made that clear in his direct testimony, calling Rakes "a piece of garbage." But if they could get the store at a reasonable price, it was a smart proposition.

Bulger and Weeks met with Rakes, who showed them the paperwork and bookkeeping for the store. Together, they arrived at a price of $100,000 for the store and its entire inventory. The deal was done. The following night, Bulger and Weeks sat at the kitchen table of the house Whitey shared with Teresa Stanley and counted out $100,000 in cash. They put the money in a paper bag and headed over to Stippo's house on Fourth Street in Southie. Weeks described what happened next: "We gave Stippo the money and told him to take it out and count it. And he had I think it was two little girls. They were running around. So Jim Bulger was playing with one of the girls. He had her on his lap and was bouncing the girl, playing with her. She was a beautiful little girl. And Stippo started talking. He says, 'Well, you know, my wife, she don't want to sell now. You know, the money. I mean, it's worth a lot more.' He wanted more money from us. We had an agreement with him for one hundred thousand, and now, all of a sudden, at the last minute, he's backing out and he's blaming his wife for it.

"He was looking to shake us down, and that wasn't going to happen. So I pulled a gun out. I had it in my waistband. I put it on the table and said, 'Stippo, we had a deal.' And then the little girl that was on Jim Bulger's lap, she reached for the gun. Jim pushed the gun away, back over towards me, and said, 'Put it away.' I put it away.

"And then Jim started with Stippo, you know, 'We had a deal. You ain't backing out. You gave us your word.'"

Rakes came to his senses. He took the money. But he wasn't happy about it. According to Weeks, Stippo began spreading rumors all over Southie about how the deal went down. "The worst rumor was that we stuck a gun in his daughter's mouth. . . . Oh, we tortured him, he was hung off a bridge. There was all kinds of crazy stuff going around."

When Rakes took the money from the sale and went on a vacation to Florida with his family, a story spread that Bulger and Weeks had killed Stippo and his entire family. "So we called him up and had him come back to Boston. . . . We had him stand in front of his store with us—it's a main drag—so people going by could see him, that he was alive. And then we went to Perkins Square, which is another main intersection of South Boston. And we stood there [with Stippo] so everybody would know he was alive and we didn't kill him."

Carney introduced the Stippo Rakes narrative into his cross-examination by focusing on what happened when Weeks first cut his deal with Fred Wyshak. During one of his first depositions regarding the Rakes matter, when asked if he and Bulger had extorted Rakes to get his store, he said absolutely not. The prosecutors had to explain to Weeks that since he had used a gun in his negotiation with Rakes, it constituted extortion. Weeks reluctantly agreed that the extortion of Rakes had taken place; from that point onward, it would be one of the crimes to which he pleaded guilty in order to secure his deal with the government. But it had always stuck in Weeks's craw. "He came to us," Kevin repeated often. In his heart, he didn't believe they had extorted Rakes. And the insistence by Rakes that he had been extorted, which he used effectively to elicit sympathy and attention from people in the media, was, to Weeks, a further example that Stippo Rakes was a devious lowlife.

"Do you agree that you extorted Rakes?" asked Carney.

The question touched off a vigorous exchange, with Weeks and Carney talking over one another. Weeks snapped, "Are you going to let me talk, or are you going to keep interrupting me?"

Carney paused. The anger in Kevin's voice suggested that the interrogator was moving closer to his goal, which seemed to be to get the witness to reveal his infamous temper and explode in the courtroom. "I'm going to ask you questions," said Carney, "because that is the rule of the court."

"Really? Well, let me talk after you ask a question."

Carney spoke as if he were a man determined to hold on to his dignity, no matter how personal this ruffian on the stand tried to make it. "Rakes said that you had taken out a gun when you were at his home and put it on the table, right?"

"Rakes told people we took the gun and stuck it in his daughter's mouth."

"Were you truthful when you pleaded guilty [to the extortion of Rakes]?"

"Yes."

"But when you had earlier spoken to the investigators, you denied extorting Rakes, correct?"

"Stippo Rakes lied about what happened and how it went down. . . . He told stories all over town. He lied. So I didn't like Stippo Rakes. I think I made it perfectly clear with you, okay. So I didn't feel any compunction to help him at all."

"So you lied?"

"I lied. I told them, you know, we didn't extort him."

"You told the investigators a lie because you didn't like Stippo Rakes, right?"

"Correct."

"So when you told me a moment ago that you never lied to the investigators, that was a lie?"

Weeks shouted, "I've been lying my whole life! I'm a criminal!"

For a moment, Carney seemed stunned. It was a statement more blunt than a lawyer is accustomed to hearing in court.

The questioning continued. Weeks's exasperation turned to surliness, as if he might explode at any minute. Carney kept looking for an opening. He asked Weeks many questions about Pat Nee, especially whether or not Nee was the man in the backseat during the Halloran-Donahue murder. Weeks answered that he didn't know. In fact, the morning after that murder he was approached in a diner by Jimmy Mantville, a former Mullen gang member who, years earlier, had pulled off one of the Boston underworld's most famous hits, the killing of Donald Killeen outside his home in Framingham. In reference to the Halloran murder, Mantville said to Weeks, "Hey, we finally got him." Mantville's enthusiasm led Weeks to believe that maybe he was the man in the backseat.

The insinuating nature of Carney's questions rankled the witness, but he mostly kept his emotions in check until Carney arrived at the subject he'd been working toward throughout the afternoon.

"Now, when you were making a decision to provide information against Jim Bulger, you were concerned that you would be viewed as a rat, weren't you?"

"To a degree."

"Well, didn't you start using a phrase when you would—"

Weeks didn't wait for Carney to finish his sentence: "You can't rat on a rat."

"What was the expression you started using?"

"You can't rat on a rat."

The subject of being a rat had become the emotional core of the trial: Bulger was denying that he had ever been a rat. The witnesses—Martorano, Weeks, and likely Flemmi still to come—all had rationalizations for why they made their deals with the government. No one wanted to be seen as a rat. Carney was suggesting that Weeks had a guilty conscience, but the witness made it clear that he walked with his head high and is not looked down upon in Southie or anywhere else in Boston.

"So no one calls you a rat?" said Carney.

"No one. . . . Maybe they don't have the balls to say it to my face. They might say it behind my back, but no one's ever said it to me."

"Because what would you do if they said it to you?"

"Well, we'd have a problem."

"What kind of problem?"

"I'd go after them."

"In what way?"

"Physically."

"What would you do?"

There was a twinkle in Weeks's eye, not one of mirth but of menace. "Why don't you call me one outside when it's just me and you and see what I would do."

"No, I'd like to hear you say in front of this jury what you would do."

"You just did."

Carney seemed uncertain whether he should show his pleasure or not. The cross-examination of Weeks was like a bout of rough sex, bracing and in-your-face. The lawyer waited a beat, and then asked, "Was prison a very reforming experience for you, Mr. Weeks?"

It was a witty non sequitur: some in the spectators' gallery laughed. Even Weeks chuckled. "Yeah," he said. "Actually, I met some nice guys in there. Got to read a lot of books."

Parry and jab, jab and parry. Weeks was channeling his time as an amateur boxer; his time on the stand was like a fifteen-rounder. Of course, the rules of the court dictated that it was not exactly a fair fight: the witness sat on the stand with his hands tied behind his back, and Carney kept probing with body blows and the occasional haymaker upside the head. Late in the day, he seemed to find the opening he'd been looking for.

"You played the system like a pro, Mr. Weeks, didn't you?"

"Objection," said Kelly, loudly. "Argumentative."

"Sustained as to form," ruled Judge Casper.

Carney rephrased the question. "You knew how the system would work, didn't you?"

"No. I hadn't been in the system. . . . This was my first arrest. I had no experience with the system."

"But you learned pretty fast."

"My lawyer was a good lawyer. I'll recommend him to you."

"You won five years"—the length of time Weeks spent in jail.

The witness seemed stunned by the suggestion. "Five people are dead," he said, repeating, "Five people are dead."

"Does that bother you at all?"

Now Weeks was truly ready to take a swing at Carney. "Yeah, it bothers me."

"How does it bother you?"

Kevin shouted, "Because we killed people that were rats, and I had the two biggest rats right next to me! That's why it—"

He didn't get to finish his sentence. From the defense table, it was the defendant, Whitey, who spat out the words, "You suck." This wasn't like when Bulger had cursed at Morris and very few heard it: everybody heard this one. YOU SUCK.

Kevin reacted immediately: "Fuck you, okay?" he shouted at Bulger.

"Fuck you, too!" shouted Whitey.

Said Weeks tauntingly, "What do you wanna do?" He gripped the railing and banged his knees against the witness stand; he was trying to rise and go after the defendant.

The armed marshals moved in, and spectators reacted with astonishment. It seemed as though pandemonium was about to ensue, a throwdown right in the courtroom. Judge Casper stood and exclaimed, "Hey, Mr. Bulger, Mr. Bulger. Let your attorneys speak in this court for you. . . . Mr. Weeks, here's how this works: You answer the questions, okay?" The judge waited for the murmuring and rustling to settle and said, "Mr. Carney, you can finish your questioning."

The cross-examination, re-direct, and re-cross continued for another hour, but nobody would remember any of it. The testimony had peaked, with an emotional exchange between the mob boss and his prize underling—his surrogate son—that would go down in the annals of Boston mob lore.

I SAW KEVIN Weeks a few days later. He invited me over to his house on Ticknor Street to talk about his time on the stand. It was a Sunday morning, and Kevin's girlfriend had set out tea and an assortment of pastries and bagels. Using fine china cups and saucers, we sipped tea, and Kevin ruminated. He seemed very relaxed, pensive, as if his testimony had been a kind of catharsis. I asked him what it had been like seeing Bulger for the first time since he last secretly met with Whitey while he was on the lam, seventeen years ago.

"It was sad," said Kevin. "That was not the way I remembered him. His eyes were blank, like he was not all there. I wonder if he's losing his mind. It was a shock, the way he's aged."

Weeks admitted that Carney got under his skin, primarily because he felt that during his direct testimony, he had gone easy on Bulger. "I was playing nice. I could have buried him. But I made it clear that I didn't know if he did the Debbie Davis murder, and I repeated what he had always told me, that he was against the killing of Roger Wheeler. I could have backed up the other testimony and destroyed him on those points, but I didn't." Given that, Weeks was annoyed that Bulger's defense lawyer seemed determined to attack his motives.

I said to Kevin, "I was worried that you were going to go after Bulger there at the end."

"Yeah," said Weeks. "It got emotional. He bared his teeth and scowled, 'You suck.'" Kevin reflected on it and said, "You know, the hardest thing is those being the last words we'll probably ever say to one another. It's a strange way to leave things after all that time we spent together."

There was one detail I found vexing: the murders of the women. Weeks had not been present for the murder of Debbie Davis. Though it was his belief that Flemmi had likely done the strangling on that occasion, as for the murder of Deborah Hussey, he reiterated what he had said on the stand: "I saw it with my own eyes."

I asked him, "Okay, but don't you find that strange? Bulger had never murdered a female before. Hussey was Stevie's problem. Isn't it out of character for him to have done that?"

Weeks pondered the question, pausing to sip his tea, and then he spoke. "I think, over time, there developed a competition between Jimmy and Stevie. They did a lot of murders together, and they were always trying to one-up each other. Stevie killed Debbie Davis, then Jimmy had to show he could do it, too. They were always testing each other. It was a sick game they played."

We talked some more about Kevin's testimony, recollections of beatings, extortions, murders, and burials. From somewhere outside, likely at nearby Gate of Heaven Church, a bell sounded. It was a fine Sunday morning in South Boston.

"Can I get you some more tea?" asked Weeks.

After leaving Weeks that day, something came into focus. In the years that Bulger and Flemmi were together, their killings became more outrageous and depraved. Why? The answer was simple: because they knew they could get away with it. They could kill whomever they wanted, plant a false version of what happened into law enforcement files, and never be held accountable. There would be no investigation. They had been doing it for years.

And the reason they had this power—the entity that made it possible for them to kill and get away with it for so long—was the U.S. Department of Justice.

10

THE HOLY GRAIL

NOT LONG AFTER Kevin Weeks finished his two-day stint on the witness stand, I was invited to come on the Howie Carr radio show to talk about the trial. I knew Carr and had been a guest on his show in previous years to promote books I had published. Nearly every day during the proceedings, I saw Howie in the third-floor media room watching the monitors and taking notes on his laptop computer, just like everyone else.

Carr is a lightning rod in Boston: some love him, some hate him. He uses ridicule and sarcasm in a way that can, at times, be sophomoric, but he is an effective entertainer. Behind his jocular on-air persona, Howie possesses a comprehensive knowledge of Boston crime history. And, as a columnist for the *Boston Herald* back in the 1980s, he had gone after the Bulger brothers—in print—at a time when others in the media rarely touched the subject.

It was a Thursday afternoon, after the trial testimony was finished for the day. Carr was broadcasting his show live from the Barking Crab, a seafood restaurant located on a dock directly across from the Moakley Courthouse. The restaurant was a classic waterfront chowder house, a wooden structure with indoor picnic tables and a horseshoe bar in the middle of the room. The menu was a chalkboard on the wall, and, on this particular day, pitchers of beer were flowing at three o'clock in the afternoon.

The Carr show was set up in an area near the back wall, next to a window overlooking Fort Point Channel and the scenic Old North Avenue drawbridge, with seagulls honking and swooping just outside the open-air windows. The place was packed with customers, most of them brought in to provide background atmosphere for the ever-popular *Howie Carr Show*. In the crowd were many familiar faces from the trial—Steve Davis was there, as were the three sons of Michael Donahue—Tommy, Michael, and Brian—as well as their mother, Pat. The CNN film crew led by director Joe Berlinger was there with cameras and a boom microphone, filming the scene at the restaurant. The atmosphere was rambunctious and circuslike, with much loud conversation and laughing and drinking. It was a slightly incongruous scene, given that many of these folks had just come from the trial where, thirty yards away at the courthouse building, the morning had been filled with the usual tales of corruption and murder.

In the crowd, I spotted Stippo Rakes. I had met Rakes earlier in the trial. I was introduced by Steve Davis, who sometimes served as a kind of liaison between the various family members and the media. By that point, I was familiar with Stippo's story. When we first met, he was friendly; he had read a book I wrote and was complimentary. But I noticed that he had the odd habit of not looking a person in the eyes when he spoke with them.

I went up and said hello to Stippo. I asked him what he'd thought of Kevin Weeks's testimony. He said, "Oh, Kevin lied. That's what he always does. It's what the government has trained him to do. The truth will come out when I take the stand."

Stippo's words were almost an exact repeat of what I had heard him say earlier in a statement to the media outside the courthouse entrance. It reinforced a feeling I had that some of the family members had become stuck in a kind of self-promotional loop, delivering sound bites and pre-digested commentary for the press. Stippo was hyperfriendly, and he gave the appearance of being accessible, but I was not alone in thinking he was the kind of guy who, with his shifty eyes and nervous smile, did not inspire trust.

After meeting with Carr and his small crew, I was given a set of head-phones and sat down to take part in his show "live from the Barking Crab."

I wasn't the only guest. Seated next to me was John "Red" Shea, a for-mer South Boston drug dealer (no relation to Billy Shea, Kermit the Frog's Irish uncle). Along with many of the mid- and street-level dealers in Bul-ger's organization, Shea had been swept up and arrested in 1990 as part of a sting operation by the Drug Enforcement Administration. In all, fifty people were pinched, though, noticeably, Bulger, Flemmi, and Weeks—the top echelon of the organization—were not among them. Some of those dealers had accepted plea bargain arrangements with the government and become informants, two of whom—Paul Moore and Anthony Attardo—would take the stand at the current Bulger trial. Red Shea, on the other hand, served eleven years in prison and kept his mouth shut. That is, until he was released and turned his years with the Bulger organization into a memoir titled *Rat Bastards: The South Boston Irish Mobster Who Took the Rap When Everyone Else Ran,* published in 2007.

Like many people, Shea had turned his feelings about Bulger into a personal vendetta, partly to promote himself and his book. He was friendly and bright. Like many ex-criminals in Boston that I met—especially those who had done an extended stretch in the joint—Shea read books and told a good story.

Howie's show that afternoon reflected the loose and jocular atmosphere of the waterfront saloon where it took place, with Carr, as he often did, obsessing about Whitey Bulger's sexuality, quoting sources who said they had seen him in the 1970s cruising the infamous gay bars in Provincetown. Red Shea suggested that Whitey had an unnatural affection for young boys in Southie, including himself. The show was set up to take calls from listeners; the calls were off the wall and took the discussion even further from anything worthwhile than had the commentary of Howie and Red Shea.

After *The Howie Carr Show* wrapped for the day, I headed back toward my lodgings in the North End with the sinking feeling that the Bulger trial was doomed. Yes, there were many dramatic moments, and the parade of old-school bookies, loan sharks, hit men, and gangsters continued to be fascinating. But the trial—and the commentary surrounding it—had become a modern version of the Salem witch trials. Any hope that the proceedings would shed light on the universe of corruption that created Bulger seemed more distant with each passing day. If I hoped to achieve a deeper understanding of the motivations behind the Bulger era, I needed to get away from the Moakley Courthouse and away from Southie.

Staying in the city's Italian North End while following the trial had been instructive. I was staying at the Bricco Suites, a set of studio apartments located behind Bricco Ristorante, a popular restaurant and bar on Hanover Street. Owned by Frank DePasquale, a prominent businessman in the North End, the Bricco was a popular spot with neighborhood old-timers. I was introduced to people with long memories, some of whom had done time in prison—or knew people who had done time—courtesy of Bulger, Flemmi, John Connolly, John Morris, or Jeremiah O'Sullivan.

In the North End, attitudes toward Whitey Bulger were scalding. People's hatred for the Bulger brothers was surpassed only by their venom for Steve Flemmi, an Italian American who had betrayed his own blood.

Few people in Boston understood the reasons behind these sentiments better than Anthony "Tony" Cardinale. Though he was not a gangster nor born and raised in the North End, Cardinale had acquired a broad range of knowledge in both areas due to his role as a prominent criminal defense attorney for many Boston-based Mafiosi.

I had interviewed Cardinale before and knew that he also had a deep professional disdain for Bulger and Flemmi. Through their relationship with the FBI and the New England Organized Crime Strike Force, they had sowed the seeds of dissension among many of Cardinale's clients in the 1980s, leading to unscrupulous convictions in court and gangland murders in the streets. Since Bulger's apprehension in Santa Monica in June 2011, Cardinale had been a frequent commentator in the Boston media, where he rarely missed an opportunity to refer to Bulger as a "lowlife" and "a piece of garbage."

I made arrangements to meet with Cardinale at Café Pompeii on Hanover Street.

One of the great pleasures of staying in the North End during the trial was that the neighborhood existed as a kind of living history of gangland Boston. Just down the street from my studio apartment was an early-twentieth-century building—formerly the C. K. Importing Company, now a bank—where Frankie Wallace was executed in December 1931. Wallace had been the leader of the Gustin gang, a group of bootleggers and racketeers from South Boson prominent during the Prohibition era. The gang was named after a street in Southie. In 1931, the Gustins hijacked some shipments of booze belonging to the Mafia. Wallace and an underling, Bernard "Dodo" Walsh, were lured to a "sit-down" on Hanover Street to discuss a truce. In the lobby of the building, they were ambushed and assassinated by two hit men.

More recent history, including key events from the Bulger trial, had taken place at locations within blocks from my living quarters. The intersection where Frank Capizzi—the witness who heard things half in Sicilian and half in English—had been shot up while riding shotgun in a car was at the end of Hanover Street. That drive-by shooting by Martorano, Bulger, and Flemmi, in which Al Plummer was killed, had been part of the hunt to find and murder Alfred "Indian Al" Notarangeli in the early 1970s.

Prince Street, where Jerry Angiulo had been born and where his headquarters was based, out of a social club at 98 Prince Street, intersected Hanover Street and was a block away from my place.

And Café Pompeii, where I was meeting Tony Cardinale, had been mentioned at the trial by John Martorano. It had been the location for a meeting between Indian Al, John Martorano, Howie Winter, and Jerry Angiulo. At that meeting, Notarangeli begged for his life and paid Angiulo fifty thousand dollars to not kill him and let him continue his business. Angiulo told him, "Okay, I will take your money. And you can live." A couple of weeks later, on Angiulo's instructions, Indian Al was murdered by Martorano—lured to Revere and shot in the head inside a car, with Bulger in a nearby boiler, or crash car, serving as an accomplice.

When I arrived at Café Pompeii, Tony Cardinale was already there, sipping espresso and grappa, chatting with the owner.

We got right to it. "Tell me about the Holy Grail," I said to the lawyer.

Cardinale smiled. "I will," he said. "But first let me come at it in a roundabout way."

As with many people in the legal profession, especially trial lawyers, Tony liked to talk. But he was one of those people from whom you didn't mind if you were going to get a roundabout answer, because within that answer would be anecdotes and layers of information that would reveal essential truths about the criminal mentality in general, and, more specifically, the inner workings of the Bulger fiasco, from the point of view of someone who also happened to be a terrific storyteller.

"Let me take you back to the roots of this case," said Cardinale. "We need to go back to the Barboza era, the 1960s."

Cardinale knew from whence he spoke: as a young attorney, having just recently passed the bar, he went to work for renowned criminal defense lawyer F. Lee Bailey. Among many notorious clients, Bailey had briefly represented Joe "Animal" Barboza. In 1970, Barboza had come to Bailey and signed an affidavit declaring that his testimony at various criminal trials was riddled with lies perpetrated in consort with devious officials of the criminal justice system. Then Barboza abruptly recanted the affidavit. Bailey ceased representing Barboza after arriving at the conclusion that the Animal was untrustworthy and quite possibly psychotic. Barboza responded by publicly vowing to kill Bailey—a threat that the attorney took seriously.

"He had to hire bodyguards," noted Cardinale.

When Barboza was eventually hunted down and taken out in a mob hit in February 1976, Bailey was quoted saying, "With all due respect to my former client, I don't think society has suffered a great loss."

Barboza's first big test as an informant witness was not the Patriarca trial, or the notorious Teddy Deegan murder trial; it had come before that in a trial involving the charge of murder against Jerry Angiulo and three others.

As an underboss in the Patriarca crime family and boss of the Mafia in the North End, Angiulo, then in his forties, had emerged as a tremendous moneymaker. Operating primarily as an organizer and financier of bookies and shylocks, Angiulo and his Boston crew became the central bank for all gambling and bookmaking operations throughout New England. The feds figured if they could take down Angiulo, they could cut off the Mafia's cash flow.

The trial took place at the Pemberton Square courthouse in Boston in January 1968. As a witness, Barboza was green and easily rattled. Consequently, Jerry Angiulo and his codefendants were found not guilty of the murder charge. Afterward, the mafia boss told a flock of reporters, "I don't want to say anything right now. I want to see my mother. She's seventy-three, and this thing has been bothering her."

Barboza went on to redeem himself as a professional witness in the trial of Raymond Patriarca and the Teddy Deegan murder trial, where he told lies that resulted in the conviction of four innocent men. Meanwhile, the feds never forgot about Jerry Angiulo, who continued to be a major player in the New England Mafia. From his perch on Prince Street, Angiulo and his brothers rubbed it in the nose of federal authorities by openly ruling the North End like Sicilian padroni from the old country.

When FBI agents John Connolly and John Morris took the baton from H. Paul Rico and Dennis Condon, they knew that a big part of that legacy involved nailing Jerry Angiulo.

Seated at a back table at Café Pompeii, away from the windows, away from the front door, Tony Cardinale chose his words carefully. "Getting Jerry Angiulo was the highest priority. It's why the FBI recruited Stevie Flemmi, whose brother Jimmy had been a Top Echelon Informant, and later Stevie recruits Bulger."

Along with Connolly and Morris, the other key inside player in the government's quest to avenge their 1968 loss to Angiulo was Jeremiah O'Sullivan. As the leader of the federal New England Organized Crime Strike Force, O'Sullivan had been on the receiving end of a baton exchange of his own. He received his mandate to aggressively pursue high-profile Mafia indictments from Ted Harrington, his mentor, the former assistant U.S. attorney who oversaw the 1968 Angiulo prosecution and other Barboza-related trials. In 1970, Harrington took over as lead attorney for the Strike Force. As a young prosecutor, O'Sullivan was part of Harrington's team; he was groomed to take over as Strike Force chief.

As with other participants inside the secretive, clubhouse world of criminal prosecutions in New England law enforcement, O'Sullivan assumed his duties as an inheritor of all that came before, with great zeal. To say that the ends justified the means was a quaint way of putting it: in a jurisdiction where FBI agents had been enabling murderers, suborning perjury, and burying exculpatory evidence for at least a generation, O'Sullivan seized his moment in history.

Noted Cardinale, "We know that, in 1979, O'Sullivan takes Bulger and Flemmi out of the race-fix case: that's a fact. He did that because he was sold a bill of goods by Connolly and Morris that without those two he couldn't get what he wanted more than anything in the world, which was to take down the Angiulo organization. He got bullshitted by two completely corrupt motherfuckers, who would have done anything to protect their informants, because they were taking money, making cases, and their star was rising in the FBI because they were doing all this great work."

The recording device that the C-3 squad was able to plant inside 98 Prince Street, thanks to a schematic provided by Flemmi, would prove to be

Jerry Angiulo's undoing. It remained in place for 105 days and picked up, among other things, killings authorized by Jerry Angiulo, who was recorded telling an underling, "You think I need tough guys? I need intelligent tough guys. . . . What do you want me to say? Do you want me to say to you do it right or don't do it? . . . Tell him to take a ride, okay? . . . Get out of the car and stomp him. Bing! You hit him in the fuckin' head and leave him right in the fuckin' spot. Do you understand? . . . Meet him tonight. . . . Just hit him in the fuckin' head and stab him, okay? The jeopardy is just a little too much for me. You understand American?"

On tape, Angiulo's diatribes sometimes came across as profane stream of consciousness, but always with a point. "Fucking, motherfucker, big-mouth cocksucker. Shut up," he said to an underling whom he was attempting to school on the proper way to fix a dice game. "You motherfucker . . . Let me tell you something. I've been in the craps business when you weren't born, you cocksucker that you are. Don't you ever, ever have a pair of dice go more than one and a half or two hours without replacing it with a brand-new set, and that set goes in your fucking pocket and they're thrown down the fucking sewer. Do you understand that? That's a fucking order because you're a fucking idiot. Now shut up."

"Yeah, but let me tell you," said the underling.

"You talk and I'll hit you with a fucking bottle."

The 98 Prince Street tapes were sometimes comical, but there was nothing funny about the charges. Cardinale, just thirty-three years old at the time, was Jerry Angiulo's lawyer during the trial. "We tried like hell to get those tapes declared inadmissible," remembered Cardinale. "But keep in mind: at the time we knew nothing about Bulger and Flemmi's arrangement with the feds."

I asked Cardinale, "Weren't your guys suspicious? Didn't they wonder who was working with the FBI from the inside?"

Cardinale was insistent: "My clients couldn't believe the FBI would ever deal with somebody as heinous as Whitey Bulger. They viewed Bulger and Flemmi as glorified hit men who would kill people for nothing. Murderous bastards. They knew Bulger had Connolly in his pocket, that he was paying Connolly for information. They were jealous and wanted in on that. That was something they would pay for. But they never believed that the FBI had such a degree of institutional degeneracy as to be in bed with Bulger and Flemmi."

In February 1986, after an eight-month trial, Jerry Angiulo and his three brothers were found guilty on multiple racketeering counts. Jerry Angiulo was sentenced to forty-five years in prison.

"So that was it, the Holy Grail," I said to Cardinale.

"No. That was a big step on the way to the Holy Grail, but that's not the Holy Grail."

In the history of the federal government's war on La Cosa Nostra, or LCN, there had never been a recording of a secret mafia initiation ceremony. In his testimony before Congress in 1963, Joe Valachi had described a mafia induction ceremony. From that point on, it had been a dream of the FBI and prosecutors to secretly record such a ceremony, and by so doing penetrate and discredit the mafia code of *omertà*.

Morris and Connolly decided, Why stop with Jerry Angiulo? Why not go for the Holy Grail?

The quest to bug a mafia induction ceremony began with the planting of yet another Title III wiretap inside Vanessa's restaurant, located at the Prudential Center, in Boston's Back Bay. Through Steve Flemmi, the FBI agents learned that the Mafia, in the wake of the devastating Angiulo convictions, had moved their meeting place outside the North End to a part of the city where, they figured, nobody would suspect a mafia confab would be taking place. Through the bug at Vanessa's, the FBI was able to record and ultimately coerce into cooperating an old-school Mafioso named Sonny Mercurio. Said Cardinale, "Mercurio was a tough guy who had done time for murder. The last kind of person you would suspect could ever be an informant." But it happened: Mercurio became the latest feather in the cap of John Connolly, who enlisted the mobster as a Top Echelon Informant.

Mercurio's job was to lead them to the Holy Grail. That wasn't going to be easy. At the time, there was a moratorium on inducting new *soldati* into the New England Mafia. So the agents and Mercurio, with an assist from Bulger and Flemmi, needed to create a scenario that would lead to the Mafia having to induct new members. Mercurio fomented a dispute between two factions of the Mafia. On the wiretap at Vanessa's, the FBI's C-3 squad heard it being decided that there was going to be a series of mob hits. What the agents did next might be considered shocking, except that it was a continuation of what had occurred during the Teddy Deegan murder twenty years earlier. The agents, though they had foreknowledge, did not warn the targets about the pending hits.

One of the targets was Frank Salemme, former partner of Steve Flemmi. Salemme had returned to Boston after a nine-year stint in prison and, in the wake of the Angiulo convictions, was looking to take over as boss. The FBI and its informants—Bulger, Flemmi, and Sonny Mercurio—were looking to use Salemme as a stepping-stone on their way to the Holy Grail.

On the morning of June 16, 1989, Salemme sat down at an outside table at the International House of Pancakes in Saugus, Massachusetts, to have breakfast and some coffee. Four gunmen opened fire. It was a sloppy attempt. Bullets flew high and off the mark, shattering glass and sending innocent bystanders ducking for cover. Salemme was hit multiple times but survived.

The second hit that had been planned—and overheard on the Vanessa wire—was successful. A New England Mafioso named William "Billy" Grasso was shot in the back of the head, his body left alongside the Connecticut River.

The FBI investigators and prosecutors had stood by and let the mayhem take place, knowing that it would lead them to their goal. Sure enough, the induction ceremony transpired, on October 29, 1989, at a private home of a mobster in Medford, Massachusetts. Present at the ceremony was Sonny Mercurio.

Numerous criminal trials rose out of the induction ceremony tapes, one of them involving a client of Tony Cardinale. The attorney still had no idea of Bulger and Flemmi's role, and he was unaware that Sonny Mercurio was an informant—though co-counsel knew there had to be a rat for the feds to have known where the ceremony was going to take place. Cardinale and the other attorneys in the case discussed who it might be. "It was beyond anything that we could imagine that a guy like Sonny Mercurio could be an informant," said Tony.

Then he listened to the tape of the induction. Just as the ceremony was about to begin, someone in the room had gone over and turned down the television. Said Cardinale to the other attorneys, "Find out who turned down that TV and we know who our informant is." The person who turned down the TV was Sonny Mercurio.

The induction ceremony tapes were a tremendous coup. U.S. attorney general Dick Thornburgh and FBI director William Sessions flew in from the nation's capital for a press conference announcing the arrest and indictment of twenty-one mobsters. Director Sessions later sent a personal letter to Connolly praising his talent for cultivating informants. Connolly was given a fifteen-hundred-dollar bonus and held up as the standard of an enterprising special agent.

"They got what they wanted," said Cardinale. "The Holy Grail. Using Bulger and Flemmi they got Mercurio, and through him they fomented a dispute. Billy Grasso was killed. They knew he was going to get killed. And Frank Salemme was supposed to get killed. And luckily a bunch of little kids and mothers didn't get killed that morning outside the pancake house in Saugus. The FBI knew it, planned it, pushed it. So this is what this Bulger trial is all about. This is why the FBI was willing to get into bed with such reprehensible lowlifes and give them the run of the town."

Cardinale finished his grappa and shook his head in amazement. When he looked back over the last thirty years in Boston, like many people, he still found it unsettling. "A big part of what I do as a criminal defense lawyer," he said, "is to try and stop cops, prosecutors, and judges from playing God. Because these guys couldn't care less if they have a guy who is guilty or not guilty. They'll manufacture evidence; they'll do whatever it takes to secure a conviction. And the way they can shave in the morning without slitting their throats is by saying to themselves, 'If he didn't do this, he did something else. Fuck him.' That's playing God. And it shouldn't be allowed to happen that way."

At the Bulger trial, there was little mention of Sonny Mercurio, the attempted murder of Salemme, or the Medford induction ceremony, nor did it seem likely that these events would be touched upon in any depth. The prosecution had no desire to cast a bad light on what had been some of the most illustrious mafia prosecutions in the very jurisdiction and office for whom they worked, the very office that was now prosecuting Whitey Bulger. As for Bulger's defense lawyers, they were claiming that their client had never been an informant, so a detailed explication of how these prosecutions came about was not in their interest.

THE BEGINNINGS OF an effort to burrow through layers of deceit in the criminal justice system in Boston occurred in May 2001. It had its origins not in the city itself, but in Washington, D.C. The House Committee on Oversight and Government Reform launched an investigation into the FBI's use of criminal informants. Chaired by Representative Dan Burton, a conservative Republican from Indiana, the committee announced its intentions to hold public hearings, both in Boston and in the nation's capital, at which many prominent players in law enforcement, both past and present, would be subpoenaed to testify.

The hearings are best remembered for bringing about the public demise of former state senator William Bulger, who since his retirement in 1996 had gone on to be appointed president of the University of Massachusetts. Bulger fought the subpoena, and when called before the committee he took the Fifth Amendment and refused to testify, on the grounds of self-incrimination. Later, the committee voted to give him full immunity from prosecution, and on June 19, 2003, Billy Bulger appeared before the committee in Washington, D.C., at the Rayburn House Office Building.

Bulger denied many things that day, including having ever heard of the Winter Hill Mob. The committee tried to get at Billy Bulger's close friendship with John Connolly and other FBI agents affiliated with the C-3 squad.

It was common knowledge in South Boston that Connolly and the senator were close. Throughout his time with the organized crime squad, Connolly routinely brought fellow FBI agents over to Bulger's office in the statehouse, where they were treated as though they were having a sitting with the pope. The understanding was that if they did right by the senator—which meant looking out for his brother, Whitey—then the senator would take care of them. When Connolly retired in 1990, Senator Bulger was a featured speaker at his retirement party and said of the agent, "John Connolly is the personification of loyalty, not only to his friends and not only to the job that he holds but also to the highest principles. He's never forgotten them." Senator Bulger helped Connolly land a cushy retirement job as head of security at Boston Edison, a public utility.

Nicholas Gianturco, John J. Kehoe Jr., Robert Sheehan, and other FBI agents also went to work at Boston Edison upon retirement. In his testimony at the congressional hearing, Bulger professed to have no recollection of having helped these people and even went so far as to produce a signed affidavit from the CEO at Boston Edison claiming that he had nothing to do with these hirings.

Then there was Dennis Condon, Whitey Bulger's first FBI handler in the early 1970s and a regular at Billy's St. Patrick's Day breakfasts over the years. On a written recommendation from the senator, Condon landed a post-FBI job as commissioner of the Massachusetts State Police.

Even though he had been granted immunity, Bulger's testimony was a study in obfuscation. One thing he couldn't deny was that since his brother had gone on the lam, he had spoken with Whitey in a private phone call that was prearranged by Kevin Weeks, who testified about the call before a grand jury. By admitting that this call took place, Bulger was acknowledging that he lied to FBI agents who had asked him, years later, if he had any contact with his brother. Bulger's immunity deal precluded his being charged with a crime, but it was an ethical impropriety that cost him his job as president of UMass.

Billy Bulger's testimony garnered the headlines, but it was not the most revealing information to be unearthed at the hearing. Most noteworthy was the committee's unprecedented exploration of the Teddy Deegan murder case. That line of inquiry immediately set off a high-stakes struggle between committee lawyers and the FBI over whether or not the bureau would be compelled to produce documents that the committee requested. The Boston SAC, Charles Prouty, made a request directly to President George W. Bush that they not be forced to turn over documents. Prouty said publicly, "We didn't conceal information. We didn't frame anyone."

One day before the committee was scheduled to begin hearing testimony, President Bush invoked executive privilege, the first time he had done so in his presidency, and ordered the attorney general to not turn over documents. The lengths the FBI was willing to go to keep the Deegan case buried were extreme. Eventually, after five months of legal wrangling, a compromise was reached. The executive privilege order was lifted and some documents were released, but they were heavily redacted.

Even for those who were aware of malfeasance in the criminal justice system in New England, the findings of the committee were devastating. Nearly forty years after Teddy Deegan was gunned down in an alleyway in Chelsea, the public learned for the first time the full magnitude of the conspiracy. They learned there was an illegal wiretap conversation in which Barboza and Jimmy Flemmi asked for permission to murder Deegan from Raymond Patriarca. The committee learned that the FBI had been told after the murder that they were pursuing a wrongful prosecution, and they buried this information. A detailed file-by-file, memo-by-memo re-creation of the Deegan case showed either knowing or willfully ignorant collaboration at many levels of the criminal justice system.

One person who was not aware of the conspiracy was Jack Zalkind, lead prosecutor at the Deegan trial, who was deliberately left in the dark. After being shown documents relevant to his case, Zalkind told the committee, "I must tell you this, that I was outraged—outraged—at the fact that if [the exculpatory documents] had ever been shown to me, we wouldn't be sitting here. . . . I certainly never would have allowed myself to prosecute this case having that knowledge. No way. . . . That information should have been in my hands. It should have been in the hands of the defense attorneys. It is outrageous, it's terrible, and the trial shouldn't have gone forward."

Over the course of the next fifteen months, in periodic public hearings in front of the committee. many key players were called to testify, including:

H. Paul Rico—Seared by his years in the Florida sun, surly and unrepentant, Rico came before the committee in May 2001. Having retired as a legendary and highly decorated agent, Rico testified as if he had nothing to fear. In the hallway outside the committee hearing room, he stuck his finger in the chest of committee counsel James Wilson and said, "What are you going to do to me, Mr. Wilson? I'm seventy-six years old. What the fuck are you going to do?"

In his testimony, Rico admitted that a memo, written by him, had first been sent to his supervisor in the organized crime squad noting that a hit on Deegan had been discussed and authorized. That memo was initialized and forwarded to the SAC of the Boston division, then sent to a regional supervisor in Washington, D.C. Eventually that memo landed on the desk of Director J. Edgar Hoover, who micromanaged every aspect of the informant program and was kept abreast of the Deegan case. The FBI, all the way to the top man, allowed the murder of Deegan to take place. They knew their star witness, Barboza, was involved. They knowingly allowed Barboza to take the stand and give a version of the killing that was markedly different from what they were hearing from other sources.

Many people within the criminal justice system had reason to believe the Deegan convictions were tainted, and they did nothing. Two of the four men wrongfully convicted were sentenced to the death penalty and incarcerated on death row. Two of them died in prison before the truth became known.

A congressman asked Rico, "Does it bother you that an innocent man spent thirty years in jail?"

Said the witness, "It would probably be a nice movie or something."

"Do you have any remorse?"

"Remorse for what?"

"So you don't really care much and you don't have any remorse. Is that true?"

"What do you want, tears?" answered the agent.

Paul Rico would accept no blame and faced no consequences for the framing of innocent men. In October 2003 he was indicted for his role in another crime, the murder of Roger Wheeler, owner of World Jai Lai. He was arrested at his condominium in Miami Shores by Sergeant Mike Huff of the Tulsa Police Department, lead investigator in the Wheeler homicide case.

Three months later, at the age of seventy-eight, Rico died in a Tulsa hospital, where he had been moved from prison while awaiting trial.[1]

Dennis Condon—As Rico's partner, Condon was another key player in the cultivation of Barboza and the fraudulent Deegan murder convictions.

---

[1]Even though H. Paul Rico, by the time of his death, was under indictment for murder and had been thoroughly disgraced, he still had his defenders. In 2012, two retired FBI agents and a former Los Angeles police officer published an ebook titled *Rico: How Politicians, Prosecutors and the Mob Destroyed One of the FBI's Finest Agents*. An obsequious defense of a man the authors describe as a "hero," the book sought to discredit the Wolf hearings, the House committee hearings, Sergeant Mike Huff, and anyone else who might have played a role in exposing Rico's misdeeds over the years. The fact that there were people still willing to act as staunch advocates for Rico, even after his death, was an indication of how such a notorious figure had been able to function and even flourish within a myopic law enforcement culture.

Condon did not appear before the committee, but he was deposed under oath by committee investigators, and his deposition was an integral aspect of the committee's final report.

Condon was forced to admit that Barboza had made it clear to him and Paul Rico that he would never testify against his friend Jimmy the Bear Flemmi, who had been an accomplice in the Deegan murder. Barboza told the agents, in so many words, If you put me on the stand I will lie to protect my friend. This fact was memorialized in FBI 209 field reports and airtels that went from field agents to supervisors all the way to Hoover.

By this time, Barboza had been a witness at the Patriarca trial and helped deliver the biggest mafia prosecution in the history of the bureau. Part of protecting the sanctity of the Patriarca conviction involved preserving the credibility of Barboza. That's why the FBI was willing to put him on the stand and have him commit perjury.

When Dennis Condon was first approached in 1997 and asked about James Bulger, he said he had no recollection of ever having met the man. It didn't take long to jog his memory; there were voluminous FBI file reports of his having opened Bulger as an informant in 1971. At the Wolf hearings in 1998, Condon's friend and fellow agent John Morris and Steve Flemmi both testified about Condon attending dinner gatherings at Morris's home in Lexington, in the company of Bulger and Flemmi.

The FBI and the criminal justice system in New England had for so long been successful at keeping their dirty secrets buried, that for someone like Condon, who was a devout Catholic with a sterling public reputation, the revelations were a nightmare come true. Though he was never indicted for his actions or legally held accountable in any way, when Condon died of natural causes in 2009, he did so knowing that his name will forever be associated with the FBI's legacy of corruption in Boston, from the Deegan murder case to the Bulger scandal.

Edward "Ted" Harrington—In the late 1960s, as an assistant U.S. attorney, Harrington seemed willing to do almost anything to protect Joe Barboza. Under questioning by the Burton committee, Harrington admitted that, previous to the Deegan murder trial, he reviewed a confidential FBI memo that revealed Barboza and Jimmy the Bear Flemmi were behind the Deegan murder and had, they believed, been given permission to kill

Deegan by Patriarca. That memo included references to the gypsy wire planted at Patriarca's office in Providence. Harrington was required by law to have released that evidence to lawyers representing the codefendants at the Deegan murder trial. He did not, which was possibly a crime or at least an act of criminal negligence. Confronted with these facts, Harrington told the committee that he simply forgot about the memo.

"For you to say you didn't remember it stretches my imagination," said Burton.

Harrington conceded nothing. When asked if he regretted having flown to California with agents Rico and Condon to testify as a character witness at Barboza's murder trial, Harrington said no. To him, defending Barboza was a consequence of the need to preserve the government's informant program, which had became the single most important tool in law enforcement's war against the mafia.

For his actions, Harrington received kudos and rose in his career from an assistant U.S. attorney to chief of the New England Organized Crime Strike Force to U.S. attorney for the District of Massachusetts, and, finally, the crown jewel, when in 1987 he was nominated to the federal bench by President Ronald Reagan. Judge Harrington presided over criminal cases in Boston for the next twenty-five years.

In 2008, during the trial of John Connolly on murder charges in Miami, Harrington put his reputation on the line and took the stand on behalf of the defense. Just as he had with Barboza forty years earlier, he was there to defend the accused on the grounds that he had been a valuable compatriot in the government's war against organized crime.

Much had changed since 1969, when, at Barboza's murder trial in California, Harrington portrayed the war against the Mob as a battle between clearly defined good and evil. By the time of Connolly's trial, the story of how Bulger and Flemmi had been protected by multiple FBI agents, a top organized crime prosecutor, and higher-ups in the DOJ, and kept out on the street to commit murders and other crimes, had entered the public consciousness. Despite Judge Harrington's testimony on behalf the disgraced agent, Connolly was found guilty of murder in the second degree.

In September 2013, Harrington retired from the federal bench as a highly lauded and esteemed veteran of the criminal justice system.

Jeremiah O'Sullivan—Members of the Burton committee were especially intrigued by the prospect of having former prosecutor O'Sullivan come before them as a witness.

Four years earlier, O'Sullivan had suffered a heart attack and missed having to testify at the Wolf hearings. At the time, defense lawyer Tony Cardinale noted that back in 1980, prosecutor O'Sullivan had fought vociferously when Mafioso Larry Zannino used a medical claim that he was too sick to come to court. O'Sullivan challenged the claim and had Zannino dragged into court, even though he was in a wheelchair and on an oxygen tank. Hearing that O'Sullivan was now utilizing a similar tactic, defense lawyers in Boston said he had "pulled a Zannino."

Though O'Sullivan had emerged as a primary inheritor of the region's systemic legacy of corruption, he had successfully stonewalled the press. He had been called to testify at the Burton committee hearings under a federal subpoena and began his testimony by reading a statement that read, in part: "I state categorically and unequivocally that, although I was made aware of the status of Bulger and Flemmi as FBI informants in the late 1970s, I never authorized them to commit any crimes and have no knowledge of such authorization."

Most of the questions for O'Sullivan revolved around his decision to drop Bulger and Flemmi from the 1979 race-fix prosecution, which led to the conviction of Howie Winter, Jimmy Sims, and nineteen other confederates of the Winter Hill Mob. O'Sullivan claimed that he had made the decision before he was approached by Connolly and Morris based on the fact that neither Bulger nor Flemmi was central to race-fix conspiracy. But then a lawyer for the committee read a January 1979 memo, written by O'Sullivan, naming Bulger and Flemmi as integral players in the scheme.

"Is this memo correct?" asked the committee lawyer.

"It must have been at the time I wrote it . . . so you got me," said O'Sullivan. He wasn't too worried. The congressional committee hearings were not legally binding; no matter how mendacious he sounded, he would not be indicted for perjury.

O'Sullivan did his best to distance himself from Connolly and Morris, saying of the FBI, "If you go against them, they will try to get you. They will wage war on you. They will create major administrative problems for me as a prosecutor."

Later, after acknowledging that Bulger and Flemmi were two of the most notorious murderers in the Boston underworld, he was asked by a congressman why, upon hearing that they were being used to make criminal cases in his jurisdiction, he didn't try to close them as informants.

Answered the former most powerful organized crime prosecutor in New England, "Because that would have precipitated World War III if I tried to get inside the FBI to deal with informants. That was the holy of holies, the inner sanctuarium. They wouldn't have allowed me to do anything about that."

IT IS NOT uncommon for people in law enforcement to joke about criminals turning on one another. Cops refer to the underworld as "a self-cleaning oven." Popular wisdom dictates that there is no honor among thieves. If a criminal is used to rat on another criminal, so be it, and if that criminal is telling lies to take down other criminals, it is, perhaps, in the minds of some, not the worst thing in the world. The reality that innocent people might become collateral damage in this provisional approach to justice is more than many in law enforcement are willing to acknowledge.

What do you want from me, tears?

Paul Rico became a player in the criminal underworld, some might say a gangster with a badge. He was rewarded for the role he played by those who sent him into battle.

Jeremiah O'Sullivan claimed that he did not trust the FBI, but he knew better than to rock the boat. When asked, specifically, if he concerned himself with troubling facts about the Teddy Deegan murder trial or other rumored injustices that he might have inherited as U.S. attorney, O'Sullivan answered, "I did not, Congressman."

"Why not?"

"It just wasn't on my turf. I didn't think that I could right the wrongs of the whole world."

Policies of law enforcement are frequently driven by public relations. For an entire generation of cops, agents, and prosecutors, the war on the LCN was the biggest game in town. Daring new techniques were created, such as the Top Echelon Informant Program and the witness protection program.

Agents like Rico and Connolly who could rub shoulders with gangsters and cultivate informants became the new stars.

In this war that spanned nearly half a century, there were many victims.

At the Bulger trial, the most obvious manifestation of the price that had been paid was the daily gathering of family members of Bulger's many murder victims. These were people who had lost loved ones, though, in most cases, the people Bulger was alleged to have murdered were fellow criminals, or others who, by choice, had tragically entered into the orbit of Bulger and Flemmi.

In the morass of duplicity that flowed from the generation of Barboza and his handlers to the generation of Flemmi and Bulger, there was another kind of victim—people who got caught in the maw of corruption, the detritus of dirty deals struck between informants and their handlers. Human waste. People for whom men like Paul Rico would shed no tears and Jerry O'Sullivan would lose no sleep. People like Joe Salvati.

At the beginning of the congressional hearings in 2001, Salvati's longtime attorney, Victor J. Garo, spoke in front of the committee. Garo had fought the government for nearly thirty years in an attempt to have Salvati's case reopened. The biggest stumbling block was the Justice Department, which consistently refused to release documents that might have exonerated Salvati. Said Garo to the committee, "The FBI determined that the life of Joe Salvati was expendable, that the life and future of his wonderful wife, Marie, was expendable, and that the four young lives of their children, at the time ages four, seven, nine, and eleven, were expendable."

Garo talked about the legal struggles to get Salvati out of prison, but most emotional of all was when he described his regular meetings with Salvati's family. He once joked with the youngest son, Anthony, that "when I get your father out of prison, you're going to say I created a monster, because he's going to follow you around, he's going to want to know everything you have done." The child got real quiet, said the lawyer, then he spoke. " 'No, Victor,' he said. 'I have never seen my father wake up in the morning. I have never had breakfast with my father in the morning. I've never taken a walk with my father, and I have never gone to a ball game with my father. I sure do want to do that in the future with my dad.' "

Joe and his wife, Marie, were at the hearings. After Garo spoke, Salvati read a statement in which he attempted to explain some of the ways his conviction had destroyed his life. "There were constant stories in the media that I was a very bad person and one not to be respected." This, said Salvati, created a tremendous burden that had to be shouldered mostly by his family. "More than once my heart was broken because I was unable to be with my family at very important times." With his wife seated at his side, Salvati looked at the collection of political representatives stretched out in front of him. "Finally, I would like to say a few things about my wife," he said. "She is a woman with great strength and character. She has always been there for me in my darkest hours. She brought up our four children and gave them a caring and loving home. . . ." Salvati's voice cracked, and his eyes welled with tears. "When God made my Marie, they threw the mold away. . . ." Then he began weeping uncontrollably.

Victor Garo, seated next to Salvati, leaned to the microphone and said, "Mr. Chairman, may I please finish those last two sentences for Mr. Salvati?"

"Sure," said Congressman Burton.

Reading from Salvati's statement, Garo continued, "When God made Marie, the mold was thrown away. I am one of the luckiest men in the world to have such a devoted and caring wife, my precious Marie."

Then Salvati's wife, Marie, read a statement about what it was like trying to raise a family while the man in their lives was in prison for a crime they knew he didn't commit. "The government stole thirty years of my life," she said.

By the time Marie Salvati finished reading her brief statement, most of the committee members were in tears or hushed in silence.

AT CAFÉ POMPEII, when I interviewed Joe Salvati, as with many events from his past, his memory of the congressional hearings was remarkably vivid. Something about the deadness of thirty years in prison had attuned his senses, energizing those moments that are outside the norm. While in prison, Salvati held on to the hope that he would one day be released, but he never dreamed that high-ranking representatives of the U.S. government, or anyone else, for that matter, would one day offer an apology.

What still rankles all these years later is that in the long fight to get released and clear his name—with Victor Garo as his Job-like point man—Salvati's biggest stumbling block were the very institutions that had perpetrated the injustice—the FBI and DOJ. Even after favorable rulings determined that these institutions be required by law to turn over documents, they simply stalled or refused to comply with court orders. It seemed as though the bureaucracy was determined to crush Salvati through indifference and institutional malfeasance. And when Victor Garo, the lawyer, did achieve a provisional victory within the legal system, there was someone else—a law enforcement representative or politician who had a vested interest in Salvati's conviction—who stepped forward and acted on behalf of the conspiracy.

Salvati remembered when he was paid a visit by Michael Albano, a member of the state parole board.

Albano's name had come up at the Bulger trial. On the witness stand, John Morris was forced to admit that he and Connolly, in 1983, had paid a visit to Albano to discuss with him his intention to vote for commutation of Salvati's sentence, along with the sentences of Louis Greco and Peter Limone.

"Albano came to me in prison," Salvati told me at Café Pompeii. "He said those two agents came up there to threaten him."

In so doing, Morris and Connolly were serving as inheritors and custodians of the conspiracy to keep buried the justice system's dirty little secrets.

Albano told Salvati that even though he had been intimidated by the two FBI agents, he was still going to vote for the commutation of his and Limone's sentence. Albano had learned enough about Barboza to comprehend that the Deegan murder convictions were rotten.

Salvati did not want to get his hopes up. His case had gone before the parole board numerous times over the years and always seemed to get mysteriously derailed. But this time, they had the votes. The state parole board voted in favor of release. Then it went to the Governor's Council, which voted nine to zero for commutation. Salvati was close; he was even transferred to a "prerelease facility" in expectation of his commutation. All that remained was a final decision from Governor William Weld.

Weld was a former federal prosecutor, a product of the same system that had conspired to frame Salvati. He had long been a fellow traveler of the Bulger conspiracy. At the annual St. Patrick's Day breakfast in Southie, Weld had shown fealty to Senator Bulger. As state attorney general, he had backed up the decision of Jeremiah O'Sullivan to not grant hoodlum Brian Halloran refuge in the federal witness protection program. Halloran and Michael Donahue were murdered by Whitey Bulger within days of Weld's decision. Even so, the odds in favor of Salvati's commutation were strong.

On May 17, 1993, Governor Weld announced that he declined to commute the sentence of Salvati, Greco, and Limone. In the case of Salvati, the governor cited "Mr. Salvati's long criminal record."

Salvati's "long" criminal record consisted of a single conviction for stealing a tool from a construction site in 1955.

It had been a crushing defeat, but four years later, in 1997, the governor reversed his decision. I asked Salvati how that came about.

"We got to Weld through Moakley," said Salvati.

I was startled. Congressman Joe Moakley? The beloved figure after whom the federal Moakley Courthouse was named?

"What happened was, my wife's aunt was sick and dying in the hospital. And in the bed next to her was Joe Moakley's wife. My wife used to go up there to the hospital every night. Moakley couldn't go often because he was in Washington. So my wife used to sit with her, keep her company. And she told her my story. Moakley's wife said, 'Make sure your husband's lawyer talks to my husband, the congressman.'

"Sure enough, one day Moakley comes in the hospital room and saw Marie sitting there. After being introduced, she told Moakley the story. He couldn't get over it. He said, 'You come by my office tomorrow.'

"Marie goes to the office. He has her sitting in the waiting area, but she can hear him say, 'Get me Governor Weld on the phone.' She hears him talking. He says to Weld, 'I want this guy home by Christmas.'"

Salvati's long nightmare was over, but there were still a few battles to wage. One of those battles was a lawsuit filed in 2003 by Salvati, Limone, and the families of the other two men who had been falsely incarcerated. The suit claimed that the FBI and the DOJ were guilty of "malicious prosecution, civil conspiracy, intentional infliction of emotional distress, and negligent selection, supervision and retention." The family members also cited "loss of consortium" for having lost their loved ones to prison for three decades. The suit would occasionally be mentioned during the Bulger trial as "the Limone case" or "the Limone matter."

The case was brought before Judge Nancy Gertner, who heard testimony at a bench trial that lasted, on and off, for years. Gertner was successful in doing what the House Committee on Oversight and Government Reform had been unsuccessful in doing; under a U.S. Supreme Court subpoena, she obtained unredacted FBI files relating to the fraudulent Deegan murder convictions and subsequent attempts to keep the truth buried. Gertner's findings were staggering, some of which she summarized in a July 2007 final ruling on the case. Declared Judge Gertner:

> Government agents suborned perjury, framed four innocent men and conspired to keep them in jail for three decades. . . . The FBI agents handling Barboza and their superiors—all the way up to the FBI Director—knew that Barboza would perjure himself. They knew this because Barboza, a killer many times over, had told them so—directly and indirectly. . . . They coddled him, nurtured him, debriefed him, protected him, and rewarded him—no matter how much he lied. . . . Indeed, they took steps to make certain that Barboza's false story would withstand cross-examination, and even be corroborated by other witnesses. . . . The FBI agents were given raises and promotions precisely for their extraordinary role in procuring the Deegan convictions. . . . The pieties the FBI offered to justify their actions are the usual ones: The benefits outweigh the costs. . . . Now is the time to say and say without equivocation: This "cost"—to the liberty of four men, to our system of justice—is not remotely acceptable. No man's liberty is dispensable. No human being may be traded for another. Our system cherishes each individual. We have fought wars over this principle. We are still fighting those wars.

Judge Gertner awarded the families of those affected a total of $101 million.

"It was a good chunk of money, sure," said Joe Salvati. His family's portion of the award was approximately $30 million. "We were able to take care of the kids, put some money away. But if somebody said, 'I'll give you thirty million, will you do thirty years?' you'd have to be an imbecile to say yes."

Mostly, Salvati has let go of the anger—"You can't hold on to it forever; it eats you up"—but there are many things about the experience that still bother him.

With the Bulger trial ongoing, Joe noticed that many of the names involved in his case—Rico and Condon and Harrington—had emerged as a Greek chorus. It is this fact that rankles Salvati most of all, that the people who cultivated and used Barboza were able to pass their skills along to those who used Whitey Bulger, and that the efforts to hide the true nature of that arrangement became not only a source of corruption but an operating mandate within the system.

"It is a shame," said Salvati. "But I'm not surprised by any of it."

The interview was over. Salvati and I exited Café Pompeii and headed out into the early evening sunlight. We shook hands and said our goodbyes. As part of his usual routine, Joe would likely go next door to Stanza dei Sigari to smoke a cigar, or farther down the block to Caffé Vittoria for an aperitif, or maybe do both.

Salvati strolled along the sidewalk, his face to the sky.

That afternoon on Hanover Street, the ghosts of the past were alive and well.

11

IRISH DAY OF THE DEAD

IN THE HIERARCHY of witnesses at the Bulger trial, where killers and those who had survived the killers garnered the most attention, few could have known that among the most enlightening would be a forensic anthropologist. In retrospect, it should have been obvious: the Bulger trial had the trappings of an excavation, an immersion deep into the molten core of various horrific acts, with gruesome details buried under layers of terror and deception. Clearly, an anthropologist would be required to get at the root of the matter.

From the witness stand, Ann Marie Mires spoke with authority, though her voice was soothing and her manner solicitous of the uninitiated. As an expert in the field of skeletal biology and the excavation and recovery of skeletonized remains, she seemed accustomed to breaking things down, explaining the most elemental facts of human decomposition.

Already the Bulger trial had led the jury and spectators through a litany of ways to die at the hands of another human being. Mires would now take us into the world of the postmortem. The forensic anthropologist was sworn in and took the stand to testify about "the diggings."

Thirteen years earlier, beginning in 2000, the city of Boston had been riveted by news of a series of excavations—three, to be exact—in which a total of six bodies were unearthed. The diggings had been initiated courtesy of Kevin Weeks, who had begun cooperating with Wyshak and Kelly. During his debriefings, Weeks for the first time told investigators about the Haunty and how the bodies that had originally been buried there were moved to another site. He told them about other murders and burials, some of which he had participated in and others he heard about over the years.

Over a nine-month period, Weeks led a team of state police, prosecutors, and anthropologists on an expedition into the heart of the city's recent gangland history.

The first of the diggings began on January 13, 2000, at a location in Dorchester across from Florian Hall, at 55 Hallet Street. This particular excavation would involve the uncovering of the most recent of the Southie murder victims, including the bodies of Bucky Barrett, John McIntyre, and Deborah Hussey, all of whom had originally been buried in the basement of the Haunty.

From the stand, Mires remembered that it was snowing that night, and it was extremely cold. She was the leader of an investigative crew that included Colonel Tom Foley of the state police and many others.

Prosecutor Wyshak directed the witness's attention to a photo projected onto a flat-screen monitor. "Do you recognize that location?" he asked.

"Yes, I do," answered Mires.

"And what is that location, Doctor?"

"That is the location of the grave site off of Hallet Street, across the street, and you can see in the picture with the American flag in the front, that's Florian Hall."

The digging had begun at 5:30 P.M. and was soon shrouded in darkness. Klieg lights were erected at the site, giving the photos presented by Wyshak an eeriness that seemed to match the task at hand.

"There's a telestrator in front of you," said the prosecutor to the witness. "If you could sort of mark the area of excavation . . . you can do it with your finger."

Mires was able to draw an arrow or a circle or an X with her finger on the monitor; her markings instantly appeared on the screen in the courtroom and also in the media room two floors below.

Said Wyshak, "I direct your attention to photo three-seventy. What does this photograph depict?"

"This is the excavation under way. We initiated the excavation with a large backhoe in order to remove the overburden. . . . We had information leading us to believe there was a seven- to eight-foot overburden, in other words, that much soil over the grave. . . . The soil consistency is going to be different inside the pit than it's going to be outside the pit. We started to feel the ground getting softer, and we consulted at that time, and we brought in the small Bobcat in order to remove the rest of the overburden."

"And showing the next photo, what does that depict?"

"This is a nice shot of the embankment, which shows you some of the stratigraphy, but right in the middle here, there's a discoloration, the soil is depressed more, it's softer, and you can see all the colors are mixed, what we call 'mottled.' This is what we believed to be the top of the grave, and soon we found out that it was."

Along with being a forensic anthropologist, Mires was also a college professor and someone who often gave presentations to other scientists and people in law enforcement. She narrated her anthropological undertaking with clarity and precision, using terminology of the trade not to impress her listeners, but to lead them into her world, so that even if you were not familiar with a term, you understood what she meant.

"The small Bobcat had disturbed the very top, so we brought in a tarp and dumped all the soil on that; we then sifted it." Mires drew a mark on the telestrator. "Here we're getting an elevation. The police officer in the center is holding a stadia rod, and we're taking a depth measurement. As I mentioned earlier, you want to lock in the horizontal and vertical dimensions of where you are; this ties it into space. Right? Ties it into Dorchester, ties it into the vertical coordinates in the world."

The doctor's manner was comforting; she was giving us observers—laypeople—details based on logic as we began our descent into what was beginning to feel spooky and ominous. "In the tines of the Bobcat we picked up some leg bones. . . . Here's a quarter-and-an-eighth-inch mesh screen that's attached to wood so we can sift the soil. And we are looking for any bones we might have missed. The large leg bones are fairly obvious, but the small foot bones are a little less obvious."

Now that Mires and her team had discovered the grave pit, they settled in for the long haul. A large tent was constructed, with lamps and electrical heat generators on the inside. Tables were set up and tarps laid out, so that the findings could be separated and laid out in individual pieces. Photos from this undertaking showed men and women wearing surgical masks and gloves along with boots and digging gear.

Once the location of the remains within the pit was identified, the process slowed to a crawl. "Essentially, now we're into a hand excavation. We're going to use what are called trowels, they're diamond-shaped hand tools;

dustpans; brushes; wooden implements. This is the more tedious and slow process of removing the layers of the soil and material."

As Mires explained it, coming upon a bone fragment, the investigators could not just grab it; they had to carefully dig around it, doing as little damage as possible, brushing it, feeling its contours, and then extract the bone from the earth. "So here we have a left and a right femur. We have the tibia, left, and the fibula of the lower leg. . . . If you'll notice, the bones are almost the exact same color as the soil. So the bones take on the same color as the soil, and they develop a patina, or covering. If the break to the bone is recent, it's like a dry twig, if you snap it, on the inside it's going to be white or light in color. The same with a bone. . . . That tells us the damage is postmortem, it occurred after the death of the individual."

Eventually, in addition to still photographs documenting each stage of the dig, the investigators brought in a video cameraman. The expedition was videotaped, with the cameraman zooming in tight on each and every major discovery.

In the courtroom, Mires narrated the video, making sense of what might have seemed to the layperson like a mysterious journey into the core of the earth. In the video, the scene looked like frozen tundra somewhere in Antarctica, with snow swirling in the night air. The archeologists and cops were dressed in huge parkas, with their breath emanating like steam from their mouths in the freezing conditions.

"What's starting to happen is we're beginning to get more than two sets of leg bones showing up. So we have a right and a left for each person, but we're now beginning to see three sets of leg bones. . . ."

Using the telestrator, Mires directed viewers to what initially appeared as streams of white in the dark soil. "Here's the body bag on top, and here's one set of leg bones, here's another set of leg bones, and I have a third. A series of ribs. And we have plastic bags and pelvic bones or hipbones over here."

For the jurors, these findings were like pieces of a puzzle falling into place.

Kevin Weeks, in his courtroom testimony, had mentioned the body bags when they moved the bodies, and now, all these years later, Mires was pointing them out, buried underground with the remains. Weeks had also mentioned the lime they had used to suppress the smell of the bodies. Mires pointed out the white chalky substance in the grave pit, which they suspected was lime but wouldn't know for sure until they sent it to the lab for analysis.

Said the witness, "With archeology, you don't exactly know what you're going to find. It's revealing itself to you as you go along. . . . Here, for instance, it appears as if this particular individual that belongs to those leg bones was buried not in an anatomical position, that they are probably disarticulated."

"What does that mean, disarticulated?" asked Wyshak.

"Articulated is when you're attached, everything is attached and the bones are attached to each other with ligaments, and that occurs when you're buried in a fresh state, right? In this situation, it appeared that this individual was disarticulated, was no longer in an anatomical position. That was probably due to the decomposition."

Occasionally, the witness would see something that pricked her enthusiasm, for instance, root growth coming up through the human remains. "There's a lot of organic material, and so it encourages root and plant growth"—in other words, fluids and the decomposition of the bodies were like fertilizer for the soil. The physical forms of the murder victims were being absorbed into the earth; they were, literally, going back to nature, causing root growth to intertwine with bones and become the organic legacy of the Bulger era.

Eventually, the remains of three distinct bodies were uncovered. Mires described how these remains were carefully moved inside the tent, where, with the heat generators, it was "a mild fifty degrees." The various bones were laid out on stainless steel gurneys. "The first thing I do is put the body in anatomical position, as if they were laying prone, faceup, with their hands out on the gurney. . . . You're going to see some photographs of those full-body shots, or, as we call them, full inventory."

On the monitor appeared an image of the reconstruction of nearly an entire skeleton, bones laid out on the gurney in the shape of a human form, complete with a skull or skull fragments. Some in the jury and spectators' gallery gasped. These disarticulated bones, which were eventually assembled for all three victims, represented all that was left of Barrett, McIntyre, and Davis, and laid out on the table like that they looked almost like people.

Said Mires, "The skeleton is like a road map. It allows us anthropologists to drive through the lifetime of that individual. We look for signs of age—how old is the person at the time they died; what sex are they, male or female; how tall are they; and ancestry. . . . There are physical characteristics in your skull, in your facial features, and in the shape of your skull that determines who your ancestors were, whether they were Caucasian, Negroid, or Asian in origin, or a mixture."

The analysis of the remains continued at the burial site for many hours. Every item found on or near the three distinct skeletons was inventoried, including, in the case of remains that were later identified as those of John McIntyre, the bullet lodged in his skull after being shot in the head at close range by Jim Bulger.

Three hours into Mires's testimony, Wyshak said, "All right, now I'd like to direct your attention to approximately nine months later. On or about September 14, 2000, did you respond to a crime scene at Tenean Beach in Dorchester?"

"I did," answered the witness.

And so began the description of the second digging, which was also well documented through photographs and video footage of the excavation. This time, the investigators were looking for the body of Paul McGonagle, who had been killed by Bulger in 1975, ten years before the victims found in the grave near Florian Hall.

The investigators were told that the body was buried in a rocky area near the shoreline. Again, the anthropologists moved slowly and methodically. The conditions were even more difficult than the previous site. "We're only three feet from the low-tide line," noted Mires. "At high tide, the grave itself wasn't submerged, but the salt water comes through the ground."

"And what does that do to decomposition?" asked Wyshak.

"It has a very caustic effect. Salt water is like acid, almost. There's a lot of salt in salt water and in the seashells. There's a lot of calcium carbonate. So it offers a contradiction because it can actually help preserve materials."

Before long, the investigators uncovered traces of a body—clothing, a shoe, organic material. "We're battling the elements. High tide is pretty much full-on now, and we're getting seepage from the bottom."

Said Wyshak to an assistant, "Okay, can we put up exhibit six-oh-six."

On the screen came a photo of what looked like a body crammed into a wet grave, decomposed, fossilized, like something out of a horror movie. "Now, what is this a photograph of?"

"This is a photograph of an individual fully exposed. . . . It's about as clear as it got. We have the shoes, platform sneakers. Here we have the knees. And this would be the trunk, the lower trunk. We have the spine, although you can't see that. Here you can see the arm. And then here it's the skull on its side and the whole—one side is removed—so it's actually kind of an open container at that point."

Wyshak called for another photo, this one a close-up of something goopy and muddy. "I'll direct your attention, right in the middle there's a gold-colored claddagh ring."

Said Mires, marking the screen of her telestrator for all to see, "Yes, the ring is here, and although I can't really make them out here, there are remnants of the finger bones in this area. They're very hard to pick out. The bones become the color of the soil the body decomposes in, so everything looks the same color because it essentially is now part of the beach after all this time."

"Did you recover this claddagh ring?"

"I did."

Wyshak produced the ring—calling it "exhibit six thirty-four for identification"—and handed it to the witness. "Is that the claddagh ring that you recovered at Tenean Beach?

"Yes, it is."

The prosecutor had Mires hold up the ring for the jury to see, and then place it in an evidence envelope.

The photos kept coming, each one more macabre than the last.

Now Mires and her team were trying to remove the remains from the grave, but they quickly discovered that the material was "almost the consistency of wet cardboard. It's very punky, almost like rotten wood, from being saturated and being in this kind of caustic environment for so long. . . . This was the only chance probably that I was going to have to measure the skull, so I set up a ruler so that I could take some very crude measurements, because once I got [the skull] out of the grave, it just kind of fell apart. So you can see here the mandible, what's left of it. A denture that was probably attached to the maxilla. It's an upper denture."

"Did you recover the denture as well?"

"Yes."

Wyshak handed the witness a plastic sandwich-size bag with something inside. "Can you open the bag?"

"I can," said Mires, opening the bag like a box of Cracker Jacks and reaching inside.

"Are the dentures in the bag?"

"They are."

"Will you display them?"

Mires held up her prize: a thirty-year-old set of dentures, extracted from the moist, decrepit skull of a Bulger murder victim from long ago.

Intoned Wyshak to Judge Casper, "Let the record reflect that the witness is displaying the dentures recovered at Tenean Beach in September of 2000."

"It may so reflect," responded the judge.

"Thank you, Your Honor."

"Counsel, would this be a good place to stop for the day?"

"Sure," said Wyshak.

And so, the day ended with the dentures of Paulie McGonagle serving as a sad coda to a long session of grisly testimony.

The lawyers and court personnel and media people spilled out into the afternoon sunshine. It was Wednesday, midweek, and the bright sky was alive with possibilities, but the dark video and photographic images from the diggings lingered in the air, befouling the shiny façade of a proud city.

THE FOLLOWING MORNING, Mires was scheduled to return to the witness stand, but, first, there was an issue that the court needed to address. The previous evening, defense counsel had filed a motion with the judge that required immediate attention.

A motion is a formal request asking the judge to do something for the "moving party" or "movant." Under Rule 7(b) of the Federal Rules of Civil Procedure, motions must be filed in writing and accompanied by a signed affidavit by the movant—in this case Jay Carney—and the motion papers must be served on all parties in the case. Carney had filed his motion papers too late for the prosecution to draft a response, so that a hearing was required in front of the judge, who would hear oral arguments for and against the motion. These hearings usually took place in the morning before the jury was brought into the courtroom.

The defense motion, docket number 1134, was headlined "DEFENDANT'S MOTION TO ADJOURN TRIAL." Bulger's lawyers were asking that as soon as Mires completed her testimony, the proceedings be adjourned until the following Tuesday. They were, in essence, asking for two extra days.

"Simply put," stated the motion, "the defendant's counsel has hit a wall and are unable to proceed further without additional time to prepare for upcoming witnesses. Counsel have struggled mightily to be ready for each day of the trial since it began . . . working seven days a week and extraordinarily long hours. . . . There is a physical and mental limitation on how much work can be done by the defense team, and a brief adjournment of the trial will allow counsel to be prepared for the upcoming witnesses."

The motion further noted, "The defendant is awakened at 4:00 A.M. every trial day, and by the end of his travel back to Plymouth, this 83-year old man is exhausted. Meaningful interaction with counsel in the evening is impossible."

Carney's motion touched off a spirited debate. It had been brought about, in part, by the prosecution's contention that the trial was well ahead of schedule and moving fast. In a strategic move, the prosecution also announced that they had dropped certain witnesses who were scheduled to testify. The defense complained on the grounds that since these witnesses were on the prosecution's list and had been scheduled to appear, the defense was put in the position of having to prepare for witnesses that the government did not intend to call. Precious time had been wasted, and now the defense was struggling to be ready to cross-examine witnesses who had been moved up the list.

It didn't seem like an unreasonable request to be asking for two extra days to prepare, but the government wasn't buying it.

"Obviously, the government opposes the motion," said Zach Hafer, who stood to argue on behalf of the prosecution. Hafer took particular exception to defense counsel's position that they had been hindered, in part, by the government not having been forthcoming with the required discovery material. "As your honor is well aware, we too have spent countless hours, mostly logistically at this point, arranging out-of-state travel, hotel accommodations, witness prep, based on daily progress of this trial. It is a massive undertaking. We've met every deadline your honor has set with respect to exhibits, witness lists. We provided daily updates to the defense as to where witnesses are going to fall in the order of proof or even just saying, 'These are the exhibits that go with this witness.' In our view, we've provided a clean road map to this trial, and there's absolutely no reason to delay it."

With a note of disdain in his voice, Hafer further addressed the point in the motion about Bulger being exhausted, saying that, as an argument for a continuance, "That's not good enough, either. The victims in this case have been waiting long enough for justice. Mr. Bulger had sixteen years to relax in California. Mr. Carney and Mr. Brennan have had the discovery in this case for years, and in our view, there's absolutely no basis to adjourn the trial for any time at all."

Judge Casper asked Hafer to run through, in order, the upcoming witnesses for the remainder of the week. He did so: John Druggan, a forensic chemist from the crime lab for the state police; Elaine Barrett, Bucky Barrett's wife; FBI agent Thomas Daly; Paul Moore, a South Boston drug dealer; Gerald Montanari, another FBI agent; Barry Wong, an unwitting accomplice to an extortion; Steve Davis; and Patricia Donahue.

Judge Casper tried to appear as though she were weighing the significance of the witnesses to judge how much time the defense would need to prepare for cross-examination, but it was clear from her demeanor and tone of voice that she had made up her mind.

Carney made one last effort. He stood to speak. There was exasperation in his voice, and in his argument astonishment that the judge would not allow the defense two measly days to be better prepared to defend their client.

Said the judge, "I'm going to cut you off there. . . . Mr. Carney, I appreciate the tone that you took in the motion in putting it forward, in laying it out without hyperbole, which I always appreciate. . . . I also take, as I take every motion that's filed before me, that you filed this in good faith and that your team has been working around the clock, matched only, perhaps, by the government team working around the clock to push this forward. So I'm not inclined to suspend the trial."

If body language is an indicator of state of mind, it was as if the defense table had taken a collective kick in the testicles. To them, the trial had become one big steamroller.

AT ITS MOST vast and far-reaching, the conspiracy to utilize Bulger and Flemmi as a means to take down the Mafia in Boston was, for the FBI and others in the criminal justice system, a theoretical exercise. Men and women who had gone to college, earned degrees, and pursued reputable lives of accomplishment in the field of criminal justice had set about to undermine and bring down a criminal underworld that they had never, nor would they ever, experience firsthand. It was this fact that led J. Edgar Hoover to make such a strong commitment to the FBI's informant program. He may have believed, instinctively, that it was the only way the Mafia could be brought down.

It was a solid strategy—in theory. Using snitches or informants from inside an organization to undermine that organization was not exactly new. John Martorano made reference to it during his testimony: Judas may have been the first Top Echelon Informant, and had he perpetrated his betrayal many millennia later, under the auspices of Hoover, he might have been relocated to Oregon or Utah, somewhere far away from the King of the Jews.

Throughout the Bulger trial, the prosecution often underscored the narrative that Whitey and Flemmi had been recruited by the FBI to help build cases against the Mafia. This was the story line that had been used in previous Bulger-related trials, and also the theory fed by prosecutorial sources to the media, where it was further expounded upon in books, documentaries, and feature films.

But the belief that Bulger and Flemmi's value to the government was based solely on their ability to make cases against the Mafia does not tell the full story. It does not explain why Special Agents Morris and Connolly would take it upon themselves to threaten a member of the Massachusetts State Parole Board presiding over a case that was initiated before either of them was even in the FBI, much less stationed in Boston. That mission had nothing to do with Bulger and Flemmi. They were acting as inheritors of the system's dirty little secrets, proprietors of a corrupt history. It was their duty to help keep it buried.

That history had been born out of a partnership between criminals—Barboza, Jimmy Flemmi, and many others less exalted—and the system. It was a central flaw of the Top Echelon Informant Program that had existed from the beginning, and if it had ever been exposed, it would have ended the program and possibly even Hoover's career.

The partnership that the system forged with Steve Flemmi and later Whitey Bulger was part and parcel of the same arrangement. By becoming informants, they also had become proprietors of this history. They knew the system's dirty little secrets. And by forming an alliance with the likes of Connolly and Morris, they were entering into a pact part of which involved helping to keep this dirty history hidden forever.

And this is where they derived their power: Flemmi and Bulger knew that by entering into this pact with the system, the system was now beholden to them. They could do whatever they wanted, not only financial crimes like loan-sharking, drugs, extortion, and robberies, but murder, any kind of murder they wanted, as long as they made the bodies disappear, so that there would be no investigation.

The murders of Debbie Davis and Deborah Hussey were a manifestation of this arrangement: killings that had nothing to do with business and everything to do with showing that they could kill virtually whomever they wanted, anytime, for any reason, and they would never be prosecuted for it.

That is partly why the burials of the bodies had become a necessity. Not only were they an effort to inter evidence belowground and out of sight; they also became a ritualistic way for Bulger to illustrate his omnipotence.

Ann Marie Mires, with her skills as an anthropologist and her pleasant demeanor, had no awareness of the motives behind the burials that she described. Part of what made her descriptions in court so chilling was the matter-of-fact way she detailed the end result of murders that had been so intimate and brutal.

The last excavation took place two weeks after the exhumation at Tenean Beach. It was centered on a location two miles to the south, in Quincy.

Approximately one hundred yards from Commander Shea Boulevard, alongside the Neponset River, a field of marshland lay at the foot of the elevated train tracks of the Massachusetts Bay Transportation Authority. Digging here was a challenge. Lumpy marshland covered an area the size of two or three football fields, and there were no markers, such as trees or large rock formations or prominent outgrowths, to help identify the exact locations of the graves. The digging crew knew that out there somewhere were the remains of two people, Tommy King and Debra Davis, whose unceremonious burials had taken place six years apart, in 1975 and in 1981.

In this instance, the excavation team brought in a geophysicist, whose "ground-penetrating radar" made it possible to examine a large area in search of "any pits and anomalies underneath the ground" before any digging had even begun.

Just as before, Mires narrated a video of the excavation, and as with the diggings at Tenean Beach, the conditions were difficult. Here high tide actually covered the entire marshland, meaning that the graves were completely submerged. It also gave a sense of urgency to the dig, since the archeologists would be forced to postpone their expedition once the tide rolled in.

A week of diggings went by, and they uncovered nothing. Pit after pit was dug up, the soil spilled out and sifted through, with nary a bone or shred of clothing. A sense of frustration set in. Then they got lucky and uncovered some skull fragments. They also uncovered a moldy, deteriorated bulletproof vest.

For the jurors, this was telling. They had heard, via the testimony of John Martorano, that Tommy King put on a bulletproof vest the night he was murdered. King believed that he, Bulger, Flemmi, and Martorano were going to kill a sad sack hoodlum named Suitcase Fidler, not realizing that his executioner was, in fact, Martorano, sitting behind him in the car. A bullet to the back of the cranium ended Tommy King's life.

At the site, the skull fragments and other remains, mixed with dirt and debris (the marshland had also been used as landfill), were dumped out on a tarp. Mires highlighted a section of the video that showed her carefully sifting through the dirt. "Here, you can see elements of the spine. Here, I'm in the pelvic area, and this is pelvic bone I'm exposing, or the hipbone. . . . This is the humerus or the upper arm bone. . . . And this is a remnant of a blue suit jacket and a vest. It was a three-piece suit."

Though the Mullen gang had largely been considered a group of ruffians, Tommy King wore a three-piece suit to his execution. Not only that, he wore what was, perhaps, the premier fashion statement of the gang. "If you look here," said Mires, "you'll see what I later determined to be driving gloves. They were the kind of gloves that only goes up to your fingers and then the fingers are exposed. But I want to draw your attention to—this is a claddagh ring. So the gloves were on the hands, and there's a claddagh ring here on the finger bones of the individual."

Said prosecutor Wyshak, "Showing you what's been marked five-six-two for identification, I ask you if you recognize what that is."

Once again, Mires held up a claddagh ring, the Irish symbol of friendship and eternal love worn by many South Boston gangsters.

It would be another month, in October, before they found the remains of Debra Davis. Her grave site was found nearer the river, in an area that was often underwater. The skeleton was found encased in a plastic body bag that had deteriorated. The body had been trussed up and tied with rope, and was tightly compacted in a fetal position. As with the other shoreline burials, some aspects of the remains had been preserved by the salt water, which served as a kind of brine. With Mires narrating, the prosecution showed a ghastly photo of the remains, where hair and some scalp tissue had been preserved though the body had been interred in its marshy grave for nearly twenty years.

As with the other remains, the bones were secured and brought to a lab for postmortem analysis. DNA tests were conducted to identify that it was, in fact, the remains of Debra Davis. Then the bones were laid out on a stainless steel table, in what had become a ritual of the Boston diggings. "Because [the Davis remains were found] in a very tight pit," said Mires, "we were able to recover almost all the material." She ran through the visual inventory of bones, a complete skeletal catalog of the human form.

Debbie Davis had been strangled to death, so there were no bullet holes to the skull or traumatic damage to the bones to help determine the cause of death.

Earlier, when Deborah Hussey's remains were found, Mires confronted a similar situation. Hussey had also been strangled to death, which was a mode of death undetectable through skeletal examination. In both cases, Mires determined that the cause of death was "homicidal violence, etiology unknown."

Wyshak asked the witness to explain what that meant.

"Cause of death is really looking at the body and trying to find that mechanism that stopped life. In skeletal remains of women that I've examined, there will not be any marks of any kind on the skeleton indicating what exactly was the mechanism that stopped life. So there's a category that we engage in or I can use, it's called homicidal violence, etiology unknown or cause unknown. It's a designation that allows us to say, 'I believe this person died of homicidal violence.' Exactly what stopped life, I do not know."

"Well," said Wyshak, "in this case what are the indicators of homicidal violence?"

"Actually, they come more from the fact that the body was buried . . . the act of or trying to disguise the location of the burial often suggests homicidal violence."

Wyshak was not satisfied; he wanted Mires to crystallize for him how the circumstances of these people's interment were the clearest indication of how they had died. "It is unusual in this day and age to find individuals who die of natural causes buried in unmarked graves?"

"Yes," said Mires. "It's unusual."

"It is unusual in this day and age to find people who die of natural causes buried in an unmarked grave with two other individuals?"

"Yes. It's unnatural."

The forensic anthropologist finished her direct testimony, and there were no questions from the defense. She was dismissed without cross-examination.

A FEW DAYS after Mires's testimony, I was standing at Tenean Beach, at the exact location where the remains of Paul McGonagle had been exhumed. I was standing there with someone who was alleged to have helped put McGonagle's body in the ground: Pat Nee.

It was a crystal-clear day. From the beach, you could see all the way to downtown Boston, an impressive skyline that hardly existed back in 1975, when McGonagle was buried.

The setting was more of a cove than a beach, hidden from the main highway and located alongside a marina. The most dominant landmark was a large gas tank from Boston Gas, which partially blocks the downtown view, depending on where you are standing on the beach. There is also a large children's play area that was not in existence back in 1975.

Nee did not really want to be there. In previous interviews, he had told me that he would show me the sites of the burials, which had previously been identified in the media. But Nee kept putting it off. As with many things relating to Whitey, and especially anything to do with the demise of the Mullen gang, it was not a pleasant memory for Nee.

The death of Paulie McGonagle had been the beginning of the descent. McGonagle was one of the original Mullen gang members who had been resistant to an alliance with the Winter Hill Mob, which was one of the reasons that he was murdered by Bulger. As a newly established partner of Bulger, Nee, it was alleged in trial testimony, had been enlisted to help dispose of the body.

All these years later, it is a topic of discussion that still bothers Nee. As we strolled over to the section of beach where McGonagle was buried, which I had recently seen depicted in video footage at the trial, Nee's discomfort was evident. He fidgeted, looked around nervously, and generally adopted the demeanor of how I imagine a person might have felt were they enlisted to dig up sand and soil, creating a small pit in which they dumped the body of a former friend and gang member.

"I was able to justify [the death of Paulie McGonagle] in my head," said Nee, "because Paulie getting killed was all about business. We were making good money at the time with bookmaking and gambling. Bulger had a conflict with the McGonagles that went back years. Now that we were in business with Whitey, his problems became our problems, in a way."

According to courtroom accounts, present that night were Bulger, Nee, and Tommy King.

Among other things, one prominent detail of the McGonagle burial was the fact that, if Nee were involved, the man standing next to him that night digging the grave—Tommy King—would be the next to go.

I said to Pat, "Somebody digging the grave of a Bulger victim, standing alongside a fellow digger who wold himself soon become a Bulger victim, wouldn't that tell you something?"

Nee thought about it and said, "Yes. It might even make that person feel that they, potentially, were next in line."

As we got in Pat's car and headed toward the next burial site, Nee pointed out locations off Morrissey Boulevard where key Bulger-related killings took place. "Right there," said Pat. "That's where Eddie Connors was shot. There used to be a phone booth there. He was in the booth when they drove up on him." A few miles down the road, Nee continued, "This is where they shot Billy O'Brien. They drove up on his car from behind and opened fire."

I had heard the details of these murders at the trial, and seeing the locations now was a weird juxtaposition, but also a historical revelation, sort of like going on a South Boston version of the city's best-known tourist expedition—the Freedom Trail.

Before we pulled into the burial site off Commander Shea Boulevard, where the remains of King and Debbie Davis were found, Nee showed me Bulger's condominium building, where he had lived with girlfriend Catherine Greig. From the outside, it was a nondescript redbrick building with many units. Nee had been inside the condo on a few occasions. "It was a nice place," he said. "A duplex. With a beautiful view of the harbor. Whitey used to stand at the window with binoculars. He could see the burial sites from there. He used to say, 'Tides coming in. Let's have a drink on Paulie.'" Nee shook his head at the memory. "Sick fuck. That was the kind of humor he had."

We parked Nee's car in a lot, crossed the street, and walked along a path that took us into a dense grove. Right away, I recognized the location from the testimony of Mires: the sweeping marshland leading out toward the mouth of the river, the elevated MBTA tracks running behind us.

"It looked completely different back then," said Nee. The path where we were standing was surrounded by a jungle of vines and overgrowth. "None of this was here. Far as I can tell, where we're standing right now is exactly where Tommy King was buried."

Even though Pat neither confirms nor denies any role in the burial, he does admit that the murder of King—committed without his foreknowledge by Bulger, Flemmi and John Martorano—had been another turning point. The realization by Nee that he might be next on the hit list loomed on the horizon like a bad case of delirium tremens.

It was around this time that a legendary IRA operative named Joe Cahill, from Belfast, reached out to the South Boston criminal underworld. Cahill was looking for money and guns in the IRA's clandestine struggle against British occupation of the six counties of Northern Ireland. At the Triple O's Lounge, Cahill met with Bulger, Nee, and a handful of others who were active in NORIAD, or Northern Irish Aid, a U.S. organization that was sympathetic to the IRA. The war in Northern Ireland had intensified in the late 1970s and would eventually culminate in the hunger strike of 1981, when Bobby Sands and ten other Irish republican prisoners in Long Kesh prison starved themselves to death as an act of protest against the authoritarian leadership of Prime Minister Margaret Thatcher.

Given that he had been born in the old country, Pat was drawn to "the struggle." Some Irish Americans saw the IRA as nothing more than a criminal organization, with a history of thuggery that included the punishment of "touts" or informants via violent means, including death. As someone who had been around violence as a marine, a Vietnam veteran, and a gangster, Nee had no problems with that side of "the Movement." And, whether you agreed with him or not, his political motivations were sincere. He viewed it as his duty to do what he could on behalf of the fight for Irish freedom. And along with all of that, he saw the IRA gunrunning operation as a way to distance himself from Bulger.

In late 1978, Nee moved across town to Charlestown, where much of the city's underground activity on behalf of the IRA was centered. There Nee met regularly with Cahill and others. As much as Nee tried to remove himself from Bulger's orbit, they remained entangled. Bulger was instrumental in securing black market weapons for the large shipment that became the basis for the *Valhalla* expedition, the gun-smuggling operation in which John McIntyre played a key role.

Bulger's involvement in the Southie Mob's IRA ventures may have been beneficial to gathering money and guns for "the cause," but it was not good for Pat Nee. Once again, Nee found himself in partnership with someone he never fully trusted. Also, it was around this time that Nee became friendly with Kevin Weeks. Nee knew that Bulger was suspicious of his relationship with Weeks. When Bulger had suspicions, he tended to scheme and manipulate as a way to control the situation.

One of Bulger's manipulations involved the use of Pat's brother's house as a site for murders and burials of bodies. It made no sense to bury those bodies down in the basement of the Haunty. Why not just take them out in the woods, as they eventually had to do anyway? Over the years, Nee had come to the conclusion that Whitey used the house as his own personal chamber of horrors as a way to compromise and entrap him in the worst of his schemes.

The other way Bulger manipulated people was by roping them into the burials, especially if the person killed was a former friend or associate—which would have been the point of having Nee put in the position of burying his former Mullen gang compatriots.

The various burials would eventually become a key element in the Bulger prosecution, and in a way may have played a role in Nee never having been indicted.

Back in 2000, after Kevin Weeks began cooperating with the government, part of his deal was based on his ability to lead investigators to the various burial sites. Weeks had no difficulty locating the grave site across from Florian Hall because he had taken part in those burials. He knew about the other burials; the general location of those graves had been pointed out to him, but when it came time to do the digging, he was unable to pinpoint the exact locations of the remains. So, according to Kevin in his testimony at the Bulger trial, he reached out to Pat Nee.

Nee was in prison on attempted armed robbery charges in 1997, when the revelations about Bulger and Flemmi first exploded in the media. In a roundabout way, he was fortunate; he avoided being subpoenaed to testify at the Wolf hearings. Through his attorney, he was told that prosecutors had every intention of charging him with being an "accessory after the fact," but the statutes of limitations at both the state and federal levels had passed.

In 2000, when Weeks reached out to Nee, Pat had no legal obligations to help locate the bodies. But by then he was disgusted by the revelations that Bulger and Flemmi had, for decades, been serving as informants for the FBI. He was having regrets about how he had been used by Bulger. Nee, according to the testimony of Weeks, told him exactly where the bodies were buried, leading to their disinterment.

Some believe that Nee's willingness to help the government locate the bodies is partly why prosecutors had taken a hands-off approach to him over the years, but Nee does not agree. "I'm sure that if those alleged crimes had taken place within the statute of limitations and I could have been prosecuted, they would have come after me," said Nee.

Of course, Pat Nee's alleged role in other crimes was still an open topic of speculation at the Bulger trial.

The day after Mires testified about the diggings, Patricia Donahue, the widow of murder victim Michael Donahue, took the stand. The night Pat Donahue's husband gave a ride to Brian Halloran down at the Southie waterfront, he met his demise in a hail of bullets. Bulger, according to Kevin Weeks, had pulled the trigger, but everyone wanted to know who his accomplice was sitting in the backseat of the hit car. There was no doubt who Bulger's defense team was trying to implicate for this crime.

"Did you learn there was a person in the backseat of the car that had a machine gun who was involved in killing your husband?" Jay Carney asked Pat Donahue.

"Yes, I did," she answered.

"And do you know that person's name is Patrick Nee?"

"From what I understood, yes."

Outside the courthouse, when talking to the media, Mrs. Donahue was reticent in her condemnation of Nee, and for good reason. Back in 1986, Donahue had sat through the trial of another person who had been identified and indicted as being the shooter. Jimmy Flynn was a well-known Charlestown criminal who had, according to Brian Halloran, made an attempt on his life before that fateful night in May 1981. The allegation was that Flynn had remained persistent and finally got the job done.

The evidence against Flynn seemed ironclad. On the evening Halloran was riddled with bullets outside Anthony's Pier 4 restaurant, as he lay dying on the pavement, he gave a last-minute identification of his assassin.

"Who did it?" asked a cop kneeling alongside Halloran.

"James Flynn of Weymouth," he replied, according to three law enforcement officials at the scene. Those were Halloran's last words before he died.

The sandy-blond, curly-haired wig worn by Bulger had apparently led Halloran to misidentify his killer. Or had it? Some speculated that Jimmy Flynn was the man in the backseat. When the arrest warrant went out for Flynn, he disappeared on the run and was not apprehended for two and a half years.

In March 1986, Flynn was put on trial. Pat Donahue was there nearly every day, listening to the testimony. The accused took the stand and was able to establish that he was nowhere near the site of the shooting on the day and at the time it took place. When Flynn was found not guilty, the Donahue family believed a travesty of justice had taken place. For the next two decades, the Donahues believed that Jimmy Flynn was the person who had killed their beloved husband and father, and that he had gotten away with murder.

Whitey Bulger's name was never mentioned in relation to the killing, until Kevin Weeks came forward in 1999 with his description of the Halloran-Donahue hit.

Now the Bulger defense team seemed determined to link Pat Nee to the double killing, not to mention other crimes for which they alleged he had played a role.

Bulger's attempts to implicate Nee persisted as a subnarrative to the proceedings. Not long after the testimony of Pat Donahue, the defense lawyers filed a motion with Judge Casper that made their intentions clear: "Patrick Nee was an affiliate of the Winter Hill gang in the 1970s and 1980s. He was integrally involved in the criminal activities of the gang. . . . The government's apparent indifference to Nee raises a legitimate question as to whether Nee has been given a 'free pass' for his criminal history. . . . Pursuant to Rule 16 of the Federal Rules of Criminal Procedure . . . the government must be ordered to provide all transcripts, reports or any other documentation of statements made by Patrick Nee to law enforcement about the criminal activities of James Bulger, Stephen Flemmi, John Martorano and any other people associated with the Winter Hill gang. . . ."

The government fired back with a written response titled, "Government's Opposition to Defendant's Mid-Trial Motion for Discovery Regarding a Nongovernment Witness," stating further, "Bulger's strange obsession with Pat Nee does not give rise to discovery obligations nor can it change the reality that Nee was, in fact, twice prosecuted by Boston U.S. Attorney's office. Indeed, Nee was prosecuted and convicted in the mid-1980s for his role in the *Valhalla* arms shipment (he was ultimately arrested by trial witness Don Defago, a U.S. Customs Agent). Shortly after he was released from prison, Nee was arrested again in 1991 and subsequently convicted for his role in an armored car robbery."

In court, Judge Casper let it be known that she would not make a decision about "the Nee matter" until the government was close to resting its case.

The fact that he had become the focus of a tug-of-war between the defense and the prosecution had, in a way, ruined the trial for Nee. He had been hoping that Bulger's long-awaited demise in court would serve as a source of pleasure and entertainment, but instead he had been subpoenaed by the defense and put in a position of concern about his own criminal liability and the legal jeopardy that might ensue.

This, of course, was precisely as Bulger had intended. In a way, much like Whitey's claim that he had never been an informant, it was another sideshow that diluted the defense case. But it was what Bulger wanted, and so his attorneys seemed determined, every chance they got, to make the issue of Nee's role in the gang a central aspect of *The People v. James J. Bulger.*

And if all this weren't rankling enough for Bulger's longtime Southie rival, the local media became involved.

In the wake of the motions filed by both sides regarding Nee, the *Boston Globe* published an article by trial reporter Milton J. Valencia headlined "Speculation on Trying Oft-Mentioned Patrick Nee." The article quoted Hank Brennan making essentially the same argument as the defense counsel motion, adding, "He's an eyewitness to many of the core allegations in this case. If the government doesn't want to call an eyewitness, we will."

Nee's attorney, Steven Boozang, responded by saying that his client would not testify in Bulger's trial. "Whitey is a professional con artist. He's trying to bring [my client] down because Pat went on with his life and became a productive member of society."

The *Globe* article also made mention of Nee's involvement in *Saint Hoods,* the Discovery Channel reality show that supposedly chronicled a group of Boston bookmakers. The Donahue family, in particular, was outraged that Nee was featured in the show, with Tommy Donahue quoted as saying, "Shame on the Discovery Channel."

Driving back toward Southie, having completed our tour of the various murder and burial sites, I asked Nee about where he thought all this was headed.

"I don't know," he said. "But this is exactly what I was concerned about, that Whitey would try to use the trial as a way to get even. Looks like I've got a real fight on my hands."

Driving along William J. Day Boulevard, looking out over Carson Beach on a sunny July afternoon, it was too nice a day to keep pestering Nee about the trial. So I gave it a rest. At a stoplight, I noticed Nee mumbling something over and over to himself. At first I thought it might be a prayer, which did not fit with the Pat Nee I had come to know.

"What's that you're mumbling?" I asked.

He repeated the phrase out loud: "On the advice of my counsel, I invoke my Fifth Amendment privilege and decline to answer on the grounds that I might be incriminated."

I told Nee that his mumbling attempts to memorize the words reminded me of the scene in *The Godfather,* when the character of Luca Brasi is at the wedding waiting to see the Don, trying to memorize his lines.

Pat laughed, because he has the Irish self-deprecating sense of humor. But he wasn't kidding.

The rest of the drive, whenever he thought I wasn't looking, I could hear him mumbling the phrase under his breath. He was committing the invocation to memory.

12

DELUSIONS OF GRANDEUR

AS I HAD most mornings for the duration of the Bulger trial, on July 17 I arose early, showered, grabbed some Sicilian olive bread at Bricco Panetteria, in the courtyard beneath my studio apartment, and headed out into the morning air. The walk to the courthouse, along Boston Harbor, was especially magnificent that morning. The seagulls sang their song, the flowers in the parkway along Atlantic Avenue were in full bloom, and the twinkling morning dew made the air seem clean and fresh as a baby's butt.

I arrived at Moakley Courthouse earlier than usual. There was potential that it would be a landmark day: Steve Flemmi was scheduled to testify, though there were still a few witnesses ahead of him on the docket, so maybe not. But with the spectator and media presence expected to be greater then usual, I didn't want to take any chances. I was there to make sure I staked out my usual spot in the media room.

When I arrived, a reporter I had gotten to know—Ed Mahoney—was already there. Mahoney had been covering the Bulger story for decades, as a writer for the *Hartford Courant*. He had been at the Wolf hearings in the late 1990s, at Paul Rico's testimony in front of the House Committee on Oversight and Government Reform, and both John Connolly trials. Perhaps his most notable accomplishment was being among the first to write about mob infiltration of World Jai Lai, whose corporate headquarters were based in Connecticut, which made Mahoney one of the most knowledgeable reporters around about the murders of Roger Wheeler and John Callahan, as well as many other aspects of the Bulger fiasco.

"Hey, did you hear what happened?" said Mahoney, cup of coffee in hand, by way of his morning greeting.

"What?" I answered.

"They found the body of Stephen Rakes this morning. He's dead." He was talking about Stippo Rakes.

"What!" I thought he might be joking, but he wasn't. "Anything on cause of death?"

"Right now they're calling it a suicide, but it sounds like they're not sure."

I instantly thought back to the day before. After the proceedings had adjourned at 1 P.M., that afternoon I went downstairs to the courthouse cafeteria for a quick bite to eat. I had seen Stephen Rakes walking down the hall, looking agitated about something. I said hello, but Rakes did not acknowledge me, which was strange. He was a friendly fellow, always quick with a greeting and usually more than willing to engage in small talk.

I later learned that Rakes had been informed that afternoon by Wyshak and Kelly that he would not be called to testify at the trial. They were concerned that Rakes's version of how he had been extorted by Bulger was at odds with that of another witness, Kevin Weeks. To present two different versions of how the sale of the South Boston Liquor Mart had transpired would only confuse the issue and provide an opportunity for the defense team to call the testimony of both witnesses into question, thus damaging their case. Rakes was out.

To say that Rakes was disappointed would be putting it mildly: his testimony was supposed to be his big moment. But would he have been so upset that he would have taken his own life?

All that was known so far was that his body was found, fully clothed, with no outward signs of trauma, on a jogging path in the suburban town of Lincoln. His car was found seven miles away in a McDonald's parking lot.

As the media people, lawyers, and trial spectators gathered for the day's proceedings, the hallways were abuzz with gossip. Many were stunned by the news, and in the absence of details there was speculation about Rakes having been murdered. Was he killed by someone connected to Bulger to prevent him from testifying? Was he killed by Kevin Weeks, who made it clear during his testimony that he had great animosity toward Stippo Rakes? Or was he killed by someone else for some reason unrelated to the trial?

The jury was brought into the courtroom that morning sharply at nine, as was the routine. There was no mention of the Rakes story, nor would there be as the day wore on. The proceedings unfolded as if nothing untoward had taken place.

At the morning break, around eleven, I received a text from Pat Nee: "Stippo Rakes killed himself."

I texted back: "Yeah, it's a big buzz here at the courthouse."

I imagined that the Rakes story was all over the local TV news and lighting up the Internet.

The primary witness that day was David Lindholm, a major marijuana dealer who had been extorted by Bulger back in the 1980s. The Lindholm testimony was fascinating and at least temporarily took everyone's mind off news of Rakes's death.

Back in the late 1960s and 1970s, Lindholm had grown from being a guy who sold joints and bags of weed to his college friends into one of the largest importers of Colombian cannabis on the eastern seaboard. He was a college-educated, middle-class kid from Milton who got involved in the trade because the profits were astounding.

On the witness stand, well past his peak smuggling years, Lindholm gave off the air of someone who was now above it all. But back in 1983, the success of his smuggling operations brought him into the orbit of Jim Bulger, who was at the time solidifying his reputation as the mob boss of all New England. Anyone making big money in his jurisdiction, according to Bulger, owed him a piece of the action. Whitey referred to it as a "tax," a variation on the term "rent," which is what the old Winter Hill Mob called it when they extracted regular payments from bookies, loan sharks, and other racketeers.

On the Fourth of July weekend in 1983, Lindholm was at a party in Nantucket, where he owned a summer home. There he ran into Joe Yerardi, a former Winter Hill bookmaker he knew, though not well, and a friend of Yerardi introduced to him as Jimmy, who he later learned was Jimmy Martorano.

Lindholm had just come off the largest shipment of Colombian marijuana in his career, a load that, he claimed from the witness stand, grossed $72 million. Approximately $40 million went to the Colombians, and another $21 million went back into the business. Lindholm estimated that he had personally cleared about $4 million, tax-free.

At the party in Nantucket, the master smuggler was careful not to reveal the full nature of his business to Yerardi and Jimmy Martorano, but they got the picture.

A few days later, back in Boston, Yerardi and Martorano paged Lindholm. They met in front of the New England Aquarium, off Atlantic Avenue near the harbor. They told Lindholm there was someone who wanted to meet him. Lindholm was suspicious, but he agreed to "go through the motions of this charade." He was taken to a place called the Marconi Club, a small function hall. There he was delivered into the clutches of Jim Bulger and Steve Flemmi.

"Did Mr. Bulger make any demands of you at this time?" asked prosecutor Zach Hafer.

"Yes," said Lindholm, in a matter-of-fact manner. "He was asking me a very specific line of questioning, and initially I thought that he might be with law enforcement. He was asking me questions that a police officer might ask. I was also concerned that the building might be bugged, so I was not forthcoming with the information or answers that he was trying to elicit from me. . . . So the conversation wasn't going too well. He demanded a million dollars from me. . . . One of the persons there fired a gun off by my head. There was a silencer on it, and the chamber was open. Five bullets were dropped on the table, along with one spent casing. A bullet was put in the chamber and spun and pointed at my head, and the trigger was pulled."

"The trigger was pulled like Russian roulette?"

"Right . . . And uh, you know, we'd been dealing with a lot of Mexicans and a lot of Colombians over the years. I knew if he killed me, he wasn't going to get any money. And I wasn't going to let down my associates. I wasn't going to drop the ball on the five-yard line. I wasn't going to give him a million dollars. So I bluffed him in negotiations down to two hundred and fifty thousand dollars."

"Mr. Lindholm, the individual that initially demanded a million dollars from you and then later agreed to take two hundred and fifty thousand dollars and was in the Marconi Club as someone fired a gun by your head, do you see him in the courtroom today?"

"I do."

"Could you point him out and identify an article of clothing that he's wearing, please?"

"He's the gentleman sitting there in the blue shirt."

Perhaps in recognition of the incongruous use of the word *gentleman,* Bulger glanced over at Lindholm, which is more than he did during most courtroom identifications.

It took Lindholm a while to get out of the Marconi Club that afternoon in 1983. Bulger continued to interrogate him about various aspects of his business. "I determined that he didn't know much about me. He knew something about me, but he didn't know much. Certainly, Yerardi and everybody else did not know the scope of what we were doing on the East Coast, from Philadelphia to New York and Boston. So I tried to downplay the level of marijuana business that we were doing. He seemed satisfied when I offered to pay two hundred and fifty thousand dollars."

At all times during his testimony, Lindholm remained relaxed, even cavalier, as he described Bulger's extortion tactics. The picture he painted seemed a tad self-serving, with the younger version of himself always in control, never frightened or panicked.

As the negotiation came to an end, said the witness, "[Bulger] shook my hand, told me that I handled myself well and some other people didn't handle themselves well. . . . He told me that if I mentioned the specifics of our discussion to anyone that he would kill Yerardi and Martorano. Well, I clearly knew that wasn't true. So when they drove me back to my car, [Yerardi and Martorano] asked me if everything was okay. I said everything was all right; I had an obligation I had to take care of, and I'd be talking to them in the near future."

Hafer paused for dramatic effect. It was late in the day, and he had held off with a particular question that, if properly posed, might supply the kind of zinger that prosecutors dream of using to end a day of dramatic testimony. "Did Mr. Bulger say anything to you at that meeting, Mr. Lindholm, about what would happen if he found out you sold marijuana on your own without informing him?"

"Yeah," answered the witness. "He'd cut my head off."

Judge Casper knew a closing line when she heard one. Without missing a beat, she asked, "Mr. Hafer, given the time, is this a good place to stop?"

"Yes, Your Honor."

Before Casper was finished with her standard cautionary instruction to the jury about not discussing the case, people flooded out of the media room, where it was prohibited to use cell phones. They wanted an update on the Stippo Rakes death mystery. The courthouse was filled with media, so it was a good place to garner the latest details.

Not much new had been revealed since the body was found that morning, but speculation had moved on from suicide to the likelihood that Rakes had indeed died as a result of foul play. The body was found fully clothed but with no cell phone and no wallet. No official cause of death had yet been announced, but the scuttlebutt among reporters—many of whom had inside sources in the state police and district attorney's office—was that Rakes had been poisoned.

By later that evening, the Rakes story had gone national. Throughout the night, I received emails and texts from friends and associates outside Boston who had heard about the suspected murder on Twitter, CNN, or the Internet. An obvious conclusion was that if Rakes had been murdered, it must have something to do with the trial. It was too big a coincidence that he wound up dead on the very day that he had been scheduled to testify. Though most everyone knew that Whitey Bulger had long since been stripped of his impregnability and no longer had a gang or contacts in the underworld, the idea that the once-powerful mob boss had somehow found a way to reach into his old bag of tricks was an irresistible angle (the headline in the *Boston Herald* that day was DEAD MEN TELL NO TALES).

The notion that Bulger had Rakes whacked was plausible, but for anyone close to the case it seemed unlikely. There was no reason for Bulger to kill Rakes. It made no sense.

The following morning, once again the volume of media people and spectators arriving for the trial was higher than usual. Stephen Flemmi would definitely be taking the stand sometime later that afternoon, and the Rakes story was unfolding by the minute. The Bulger trial was the place to be.

As I grabbed my morning coffee and settled in for the day, I was approached in the hallway outside the media room by a local reporter I knew. "Hey," said the female journalist, excitedly, "did you hear the latest?"

"What?" I asked, ready for a bombshell.

"Pat Nee is being investigated for the murder of Stephen Rakes. He left a threatening note in the mailbox at Rakes's house the day before the body was found."

The reporter worked for a prominent news website; she had been covering the trial and had filed a number of stories since the trial began.

"Are you working the story?" I asked.

She nodded. "Me and others. It's ready to go. Only thing holding it back right now is the legal department."

A couple of questions raced through my head, the first being the possibility, or plausibility, that Pat Nee killed Stippo Rakes. That seemed unlikely, bordering on absurd. Not that Pat Nee wasn't capable, if he had a motive and felt that such an act was necessary. I knew that decades ago Pat sought to kill the person he believed had killed his brother Peter, shot him and left him for dead. I knew that Pat had wanted to kill Whitey Bulger, and probably still would if he could do it and get away with it. Obviously, Nee was capable of killing—at least the Pat Nee of twenty-five years ago, who was involved in gangster activity that reportedly included the burial of bodies.

But Nee had no beef with Stippo Rakes. It made no sense that he would be involved. Nee had been out of the killing business for a long time. He had written a book about his criminal career, was involved in his Discovery Channel reality show, and was now a grandfather who doted over his grandkids and gave talks to young males about not getting involved in the criminal life.

The second question that crossed my mind: why is this person telling me this? Journalists are not in the habit of sharing hot tips with other journalists. The idea that a reporter would give away their story before it had been published or broadcast was suspicious. Clearly, this tidbit was being thrown my way in the expectation I would look into it, thus helping to spread the rumor that Pat Nee had murdered Rakes.

As far as I could tell, this reporter had no idea that I knew Pat Nee, much less that Nee was a key source of mine whom I spoke with frequently about different aspects of the Bulger story. She had leaked this story to me figuring I was a writer from outside Boston who might not know the lay of the land and would jump on what appeared to be inside information on the hottest story in town.

I asked the reporter some questions about the source or sources of her information. She mentioned something about cops and family members, but her answers were vague, leaving me with the conclusion that not only was the story fraudulent, but that the reporter was deliberately feeding me disinformation. The question remained: why was she giving me this information, and who was behind it?

As the day's proceedings got under way, my head was swimming.

Much of the day was spent with Lindholm finishing his testimony. There was cross-examination and re-direct and re-cross. The proceedings were scheduled to end that day at 1 P.M. At around 12:45, the moment everyone had been waiting for arrived: Steve Flemmi was brought into the courtroom.

In his khaki pants and light green jacket, Flemmi looked like a union delegate who had just come from a work site, or a plumber, which was ironic; other than his duties as a full-time hoodlum, he'd never worked an honest day in his adult life.

Among the media, everyone had his or her own expectations about the testimony of Steve Flemmi. For the local Boston press, it was a momentous occasion, the first face-to-face showdown between two gangsters who had, over the course of a quarter century, conspired together to eliminate all underworld competition in the city and take over the criminal rackets. As with the testimony of Kevin Weeks, Flemmi would for the first time be making his accusations about "the Bulger years" with Whitey right there in the room.

The personal aspect of the testimony—the fact that Flemmi and Bulger were facing each other for the first time in a courtroom—was less significant to me than the fact that here was an opportunity to finally put all the pieces together. Steve Flemmi had been an FBI informant since the mid-1960s. He had served as an informant under Paul Rico and Dennis Condon during the Boston gang wars. He was the person who, at the behest of those two men, convinced Joe Barboza to become a cooperating witness. He also was the person who, along with Frank Salemme, planted a bomb in the car of John Fitzgerald, Barboza's lawyer, blowing off Fitzgerald's leg. He had committed that crime on behalf of the Mafia, as ordered by Jerry Angiulo. Flemmi had also been at the center of interactions between Bulger, Connolly, Morris, and the FBI.

Steve Flemmi was the Zelig of the Boston underworld. He played all sides of a complex criminal universe, including the side of law enforcement. The fact that, in the end, he betrayed everybody he ever did business with was beside the point. More than anyone else, including Jim Bulger, Flemmi was in a position to open Pandora's box and let the demons fly.

From the moment Flemmi took the stand, I sensed a problem. Partly, it was his demeanor. At seventy-nine years old, Flemmi was somewhat doddering, with limited hearing in one ear. If there were an old folks' home for once-feared and now-diminished gangsters, he would be the sergeant at arms. But it wasn't so much the physical frailties that didn't bode well as it was an issue of intellectual acumen.

There are many kinds of people operating in the criminal underworld. Some, like Bulger, are known for their self-discipline. Others are good with money. Still others are outright sociopaths and psychopaths, valuable because of their facility and enthusiasm for violence. Over the years, I made a mental note that some Boston gangsters I had met, people like Kevin Weeks, Pat Nee, and the Martorano brothers, were seemingly no different than many other working-class people I knew from the city's neighborhoods. They had been raised in the same general environment as many cops, firemen, and other civil servants. Most had, at some point, dropped out of school, but they were reasonably well-read individuals who had an active intellectual curiosity and seemed to have a sense of the world beyond their own atavistic needs of eating, sleeping, screwing, killing, and shitting.

Steve Flemmi, on the other hand, seemed to be only a step or two above an outright thug, and that was surprising. I was aware of his criminal history from having burrowed into his government debriefing file, hundreds of investigative DEA-6s from when he first became a cooperating witness and gave detailed personal versions of criminal activity going back forty years. Those facts had been further expounded upon by Flemmi having testified at three previous trials and three civil proceedings. For Flemmi to have had the criminal career he did, I was expecting someone more along the lines of Bulger, or someone like the late Buddy McLean from Somerville, or Howie Winter—criminal figures from the annals of Boston mob lore who had become key players through guile or force of personality.

But then it occurred to me—these men had all been leaders. Steve Flemmi was a follower. It could be argued that he was a master follower who had functioned and even excelled from within many different camps, and that took skill. On the streets, Flemmi had certainly been a survivor, and he had made money for himself and his partners. As a gangster, he had a long and fruitful career. But after seeing and hearing Flemmi on the stand, after observing the vacuous gaze, the slowness of his ability to mentally process information, the stuttering speech, my initial impression was that his long, highly profitable run as a gangster was an act of prestidigitation worthy of Harry Houdini.

Except, of course, that Harry Houdini escaped, and Flemmi was now in captivity. Once he was arrested in December 1994, his lack of mental capacity became a huge liability. Incredibly, in all his time as a criminal, he had never even been through a trial, much less been convicted of anything. He had never faced an extended period in jail. When Flemmi first went public with the astounding revelation that both he and Bulger were FBI informants and that they had been promised immunity from prosecution by the FBI, he believed he had the upper hand. But he and his attorney were no match for Wyshak and Kelly, who ultimately defeated Flemmi and crushed his will.

And so now, here he was, working for those very same prosecutors, a none-too-bright former gangster with many stories to tell.

Fred Wyshak stood at the lectern and led the witness through a series of questions that established his personal history: born and raised in Boston; two siblings, the infamous Vincent "Jimmy the Bear" Flemmi, and Michael Flemmi, former Boston cop convicted on criminal charges; two tours of duty as a paratrooper in Korea. The prosecutor had Flemmi point out the defendant and asked, "How long have you known Mr. Bulger?"

"Well, I met him once on one occasion in 1969, and I met him again in '74, in the middle of '74 when I came back off the lam. I met him up in the Winter Hill section of Somerville."

"Okay, and when was the last time you saw him?"

"I saw him about a week prior to Christmas in 1994."

"And did you know him from between 1974 and 1994?"

"Yes."

"What was the nature of your relationship during that twenty-year period?"

"Strictly criminal," said the witness—emphatically—as if he were concerned that someone might misinterpret the nature of their union.

Like John Martorano before him, Flemmi came to the stand having admitted to multiple murders, in his case ten. As part of his plea deal with the government, Flemmi was allowed to plead guilty to the murders he had committed along with Jim Bulger and would not be prosecuted for any others. Wyshak established that, unlike Martorano and Weeks, who had done time and were out on the street, Flemmi was a ward of the state. From deep within the prison system, where he was held in a special witness protection unit, he was every few years dusted off, prepped like a contestant on a television quiz show, and brought into court to testify at a Bulger-related legal proceeding. This time his mission was to seek and destroy the man himself.

Flemmi's time on the stand was a teaser: after fifteen minutes the trial was adjourned for the day. It was just enough of an introduction to guarantee that everyone would be back again the following morning for the big show.

I MADE ARRANGEMENTS to meet Pat Nee that night, without saying anything about the story I'd heard regarding his being investigated for the murder of Stippo Rakes. I waited until he picked me up in his Jeep on Hanover Street, and then I said, "Let's drive around a bit. There's something I heard at the courthouse today that we should talk about." As we drove around the narrow, quaint confines of the North End, past the former Angiulo brothers' headquarters at 98 Prince Street, I told Pat what I had heard from the journalist that day.

"Are you joking?" he said. "Why the hell would I want to kill Stippo Rakes?"

Nee was as curious as anybody about who might have killed Rakes. But now his curiosity was consumed by the question of who might be trying to rope him into the picture. One possible culprit was Bulger. "Could he be pulling the strings on this?" Nee said, more of a rhetorical question than a serious line of inquiry. We both doubted that Whitey had that kind of sway anymore; his power to control events in Boston had ended long ago when he went on the lam.

"Let me ask around a bit," said Nee, "see what I can find out." My guess was that Pat still had friends or contacts in law enforcement. If investigators were looking into anyone specific for the Rakes murder, no doubt that information would be spreading on the city's law enforcement grapevine.

"I've got another potential problem that has come up," said Nee.

"What's that?" I asked, wondering what could be worse, or equal, to being investigated for the most notorious murder in town.

"I was contacted the other day by some people here in the North End," he said. I knew what that meant: the Italians, that is, whatever was left of the Mafia in the neighborhood. "Kevin's testimony opened some old wounds. They're unhappy with certain things that came out at the trial. They want to have a meeting and talk about it."

"They're unhappy about what, exactly?" I asked.

"I don't know," said Nee. "That's what they want to talk about, I guess."

It seemed unusual to me that there was still any kind of a mafia faction remaining in the city, but I had been informed otherwise by a cross section of Bostonians. It was thought of as common knowledge that the boss of the neighborhood was Vincent "Vinny" Ferrara. Now sixty-three years old, Ferrara had been released from prison in 2005, after serving sixteen years on a racketeering conviction. Ferrara's twenty-two-year sentence had been reduced by Judge Mark Wolf when it was revealed that Assistant U.S. Attorney Jeffrey Auerhahn withheld evidence during Ferrara's plea negotiations. Ferrara had pleaded guilty to a second-degree murder charge—on a murder he didn't commit—believing that if he went to trial and was convicted he would spend the rest of his life in prison. What he didn't know was that the primary witness against him had tried to recant his accusations but was talked out of it by the assistant U.S. attorney.

In court, Judge Wolf excoriated the U.S. attorney's office and released Ferrara six years early.

Though he was under "supervised release" for three years and had agreed in court to a stipulation that he would not return to his life of crime, there were some who believed that Ferrara, over the last decade or so, had resumed his role as a boss of the North End.[1]

I had been wondering how remnants of the Mafia in town might react to the Bulger trial, or, for that matter, to Bulger in general. The attorney Tony Cardinale, for one, had told me on numerous occasions that his clients didn't think much of Bulger and Flemmi, referring to them as lowlifes and scumbags. The fact that the former Winter Hill mobsters had used the FBI to take down the Angiulos and others put Bulger and Flemmi—and FBI agent John Connolly—in a special category as reviled figures among mafia aficionados in Boston.

Over the years, in interviews with Nee and others in the Southie gang world, I asked if there were concerns about retribution. But by then many former Southie gangsters were being used to testify in various Bulger-related prosecutions. It didn't make much sense for the Mafia to attempt to kill, say, Weeks or Flemmi, since they were the very people who were being used to take down Connolly and Bulger.

There had been concerns, Nee told me, that the Mafia might try to kill Billy Bulger as a way to get revenge against Whitey. Or maybe they would go after one of Billy Bulger's sons, one of whom was a visible figure in city government. It was the kind of act that the Mafia in its heyday might have considered, but by the early decades of the twenty-first century, the Mafia didn't have the wherewithal to pull off such a high-profile hit, which would bring down a level of heat and attention that would eliminate whatever little rackets were left for them to muster a living from.

A more realistic possibility, thought Nee, might be that "the Italians" would attempt to harm Kevin Weeks. Now that Weeks had completed testifying against Whitey, he was vulnerable. "If they want to do anything to Kevin," said Nee, "I won't go along with that."

We drove around and talked some more. Up until then, the Bulger trial seemed to exist mostly as an artifact of history, with events from long ago, and

[1]In 2014, federal investigators leaked to local Boston media an updated assessment of the Mafia hierarchy in New England. Vincent Ferrara was not mentioned, suggesting, as Ferrara himself has claimed, that he is retired. The man federal authorities now claim is boss of the New England mafia is none other than Peter J. Limone, the man who, along with Joe Salvati, was falsely convicted for the murder of Teddy Deegan in 1968.

players whose criminal reputations had faded like the sun that was now setting over the North End, casting a golden hue. The murder of Stephen Rakes seemed to change all that. The dark uncertainties surrounding his death, the speculation over who or what was behind the circumstances of this possible homicide, seemed to pull the proceedings into the orbit of the Bulger era from long ago.

For Pat Nee, this was not a good thing. I could see his mind was working. He was back in Whitey's world trying to figure out what the hell was going on, who was pulling the strings, and whether or not he needed to watch his back.

THE FOLLOWING MORNING, Steve Flemmi was back on the stand, wearing the same clothes as the day before. He settled in for the long haul.

Flemmi would be on the stand for the better part of the next five days. His testimony lasted so long that twice it would be interrupted to bring in short-term witnesses who had been flown in from elsewhere in the country. They had been scheduled to testify on a specified date, and their travel plans needed to be accommodated. Flemmi, on the other hand, was not going anywhere.

The area of testimony that seemed to garner the most intense focus from trial observers was Flemmi's versions of the Debbie Davis and Deborah Hussey murders. The killings were so obviously outside the bounds of any ethical code, gangster or otherwise, that both Bulger and Flemmi had, over the years, been attempting to deflect culpability. Both claimed that the other had done the deed, with Flemmi taking things a step further and claiming that he had been against undertaking these murders but was talked into it by Bulger.

For sheer depravity and shock value, the witness's description of these murders belonged in a category by itself. Flemmi had described these acts in public before—in various hearings and trials—but he was now doing so within the context of his relationship with Bulger, who sat nearby in his usual Hensley shirt, blue jeans, and white sneakers, his face buried in his notepad as the witness detailed acts that stripped away any last vestige of humanity that these two men might claim to possess.

The story that Flemmi had told in previous accounts was that Debbie Davis was murdered because she had become a threat to the "organization." As the relationship between the attractive young woman and Flemmi, her much older gangster boyfriend, seemed to be coming to an end, Bulger was worried that Davis knew too much. Flemmi admitted to his partner that he had "blurted out" to Davis the fact that they met regularly to exchange information with FBI agent John Connolly. Bulger was "angry." He was especially concerned because Davis's brother, Mickey, who was an inmate at Walpole state prison on narcotics charges, was believed to have become a cooperating informant. Bulger believed that if Debbie told her brother about the Connolly connection, there was a good chance that Mickey Davis would seek to use the information to barter a deal for himself.

From the stand, when attempting to relate the detail about Debbie's brother Mickey, Flemmi mistakenly said, "Steve Davis." He was about to correct the mistake, when suddenly, from the spectators' gallery of the courtroom, Steve Davis exploded.

"That's a lie!" Davis shouted. "That's a fucking lie!" He bolted to his feet. Davis's wife, seated next to him, sought to hold him back. Armed marshals moved in from all sides.

"Mr. Davis!" shouted Judge Casper.

"There's no testimony on me being a rat, you piece of shit," declared Davis.

"Mr. Davis," repeated the judge.

Flemmi was startled, saying across the courtroom to Steve Davis, "I just told you I inadvertently made a mistake. I said it wasn't you that I was referring to."

"Mr. Davis, I need you to be respectful of these proceedings, okay? I need you to promise that you can do that."

Davis caught his breath and said, "Yes. Okay." His wife pulled him back down to his seat on the spectators' bench.

The judge turned to the jury box. "Jurors, you'll disregard anything that was said from the gallery."

Some of the jurors sat wide-eyed; they were riveted by the sudden pandemonium. Once matters settled back down, Flemmi was able to resume his tale of strangulation and murder.

On December 10, 1981, Flemmi told Davis to meet him at the house on Third Street in Southie that he had recently purchased for his mother. Among other things, the house was a symbol of the strong bond that had developed between Flemmi and Bulger. Located next door to the house of Whitey's brother, Senator Bill Bulger, the two front doors facing each other, it was also less than half a block away from the Haunty.

These two homes, Flemmi's and Bulger's, brought into proximity blood relations of both families, solidifying for these two gangsters that they were in it together. The fact that down the street was a basement burial ground connected to the two only made their bond stronger.

When Debra Davis arrived at the house, the interior was being remodeled. There was no furniture yet in it. Plastic tarps were spread around, stepladders still standing, and construction tools and equipment lying around on the floor.

According to Flemmi, as soon as Debra Davis entered the front door of the house, Bulger grabbed her around the neck. He dragged her down some stairs into the basement, never letting go of her neck. In the basement, he strangled her to death.

"I've never been able to forget it," said Flemmi from the witness stand. "It's affected me, and it's going to affect me until the day I die." He was talking about watching Bulger squeeze the life out of his former girlfriend. He claimed to have said to Bulger, "Let her pray."

"If she was already dead before you brought her downstairs, why did you say 'let her pray'?" asked Hank Brennan during cross-examination.

Said Flemmi, "Because that was a reaction on my part. . . . Because I was in a semi-traumatic state, I said, 'Let her pray.' I might have said it upstairs, I might have said it on the way downstairs, I don't remember. But that's exactly what happened, and nothing's going to change that."

Then Flemmi helped Bulger strip the clothing off Davis's dead body. Bulger went upstairs and lay down on the floor. Flemmi began pulling the teeth from the mouth of Davis, using a set of dental pliers. "It was distasteful," said Flemmi. "It bothers me now to think about it."

In court, the witness wanted everyone to know how abhorrent the killing had been and how bad it made him feel. This had validity only if you turned a blind eye to how calculating Flemmi had been following the murder: how he went to Olga Davis, the mother, and told her how concerned he was, later telling Mrs. Davis that he located travel records that showed Debra had flown out of Logan International Airport to Mexico. Flemmi paid someone to steal Debra's dental records from her dentist's office, so he could destroy them. He even made sexual advances toward Debra's younger sister, Michelle, who was sixteen at the time. And, most damning of all, a few years later, Flemmi took part in another gruesome murder of a woman in his life, his stepdaughter Deborah Hussey, under circumstances that were remarkably similar to the killing of Debra Davis.

In the annals of depraved acts by Flemmi and Bulger, the Hussey murder was another benchmark.

In his direct testimony, Flemmi insisted that, once again, it was Bulger who wanted Deborah Hussey murdered, that he was initially against it. Flemmi's story was that Deborah had become a drug addict and a part-time prostitute. She was at Triple O's one night and made a spectacle of herself, which had caused the owner, Kevin O'Neill, to warn Bulger and Flemmi that she was out of control. According to Flemmi: "[Bulger] wanted to kill her, and I told him, I said, 'Well, why don't we just send her off? I'll send her off somewhere.' I kept sending her off and she kept coming back. So it came to the point where he wanted to kill her."

On cross-examination, Hank Brennan dug a little deeper. Through a series of pointed questions, he led Flemmi into an admission that he'd been having a sexual relationship with his stepdaughter. "It was consensual," said Flemmi. No intercourse, just oral sex. The mother, Marion Hussey, had been unaware of this relationship until one night—six months prior to the murder—there was a heated argument between the three participants. Deborah Hussey told her mother that Flemmi had been molesting her for years. Marion demanded to know if this was true. Flemmi admitted that he and Deborah had been having sex but insisted that it was consensual.

"You knew that having this relationship with your stepdaughter was wrong, didn't you, Mr. Flemmi?" asked Brennan.

Flemmi squirmed in his seat. Throughout his testimony, he had exhibited a slight tic: whenever he became distressed, he began to sniffle, which he did now. "What about Mr. Bulger?" he said defensively. "We shared a lot of information, both of us, Jim Bulger and myself. And he had a young girlfriend, sixteen years old, that he took to Mexico. That's a violation of the Mann Act. So if you want to come down on me, I just want to relate to you—"

Judge Casper raised a hand and cut Flemmi off, telling him to stick to the question at hand.

"Yes, Your Honor," said Flemmi.

Brennan paused a moment. He was doing what good defense attorneys do—improvising, trying to capitalize on the fact that Flemmi was riled. "When you were asked questions [on direct examination] about why you killed Miss Hussey that day, there's something you left out about your motives, isn't there, Mr. Flemmi?"

"What did I leave out?"

"Well, you know that having a reputation as a murderer, although some people may look at it negatively, you enjoyed that reputation, didn't you?"

Flemmi shook his head. "Mr. Brennan, when I was in the military I killed a lot of Chinese. I never enjoyed that. I never enjoyed killing anyone my whole life. It was distasteful."

"There's a word in jail that's worse than 'murderer,' isn't there, and that's 'pedophile,' isn't it, Mr. Flemmi?"

"I wasn't a pedophile. You want to talk about pedophilia," said Flemmi, nodding toward Bulger, "right over there at that table."

Again, Judge Casper snapped; Flemmi was trying her patience. "Mr. Flemmi, you need to answer the question that's asked. No ad-libbing, no adding commentary, just listen to the question and answer it, okay?"

Flemmi said yes.

All eyes were on Whitey; if he were going to explode, now would be the time. But he kept his eyes down and continued to doodle on the notepad in front of him.

"In jail they call pedophiles diddlers or skinners, don't they?" asked Brennan.

Wyshak rose to his feet. "Objection. He's trying to goad the witness."

"Sustained," said the judge. "Mr. Brennan, next question."

Apparently, the defense counselor had squeezed all he could out of this exchange. So he turned his attention to the specifics of Deborah Hussey's cruel demise.

Unlike the Debra Davis homicide, where Flemmi and Bulger were the sole participants, there had been an additional witness to the Hussey killing—Kevin Weeks. In his testimony, Whitey's henchman described how he had come down from the upstairs bathroom at the Haunty to discover Bulger with his hands around Hussey's neck, rolling around on the floor. Hussey frothed at the mouth and her eyes rolled back in her head until Whitey had squeezed the life out of her petite five-foot, two-inch frame. Then they dragged her down in the basement.

Flemmi was in accordance with this description until the point where they were all in the basement. Weeks had testified that Flemmi put his ear to Deborah's chest and proclaimed, "She's not dead." He then affixed a rope around a stick, placed the stick across Hussey's windpipe, and twisted the stick so that the rope pulled tighter and tighter, cutting off every last molecule of oxygen.

Flemmi denied that any of that took place. "I definitely didn't strangle her," he said.

They stripped the body, and Flemmi, as was the routine, extracted the teeth. Then Weeks and Flemmi dug the hole in the basement, while Bulger, as per usual, went upstairs and lay down.

Asked why Bulger always lay down, Flemmi said, "I don't know. Maybe he was mentally, physically exhausted. I don't know. Maybe he got high on it or something, and he was exhausted. That's my interpretation."

For the jurors, or anyone else soaking in the testimony surrounding the murders of the two Debbies, these were among the trial's darkest days. The intimacy of the killings, and the fact that these defenseless young women stood no chance against these brute men of violence, was more than many could bear. At least two female jurors were brought to tears, and there were sniffles among the family members in the courtroom.

The details were so horrifying that they obscured an even deeper horror. For two men who took such pride in their reputations as professional gangsters, these two murders were a leap into the unknown. Although Flemmi spent considerable energy trying to explain how the killings were connected to the criminal enterprise, to anyone with a discerning intelligence this rang false. Two twenty-six-year-old women who were not part of the group and knew little or nothing about the gang's criminal activities, strangled to death. In the universe of organized crime, or any other universe, there was no justification.

Why, then, had Flemmi and Bulger engaged in these depraved acts that were an affront even to the gangster code?

Because they could.

These two men routinely murdered people, made the bodies disappear, and walked away clean. The result was that they had entered into a world of magical thinking: the belief that they were invincible had led them to increasingly more depraved acts, many of which had nothing to do with the business of crime. Having sex with underage girls, murdering young women with your bare hands, extorting people at will with no fear of ever being caught—these were the acts of men who not only thought but *knew* that they were above the law.

Delusions of grandeur? Certainly. But they could hardly be blamed.

The FBI's commitment to their two informants was all-inclusive. Amid speculation on the street and in the halls of law enforcement that Flemmi and Bulger may have played a role in the disappearance of Davis and Hussey—among other victims—special agents from the Boston division paid visits to Olga Davis and Marion Hussey. The mothers were told that the bureau was doing everything in its power to locate their missing loved ones. They were also told not to talk to any other law enforcement agencies. In the case of Olga Davis, she was eventually told by an agent that she had "nine other children to worry about" and should move on with her life.

At the same time, false theories and disinformation about the murders were disseminated through FBI reports, supposedly based on inside information from their Top Echelon Informants, who just happened to be the two men who committed the murders.

BY DAY THREE of Flemmi's testimony, defense attorney Brennan began to zero in on a line of inquiry that had gone cold weeks earlier.

Flemmi was the last chance the defense had to burrow into the history of Boston gangland and show how the Bulger era was a logical outgrowth of all that had come before. The opportunity had presented itself when, during Flemmi's direct testimony, Wyshak led the witness through a series of questions about Special Agent Paul Rico. Flemmi explained how, in the early months of the Boston gang war, he and his partner at the time, Frank Salemme, had been approached by Rico and a Boston police officer named Bill Stuart. At the time, Flemmi and Salemme were based out of Roxbury, a rough-and-tumble Boston neighborhood, and they were aligned with a criminal gang led by the three Bennett brothers, Walter, Billy, and Wimpy.

The year was 1965. Paul Rico had by then inserted himself into the gang war as an agent provocateur. Although no one knew it at the time, Rico had enlisted Buddy McLean as an informant and had sided with what would eventually become the Winter Hill Mob, based in Somerville, in its war with the Charlestown gangsters led by the McLaughlin brothers and the Hughes brothers.

The Bennett brothers of Roxbury were aligned with the Charlestown Mob, which meant that Flemmi and Salemme were, too.

At the auto garage in Roxbury, Rico convinced the two hoodlums that they should switch sides. He explained the benefits of having an FBI agent like himself backing them up. Flemmi and Salemme agreed, forging a pact with Rico that immediately escalated the gang war, leading to the murders not only of two of three McLaughlin brothers and two Hughes brothers, but also all three Bennett brothers.

Fred Wyshak, during Flemmi's direct testimony, had been willing to detail this early alliance between Rico and the witness because it showed the earliest link between the FBI and the Winter Hill Mob. In the interest of full disclosure, the prosecutors knew that they needed to be forthcoming about this "unholy alliance." Portraying Rico and later John Connolly as rogue agents was a way of controlling the narrative. This strategy had some obvious pitfalls, though.

For one, neither Connolly nor Rico was a rogue agent. Paul Rico had inserted himself in the Boston gang wars as a matter of policy; it had been a deliberate strategy on the part of the FBI to pit differing sides of the underworld against one another. The idea was to stir up acrimony so that agents like Rico could use this discord to cultivate informants by offering to take their side in the war. It worked. The cultivation of informants made Rico a star within the FBI universe, with pay raises, in-grade promotions, and letters of commendation from Hoover to prove it.

Having Flemmi detail Rico's Machiavellian ways ran the risk of exposing the immorality of what had become an unwritten strategy of law enforcement. Judge Casper, however, was not likely to let the proceedings stray too far in that direction. A far more perilous possibility was that by picking at the scab known as Paul Rico, the prosecutors might inadvertently reopen old wounds and pave the way for questions about Joe Barboza, the framing of innocent people for the Deegan murder, and the larger narrative of corruption and culpability that the government had spent the entire trial attempting to conceal.

"Mr. Flemmi," Brennan asked the witness, "at some point you learned about the Deegan murder, didn't you?"

The mood of the proceedings shifted; the ghosts of Deegan and Barboza had entered the courtroom. No creaking chairs, no coughs. The room went silent.

"Teddy Deegan was a friend of mine, yes," answered Flemmi.

"And you learned that Mr. Barboza and your brother Jimmy Flemmi were involved in that murder, didn't you?"

"I found that out after they told me. . . . I was very upset . . . If I had known about it previously, I would have prevented it. I would have told them to back off the guy."

"You knew that Mr. Barboza was working at some point with Mr. Rico as a cooperating witness, didn't you?"

"After he started cooperating, yes."

"And after Barboza started cooperating, he started implicating people in that murder that weren't even there, isn't that true?"

"Yes, that's true."

Brennan paused, knowing that his next question would likely bring an objection and a lengthy sidebar. "Mr. Rico had conversations with you about that murder and the prosecution of that murder, didn't he?"

Right on cue, Wyshak stood. "Objection. Can we have a sidebar on this?"

The five lawyers all gathered at the far side of Judge Casper's perch, away from the jury box.

Said the judge, "Counsel, what's the nature of your objection?"

Wyshak launched into what had become a well-worn melody: "Your Honor, I think that Mr. Brennan is seeking to insert the whole Limone matter into this trial. I think Mr. Carney raised it and has previously raised it. The fact that Mr. Rico and Mr. Condon may have been aware of exculpatory information during the sixties and did not provide that to state authorities, which resulted in the unlawful incarceration of certain individuals, I think is not relevant to this trial. They're just trying to insert government misconduct into this case for—I don't know. Jury nullification is the only kind of argument I think they can make."

The concept of jury nullification was obtuse, even to legal experts, but ever since opening statements Wyshak and Kelly had been trying to figure out where the Bulger defense was headed. Caught off guard by Bulger's willingness to admit to many of the charges in the indictment, they had taken a defensive posture in relation to the dirty history of Barboza and the Deegan murder, what Wyshak referred to as "the Limone matter." For the prosecution, the concern was that if the defense was allowed to give a detailed explication of the corrupt universe that had created Whitey Bulger, they would be able to say, "Yes, our client was a criminal, but he was a criminal in partnership with a corrupt criminal justice system. For you to find the defendant guilty, you must also find guilty the entire justice system. And since the justice system does not accept responsibility and cannot be held accountable, it would be unjust to pin it all on Whitey Bulger."

As a tactic, jury nullification was rarely attempted, much less successful. It had been used in the 1950s in the Deep South in cases involving the Ku Klux Klan and acts of racial violence. Racist Caucasian juries voted not guilty to crimes that had been charged, even though they knew the accused had committed the acts, because they sympathized with the defendants.

If Brennan and Carney were angling for an acquittal based on the supposition that they could so tarnish the U.S. Department of Justice that the jury would react with disgust and vote not guilty, they had work to do. That case had not yet been made. Brennan seemed to realize that if he were to make that case, now was his best opportunity.

Responding to Wyshak, Brennan explained, "This conversation [between Flemmi and Rico] about the Deegan murder and the prosecution's involvement in Limone go to the heart of this witness's state of mind. . . . What this is, it's the earliest point that we have of the formation that Flemmi knows the Department of Justice will protect their own if they become informants or cooperating witnesses and the extent that these people will go to protect them."

Judge Casper listened, then turned to Wyshak: "Counsel, why isn't it permissible, in your view, for Mr. Brennan to inquire about Mr. Flemmi's understanding of the relationship between Rico and Barboza when this was the subject, as I recall, of some questions on direct examination?"

Wyshak answered that his direct examination on this issue had been limited. "Furthermore," he added, "I don't think Mr. Rico was protecting Mr. Barboza. You know, the word *protecting,* I don't really understand what it means in this context. Rico at some point developed Barboza as a witness, quite frankly, because the Mafia had murdered two of Barboza's underlings, Mr. [Arthur] Bratsos and Mr. [Thomas] DePrisco, and Barboza agreed to cooperate against the Mafia regarding the Teddy Deegan murder. To the extent that Barboza was providing false information to the FBI about the participation of certain individuals in the murder and Rico and/or Condon supposedly knew about that and didn't disclose it to the state prosecutors, I just don't think Flemmi had that information or was part of that conspiracy. . . . We're going to have a little mini-trial about what was happening in the Limone case. . . . I just think that the probative value is very low and the prejudice is very high."

Brennan did not budge. It was his contention that Flemmi became an informant for the FBI back in 1967 expressly because of what Rico and Condon had been willing to do for Barboza. The implication was that Flemmi later carried this knowledge into his relationship with Whitey Bulger. If you were to accept the claim that Bulger had become an informant, it is probable that his willingness to do so had its roots in the Rico-Barboza-Flemmi relationship. "This issue can be no more central," said Brennan. "It goes right to the relevant issues in this case. The government has opened the door. And I know it is a damaging issue for the federal government, but it's one that exists."

The discussion did not end there. Sensing that this was a crucial moment that needed to be given its due, Judge Casper dismissed the jury for the day. The lawyers debated the issue for another half hour. Ultimately, Casper decided that she would let Brennan ask the witness certain questions on this subject, but how far she would let him go was dependent on how much Flemmi was willing to admit he knew about the nature of Rico's deal with Barboza.

The following morning, cross-examination resumed. Given the discussion that had taken place the day before, there was considerable expectation that this could be a turning point in the defense's case. If Brennan were able to make the connections he wanted to make, it was possible that the full narrative thread of corruption in Boston over the last half century could be established, helping to shed light on how the entire Bulger era had come into being.

Unfortunately, the witness was either unwilling or unable to provide the smoking gun.

At his age, with diminished hearing and somewhat attenuated mental capacities, Flemmi spun his wheels. At issue was a task that Flemmi had carried out for Rico. At the FBI agent's request, he visited his brother Jimmy the Bear at Walpole prison. His job was to make sure that Jimmy did not interfere with Barboza's cooperation in any way.

Brennan had hoped to establish that Flemmi carried out this mission because he knew, based on earlier conversations with Rico, that it would enhance his relationship with the government and provide certain benefits. Brennan asked Flemmi about his "state of mind," which was the legal ground upon which the judge had allowed him to pursue this line of inquiry.

"Mr. Brennan," said Flemmi, "all I know is [Rico] told me what to say. I went up and told my brother not to get involved. He was part of the murder."

Flemmi seemed to think that Brennan was trying to rope him into the conspiracy that resulted in the false convictions of Salvati, Limone, and others for the Deegan murder, and so he became prickly and defensive on the stand: "I had a very small role. . . . I just did what he asked me to do."

"But you knew that the government had a lot of power as far as who they were going to place in the prosecution and who they would avoid prosecuting, right?"

Flemmi sniffled and shook his head. "I can't put myself with the government, how they felt and what they were going to do. I just did what Rico asked me to do."

It was clear that Flemmi was not going to be the bombshell witness that the defense hoped he would be. Brennan dropped the subject and moved on to other issues of murder, corruption, body disposal, and the ins and outs of Flemmi becoming a cooperating witness against everyone he had ever known in the criminal underworld.[2]

---

[2] A seminal event in the Bulger saga that was, curiously, only mentioned in passing during Flemmi's testimony was a dinner meeting that took place at the home of Steve Flemmi's mother. At this meeting were Flemmi, Bulger, FBI agents Connolly, Morris, and Jim Ring,

THE GOVERNMENT PUT on the stand four more witnesses after Flemmi. Two of those witnesses—Kevin O'Neill and Richard Buccheri—were significant to the case.

O'Neill, a hulking, three-hundred-pound son of South Boston, was called to illustrate how Bulger had commandeered Triple O's as his unofficial headquarters, and how he had used the South Boston Liquor Mart and the nearby Rotary Variety store as a way to launder his illegal proceeds from drugs, extortion, gambling, and other rackets. Asked why he didn't ever say no to Bulger, O'Neill answered, "I didn't think that was smart. . .̇. He wasn't a guy to fool with."

Buccheri was an extortion victim. In the summer of 1986, he had intervened in a dispute between Kevin Weeks and a neighbor over demarcation boundaries on their properties. Buccheri got a call from Steve Flemmi, who told him that Bulger was not happy that he had stuck his nose in their business. He had to go see Bulger at Flemmi's mother's house on East Third Street.

---

who had recently taken over as head of the C-3 squad. Also present as a special guest was former agent Joe Pistone, whose exploits as an undercover agent who penetrated the Mafia would be lionized in the movie *Donnie Brasco*. It was an esteemed gathering, with the bosses of the Southie underworld socializing with the leaders of the FBI's organized crime squad in Boston. If that weren't enough, at one point Senator Billy Bulger, who lived across the courtyard from Mrs. Flemmi, entered the room so that he could view a program on Mrs. Flemmi's television. If Billy Bulger thought it was strange to see this unusual mix of good guys and bad guys dining together, he did not say so. In fact, years later, when called to testify at congressional hearings, Billy Bulger claimed to have no memory of the occasion.

The wining and dining of Bulger and Flemmi became a tradition in the Boston division of the FBI. It was revealed at the 2008 Miami trial of John Connolly that before and after his retirement in 1990, his successor as informant handler, Special Agent Nicholas Gianturco, hosted dinner parties for Bulger and Flemmi at his home that were attended by other agents, with his two young children also present in the house. At the Connolly trial, it was alleged by witness Steve Flemmi that Gianturco and at least five other agents—Connolly, John Morris, John Newton, Mike Buckley, and Jack Cloherty—received cash bribe payments from the Bulger/Flemmi organization. Gianturco took the stand and denied the payments (as have all of the agents, except for Morris), but he admitted receiving gifts from Bulger—with John Connolly acting as middleman—that included a black briefcase, a bottle of cognac, and a Lladro vase. Testified Gianturco, "They were informants. Informants were important. You don't make organized crime cases without informants. They were giving us information about the Mafia." Gianturco added that presents "didn't mean anything. They weren't getting any information from me. They weren't getting any assistance from me. Again, they were informants. They were important, and it just didn't mean anything to me other than a Christmas present."

Buccheri knew the house. He was a real estate developer who had helped Flemmi find contractors to build the cabana behind the mother's house. It was during the building of that cabana that Buccheri first met Jim Bulger and his brother, the senator William Bulger, who lived next door.

Buccheri met Flemmi at his mother's house and was led to the cabana that he had helped build, where Bulger was waiting.

"Richie," said Bulger. "Sometimes you should keep your mouth shut." Bulger banged on the table and added, "Did you know that Kevin Weeks is like a surrogate son to me?"

Then, according to Buccheri, Bulger put a shotgun to his head and threatened his family. "Richie, you're a stand-up guy. I'm not gonna kill you now, but you're gonna have to pay me."

"How much?" asked Buccheri.

"Two hundred," said Bulger.

The real estate developer was somewhat relieved. "Two hundred dollars?" he asked.

Bulger smiled. "Two hundred thousand."

When Buccheri balked, Flemmi stuck a revolver in his mouth until he nodded.

"Will you take a check?" asked Richie.

Flemmi nodded.

A check for two hundred thousand dollars was made out to Stephen J. Flemmi. The next day, Buccheri received a call from his bank requesting authorization to cash the check. "Go ahead and cash it," he told the bank manager. Then Buccheri had his secretary draw up some fraudulent paperwork to make it appear as if the transaction were a real estate deal.

It was a high price to pay, but Buccheri was happy to be alive. A few days later, he received a phone call from Steve Flemmi, who told him, "Jim Bulger says you're a friend now."

On Friday, July 26, the jury heard from the government's final witness, FBI special agent Scott Garriola, who testified about the arrest of eighty-two-year-old James Bulger in Santa Monica. After Garriola left the stand, Wyshak walked to the podium and declared, "Your Honor, the United States rests its case against James J. Bulger."

13

THE MUGGING OF FITZY

THE MYSTERIOUS DEATH of Stippo Rakes continued to hang over the proceedings for a couple of weeks, and then the mystery was solved. Rakes's murder, it turned out, had nothing to do with the Bulger trial.

Rakes had always been a bit of a hustler, an independent businessman looking to make deals. One of his deals was with a man named William Camuti, age sixty-nine. Rakes had given Camuti a significant amount of money as a loan, and Camuti, apparently, had not been able to pay him back.

The two men made arrangements to meet in the parking lot of a McDonald's in Waltham to discuss Camuti making a payment. They met in Camuti's car. When Rakes climbed into the passenger seat, Camuti had already purchased two cups of coffee at the McDonald's, one of which he gave to Rakes. What Stippo didn't know was that the coffee was laced with a fatal dose of potassium cyanide that Camuti had bought via the Internet.

Rakes complained about the coffee being bitter, but he drank enough of it to die. Camuti drove around for a while with the dead man next to him, then he dumped the body of Stippo Rakes on the jogging path in Lincoln.

Investigators were mystified until, a week later, Camuti tried to commit suicide. Detectives visited him at the hospital, and there the assailant confessed to the entire scheme.

Death has a way of exerting its presence, and the weirdly timed demise of Stippo Rakes became absorbed into the proceedings at the Moakley Courthouse, like a smell that persists even after the cause of the odor has passed. The trial was about death, or, to be exact, many deaths, and so the idea that a fresh corpse might be added to the mix had a perverse logic. The murder of Rakes became part of the ether surrounding the trial, one more violent detail in the penultimate chapter of the Bulger saga.

Now that the government had rested its case, it was the defense lawyers' turn to call witnesses to the stand.

It is a well-worn jeremiad that the burden of proof in a legal proceeding is on those making the accusations. The defense does not have to put forth a case at all, and often they will not, especially if it is believed that the accuser's case is weak or has been sufficiently undermined through cross-examination of the prosecution's witnesses. But the Bulger case was unusual. Carney and Brennan were, to an extent, attempting to put the government on trial and therefore were in the position of needing to make their case. This had been a point of contention throughout the trial, both as a philosophical position and as a legal matter. It was the position of the government that the defense did not have the legal right to pursue such a strategy, especially if their goal was jury nullification, a specious tactic not supported by case law. The battleground for this particular conflict was the defense counsel's proposed witness list.

When the trial began, the defense submitted a list of eighty names that included everyone from recent FBI director Robert Mueller to Howie Carr. The prosecutors let it be known that they would be contesting most of the names on this list on the grounds that any testimony these witnesses might offer came under the heading of "collateral matters" that had nothing to do with the trial.

Midway through the trial, defense counsel submitted an amended list of fifty names. Once again, prosecutors made it clear that, in their opinion, the list was filled with proposed witnesses who had little or nothing to do with the trial at hand. They intended to object to each and every name on the list.

Judge Casper had been avoiding this battle. Whenever the issue came up during the trial, she advised the counsel on both sides to work it out. But by the time the government was ready to rest its case, after the defense lawyers had revised their list downward again with no relenting from the government, it was clear there needed to be a hearing in open court.

The judge's ruling on the defense team's proposed witness list turned out to be one of the final indignities for the defense in a proceeding that had consistently not gone their way. Carney and Brennan came into this hearing with a list of thirty proposed witnesses that included people like Joe Salvati and Michael Albano.

Some of the names on the list were people designed to impeach the testimony of individual witnesses in the government's case, but others were there to give credence to the defense contention that Bulger's criminal career was the consequence of corruption and collaboration from within the system, and that it went back half a century. The government had been objecting to this argument all along, with support from Judge Casper, and it seemed unlikely that the parameters of the trial would change now.

Said Wyshak, "I mean, really—Joe Salvati, Your Honor? Joe Salvati?"

With a tone of incredulity, the lead prosecutor stood before Casper at the late afternoon hearing and sought to discredit and derail the defense counsel's witness list and therefore their entire case. He was largely successful. When the hearing was over, there were a total of twelve people that the judge was going to allow the defense to call as witnesses for their case.

Whatever last semblance of hope there was that the defense would be able to make a grandiose case that encapsulated the full sweep of the Bulger era had been crushed, once and for all.

Still, there were a few witnesses to be called who promised to shed new light on the Bulger fiasco, one of them being Robert "Fitzy" Fitzpatrick, the former assistant special agent in charge (ASAC) of the FBI's Boston division from 1981 to 1986.

I had come to know Bob Fitzpatrick well since the summer of 2011, when Bulger was apprehended in Santa Monica. Around that time, Fitzpatrick published a memoir about his experiences in the Boston division of the FBI. The book was called *Betrayal: Whitey Bulger and the FBI Agent Who Fought to Bring Him Down.* A scathing insider's account of the FBI's duplicitous efforts to protect Bulger and Flemmi, the book stirred up controversy and enmity among former FBI agents and members of the Boston U.S. attorney's office who had been on the job during the years of the Bulger fiasco.

After reading *Betrayal,* I contacted Fitzpatrick and we began an ongoing friendship based primarily on a desire to understand how the Bulger era ever could have been possible in the first place.

I met Fitzpatrick for the first time at his home in Rhode Island, a bucolic setting overlooking Narragansett Bay. Having read his book, I knew he'd been through hell in his efforts to challenge the FBI's insistence on protecting Bulger and preserving his status as a Top Echelon Informant. After years of making a pest of himself, and after an exemplary twenty-one-year career, Fitzpatrick was drummed out of the bureau a few years before becoming eligible for a pension.

In his early seventies, still vigorous, with skin and hair permanently bleached by the ocean air and sun, Fitzy was the classic G-man in retirement. At his home office in Rhode Island, he dug out old files on the Bulger case; we traded information and began constructing a narrative that might explain how Whitey had been able to remain in power for so long, even though, during the 1970s and 1980s, he was suspected of being involved in many murders.

"At the time," said Fitzpatrick, "I couldn't see it. Bulger was being protected by forces beyond my comprehension. I knew he was being protected, of course. Every time I tried to challenge the in-house position on having a guy who was himself a mob boss—a real no-no as far as confidential informants are concerned—I received pushback at every level. But it took a long time for me to begin to see the big picture. Probably not until the Wolf hearings and the various trials that came after that."

One of the reasons that Fitzpatrick ran into problems in Boston had been simply that he was an outsider. In 1981, FBI headquarters in Washington, D.C., made the decision to transfer Fitzpatrick from his posting in Miami to Boston, where, as ASAC, he would be second in command to Lawrence Sarhatt, who was the SAC of the entire Boston division.

Specifically, Fitzpatrick was sent to Boston to sort out what had become a nasty jurisdictional dispute between the FBI and other law enforcement agencies in the area, namely the Massachusetts State Police. There were accusations being made that the FBI's C-3 organized crime squad was interfering with other agencies' investigations into Bulger and Flemmi's activities.

Part of Fitzpatrick's mandate involved meeting Bulger, assessing his "suitability" as an informant, and filing a report with the supervisor of the Boston office.

"It was Morris who drove me to Bulger's condo in Quincy," said Fitzpatrick. "All the way there, he's telling me how much I'm going to like this guy Bulger. He's building him up, so much so that I became suspicious.

So we get to the location, Morris stays in the car. I go to Bulger's door. He answers. He's wearing a Boston Red Sox cap and sunglasses, even though he's indoors. I mean, they say the eyes are the window to the soul, and right away, I can't see this guy's soul." Fitzpatrick laughs, not so much with mirth but as if to say, What else can you do but laugh. "I put out my hand to shake his, and he ignores the gesture, leaves me standing there with my hand out. Oh, well, that's not good."

Fitzpatrick had dealt with many confidential informants in his career. He had been assigned to teach a course on the cultivation and management of informants, which is one of the reasons he'd been assigned to Boston to assess the Bulger situation. With Whitey, right away he saw that the signs were not good. Usually, an informant is solicitous when meeting someone higher up in the law enforcement chain of command. Explained Fitzpatrick, "Their entire deal with the government is based on their delivering the goods, so to speak. So they are often eager to convince you that what they have to offer is 'singular information,' as we call it. But with Bulger, it was the opposite. He was unfriendly bordering on hostile. He wanted to make it clear that he was the one in charge, not the other way around."

Once inside the apartment, Bulger did not offer Fitzpatrick a seat. They stood in the kitchen. Fitzpatrick asked, "So, what are you doing for us?" Bulger launched into a long dissertation on how he would never testify in court and how he did not expect nor did he want to be paid. "I have my own informants," he said. "I pay them for information. They don't pay me."

"I didn't say much," remembered Fitzpatrick. "I let him do most of the talking. And none of it was good, from my perspective. He was boasting that he was the boss of his own group, that he called the shots. After a few minutes of hearing this, I asked myself, What the hell am I doing here? I mean, clearly this guy thinks we work for him."

If that weren't enough to throw Fitzpatrick for a loop, all of a sudden, from another room in walks John Connolly. "He's not supposed to be there. This was supposed to be a one-on-one between Bulger and me. Connolly knows that. It was improper for him to be there."

The meeting lasted twenty minutes, then Fitzpatrick left and went back to the car. When he sat in the front seat, Morris asked, "So, what did you think?"

Fitzpatrick said, "I'm going to close him."

Morris became deadly serious and said, "No, you're not."

Decades later, Fitzpatrick remembered the moment vividly, as if he could still feel the sting. "Morris was the supervisor of the organized crime squad, but he was under me. I was his manager. For him to say that to me was an act of insubordination. I was angry. But I let it pass. I was still new to the division, had only been there three months or so." Fitzpatrick shook his head in dismay. "It was the first indication of what I was up against. And it got worse after that."

After his meeting with Bulger, Fitzpatrick returned to the office and composed a two-page memo recommending that Bulger be closed as informant.

I knew after meeting Fitzpatrick that first time that he was the kind of source a journalist or writer dreams about, someone who has been inside a particular system and then, through some sort of cataclysmic experience, is cast out of it. Bob had gone to Boston a die-hard FBI agent, a true believer and good soldier, and through his long process of disillusionment he was able to see things from a unique perspective, like a cult member who has left or been forced out of the cult.

On July 28, the evening before he was scheduled to take the stand, I met Fitzpatrick at Champion's bar, near the Westin Copley Place hotel, where he had been booked into a room by the Bulger defense team. He was with his wife, Jane, whom I had met in Rhode Island. Jane went through Bob's travails with him back in the 1980s, when he was ASAC, and also during his extended and acrimonious parting of ways with the bureau.

I said to Bob, "I hope you're ready for this. Turns out you are pretty much the one and only major witness for the defense. You are their entire case."

Fitzpatrick laughed at the obvious absurdity of his being called to testify on behalf of the defense. He was not a supporter of Bulger. "I hope they fry the bastard," he told me when we first met in 2011. But he was sympathetic to the argument that Bulger had been protected by people within the criminal justice system and was therefore, in some ways, a creation of that system. And certainly Fitzpatrick welcomed the opportunity to explain to a jury and the public what happened to someone within the system who went against the grain.

"I'm hoping that testifying at this trial can maybe bring us some closure," said Bob. "Because that's what Jane and I have never had."

"Well," I said, "one question you will need to answer for yourself before you take the stand: was Bulger an informant or not?"

Bob had been following the trial; he knew the defense had been attempting to make the argument that Bulger never was an informant, that his role as a TE was a fictional creation of the FBI.

"He was an informant," said Bob. "But that was the problem. He had been allowed by Connolly and Morris to believe that he wasn't an informant, or at least that he didn't have the obligations that were expected of someone who was an informant."

Fitzpatrick remembered how every time someone from the bureau was taken by Morris and Connolly to meet Bulger, they were told, "Don't treat him like an informant. He's sensitive about that." Apparently, Bulger's handlers had finessed the relationship in such a way that for them to receive information from Bulger and Flemmi, they allowed Bulger to believe whatever he wanted to believe. Meanwhile, they hyped up his informant file with information sometimes pilfered from other files. Said Fitzpatrick, "Anything of value that could be used against LCN, that came from Flemmi. Thanks to Connolly, Bulger got equal credit for anything that came from Flemmi. That also went into Bulger's file."

I asked Fitzpatrick about a particular FBI summit meeting that I knew would come up. An earlier witness, Special Agent Gerald Montanari, had testified about a meeting that he attended, along with Fitzpatrick, in Washington, D.C., at FBI headquarters. The meeting had taken place in the wake of the Wheeler, Callahan, and Halloran murders, all of which stemmed from the alleged involvement of the Winter Hill Mob in the World Jai Lai operations. At the time of this meeting, the FBI field office in Oklahoma was investigating the Wheeler murder and had made accusations that they were not receiving full cooperation in Boston.

The D.C. meeting was attended by Boston supervisors, supervisors from FBI headquarters, and other representatives of the Justice Department. It was the most high-level meeting to ever take place on the issue of Bulger and Flemmi. At this meeting, everyone had a chance to speak his mind. If there was to be a point of recognition or understanding on the part of DOJ that the Bulger-Flemmi relationship was out of hand or had gone bad, now was the time to take action. Instead, the primary concern of those gathered at this meeting was to protect their informants and see to it that the Bulger-Flemmi connection was kept confidential.

I asked Fitzpatrick, "In retrospect, do you wish you had spoken up at that meeting?"

I could see the cloud come over Bob. I knew this was a sore subject. Even though Fitzpatrick's book, *Betrayal*, portrayed him as a crusader and quasi-whistle-blower, I knew that in many ways Bob was haunted by the belief that he could have done more. His efforts to close Bulger as an informant had been met with such vehement resistance that, in some ways, he eventually became defeated and stopped trying. The meeting in Washington, for Fitzpatrick, had been the ultimate missed opportunity.

"I think by then, I had lost my faith in God," he told me.

The loss of faith was no small thing. Fitzpatrick had grown up in a Catholic orphanage in New York City. Early in his young adulthood, he entered a pre-seminary with the thought of becoming a priest. He left to join the military and later the FBI, but issues of devotion and faith remained paramount in his life and career.

I let the subject drop. Bob's daughter was also in town and had joined us at Champion's; the gathering had turned into a family get-together for the Fitzpatricks rather than a pre-testimony strategy session. Bob was concerned about whether or not he was prepared for what he anticipated might be a vigorous cross-examination by the government. He'd had a couple of conversations with Carney and Brennan to discuss his testimony, but not as much preparation as he would have liked. "I'm not sure that I'm fully ready for this," he said. But family matters had taken precedence; he would take the stand the following morning whether he was ready or not.

I left Fitzpatrick that evening with the hope that everything would be okay, though, in truth, neither Fitzpatrick nor I had any idea what he was likely to encounter in his time on the stand.

ON MONDAY, THE trial resumed with a renewed air of expectation. Partly, this was due to the fact that it was the first day of the defense case, time for a new angle on the evidence and fresh issues to be raised.

There were unresolved matters: For one, would Pat Nee be called to the stand? The defense was still claiming that they intended to call Nee, but the prosecution countered that for Nee to take the stand and be made to take the Fifth in front of the jury would be improper. The judge had been kicking this issue down the road but made it clear that it would need to be resolved shortly.

Another issue: would Bulger testify? On numerous occasions, Carney had been asked about this. If Bulger were to take the stand it would require scheduling issues. There would need to be a hearing to discuss what issues Bulger would be allowed to testify about. It would likely extend the trial another week or more. Not to mention that it would create a media frenzy that might require special security measures at the courthouse.

"My client has not yet made up his mind," is all that Carney would say. If Bulger did testify, added Carney, he would be brought to the stand as their closing witness.

Meanwhile, Robert Fitzpatrick was brought into the courtroom and led to the witness stand.

"Good morning, sir," said the judge.

"Good morning, Your Honor," said the witness.

Hank Brennan, standing at the podium, asked, "Over the course of your life, sir, did you work in a particular area?"

"Yes, I did."

"Could you tell the jury where?"

"In the FBI for twenty-one-plus years."

Brennan led Fitzpatrick through his resume, which involved many significant cases, including, as a young agent, being at the scene of the Martin Luther King Jr. assassination; working undercover to infiltrate white supremacist organizations in Mississippi; and the ABSCAM political corruption investigation of the 1980s that led to the conviction of a sitting U.S. senator.

Fitzpatrick likes to talk; he's an Irish storyteller whose stories lead from one story into another. Brennan seemed content to let the witness ramble, which brought vigorous objections from prosecutor Brian Kelly on the grounds of "unnecessary narrative," "hearsay," and "lack of relevance."

Through it all, Fitzpatrick painted a picture of an FBI conspiracy to protect Bulger that boggled the mind. His efforts to close Whitey as an informant touched off a chain reaction within the Justice Department that only deepened and broadened, the more pressure he applied. The clearest indication of what Fitzpatrick was up against was when he attempted to get informant Brian Halloran into the witness protection program.

The South Boston hoodlum was being handled by the team of Special Agents Montanari and Brunnick. At the time, the investigation into the murder of Roger Wheeler in Tulsa was gaining steam. Halloran was claiming to have been originally given the task of killing the owner of World Jai Lai that was eventually carried out by John Martorano.

As ASAC, Fitzpatrick played a role in the management of Halloran as a potential informant against Bulger and Flemmi. "It was creating problems," explained the witness. "I told headquarters the we were in a double-bind situation. . . . I continually voiced my opinion that you can't have Bulger as an informant given the situation that I discovered in my initial meeting [with Bulger]. You have a guy telling you he's not an informant, that he's never going to testify. . . . That automatically in my opinion and according to the book would nullify him as a trusted informant. He may be an informant in name. You can call him whatever you want, but if the subject doesn't believe that, as far as he's concerned, that he's an informant—it's a rather unique and complicated way of expressing that a lot of informants don't want to be labeled as informants, and they say they're not. In some cases, they're not; in other cases, they say that for ego gratification, for power, and for a host of other reasons they don't want to be called an informant."

With Halloran as an informant and potential witness against Bulger, Fitzpatrick had a more immediate reason for not wanting Bulger's informant status to stand. "We couldn't have Bulger giving us information on murder cases because he had now become the subject of a murder investigation."

"Did you make that clear to Washington?" asked Brennan.

Fitzpatrick pointed out that in his memo to headquarters he not only made it clear, it was in the title of his report.

"And when Washington wouldn't do anything to close [Bulger's file], what did you do?"

"Well," said Fitzpatrick, "in a quasi-military organization, there's a fine line between insubordination, telling my superiors what to do, and making recommendations. I could express the fact that I didn't like things, but I can't come right out and say, 'Close this guy.' I can be very vocal, and I was. I could be adamant about my position, and I was. I explained to them that we have a problem here."

"Did Washington follow your advice?'

"No."

The FBI agents handling Brian Halloran felt they needed to get him off the street—pronto. "We thought he was going to get whacked, murdered," said Fitzpatrick.

As ASAC, it fell on Fitzy to contact Justice Department New England Strike Force chief Jeremiah O'Sullivan, from whom he needed authorization to initiate Halloran into WITSEC, the Witness Security Program.

"So when you went over to see Mr. O'Sullivan," asked Brennan, "what happened during that conversation?"

Fitzpatrick opened his mouth to speak.

"Objection!" shouted Brian Kelly.

"Sustained, sustained, sustained," said the judge, drowning out the witness, who had started to give an answer.

Brennan said to Fitzpatrick, "Without saying what the conversation was, did you have a conversation with Mr. O'Sullivan?"

"I did."

"Did he agree to put [Halloran] in the witness protection program?"

Again, Kelly was on his feet. "Objection. Leading."

"Sustained as to that question," said Casper. She turned to Brennan: "Do you want to ask him what did you do as a result of that conversation?"

Said Brennan to Fitzpatrick, "As a result of your conversation with Mr. O'Sullivan, was Halloran placed in the witness protection program?"

"No, he was not."

"During that conversation with Mr. O'Sullivan, without saying what was said, what was your temperament?"

"Anger."

"What was Mr. O'Sullivan's temperament?"

Kelly stood to object, but Fitzy got his answer in before the objection: "He was adamant against."

"Objection!" shouted Kelly. In making so many objections, the prosecution was following legal protocol, but they were also protecting the reputation of the Boston U.S. attorney's office—their office—formerly led by Jeremiah O'Sullivan.

As Fitzpatrick recalled it, after getting no satisfaction from O'Sullivan, he sought to go over his head to William Weld, the U.S. attorney who would later become governor.

Asked Brennan, "When you went to see William Weld, was your objective the same as when you went to see Mr. O'Sullivan?"

"My objective was to complain that we're not doing enough to put Halloran in the witness protection program and get him out of harm's way."

"When you spoke to William Weld about your complaints, was Brian Halloran put into the witness protection program?"

"No."

"How many days after you spoke to William Weld was it that Mr. Halloran and Mr. Donahue were murdered?"

"Two days."

With their key witness now dead, the FBI's investigation of the murder of Roger Wheeler had been dealt a potentially insurmountable blow. In the wake of this fiasco, Fitzpatrick, on May 25, 1982, was called to the big conference in Washington, D.C., attended by Special Agent Montanari, as well as Jeff Jamar, unit chief for the Boston organized crime division; Randy Prillaman, the FBI's national informant coordinator; and Sean McWeeney, chief of the bureau's Organized Crime Section. At this summit meeting, which took place at FBI headquarters, inside the building of the U.S. Department of Justice, Fitzpatrick assumed there would be a discussion about the Wheeler and Halloran murders. Instead, the primary concern, as expressed by Chief McWeeney, was the New England Strike Force's budding case against Jerry Angiulo and the Mafia.

Fitzpatrick was stunned. In his view, FBI headquarters should have been concerned that people were being murdered by gangsters whom they were operating as informants. Instead, their main concern seemed to be, How do we protect our informants from exposure?

The result of this meeting represented a watershed moment in the conspiracy to cover up the Bulger fiasco. In a memo written by ASAC Fitzpatrick, summarizing this meeting and a series that followed, it was stated: "It was mutually agreed that agents actively working the Wheeler case would coordinate information with SA Connolly's sources so that this matter can be quickly and effectively resolved."

In other words, headquarters was kicking the ball to John Connolly, a street agent, designating him to coordinate with Bulger and Flemmi, meaning they were setting up Connolly as a fall guy in the event of future exposure.

In court, after reading from the memo, Brennan asked Fitzpatrick whether he agreed with what was being suggested by headquarters.

"Well," said Fitzpatrick, "again, that was one of the problems, the double bind. Here we are being instructed to deal with Connolly, where his source, Bulger, is a subject in the murder that we're going to go talk to the informant agent about. It didn't make much sense. And, quite frankly, we discussed that. We discussed that it was like leading the fox into the chicken coop."

"Did you discuss that in Boston or did you discuss that in Washington?"

"Both."

Fitzpatrick's direct testimony lasted two hours. His time on the stand ended with the agent detailing how his attempts to close Bulger as an informant ended with his being forced to take a demotion and cut in pay and the loss of his pension. It was a sorry statement on the nature of institutional retribution and designed to elicit sympathy for a man who had gone against the grain and paid a heavy price. Fitzpatrick's story was a cautionary tale, one that—the jury was encouraged to believe—made him worthy of respect, if not admiration. Then Brian Kelly stepped up to the podium.

As a prosecutor, Kelly had during the trial shown occasional moments of belligerence and scorn. In various hearings before the judge, with the jury out of the room, and at sidebars, he could barely contain his contempt for the defense, especially when their arguments veered toward a critique of the Boston U.S. attorney's office or the Justice Department's role in enabling Bulger and Flemmi. For Wyshak and Kelly, the Bulger case was personal. Their mandate was to convict Bulger, but it was also understood that part of their role was to protect and salvage the reputation of the system they served.

As his first question, in a tone both blunt and accusatory, Kelly asked, "Sir, it's fair to say, isn't it, that you're a man who likes to make up stories?"

Fitzpatrick was taken aback: "I beg your pardon."

Kelly became even louder and more insistent: "You're a man who likes to make up stories, aren't you?"

"No," said the witness.

"In fact, for years you've been trying to take credit for things you didn't do, isn't that right?" Kelly was not asking questions that required an answer; he was calling the witness a liar. "In the beginning of your testimony, didn't you gratuitously claim credit for arresting the mob boss Jerry Angiulo?"

"I did arrest Angiulo," said Fitzpatrick.

"Okay. That's your testimony under oath, sir?"

"Yes."

"Sir, isn't it a fact that the case agent on Angiulo was Ed Quinn?"

"Yeah, he was a ride-along with me. I was the ASAC in charge. I went to the table and put the arrest right on Angiulo." The mafia boss had been arrested at Francesca's restaurant while eating lunch.

"That's a total bald-faced lie, isn't it?" bellowed Kelly, in a voice so loud that it startled some in the jury. "You had nothing to do with that arrest, did you?"

"Were you there?" asked Fitzpatrick, facetiously.

Kelly showed the witness an FBI 302 arrest report, written by Special Agent Ed Quinn. There was no mention of Fitzpatrick.

Said the witness: "This is [Quinn's] report. I can tell you categorically that I arrested Angiulo. I advised him of his rights. I was there at Francesca's."

This particular line of attack on Fitzpatrick was inside baseball, Boston-style. Ed Quinn was one of the agents whose role in the Angiulo investigation had been highlighted in the book *Underboss*. Quinn had served in the FBI's Boston office for many years and was friendly with people in the U.S. attorney's office and also with reporters and book writers in Boston. Who deserved credit for the Angiulo arrest had been a bone of contention ever since Fitzpatrick published an account in his own book. By seeking to expose Fitzpatrick, Kelly was acting, in part, on behalf of Quinn and others in Boston law enforcement who were no fans of Bob Fitzpatrick.

Kelly spent a significant amount of time on the details of the Angiulo arrest, using Quinn's report to berate the witness, then he turned his attention to the Martin Luther King Jr. assassination. "Haven't you in fact pretended that you were the one who found the rifle that killed Martin Luther King? Haven't you made that claim in the past?"

"I found the rifle when I was at the scene. I was the first FBI agent at the scene, and I found a rifle coming down the stairs, having just missed James Earl Ray, the shooter. The rifle was in the alcove, and there's a report on that, a court report."

"That's another outright lie, isn't it, sir?"

"The court report?"

"No, your testimony just now. Isn't it true that three Memphis police officers found the rifle that was used to kill Martin Luther King, not Bob Fitzpatrick?"

"I found the rifle along with them. They could have been there . . . but I'm the one that took the rifle, transported it to the bureau, submitted it to the forensic people."

Kelly pounced. "Wait a minute, wait a minute." His voice rose in indignation. "Transporting something is like being a courier, a gofer. That's not finding it, right?"

Kelly had worked with detectives and federal agents his entire career; he knew that some in law enforcement have a tendency to overstate their role in a particular case, especially a high-profile one. Retired lawmen often refer to a case they were involved in as "my case," even if their role was merely supportive. Fitzpatrick had this tendency, and it was now being used as a broad, sweeping brush to portray him as an inveterate liar.

The first thirty minutes of Kelly's cross-examination were a relentless assault. No witness thus far in the trial had been on the receiving end of such aggressive and accusatory questioning, not even gangsters like Martorano and Weeks. The prosecutor was seeking to decimate Fitzpatrick's credibility. And he was doing so by using subjects that, thus far, had nothing to do with the Bulger case.

Kelly and Wyshak knew that Fitzpatrick's status as a loyal public servant gave added weight to his allegations about the system's coddling of Bulger and Flemmi. In order to undermine the witness's testimony about the government's complicity in the Bulger fiasco, Kelly apparently felt that he first needed to destroy Fitzpatrick's credibility as a man of honor.

The trial adjourned for the day at a point where Kelly was just getting warmed up. Fitzpatrick would have to return to the stand the following morning, for more of the same.

I was supposed to meet Fitzpatrick that evening. When I called him, he was busy doing an interview for the CNN documentary crew that had been covering the trial from the beginning. I could tell from Fitzpatrick's voice that he was disappointed by the tone of Kelly's questioning, that once again, as during his time on the job, he was under attack for questioning the government's role in enabling Bulger.

"Let's meet tomorrow when I'm off the stand," he said.

The following morning, Fitzpatrick arrived at the courthouse, knowing that he was going to again be pummeled. The prosecutors seemed to be acting on behalf of people whom he had named in his book, maybe former colleagues of Wyshak and Kelly. As they say on the street and sometimes in the halls of justice: payback is a bitch.

Sure enough, for the remainder of Fitzpatrick's cross-examination Kelly referred frequently to *Betrayal,* sometimes quoting from its pages and even calling into question the placement of certain photographs in the book.

Betrayal was indeed problematic for Fitzpatrick. The book had been written by a crime fiction writer chosen by the publisher. Fitzpatrick had been interviewed extensively by the writer, but his contributions to the actual writing of the book were minimal. The author leaned heavily on fictional storytelling techniques, including reconstructed dialogue and instances of dramatization. The same could be said about the books of other witnesses, most notably Colonel Thomas Foley, John Martorano, and Kevin Weeks. Tom Foley's book had been portrayed as peripheral and insignificant by Fred Wyshak. The books of Martorano and Weeks were hardly mentioned.

In Fitzpatrick's case, his book was used as Exhibit A to portray him as an unrepentant fabulist.

"Didn't you use phony dialogue between James Bulger and John McIntyre in your book?" asked Kelly.

"It's probably part of the research," explained the witness.

Kelly read a particularly hyperbolic passage of hard-boiled dialogue between Bulger and murder victim McIntyre. There were titters in the court-room. "That's completely made up, isn't it?" asked Kelly.

"I had a coauthor," said Fitzpatrick. "So it could have been part of his narrative."

"So it's your coauthor's fault, you think?" Kelly's tone was thick with sarcasm.

"I don't know."

"Like sometimes it's headquarters's fault when you couldn't get things done in Boston, now it's your coauthor's fault here?"

"I didn't say it was his fault. I just said he coauthored it, and I don't recall that particular aspect of the writing of the book."

Kelly pondered that and asked, "Do you think the McIntyre family, upon reading a little dialogue like that, would be pleased to see this phony dialogue?"

Using the McIntyre family was rich. The U.S. government, whom Brian Kelly represented, had fought the McIntyre family tooth and nail, along with all the families of Bulger's victims, in their civil lawsuit against the U.S. Justice Department and the U.S. attorney's office. Now Kelly was shamelessly using the aggrieved party as a cudgel to beat Fitzpatrick.

The onslaught continued. Kelly noted that in Fitzpatrick's testimony in the Wolf hearings, he never expressed that he was angry with Jeremiah O'Sullivan for not putting Halloran into the witness protection program. Said Kelly, "Back in 1998, when you were testifying under oath, [O'Sullivan] was still alive and could refute your claims, couldn't he?"

"I don't recall the exact date he died," answered the witness.

"Well, he's dead now, right?"

"As far as I know."

"Pretty easy to blame a dead guy, isn't it?"

Fitzpatrick had been mostly unflappable, but now he snapped. "Listen, that's an insult as far as I'm concerned."

"Isn't that what you're doing?"

"No, that's not what I'm doing. And that's a blatant insult."

The prosecutor and witness began talking over one another in a verbal scrum until the judge interceded: "Mr. Kelly, let him finish his answer."

The defense team rarely objected; they did not come to Fitzpatrick's defense, which seemed odd. The previous day, as Kelly's questioning became more and more vituperative, Brennan had objected. But today he was willing to let Kelly swing away. It seemed as though the defense team, the day before having seen the tenor of Kelly's cross-examination, overnight made a strategic decision to let the prosecutor beat up on the witness, and in so doing reveal to the jury how the government treats someone who goes against their program. Kelly's bullying posture and general temperament was so over-the-top, so disrespectful of a legitimate public servant, that he ran the risk of alienating the jury. Thus Fitzpatrick became a sacrificial lamb; he would be relentlessly pummeled without objection, in the interest of Whitey Bulger's legal defense.

AFTER FITZPATRICK FINISHED his testimony, I met with him at the Marriott Long Wharf hotel, where he had moved from his previous accommodation. We sat down at the bar of the hotel, overlooking the inner harbor and Christopher Columbus Park. It was fair to say that Fitzpatrick was shell-shocked, but he remained jocular.

"Jane's taking it badly," he said, referring to his wife. She had not been in the courtroom during the cross-examination but followed it via Twitter. Said Fitzpatrick, "This has been going on for decades. I felt like I was the one on trial, back in the mix, defending myself."

It was a glorious summer day, with seagulls swirling and tour boats pulling up to the dock just outside our window on the second floor of the hotel. The pleasant conditions belied the brutal display that Fitzpatrick had just undergone.

"I knew they'd throw stones," said Bob. "Some of it had come up at other trials. But Kelly's attitude was something new. He was acting like a hit man."

Fitzpatrick was especially upset that as his closing volley, Kelly had quoted from his settlement agreement with the FBI. Fitzpatrick's understanding of that agreement was that it would remain confidential. Fitzpatrick had signed that agreement with the U.S. Justice Department, and now here it was being used against him by a representative of that same department.

I asked Fitzpatrick about his now-famous memo, the one he wrote after meeting Bulger at his condo in Quincy. In that memo, he suggested that Whitey Bulger be closed as an informant. Kelly had made an issue of the fact that the memo was never located, suggesting that Fitzpatrick lied and the memo never existed. Bob shook his head. "Don't you think I'd like to know what happened to that memo? I sent it to Larry Sarhatt, who I believe wanted to close Bulger. He might have put it in his office safe and the memo was later destroyed by James Ahearn [Sarhatt's successor]. Or maybe Sarhatt forwarded it to HQ and it was buried. I don't know."

As with everyone I knew whose life had been drawn into the Bulger fiasco on both sides of the law, Fitzpatrick could not shake the past. In his mind, one of the FBI men most responsible was John Morris, even more so than Connolly. "He was Connolly's direct supervisor. If Connolly's tendency to identify with his informant, to kowtow to Bulger, was to ever be corralled it should have been done by Morris."

Fitzpatrick remembered Morris back in the early 1980s showing him a book he was reading on the pathology of lying. To Bob, Morris was a classic example of the "superego lacuna," the psychological term for someone who has holes in his or her conscience. "He conned Connolly, the bureau—everybody."

Then there was Jeremiah O'Sullivan, who used to distribute pamphlets to fellow prosecutors and agents about how to root out corruption.

As Fitzpatrick sipped his drink and nursed his wounds, he was still having a hard time understanding how, in the eyes of those who took an oath and pledged allegiance to the concept of morality and justice, he was seen as the bad guy.

In retrospect, the mugging of Fitzy had been inevitable. Fitzpatrick's presence in the courtroom was a rebuke to generations of cops, agents, and prosecutors, from New England to Washington, D.C., who were part of the universe that helped create Whitey Bulger. After his direct testimony, Brian Kelly could have said, "No questions, Your Honor," and it would not have affected the government's case. Fitzpatrick's testimony had little or nothing to do with the specific charges against Bulger. But Kelly, in his role as interrogator, was not there to serve the case. He was there to settle old scores, to assume the role of the Great Avenger on behalf of a system that still had much to hide.[1]

THE DAY AFTER Bob Fitzpatrick left town, the issue of Pat Nee finally came to a head. Ironically, it was Nee himself who forced the issue.

As a consultant and also one of the key on-camera performers in *Saint Hoods,* the Discovery Channel reality show, Nee and the rest of the cast had been invited by the producers to a promotional screening and after party in Los Angeles. They would all be flown out to the West Coast and put up in a nice hotel for what amounted to an all-expenses-paid, four-day vacation in Southern California.

The date for the screening and party was set for August 2. But Nee was still under subpoena and required to stay in the area as long as the likelihood remained that he would be called to the stand. So Nee and his lawyer, Steve Boozang, decided to force Bulger's hand. In a written motion filed with Judge Casper, Boozang requested that Bulger's defense counsel be required to put up or shut up. Boozang stated that his client had an out-of-town commitment that had been scheduled for months, and that if Nee were, in fact, to be called to the stand, it should take place immediately so that his client could honor his commitment. He should not be held under subpoena indefinitely.

Early on the morning of July 31, before the jury was present, Boozang and Nee arrived in courtroom number eleven at the Moakley Courthouse.

---

[1] The desire on the part of Bulger prosecutors to punish Robert Fitzpatrick continued after the trial was over. On April 30, 2015, Assistant U.S. Attorney Fred Wyshak announced that Fitzpatrick was being indicted on six counts of perjury and six counts of obstruction of justice stemming from his testimony at the trial. Specifically, the indictment stated that Fitzpatrick had "knowingly made false and misleading declarations" in his retelling of criminal cases he was involved in previously in his career, most notably his claim that as a young FBI agent in Memphis he had been among the first to arrive at the scene of the assassination of Martin Luther King Jr., and also that he had physically made the arrest of mafia boss Gennaro Angiulo at Francesca's restaurant in 1986. Fitzpatrick was arrested and brought handcuffed into court to face the charges. It was an astounding turn of events, and a seemingly blatant act of retaliation on the part of prosecutor Wyshak. Even *Boston Globe* columnist Kevin Cullen, who had ridiculed Fitzpatrick in print during his time on the stand, referred to the indictment as "vindictive." Facing charges that could, upon conviction, result in up to sixteen years in prison, Fitzpatrick was slated to go to trial in fall 2015.

Pat took a seat in the back. Though the spectators' gallery was mostly full with media, family members of victims, law enforcement people, and others, Nee was struck by the fact that no one seemed to recognize him. Except for one person: Jackie Bulger, Whitey's brother.

Jackie had been a mainstay at the trial, the only member of the Bulger family to attend every day. The younger Bulger looked over, saw Nee, and quickly looked away. Whitey, on the other hand—seated at the defense table with his back to the spectators' gallery—seemed unaware that Nee was even in the courtroom.

Whitey's former partner and current nemesis had no idea whether or not he was going to be called to the stand. He had been told by his lawyer that it was possible. To Nee, it hardly mattered. He had committed to memory his Fifth Amendment invocation, and if called to the stand he would take the Fifth.

After Steve Boozang introduced himself to the judge and counsel from both sides as Nee's lawyer, Judge Casper called them all over to a sidebar. The entire discussion about Nee's fate took place beyond earshot of everyone in the courtroom, including Nee.

Boozang started by saying, "Your Honor, Mr. Nee intends to assert his Fifth Amendment privilege on each and every question other than his name and where he lives. I think Mr. Bulger has ensnared him in some very serious allegations. I think that questions from Mr. Carney, whatever circus he intends to perform today—"

Carney jumped in: "Your Honor, I object. I object. There's—Mr. Boozang—I don't think he is aware that he is prohibited from this kind of commentary instead of just providing legal argument. I know he doesn't understand it. And—"

Casper cut off Carney, saying to Boozang: "Counsel, obviously, just focus on the arguments."

"Certainly, Your Honor," said the lawyer. He was hopped up and had come to the courtroom ready to rumble.

Judge Casper sought to get to the heart of the matter. The burden was on Carney to provide some sort of explanation for why they should call Nee. "I've reviewed the case law on this," she said. "Mr. Carney, can you make a proffer to me about what you're planning to inquire about?"

Carney explained that he was going to ask Nee about a video currently on the Internet, a promotional spot for the Discovery Channel reality show where Pat Nee talks about being a bookmaker in South Boston. "[Nee] has the confidence to not only put this in a video, but to publicize it. I suggest that this supports the fact, an argument we've made, that he is receiving special protection from the government." Carney then offered that there was a second matter he planned to ask about. "I intend to ask him a question concerning whether or not he is a Top Echelon Informant. That is not a question to which he could assert a privilege, because if a person is a Top Echelon Informant, he isn't committing a crime by answering that."

Said Casper, "And, Counsel, how are either of those areas relevant to the charges in this case against Mr. Bulger?"

"Because it will present evidence to the jury of how they pick and choose who they want to have prosecuted. And they make deals, and sometimes those deals involve not even charging someone with a crime."

"May I respond, Judge?" asked Boozang.

"Yes, you may."

"When most of us have grown up, we didn't have reality TV shows. It's a reality-based show. They had lawyers on the show to make sure nothing they did was improper. It's a reality-based show; he's earning a living. It has nothing to do with bookmaking. He was never a bookmaker."

In response, Carney continued to make his argument, though it was apparent that his main motivation was to get Nee into the courtroom, to put him on the stand before the jury, even though he knew that no matter what questions he asked, Nee would claim the Fifth. The only interesting point behind Carney's argument was: why was he even making this argument?

"I racked my brain over the weekend," said Boozang to Judge Casper. "What could Mr. Carney possibly think up to ask Mr. Nee? Then I said, forget that, let's get to the real source here. It's Mr. Bulger." Boozang speculated that the entire matter was a ploy by Bulger to drag Nee into the proceedings. "He's doing the same thing he's done before, except it's Mr. Carney and Mr. Brennan who are his handlers, his FBI handlers, and he's going to—"

Casper raised a hand and cut the lawyer off before he could extend his metaphor, saying, "All right, Counsel, I get your argument. . . . I have heard the proffer from Mr. Carney about the areas of questions, that he's planning to inquire about this YouTube show and Mr. Nee running some bookmaking crew in South Boston, and also inquire about whether he's a Top Echelon Informant. . . . I don't see how this is relevant to the case."

The judge's ruling was clear, but still Carney pleaded. "I accept your honor's ruling regarding whether or not it's relevant that he has been a Top Echelon Informant against the Irish Republican Army on behalf of the Central Intelligence Agency."

Boozang glared at Carney, dumbfounded. Where was this coming from? And why was Carney attempting to slip it into the record? There was only one answer: Bulger.

Carney continued with his argument, until Judge Casper finally drove a stake into his proffer and declared, "I'm not going to allow any of that, Counsel. Okay?"

"Okay," said Carney, finally conceding defeat.

With the sidebar concluded, Boozang strolled to the back of the courtroom, nodding for Nee to follow as he exited through the swinging doors. Out in the hallway, he told his client, "That's it. You can go. Have a good time in California."

Nee left the courthouse with a bounce in his step. There was a reporter and a photographer out on the sidewalk; they shouted a couple of questions at Nee. But he kept strolling purposefully toward a car that was waiting for him.

Later that day, I spoke to Pat on the phone.

"I had no idea what was going to happen," he explained about his brief time in the courtroom. "I was ready to take the stand if I had to. I was ready to take the Fifth. But luckily that never happened." There was a lightness in Nee's voice, as if a weight had been lifted. He could hardly believe that he was now free and clear of the Bulger trial.

We spoke a few more minutes before Nee said, "Hey, I gotta go. Busy packing for my flight. I'm off to Hollywood."

14

OUT WITH A WHIMPER

IN ITS LAST week of testimony, the Bulger trial sputtered toward the finish line. Since the defense counsel's case had been gutted and their witness list decimated by Judge Casper, the defense of Whitey Bulger came down to a handful of former FBI agents, none of whom was a defender of the defendant. One by one, the retired agents were called to the stand, men mostly in their seventies far removed from their years in the Boston division of the FBI. They had been called by the defense to detail their personal experiences within a division of agents that, over time, began to feel more and more like an appendage of the city's criminal underworld.

On the outside, special agents and supervisors of this era looked like any other legitimate FBI agent. They showed up for work on time and wore the requisite suit and tie. You could not tell by looking at them that anything was amiss. When there were problems related to strange happenings in the office, honest agents turned to other agents and supervisors in the chain of command because they thought they could be trusted; that they would keep their entreaties confidential in accordance with bureau procedure; and that they would share the concern that crucial confidences and procedures were being violated and, as a result, investigations were being compromised and potential informants were being murdered. Honest agents turned to fellow agents and supervisors because they believed—they hoped—that their colleagues were loyal to the oath they had taken when they were sworn in as federal agents. But then the truth revealed itself.

Retired agent Matthew Cronin was a ten-year veteran when he was assigned to the Boston division in 1978. He was assigned to a hijack and property theft unit known as the C-7 squad. Not long after he arrived, he had begun to get the impression that something was amiss. There were rumors of a leak in the office; someone was stealing confidential information from the rotor file and passing it along to criminals.

It didn't take long to trace the source of contention. The organized crime C-3 Unit was accorded privileges that other units were not. For one thing, they monopolized all of the division's surveillance teams; when other units wanted to conduct surveillance they could not get a team, unless the supervisor of C-3, John Morris, cut one loose. C-3 did whatever they wanted, and no one could call them on it; they were protected from above.

Testifying all these years later, white-haired and stoop-shouldered, Cronin seemed relieved to finally get a chance to describe what he called "an aura" in the Boston FBI. Along with Bob Fitzpatrick and a handful of others, he was an honest agent and good man who had been at first stunned and eventually defeated by what he encountered. In Cronin's voice and demeanor there was also the sense that he had been haunted by how it played out, with Bulger and Flemmi killing people while being protected from within his own division.

From the witness stand, Cronin described one investigation that he remembered well. He and his partner, James Crawford, were on to the Laffey brothers, a crew of criminals out of Chelsea. The Laffey brothers were connected with all the major players in South Boston. The C-7 Unit was working on this investigation with the Strike Force led by Jeremiah O'Sullivan.

Cronin and Crawford became concerned that their investigation was being undermined by an internal leak. They approached a Strike Force lawyer, Dave Twomey, to lodge a complaint. Twomey told them he would look into it. Years later, Cronin and Crawford learned that Twomey himself was the leak.

On this same investigation, the agents finally reached a point where they drafted an affidavit that was to be submitted to a judge to secure authorizations for wiretaps and search warrants. The day they planned to submit the affidavit, which included the names of seventeen criminals targeted by the investigation, Cronin and Crawford were approached by Morris, Connolly, and James Ring, who had recently taken over as the new supervisor of the C-3 Unit. The men from C-3 told them there were three names they wanted removed from the affidavit. Two of the names were Bulger and Flemmi.

Morris and Connolly told Cronin that they were conducting a case on the three names and were concerned that having them named would alert them. That, as it turned out, was a lie.

Cronin's voice, all these years later, still strained with incredulity as he said, "Those three were confidential informants. We should have been told that, but we weren't." Cronin added that never in his career had he been instructed to remove names from a sworn affidavit.

Cronin and Crawford wanted to complain, but where could they turn? Eventually, they did turn to their Justice Department supervisor, Jerry O'Sullivan. Of that meeting, Cronin testified, "Initially, I was very pleasant but I turned angry. . . . Mr. O'Sullivan ordered us out of his office." Cronin and Crawford were experiencing the same creeping sense of dread that Fitzpatrick had felt, the knowledge that those you hoped you could trust were, in fact, members of the conspiracy.

When asked why he didn't contact FBI headquarters with his concerns, Cronin said, "You learn pretty quickly to keep your cards close to your vest." To lodge a complaint with headquarters would have required going through the chain of command; Cronin was worried that there would be "consequences."

THE DEFENSE HAD hoped to explore the outer reaches of the conspiracy to protect Bulger but were thwarted at every turn. On their original witness list had been names such as ex-governor William Weld and FBI director Robert Mueller, who served as U.S. attorney in Boston after Jeremiah O'Sullivan. These names never made it past the first cut. If the defense was to be prohibited from following tributaries of corruption to the top, they could at least wallow in the lower depths. Since the prosecution was contending that the corruption began and ended with the Boston FBI, there were few objections from Wyshak or Kelly. The retired agents were paraded to the stand, like survivors from the Battle of Bunker Hill.

Among them was Cronin's supervisor in the C-7 squad, Fred Davis Jr., who ambled into the courtroom, was sworn in, and took his seat in front of the microphone.

Lanky and laconic at age seventy-four, Davis was a cowboy from Missouri who had served most of his career in Houston, where he likely fit in, before being transferred in September 1979 to Boston, where he likely did not. It wasn't that Davis wasn't a likable fellow; he was. But the ways of the northeastern big city were a hornet's nest unlike anything Davis had ever experienced in the West.

After being asked to give the standard recitation of his various postings and duties within the FBI food chain, the witness was asked, "Did you notice something about the atmosphere in Boston . . . that was different than your previous positions?"

"Yeah," said Davis. "I call it paranoia. . . . The working agents were a little more nervous than they might have been in some other situations in another office. . . . They were nervous about an internal situation. . . . They were concerned that there were agents in the office who might be leaking information."

Davis described a time when he had been in the office for only three months, when an agent whom he did not know seemed to be sniffing around his unit's rotor file. Normally, when an agent from another unit wanted to see the files of a different squad, he went first to that squad's supervisor and asked permission. Davis asked the agents on his squad, "Who is that fella?" He was told, "John Connolly from the C-3 squad."

The agents did not like Connolly snooping around their files; they warned Davis that he "was up to no good." Said Davis, "Everyone in the office seemed to know that Connolly was the leak."

Hank Brennan asked Davis what, if anything, he did about it.

"Well," said Davis, "I went to John Morris, whom I personally liked the fellow. . . . I said, 'Look, my guys are nervous about Connolly being in our area. I want you to do whatever you need to do to keep him out of there. Otherwise I'll run him out, and then I'll take it up front.' Meaning the SAC."

"Based on your limited experience at that point with Mr. Morris, did you trust him and his integrity at that point?"

"I had no reason not to."

Morris said he would take care of it, but the pilferage of files did not cease. Eventually, Davis began gathering up certain sensitive files and, at the end of each day, locking them in a fireproof safe inside his private office.

"Did you find that to be consistent with or normal compared to your experiences in other offices?"

"No."

"As an FBI agent who is sworn to truth and integrity, did you have an expectation that you would be able to trust all your colleagues in your office without putting case files under lock and key?"

"Yes."

One case that Davis's squad was especially concerned about involved Frank Lepere, a major marijuana dealer who had become a tremendous source of revenue for the Bulger organization. The C-7 squad was investigating Lepere for the theft of trucks and other transportation equipment that he used in his narcotics business.

While asking about the Lepere investigation, defense lawyer Brennan asked Davis, "While you were in the Boston office, were you there during the time allegations arose against a Strike Force member by the name of David Twomey?"

This question brought an immediate objection from Fred Wyshak.

"Let me hear you at sidebar," said Judge Casper.

The case of David Twomey was another that Wyshak referred to as a "rabbit hole." Twomey was an assistant U.S. attorney and member of Jerry O'Sullivan's Strike Force who would eventually be convicted at trial and sent to prison for leaking information to Frank Lepere. Twomey also took money from the smuggler in exchange for inside information. Eventually, after first going on the lam, Lepere was apprehended and cut a deal with the feds, ratting on Twomey and testifying against him at trial in 1986.

Huddled together at sidebar, separated from the jury and spectators, the lawyers and judge struck a familiar pose. Wyshak explained his objection to the woman in the black robe: "This is just another demonstration of how the defense continues to put in irrelevant information about government misconduct in the main hope that somehow it's going to result in jury nullification and mistrial. What the case involving David Twomey has to do with the charges against Mr. Bulger in this indictment totally escapes me. . . . They're inserting it because they're trying to put in every incident that something went wrong in Boston hoping that it's going to impact the jury and somehow affect their decision making."

Wyshak's objection was passionate bordering on emotional. It was not easy attempting to keep the Bulger trial from spilling into other potentially damaging areas. It required diligence, and the prosecutor had, throughout the course of the trial, honed his argument around this issue that the defense was attempting to stack the deck. The problem was that most racketeering-related crimes in Boston during the Bulger era were only a step or two removed from Whitey, and the Lepere-Twomey case was no exception.

Not only had Lepere been a major moneymaker for Bulger and Flemmi; he was also a crucial link to the Strike Force. There was a rumor in Boston crime circles that it was the Bulger organization that had forced Lepere to cut a deal with the feds and testify against Dave Twomey. They had sacrificed Twomey to protect his boss, Jerry O'Sullivan, who was by that time operating in collaboration with Bulger and Flemmi.

Hank Brennan, for his part, had been listening to Wyshak and Kelly deflect responsibility for government corruption for two months. In a sometimes sanctimonious manner, the prosecutors sought to ridicule the very idea that someone would question the motives or veracity of reputable public officials. Given the steady flow of law enforcement sleaze that had been revealed during the trial, it was reasonable to surmise that Wyshak would be circumspect in his protestations that defense counsel was reaching far and wide to bolster their accusations of deep-rooted institutional corruption in the Justice Department. Brennan seemed more bemused than offended when he said to Judge Casper, "I know the government's position is that John Connolly was a rogue agent. We don't necessarily share that theory. . . . If there are leaks in the Boston office that extend beyond Connolly and there's impropriety, why should that be sanitized from the jury? Why shouldn't the jury hear that this information exists, that there was not just one source of corruption, John Connolly, like the government is purporting, but there's more than one source?"

Brennan and Judge Casper went back and forth. As always, Casper was polite and patient; she allowed Brennan to flesh out his position, although it seemed as if she knew what her ruling would be before the lawyer opened his mouth. She sustained the objection by saying, "I understand the relevance to your defense of this line of questioning, but I don't see how the Lepere-Twomey matter relates to that."

Brennan acknowledged her ruling with a nod; by now, he knew better than to waste time shadowboxing in an empty ring.

OF ALL THE FBI witnesses called by the defense, perhaps the most eagerly anticipated was a woman in her mideighties by the name of Desi Sideropoulos. Gnomelike and gray-haired, Sideropoulos had been an executive secretary with the Boston division of the FBI for an astounding sixty-two and a half years. For fifty of those years she had been secretary to the SAC. In her time, she had worked for eighteen different SACs. If anyone knew where the memos were buried, it was Desi.

In 1980, Sideropoulos was working for Larry Sarhatt. Part of Desi's job as secretary was to take dictation; Sarhatt would verbally compose confidential memos, with the secretary writing down notes and then typing the memo out in written form. Though she had probably helped create thousands if not millions of memos in her career, there was one she remembered very well.

The context for this memo had been established for the jury earlier in the trial, during the testimony of James Marra from the Inspector General's Office. Marra had read from a series of memos that were generated when the Lancaster Street garage investigation, led by the Massachusetts State Police, had been compromised. The staties were angry; they believed that Morris and Connolly had leaked information to Bulger, who they suspected but could not prove was an FBI informant.

The Lancaster Street garage fiasco had reverberated throughout the Justice Department. Accusations were flying back and forth between various law enforcement agencies. Since his arrival, Sarhatt had concerns about Connolly and Morris's management of the Bulger situation, which he had inherited. He knew that it was a potential hot potato, with powerful forces—including Strike Force chief O'Sullivan—acting as an advocate for Bulger and Flemmi. But Sarhatt felt that he could no longer operate in the dark. He figured he'd better look into the Bulger situation for himself.

On the day after Thanksgiving—November 25, 1980—at the Logan Hilton Inn, a hotel near the airport, Sarhatt met face-to-face with Whitey Bulger. Morris and Connolly were also present. It was a long meeting—four hours—at which the top man in the FBI Boston division and the boss of the Irish Mob had a lengthy conversation. Afterward, back at the office, Sarhatt dictated the details of the meeting to secretary Desi Sideropoulos.

In part, the memo read:

Met with BS-1544 TE [Bulger] for the purpose of debriefing source regarding various criminal matters. . . . Source furnished information about his early childhood, his criminal activity, incarceration and association with the FBI. . . . Informant's intention to help the FBI stems from favorable treatment received by his family from SA PAUL RICO after SA RICO was responsible for his incarceration. His family indicated to him that SA RICO was such a gentleman and was so helpful that he, Informant, changed his mind about his hate for all law enforcement. . . . He is fully aware that the MSP [Massachusetts State Police] is aware of his Informant role with the FBI; however, he is not concerned with his personal safety because no one would dare believe that he is an informant. It would be too incredible. . . .

One of the reasons Sarhatt wanted to meet with Bulger was that he had been told the mob boss had on his payroll a corrupt state trooper. The name of that trooper—David Schneiderhan—had not yet been revealed. Sarhatt wanted to know the name of the dirty trooper.

Informant was asked whether he would divulge the identity of the State Police source that had been furnishing information to him and he stated that he would not because this source is not doing it for monetary benefit but as a favor to him because of his close association with him.

This, of course, was not true. The Winter Hill Mob had for years been paying Schneiderhan. Whitey had other lies to pass along:

Informant also related that he is not in the drug business and personally hates anyone who does [sic]; therefore, he and any of his associates do not deal in drugs.

At the end of his memo, in a section headlined "Observations," Sarhatt gave his personal opinion on Bulger's value as an informant:

I am not certain that I am convinced that informant is telling the full story of his involvement. As much as we no longer need his information concerning another sensitive matter, consideration should be given to closing him and making him a target.

SAC Sarhatt was not only recommending that Bulger be closed, but that he be targeted for criminal investigation.

As she took down her boss's dictation, secretary Sideropoulos did not know the identity of BS-1544 TE. Even if she had been told the name James Bulger, it probably would not have meant anything to her. Desi had no clue that this memo was any different than the many others she wrote up, until she was finished.

"Did [Sarhatt] give you any instructions about where to keep the original of this document?" asked defense lawyer Carney.

"He told me to keep it in an envelope, a sealed envelope."

Sideropoulos then explained that back in the 1970s and early 1980s, the SAC's office had a private safe. Occasionally, the secretary was asked to label a document "strictly eyes only," meaning that it was personal and confidential to the SAC, and place it in the safe. No one else in the division had access to the safe. It was a place where memos went to die.

Sarhatt instructed Sideropoulos to put the sealed memo into the private safe.

At the time, Sarhatt had already been designated for a new assignment; he had only a few months left in Boston. He told the secretary, "Whoever the new SAC is, make sure they read that document."

Later, when the new SAC took over, Sideropoulos did as she was told. She referred James Ahearn, the new SAC, to the controversial memo.

"After Ahearn read the memo," asked Carney, "did he give you directions what to do?"

"He told me to destroy it."

"What did he say when he told you that?"

"He told me to destroy it or we'll all get fired."

Again, Sideropoulos did as she was told. She destroyed the document that had been locked away in the safe.

For the defense case, this revelation was akin to a "smoking gun" moment. What was so dangerous about a memo suggesting that James Bulger be closed as an informant? Why was the bureaucracy, in the person of a respected supervisory agent, seeking to protect itself by destroying potential evidence?

The defense did not have the answers to these questions, but by planting the seed of doubt in the collective mind of the jury, they were hoping to undermine its confidence in the government's case.

Thirty years passed before Sideropoulos was ever asked about the memo. In preparation for the Bulger trial, she was contacted by Wyshak and Kelly. They had uncovered a version of this memo that existed in the FBI's administrative file in Washington, D.C. A version of the memo had been sent to headquarters, but was it the same version that had existed in the SAC's safe?

When Sideropoulos was asked about the memo, she admitted that she had destroyed the original pursuant to an order from her boss. They asked if she could re-create the memo based on her original dictation notes. She said that she could—and did—re-creating a memo that she believed was identical to the one that had been destroyed. Which led to another startling revelation: the memo that existed in the files at headquarters was identical until the last section, under the heading "Observations," where Sarhatt recommended that Bulger be closed as an informant and targeted for investigation. That section had been deleted from the memo.

Someone had doctored it.

Was it altered in Boston before it was ever sent to headquarters? Or had someone in Washington deliberately deleted the section advising that Bulger be closed as an informant and prosecuted?

More confounding questions, especially since the passage of time made it possible for those responsible to scurry into retirement and disappear. The deceit that had contributed to this blatant obstruction of justice was absorbed into history and successfully buried within binary modes of concealment deep within the system. Those entrusted with the role of safeguarding the Bulger conspiracy had fulfilled their duties. Seemingly, the system did what it was supposed to do: protect itself from exposure and criminal liability.

THERE WAS ONE final witness after secretary Sideropoulos. John Martorano was called back into the courtroom to testify regarding one limited matter.

It was almost nostalgic to see Martorano again take a seat on the witness stand, two months after he first appeared. As before, he was dressed in a tailored blue suit, only this time with no tie, collar open, with a light blue, striped shirt. He had a silk hanky in his breast pocket and designer glasses with tinted lenses. His deep tan and who-gives-a-fuck physique, redolent of an independent life of leisure, seemed to reflect his inner self: he looked like a mob hit man just flown in from South Florida.

Johnny had been re-called to set the record straight. Back in the early 1980s, while he was on the lam down in Clearwater, the hit man had spoken on the phone with Steve Flemmi about the demise of Debra Davis. According to Martorano, Flemmi had more or less admitted that he killed his ex-girlfriend. He told Martorano that he "accidentally" strangled her. Martorano asked his Winter Hill partner, "Stevie, how do you accidentally strangle somebody?" Flemmi gave a half-assed answer that, to Martorano, was none too convincing.

When defense lawyer Carney presented the witness with a transcript of previous testimony he had given at another proceeding, Martorano removed his tinted shades and replaced them with reading glasses. When he had finished reading the section he had been instructed to read, he switched back to the shades.

In less than fifteen minutes, the questioning went from direct to cross to re-direct and back again. The defense had put Martorano on the stand to deflect responsibility for the Davis murder from Bulger to Flemmi. The prosecution kept wanting to bring it back to Bulger. In a final question, Fred Wyshak asked the witness, "Mr. Martorano, when you were in Florida in 1981 when Ms. Davis disappeared, who was Mr. Flemmi's criminal partner in Boston?"

"Whitey," said Martorano.

It was the final word spoken during testimony in the trial of James Bulger.

After Martorano was dismissed, an air of restless expectation rustled through the spectators' gallery in the courtroom. The moment of reckoning had arrived: would Whitey take the stand and testify in his own defense?

The suspense was palpable but also artificial, like a nondairy sweetener with a stale aftertaste. Carney had begun the trial by all but promising the media that Bulger would testify, but he had tellingly not promised that to the jury, either in his opening statement or during the trial. Most legal experts and observers noted that it would have been unprecedented for Bulger to take the stand in a trial of this type. It was highly unlikely. And as the proceedings unfolded, with the defense lawyers being restricted by the judge from pursuing avenues of evidence that were to Bulger's liking, the possibility of him taking the stand diminished even more.

As much as everyone—including the media, the lawyers, the community, and probably the jury—would have welcomed hearing directly from the man who had been the focus of so much testimony over the last two months, there was never much chance that Whitey would take the stand.

The jury was removed from the courtroom. The judge called the lawyers over to her bench for a sidebar conference. There, Carney informed legal counsel and the judge that the defendant had decided not to testify. Casper indicated that she would like to ask the defendant a few questions about his decision, and that this should be done in open court.

The lawyers walked back to their respective tables.

Judge Casper looked directly at the defendant. "Mr. Bulger, I just want to address you directly."

Whitey stood up. It had been noted by those who had been following the trial on a daily basis that, as the proceedings continued over the summer, it seemed as though the defendant was physically diminishing in stature. Certainly, he had become more pale and, given the likelihood of less-than-stellar prison cuisine and a limited diet due to heart health concerns, Bulger had thinned down until he looked like exactly what he was: a frail, aging man in his eighties. The disparity between what he had been and what he had become was enough to hush the room into silence.

The judge continued: "You understand that this is the juncture of the case at which I ask for a decision about whether or not you're going to testify. Mr. Carney has represented on your behalf that you're choosing not to testify. Is that correct?"

"That is correct," said the defendant.

It was not the first time we had heard Bulger's voice. Earlier in the trial, the prosecution had played two recordings of conversations that Bulger took part in while incarcerated at Plymouth County Correctional Facility. One of the conversations was with Bulger's brother Jackie, and another with his nephew, a son of his brother Billy. Bulger would have known that all phone conversations at the prison were recorded. The prosecutors tried to suggest the recorded conversations had probative value, but really they seemed like a stunt by the government to show that they finally got Whitey Bulger's voice on tape.

Bulger's voice was reedy and taciturn, the Boston accent diluted somewhat, perhaps by his having spent sixteen years in Santa Monica trying to disguise his Southie roots.

Judge Casper asked Bulger if he had made his decision not to testify after careful consultation with his lawyer.

"Yes, I have," he said.

"Are you making the choice voluntarily and freely?" she asked.

Bulger was ready with a little speech that he likely prepared: as he began to speak, his voice wavered—he was nervous, no doubt, having to play the role of Whitey Bulger, the legend whose motivations and exploits had come to dominate the lives of all who had followed his life story over many decades.

"I'm making the choice involuntarily," said Bulger. "I feel that I've been choked off from having an opportunity to give an adequate defense and explain my conversation and agreement with Jeremiah O'Sullivan. For my protection of his life, in return, he promised to give me immunity."

At the word *immunity,* the judge jumped in: "I understand your position, sir, but certainly you're aware that I have considered that legal argument and made a ruling."

"I understand," said Bulger.

"And I understand, sir, if you disagree with it, okay?"

"I do disagree. And that's the way it is. And my thing is, as far as I'm concerned, I didn't get a fair trial, and this is a sham, so do what youse want with me. That's it. That's my final word."

From somewhere in the spectators' gallery, a voice rang out: "You're a coward!" It was Patricia Donahue, widow of Michael Donahue, shouting from among the spectators.

Announced the judge, "I need silence in the gallery." She waited until the rumbling and rustling subsided.

Turning back to the defendant, she noted, "Mr. Bulger, I understand your position, but my question to you was a simple one about whether you've decided not to testify in the case."

"That's my answer," snapped Whitey.

"Okay, so you've decided not to testify in the case?"

"Correct."

And that was it; Bulger sat down. The defense rested its case.

OVER THE FOLLOWING news cycle, there was much verbal hyperventilation in both the local and national media. Whitey had spoken. It certainly wasn't anything like the "full truth" or "stunning revelations" that his lawyers had suggested would be forthcoming, but he had slipped into the public record at least one lollapalooza by suggesting that his arrangement with Jerry O'Sullivan had something to do with protecting the prosecutor's life.

It was an explanation from out of the blue. Never in the long history of O'Sullivan's career as a prosecutor had there been allegations on record of attempts on his life by the Mafia. It sounded like something out of a comic book version of organized crime, or a worldview informed by iconic fantasy depictions of crime like *Dick Tracy*, where good and bad is colored in black-and-white, or *The Untouchables*, a sophomoric depiction of the underworld that Bulger may have watched on TV in his youth. In reality, the Mob in the United States, especially the Mafia, rarely attempted to murder government officials. Such an act would bring about a reaction on the part of the criminal justice system that would make it impossible to conduct business.

Even so, Bulger's highly imaginative explanation might have been worthy of consideration were there any details to back it up, such as, Who set up his liaison with O'Sullivan? How many meetings were there? Where did they take place? And what, specifically, was promised? None of these details were provided by Bulger before or during the trial. All that was given was this glancing suggestion by Whitey that in exchange for protecting the prosecutor's life, he had been given a blank check to commit crimes.

What made Bulger's fantasy all the more vexing was that it seemed designed to obscure a more realistic version of his deal with O'Sullivan.

From prison in Florida, before the trial began, John Connolly had told me the story of Bulger and O'Sullivan meeting at a hotel room in Boston around Christmas of 1978. Connolly set up the meeting, at O'Sullivan's request. Connolly was there. "Jerry and Whitey seemed to like each other," Connolly had said. It was at this meeting that Bulger and O'Sullivan allegedly formed their pact. It was based on the concept that O'Sullivan would drop Bulger and his partner, Flemmi, from the massive race-fix indictment, and presumably, protect them from future prosecution, if Bulger and Flemmi delivered as informants in the feds' ongoing dream of taking down the Mafia in Boston.

This was a far more plausible scenario than the one Bulger floated during his brief statement in court. But Whitey could not admit to this scenario, because it would require his acknowledging that he had been an informant. Since he was not willing to admit that he had been a TE, it required that he come up with an explanation for his so-called immunity deal that was devoid of details or rational explanation.

For anyone who had hoped the Bulger trial would serve as a final unmasking of the conspiracy that created Whitey Bulger, this was the final nail in the coffin. Apparently, the full truth would never be known—not only because the government wanted to keep it covered up, but because Whitey did not have the wherewithal to look himself in the mirror and admit what he had become.

And so the trial shifted into its final stage; all that remained to be heard were the closing summations.

For the prosecution, in particular, the closing statement was to be an effort of Herculean proportions. The team of Wyshak and Kelly had been gathering evidence and developing the case against Bulger for twenty years. It had been an unprecedented marshaling of forces. Even after Bulger went on the run back in 1995, they had continued developing their case. Patiently, they had accumulated evidence and witnesses and designed a strategy, as if they were architects laying the groundwork for an edifice that might not ever be built. Previous trials of John Connolly had been a prelude, significant projects, yes, but small and manageable compared to the Bulger trial, which had the potential of becoming a sprawling, three-ring circus.

There had been other historic RICO cases against organized crime entities that included criminal acts from over a period of decades. But there were few that had begun with an indictment and then remained open for the next twenty years. While Whitey had been a fugitive, Wyshak and Kelly kept adding pieces to the puzzle. Jimmy Katz, Dickie O'Brien, Joe Tower, Billy Shea, and many other former criminals had cut deals with the government hoping and believing that Bulger would never turn up or be apprehended. Their appearances on the stand, along with the more significant testimony of Martorano, Morris, Weeks, and Flemmi, resulted in an unprecedented kaleidoscope of evidence against Bulger.

In his summation Wyshak sought to lay it all out as if he were Ann Marie Mires, the forensic anthropologist, reconstructing a human body with bones, teeth, and other found objects. Standing at the podium, looking straight at the jury, the prosecutor spoke with a firm sense of purpose: "The evidence at this trial has convincingly proven that the defendant in this case, James Bulger, is one of the most vicious, violent, and calculating criminals ever to walk the streets of Boston. . . . [He] was the leader of a very wide-ranging, broad organization that was involved in many different types of crimes, from illegal gambling, loan-sharking, extortion, money laundering, narcotics distribution, to murders."

At its most grandiose, the trial had been a historical pageant. Wyshak wanted the jury to feel as though they were a part of something monumental. He referred the jury to the video monitors, which were positioned facing the jury and the spectators' gallery, on which were displayed the leadership of the Winter Hill gang. This chart, complete with thumbnail photos of the various gang leaders, had been shown to the jury numerous times during the trial. Said Wyshak, "The men who led this group—Bulger, Flemmi, Martorano, Winter, McDonald, Sims—these men were the survivors of the gang war during the sixties. . . . You heard about how these neighborhood groups in Charlestown and Somerville and Roxbury and Dorchester were involved in this shooting war, where over sixty people died. The Mafia sort of sat on the sidelines taking potshots at both sides in the gang war, but these men were the victors, these men were the survivors. They were armed to the teeth. They were organized. They were feared. They acted like a paramilitary organization. You heard the evidence. When they engaged in criminal activity, they had this armory of weapons, they used stolen cars. Mr. Martorano described them as boilers. They had backup cars in order to crash into police vehicles that may come onto the scene. They communicated via walkie-talkies. They obtained intelligence from law enforcement. They hunted their targets.

"These men didn't hunt animals, ladies and gentlemen, they hunted people. That's why they were so successful. These men were the scariest people walking the streets of Boston."

The prosecutor reminded the jury how all the mid- and street-level gangster witnesses in the trial made it clear that Whitey was the boss. Even though Bulger and Flemmi emerged as equal partners, in Southie there was never any question that Whitey was the man. He was the one who was rumored to have FBI agent Connolly in his pocket. He was the one who had a brother in the statehouse.

Said Wyshak, "William Bulger was one of the most powerful politicians in Massachusetts at the time. You heard the stories about the St. Patrick's Day breakfast, how politicians stood in line outside waiting to get in, but John Connolly and a select group of FBI agents were brought to the back door and given a seat right up front.

"That's another reason why John Connolly aligned himself with James Bulger. Not only did it enhance his personal career, it cemented his relationship with William Bulger for his dream job as police commissioner of the city of Boston."

The subject of Connolly was a touchy one for Wyshak. Certainly, the prosecution had no hesitation in linking Connolly to Bulger's organization and making it appear as if "Zip" was the mastermind behind the corruption of the Boston FBI. Wyshak shrewdly acknowledged, "The defense probably did a better job of [exposing the corruption] than the government did." The Boston FBI, admitted Wyshak, was "a mess." But then the prosecutor executed a ninety-degree pivot to deflect attention from the U.S. Justice Department, which had consistently rewarded Connolly and his partner, Morris, with commendations and financial incentives, and the U.S. attorney's office, which built prominent criminal cases against the Mafia in partnership with Morris and Connolly's C-3 Unit.

As Wyshak put forth an argument designed to exonerate the upper reaches of institutional authority, his voice turned shrill. He used one of his favorite phrases, "make no mistake about it," and used sweeping phrases such as "every piece of evidence that's before you at this trial." Generations of corruption in the criminal justice system in New England were narrowed down by Wyshak to one element: a "failure of management" on the part of the Boston FBI office. Not surprisingly, the prosecutor attempted to put the blame on Robert Fitzpatrick.

Wyshak called Fitzpatrick "the poster boy for what was wrong with the Boston FBI at the time," even going so far as to imply that Fitzpatrick was personally responsible for the deaths of Debbie Davis, Roger Wheeler, John Callahan, Brian Halloran, Michael Donahue, John McIntyre, and Bucky Barrett, all of whom were killed while he was ASAC of the Boston office. This expression of moral outrage on the part of the prosecution was not only unusual, it was singular. Wyshak's condemnation of Fitzpatrick did not extend to any of the other ASACs, SACs, special agents, or Strike Force prosecutors who were on duty during the Bulger era.

The prosecution had been allotted three hours for their summation. Wyshak exceeded that amount of time. A significant portion of his argument was spent defending his brand. The U.S. government, in the form of the Department of Justice, had taken a beating during the trial, and the prosecution, along with convicting Bulger, was entrusted with the duty of cleaning up after the elephants at the parade.

Said Wyshak, "The defense would have you think that the entire Department of Justice, the U.S. attorney's office, the Strike Force, is corrupt. Not so, ladies and gentlemen. Use your common sense. You know, there's an old saying: a few bad apples spoil the barrel."

Finally, Wyshak did something he had not done during the entire trial: he resorted to invective. In response to an implication put forth by the defense counsel that prosecutors secured cooperative testimony from criminals through financial inducements, the lead prosecutor snapped, "The concept that the government buys testimony, well, that's just a slanderous and lowlife remark from Mr. Carney. It's not how the system works."

A lowlife remark?

John Martorano was paid twenty thousand dollars on release from prison. Many of the criminal witnesses who testified acknowledged receiving payments from the government. Whether or not this constituted "buying testimony" or was simply a case of the government offering financial aid to people who had already agreed to cooperate was an argument that had been going back and forth for decades in courtrooms all across America. Criminals are persuaded to testify through all kinds of inducements—from reduced sentences to improved incarceration conditions and financial remuneration. Assistant U.S. Attorney Wyshak's shot at Jay Carney for making what was arguably a legitimate observation was—uncharacteristically—a punch below the belt and after the bell.

IN MARSHALING TOGETHER the evidence and intellectual wherewithal to formulate a cohesive closing summation, the defense team of Carney and Brennan were caught in a conundrum. They could spend the better part of their three-hour time allotment making the case that Bulger had never been an informant, which, no doubt, would have been to the liking of their client. But as longtime members of the Boston bar, first as prosecutors and now as defense attorneys, they knew that as they addressed the long-gestating case against Whitey Bulger the eyes and ears of an entire city and part of the nation would be fixed on their closing statement. It might have been an overstatement to say that their entire careers depended on it, but it was not far-fetched to surmise that for the remainder of their years on the bar they would never again have such a high-profile case.

In their opening statement they had suggested that their defense of Bulger would be historic and monumental. Much of this hyperbole was predicated on the possibility that Whitey himself would take the stand. With that fantasy finally having been disposed of, the lawyers were faced with a challenge: deliver a closing statement that was worthy of their case.

They had decided to divide their presentation into two parts, with Brennan delivering a ninety-minute summation and Carney following with a statement of equal length.

"About an hour ago," said Brennan, standing at the lectern addressing the jury, "Mr. Wyshak was telling you about the fact that some of the most dangerous murderers in the history of Boston were walking the streets." Brennan identified Martorano, Weeks, and Pat Nee as among the men Wyshak had been referring to, saying to the jury, "You have to sit there and ask yourself: if they're so vicious and violent and our government knows about it, why are they out there right now?"

From the start, Brennan sought to plant the seed: "There's got to be more to the story. . . . To understand what the government's motives are, we have to go back to the 1960s. . . . And after we talk a little bit about the history, we're going to talk about today, what the government has done to cover up their liability and their responsibility for what they have done."

It was a promising opening salvo, and for a good thirty minutes Brennan laid it all out. He started with Steve Flemmi and constructed a narrative that, in all the journalism and books on the Bulger era, had been insufficiently explored. It was Flemmi who, during the city's gang wars, while Bulger was away in prison, first became a Top Echelon Informant. Flemmi entered into a partnership with Special Agents Rico and Condon.

Noted Brennan: "[Flemmi] was at war with other criminals. He was at war with other gangsters, and when he needed help, all he needed to do was draw on his friends, the federal government. Condon and Rico, they'd tell him where Punchy McLaughlin was, where Wimpy Bennett was. 'You want to murder him? I'll give you the bus stop he's going to be at.' They're in partnership with him. And when they needed his help, they needed some information, they needed a gun, they needed a car fixed, they'd call on their friend. This is the type of relationship that they had, and they accepted it."

It was a cogent point: Brennan was suggesting that the seed that had been planted that gave flower to the ugliness, corruption, and murder that were to follow for the next thirty years had been planted not by Bulger, Connolly, and Morris, but by Flemmi, Rico, and Condon.

To illustrate his point, Brennan reminded the jury how, after Flemmi and his partner Salemme blew up the car of Joe Barboza's lawyer, blowing off his leg, they were told to get out of town by Special Agent Rico. During his time on the lam, Flemmi remained in touch with Rico. At the same time, he murdered a criminal partner in the Nevada desert. There was a warrant out for his arrest. But Flemmi kept moving. He wound up in Montreal, where he hid out until receiving a call from Rico telling him it was safe to return to Boston. Brennan reminded the jury, "[Flemmi] didn't even want to come home. He said that. He felt like it was a threat." But Rico insisted. Flemmi's services were needed back in Boston.

"Then we have the transition," said Brennan. "As agents get older and Mr. Rico and Mr. Condon start to move on, who comes in to take their place? Special Agent Connolly and Special Agent Morris. They hand off the baton, and it's business as usual. It's not a rogue agent. It's systemic. It's what they do."

So far, so good: Brennan was spinning a tale that implied that the purveyors of the system, the FBI field agents and their supervisors, were manipulating the gangsters like pieces on a chessboard. Brennan even took the argument a step further, explaining how the efforts of the FBI became the foundation for the federal Strike Force and the U.S. attorney's office.

"When we near the late 1970s, we know the temperament of the Department of Justice. We know the Strike Force, headed by Jeremiah O'Sullivan, wants the national attention. They want everybody to look at Boston and say, 'This is the prototype. These guys are the best at what they do.' They want the accolades, they want the glory, and they're willing to make deals. They're willing to protect criminals, murderers, because of pride. Because when law enforcement puts pride and self-importance in the equation, something about it gets distorted, something gets perverted, and something gets corrupted."

And this is where Brennan's presentation became derailed. After constructing a compelling narrative, Brennan found himself at a dead-end street with nothing visible except for the disembodied visage of Whitey, hovering in the darkness, like the face of Obi-Wan Kenobi. It was logical to surmise—and there was plenty of evidence to back it up—that Flemmi was called back to Boston, in part, to help recruit Bulger as a Top Echelon Informant. But Brennan could not make that argument because his client was not willing to admit that he ever was an informant. And so Brennan was left with a less than startling conclusion to his story. He ended by suggesting that Flemmi's historical relationship with the government was the reason that Bulger's partner was now a witness telling lies about his client. This may have been true, but it was a far less epic explanation for Flemmi's motivation than the likelihood that he was an essential facilitator of Whitey's relationship with the feds, thus ushering in the Age of Bulger and all the bloodshed that followed

The defense team's closing argument became even less probative when Brennan handed over the reins to his co-counsel.

Throughout the trial, J. W. Carney had seemed to become increasingly unfocused. Carney was the one who had been saying to the media from the outset that his client would take the stand, and when Bulger chose not to do so, the lawyer appeared deflated. He remained vigorous in his legal arguments before the judge, but his grasp of the particulars of the case at hand unraveled in the final days, culminating in a closing argument that was slipshod and uninspired.

He went for the folksy approach, mentioning to the jury before he began that if he seemed nervous it was because, for the first time in his thirty-five-year legal career, "my mother is in court watching me." The attorney then began his summation with a rambling example of why the government's witnesses couldn't be trusted, citing the television show *The Brady Bunch*—an oddly outdated reference—and then segueing into an anecdote about buying a television from a youthful but untrustworthy sales assistant, all of which was unnecessary if you, the jury, had first utilized a copy of *Consumer Reports* magazine. And if all of this weren't enough to underscore the jury's need to make wise evaluations, Carney free-associated on the subjects of elective surgery, childbearing, and consulting a guidance counselor as further obtuse examples of informed decision making.

Carney delivered some tart one-liners: Of Martorano, he noted, "I think if you did a CAT scan, you'd have troubling finding a heart in this guy." After quoting from the testimony of Kevin Weeks where he declared, "I've been lying my whole life; I'm a criminal," Carney waited a few beats before saying wryly to the jury, "May I kiss you, Mr. Weeks, for your candor?"

The one-liners elicited chuckles from some in the jury and the spectators' gallery, but Carney's attempts to make substantive points often led to dismay. He sought to link Martorano to the historical quagmire of Joseph Barboza, noting that the witness was a protégé of Barboza. But in his reference to the Teddy Deegan murder and Barboza having framed innocent men for the crime with the help of the FBI, Carney mistakenly identified

Jimmy Martorano as one of the true killers when he meant to say Jimmy Flemmi. He repeated this mistake throughout his summation. Elsewhere, he referred to Kevin Weeks as Kevin Nee, once correcting that mistake only to repeat it twice more before he was finished.

Carney used barely half of his allotted time, ending with a boilerplate plea to the jury that they live up to their constitutional duties by saying, "No, we don't find the evidence to be proof beyond a reasonable doubt. You can say it with courage that the prosecutors have not met their burden of proof, and then you will embody our constitutional protections."

Given the tepid nature of Carney's portion of the closing argument, and the overwhelming evidence aligned against Bulger, it was a surprise that the jury deliberations took as long as they did. For five days, the jury gathered to deliberate behind closed doors. The media and interested spectators also gathered. These days were a time for followers of the Bulger saga to kibitz and speculate. Waiting for a verdict had an air of expectation not because there was much question how the verdict would go, but because the verdict represented the end of a story that had held the city in its grip for at least three decades.

Finally, the jury announced that they were ready with their verdict, the word spreading via texts and Twitter. The media and trial observers flooded into the Moakley Courthouse and took their positions. Bulger was brought into the courtroom. By this time, Whitey had adopted a nonchalant attitude, as if the verdict meant nothing to him. He sat down at the defense counsel's table and immediately began scribbling notes on a legal pad, as he had often throughout the latter weeks of the trial.

The jury was brought into the courtroom.

Bulger was asked to stand.

The court clerk began to read the verdict. It was going to take some time. There were thirty-two counts and multiple criminal acts within each count.

Many of the counts were pro forma: Bulger had already admitted to racketeering, loan-sharking, illegal gambling, drug trafficking, and gun possession. The clerk announced the word *guilty* in relation to these charges as if he were reading from a grocery list. It was when the clerk reached the portion of the verdict sheet that involved the nineteen murders that the entire gathering was riveted to attention.

Almost immediately it was clear that the prosecution had not scored an across-the-board victory on these charges. With the clerk announcing "proved" or "not proved" to each of the murder counts, it was a mixed verdict. Overall, Bulger was found guilty on eleven of the murders, with seven being declared "not proved," and one, the murder of Debra Davis, resulting in a declaration of "no finding."

The reading of the verdict had taken twenty minutes. When it was over, Bulger was asked by Judge Casper, "Do you fully understand the verdict reached by the jury in this case?"

"Yes, Your Honor," said Whitey.

Bulger sat down and resumed scribbling on his notepad.

The judge thanked the men and women of the jury for their service, and they were dismissed. After they were gone, Casper announced a date two months hence when the guilty party would be sentenced for his crimes.

A gaggle of U.S. marshals gathered around Bulger; he stood and was led from the courtroom. The trial was over.

It had been a long haul: thirty-five days of testimony spread over two months. Seventy-two witnesses. After two days of closing statements and the judge's official charging of the jury, deliberations had lasted for thirty-two and a half hours over five days.

Not everyone was happy with the verdict. Family members of those murdered for whom Bulger's involvement was not proved were vocal in their displeasure. William O'Brien, whose father, also named William O'Brien, had been gunned down in the shooting so dramatically described by witness and shooting survivor Ralph DeMasi, was livid. He stormed into the hallway outside the courtroom and cursed loudly. Other family members expressed outrage and dismay outside the courthouse, where the media horde was the largest it had been, double its usual size, with helicopters buzzing overhead and well-known local television reporters conducting live remotes for their various news agencies, cable shows, and podcasts.

Patricia Donahue, who had become a favorite of the media because of her dignity and politeness in the face of such trying circumstances, seemed relieved. She told the press that she had cried during the reading of the verdict, adding, "I think there was justice for me, but maybe not for some other victims."

William O'Brien continued to vent his anger, saying to the media, "My father was just murdered again, forty years later, in the courtroom. The prosecution dropped the ball. . . . That jury should be ashamed of themselves."

Steve Davis, who had become such a ubiquitous figure in and around the courthouse and with the media, also expressed displeasure. He said that he was certain Bulger had played a role in his sister's death, no matter what the jury decided. "It's not over for me," he said, and then he broke down in tears and stepped away from the microphone.

After the family members had spoken, Carney and Brennan stepped up and claimed that they were satisfied with how the trial had gone; they declared victory. Said Carney, "Mr. Bulger knew from the time that he was arrested that he was going to be behind the walls of a prison for the rest of his life, or be injected with a chemical that would kill him. . . . This trial was never about Jim Bulger being set free." Carney and his co-counsel both noted that an unprecedented level of corruption had been exposed during the trial, which had been Bulger's primary goal.

In the warm summer breeze that blew in from Boston Harbor, the lawyers' rhetoric rang hollow. By attempting to oversimplify their client's relationship with the FBI and others in the criminal justice system, they had contributed to a further muddling of the facts. This was partly what they had been paid to do, the bulk of their fees, in the end, covered by U.S. taxpayers.

The final group of interested parties to speak to the media were those representing the federal government. U.S. Attorney Carmen Ortiz, in the job once held by Jeremiah O'Sullivan, stood at the bank of microphones flanked by eight men representing various branches of the U.S. Justice Department. None of these directors and supervisors had been in their current positions when James Bulger was active in Boston. Likely they knew no more or less about Bulger than the average citizen who followed his story through journalism accounts and books. Nonetheless, these people were there to dance on Whitey's grave. The conviction of Bulger was a big moment in their careers, and they were there to receive the accolades and take part in throwing the last few shovels of dirt over the remains of the Bulger legacy.

"Today is a day that many in this city thought would never come," said Ortiz. "We hope that we stand here today to mark an end to an era that was very ugly in Boston's history." Ortiz went on to say, "The myth, the legend, the saga of James Bulger is now finally over. He is ancient history."

The emphasis on history, putting the story of Bulger in the distant past, was the key talking point as leaders of the federal Bulger Fugitive Task Force, DEA, U.S. Marshals Service, and other law enforcement agencies followed Ortiz to the microphone. Said Vincent Lisi, a man who had only recently been appointed SAC of the Boston FBI office, "I realize that the actions of a small percentage of law enforcement many years ago caused some people to lose faith and confidence in us. . . . We went through a dark period where there was corruption, but we're beyond that now."

It was a mighty act of prestidigitation: now you see it, now you don't. Through a collective expression of relief and pride on the part of various governmental representatives of the criminal justice system in Boston, Whitey and his legacy was no more. Never again would a federal official be compelled to explain—nor would anyone, outside of John Connolly, be held criminally accountable—for having protected and underwritten the career of one of the most notorious U.S. gangsters of recent times. Case closed.

ON HANOVER STREET, in the North End, Joe Salvati stopped to have a smoke at his favorite cigar lounge not far from Café Pompeii. In those days when the jury was deliberating over Bulger's fate, Salvati paid little attention. There was no real suspense, after all. Whitey was going down, and he would no doubt live out his dying days in prison. Like everyone else in Boston, Salvati was pleased to see Bulger get what he deserved. But Joe felt no great sense of closure from the verdict.

"I'll never get those thirty years back," he told me.

Like the family members of Bulger's victims who had received copious attention during the weeks of the trial, speaking with the media on a near-daily basis, Salvati was among the walking wounded. But Joe sought little attention during the trial, and few came asking for his opinion. Salvati's history represented yet another unseemly side of the Bulger saga—the poisoned root that spawned the entire rotten organism—that the prosecutors had been working to keep buried since the first day of the trial.

Now that it was over, I asked Salvati if he believed the results of the Bulger trial would lead to more honest agents and prosecutors.

Joe the Horse pursed his lips—a smile not of mirth but of resignation. "They protected Bulger the same way they protected Barboza. A lot of people in the government got away with that, with no repercussions."

"Yeah," I said, "but do you think the government has finally learned its lesson?"

"What's to learn?" he said. "They got away with it. A lot of people were in on it, and they were able to retire with a pension, go home, and spend time with their grandkids. And any new agents or prosecutors in there now, the lesson is, you can get away with it, too."

Salvati and I sat in glum silence for a few seconds. It was not a pleasant thought, what Joe was saying, but I could think of no counterargument. And then Salvati put the cherry on top. "You ask me," he said, "I don't think they learned nothin'."

EPILOGUE

TWO MONTHS AFTER the verdict, I met juror number twelve, Janet Uhlar. The occasion was the official sentencing of James J. Bulger in November 2013. We met at the Palm restaurant, not far from the Moakley Courthouse. Uhlar was well known there; during the trial, the jury often was taken to the Palm for their meals. To the maître d' and the managers, Uhlar's face was familiar, and as we entered the restaurant for our midday meeting, a manager saw Janet and congratulated her on the jury having reached its verdict.

In the weeks since Bulger was found guilty, Uhlar had been vocal in her criticisms of the government's case. She had, of course, reached the same verdicts as the other jurors, with the defendant being found guilty on thirty-one of thirty-two counts, which included eleven of nineteen murders. But it had been an excruciating process. "Yes, Bulger was involved in some horrible crimes," she said, once we sat down in a quiet corner. "He admitted to some of those crimes in the opening statement. But to me the government's case was a travesty of justice."

The day before, in front of the courthouse, Uhlar had given an impromptu press conference to some of the media. She excoriated Wyshak and Kelly, characterizing the deals they made for the testimony of Martorano and Flemmi as "immoral." She suggested that the trial had likely barely skimmed the surface in its presentation of who was responsible for enabling Bulger's career, and she criticized the media for not being more diligent in investigating corruption. "The media needs to start doing its job," she said angrily.

Her comments were aired on the local Fox News affiliate and created a stir. Other jurors were quoted in the press criticizing Uhlar. Howie Carr, on his radio show and also in his column in the *Boston Herald,* referred to Uhlar as a "nut job" and suggested that she must be in love with Bulger.

The assault on Uhlar continued. That morning, in front of the courthouse, Steve Davis got in Uhlar's face and demanded, "What are you trying to prove?"

"I'm concerned about the integrity of the Constitution," she replied.

"The Constitution?" Davis was incredulous. "Forget about the Constitution. This is real life."

Davis was angry. He blamed the jury for having reached a verdict of no finding in relation to his sister's murder. More recently, Uhlar, specifically, had further raised his ire when she and two other jurors drafted a letter to Judge Casper arguing that Steve Davis should not be allowed to present an impact statement before the court, as other family members of Bulger's murder victims would be allowed to do at the time of sentencing. Uhlar's argument was that the jury had taken their duties very seriously and reached their conclusion on the Debbie Davis murder after careful deliberation. To allow Davis to speak was an affront to the jury.

Uhlar's position was distressing to Davis, partly, perhaps, because he had already begun promoting his yet-to-be-published book, entitled *Impact Statement,* on Amazon.com and other Internet sites.

In front of the courthouse, Davis cursed at Janet, calling her "crazy" and other insults not fit for print. Uhlar walked away from the courthouse in tears. Later, she claimed, she was lectured by a female reporter from the *Globe* and told, "You don't know what you're talking about. The media in Boston has been covering this story for twenty years and doing a great job."

In many ways, the reaction that Janet Uhlar experienced was akin to what Bob Fitzpatrick had also undergone in his attempts to shed light on the Bulger conspiracy. To adopt a position different from the status quo was to engender the wrath of the Boston establishment, including the media.

At the Palm restaurant, Janet had regained her composure. Her argument, she told me, was not with Steve Davis. "The U.S. attorney's office has been masterful in how they're doing this," she said. "They're playing the victims' families again and again and again. They smash them down and then raise them up to give impact statements. It's this game they're playing with everybody."

Uhlar had become especially disgusted by Wyshak and Kelly, who, she had come to believe, should be prosecuted for some of their actions. She cited the testimony of Kevin O'Neill, owner of Triple O's, who described from the stand how prosecutor Brian Kelly had manufactured false accusations against him so that a judge would hold him in jail. Kelly was engaged in a heavy-handed effort to force O'Neill to cooperate with the prosecution. Said Uhlar, "They held him on trumped-up charges. I was in shock listening to that whole thing. It wasn't until [O'Neill] gave Kelly what he wanted that they let him out of jail. That was such a violation of that man's civil rights. And Brian Kelly was so arrogant about it. He wasn't even ashamed."

Eventually, Uhlar had begun to ask herself, "Why is Bulger so much worse than Martorano and Morris and the others? Why are they free today and all this effort and money is spent on convicting Bulger? How do [the prosecutors] weigh that out? How can they justify that? It didn't make sense to me. It still doesn't make sense to me."

At certain points in the trial, Uhlar had begun to sense that there was an explanation outside and beyond the scope of the evidence. Something was being hidden. She had tried to bring her concerns into the jury room during deliberations, to no avail. Most of the jurors bought the prosecution's case without serious questions. Why? "Because it's the government," said Uhlar. "In this country, people want to believe their government. And if you say something long enough, they believe it. People have been deceived for so long, they don't know how to ask the questions."

With a jury overwhelmingly inclined to vote "guilty" across the board, Uhlar had to settle with getting the jurors to at least evaluate the various murder charges individually. Enough of the jurors were disgusted with Martorano, Weeks, Morris, and Flemmi as witnesses that they acknowledged you could not take the word of any one of them without corroboration. And so, if the charge rested on the sole testimony of any one of those four witnesses, the jurors agreed to rule "not proved."

It was a modest repudiation of the government's case, but Uhlar wishes she had done more. "I do have regrets. I regret that I didn't dig my heels in and go for a no finding."

As for the concept of jury nullification, which the prosecutors had claimed was a subterranean goal of the defense, Uhlar says it never crossed her or anyone else's mind. "The way the crimes were packaged made it hard to declare anything but guilty. If Bulger was part of the enterprise, he was guilty of crimes committed by the enterprise. Judge Casper reiterated that during her charge to the jury. She made it clear that she did not want 'no finding.'"

At the Palm, Uhlar hardly touched her food. She talked nonstop. She had kept her feelings about the trial bottled up for so long that it now came out in a torrent. In her worst moments, she said, she feels as though by voting guilty she had become part of a cover-up on the part of the Justice Department. "We were held captive for ten weeks. I was deceived. The first thing I did when the trial ended was to google 'Jeremiah O'Sullivan.' There's a name—every time it came up the prosecutors objected. There's so much about this case that we weren't allowed to know. . . . This trial was a fundamental violation of the Constitution."

THE DAY AFTER I met juror number twelve, the court was scheduled to hear impact statements from the family members. It was an emotional day. Most of the people speaking before the court were now in middle age; they had been mere children when their loved one was murdered by Bulger or others associated with his crew. Most of these people had grown up knowing that the notorious Whitey Bulger had played a role in the killing of their father, uncle, sister, or daughter. Within the community, these were intimate murders, hushed in silence because they had occurred under the umbrella of organized crime. These people had grown up consumed with fear and hatred for the man who through his powerful political brother, his connections in law enforcement, and his control of the underworld had, for decades, seemed to be above the law.

One by one, they stood to speak, twelve of them in all. Many were consumed with emotion. Here was the murderer sitting in front of them, dressed on this day in an orange prison jumpsuit, looking even older and more withered than he had just two months earlier. Here was the man they had hated as far back as they could remember. It was almost too much to process.

Sean McGonagle, the son of Paulie McGonagle, stood at the podium and referred to Bulger as Satan. He was eleven years old when his father disappeared; he's now forty-nine. His voice choked with emotion, he vividly recounted how a few months after his father's disappearance, he received a phone call one day. The voice on the line said, "Your father's not coming home for Christmas." Sean McGonagle recognized the voice. It was Whitey Bulger. The voice was unmistakable. But still he asked, "Who is this?" The person answered, "Santa Claus," and then hung up.

In the pantheon of cruelty in the life of a mobster, there are bound to be many indefensible acts, but calling the young son of someone you murdered and taunting them with the knowledge that his father would not be home for Christmas was in a category all by itself.

Bulger looked down at his legal pad, scribbling notes. He never once made eye contact.

McGonagle concluded by saying, "You thought you carried yourself as an Irish icon. Nothing could be farther from the truth."

The son of Al Notarangeli stood to speak, and the daughter of Billy O'Brien. Patricia Donahue spoke, as did the daughter of Stephen Rakes, a son and daughter of Eddie O'Connor, and the son of John Callahan.

Steve Davis was allowed to speak. "It's been a long thirty-two years," he said. "I have fought hard for justice for my sister Debbie." Davis became overwhelmed with tears, struggled to get out the words. "This man has built up so much hate in my heart. I'd like to strangle him myself. The son of a bitch should have to look in the eyes of his victims." Davis yelled at Bulger: "You piece of shit, look at me!" Whitey glanced up briefly, then looked away.

Davis ended by saying, "I hope Whitey dies the same way my sister did, gasping for breath as he takes his last breath."

The daughter of Bucky Barrett stepped forward. Her name was Theresa Bond, and she was strangely calm. After introducing herself, she said in a soft, almost kindly voice, "Mr. Bulger, would you please look at me?" Her tone was so different than the others who had spoken that it caught Bulger off guard. He looked up. She reminded Bulger that on the night her father was murdered, he had been praying to a photo he had in his wallet, a photo of a young girl. "That was me," said Bond. "I was that little girl."

Bulger looked down. He betrayed no emotion, but it seemed as though

Theresa Bond had reached Bulger in a way the others had not—not through invective or hatred, but through forgiveness. "I just want you to know that I don't hate you," she told him. "I don't have that authority. That would be judging you. I do hate the choices that you've made, along with your associates, but more so, I hate the choices our government has made in allowing you to rule the streets and perform such horrific acts of evil."

Whitey hung his head in what seemed like shame, and Bond finished by saying, "Mr. Bulger, do you have remorse for taking my father's life? I think you do. I forgive you."

There was so much personal animosity toward Bulger, built up over a lifetime of suffering, that few of the victims' family members could see beyond Whitey. He had become the symbol of an evil that lurked in their community and the city; he had shattered lives almost beyond comprehension. None thought to reflect upon the context that made Bulger possible—except for one.

David Wheeler, the son of Roger Wheeler, had turned his father's murder into something of a crusade. Not long after Roger Wheeler had been murdered in Tulsa, shot in the face by John Martorano, the Wheeler family had begun to suspect that the killing had been facilitated by retired FBI agent H. Paul Rico. This was especially shocking, since Rico had been hired as a security consultant for World Jai Lai by Roger Wheeler. As the son noted in his courtroom statement, "My father's fatal mistake proved to be his faith in the FBI. . . . A team of retired FBI agents, led by former agent H. Paul Rico, assured him that they would protect his business and 'keep it clean.' "

Standing at the podium, Wheeler was a son of wealth and privilege, as distinguished from the working-class Boston folks who had given impact statements. His father had been CEO of an international company. The Wheeler family had been slow to comprehend the conspiracy of corruption that led to his father's murder. After the killing, said Wheeler, "I was confident that we would quickly catch Rico and his criminal associates. Sadly, my faith in the American government was misplaced."

It wasn't until sixteen years after Roger Wheeler was murdered that the family learned the truth. John Martorano provided the details at the Wolf

hearings in 1997. It was also then that the family learned that John Callahan and Brian Halloran had both been killed to keep them from talking
about the Wheeler murder, a cycle of killing that involved not only former FBI agent Rico, but also Agents Connolly and Morris. This raised
many unanswered questions. Asked David Wheeler, "How many others
were involved in these and other FBI informant murders? Who else at the
bureau knew about these secret relationships with these vicious criminals
but turned away, said nothing, as others were murdered? Did any supervisors or other agents care to ask any questions, connect the few simple dots
between these murders and their own informants? Where was the Justice
Department in all this?"

Eventually, the Wheeler family filed a lawsuit against the FBI and the
Justice Department for their role in their father's wrongful death. The government responded that it was too late; that the Wheeler family should have
filed their suit against the government years ago. The statute of limitations
had passed.

It was as if the family were to blame for not fully grasping the conspiracy
behind their father's murder until it was too late. After all these years, it still
riled David Wheeler, who grasped the podium with both hands and almost
shouted: "Everyone within the sound of my voice should understand this:
the FBI, entrusted with the greatest law enforcement powers in the nation,
is responsible for my father's murder. They are as responsible for that murder as this defendant sitting here before you."

Wheeler's statement was a barnburner. The problem was that Wheeler's
words seemed aimed at issues barely touched upon at the trial.

The day after the impact statements, Bulger was brought back to the
courthouse for his final appearance. He stood before Judge Casper, who
prefaced her sentencing of Bulger with a statement. She called Whitey
"evil," "reprehensible," "monstrous." Her words were the culmination of
what the trial had been for many Bostonians: a demonization of Whitey
Bulger as the greatest criminal mastermind the city had ever seen.

Casper sentenced Bulger to two life terms, plus seventy-five years.

Bulger was asked if he had anything to say.

"No," he answered.

He was led from the courtroom for the final time.

IN THE DAYS and weeks following the trial, I spoke with Kevin Weeks and Pat Nee. Both were satisfied with the verdict but seemed to derive no great sense of pleasure or closure from the proceedings. Weeks, in particular, saw the trial as a public disgrace for Bulger that could have been avoided if Whitey had simply pleaded guilty to the charges. For Kevin, closure was a pipe dream: he has two sons entering young adulthood who will be made to answer for his legacy as Bulger's protégé and also the man who brought him down by testifying against him in court.

"It hasn't been easy for them," Weeks told me. "All I can do is be there and give them the support that I never really had when I was their age."

As for Nee, the concerns were more of a legal nature. Rumors persisted after the trial that local prosecutors would attempt to bring charges against him for various crimes in which he was alleged to have played a role, including, most notably, the double murder of Brian Halloran and Michael Donahue. Nee makes no attempt to hide from these allegations. The fact that he continues to circulate in Southie and, in some quarters, remains a well-respected member of the community is Nee's way of saying, "You have no case against me."

Following the trial, Nee's more immediate concern was that *Saint Hoods,* his reality show on the Discovery Channel, was canceled after only two episodes had been aired. The former gangster had mixed feelings. "The money was decent," he told me. "I'll miss that. But the notoriety was more trouble than it was worth. I never wanted to be a media sensation. I'll leave that to Whitey."

FROM THE PERSPECTIVE of the U.S. Department of Justice, the trial of Whitey Bulger was an unequivocal success. The devil had been burned at the stake in the town square, and the town had reveled in his demise. The trial provided the government with the self-justification they had been denied while Bulger was on the run for sixteen years. Not only had they nailed Bulger, silencing those who claimed they had no interest in prosecuting the well-connected gangster, but they had done so in a way that effectively shut all doors leading to further official areas of inquiry. The historical framework that created Bulger—and the law enforcement strategy that gave him his power—remained mostly unexamined. The individuals responsible, aside from John Connolly, would not be legally held to task.

The cost of the trial was considerable: U.S. taxpayers paid approximately $6 million to stage the trial at the Moakley Courthouse. Prosecutors, defense lawyers, and their staffs had to be paid. The expense of transferring Bulger on a daily basis to and from Plymouth County Correctional Facility, escorted by a law enforcement motorcade, was considerable. Witnesses had to be flown in from around the United States and put up in hotels. The jury was paid transportation expenses and fed on a daily basis. The security detail at the courthouse was twice its normal size.

With the expense of such a high-profile proceeding, a discerning citizen might have expected more than a show trial. Given that there never was any doubt that Bulger would be found guilty of crimes that would result in him being put away for life, the trial could have been a legal exploration of the law enforcement policy that makes it possible for a man like Whitey Bulger to thrive. Instead, the trial was largely a strategic rope-a-dope designed to contain and focus all venom on Bulger, while the many players who had enabled and protected his reign—for personal or institutional reasons—were allowed to fade into retirement.

For anyone who thinks this a minor injustice, or a local issue only relevant to Boston, consider the following: the policies that created Whitey Bulger are still in place. The Top Echelon Informant Program has been discontinued in name only. Local cops and federal agents still cultivate and pay criminal informants, and sometimes those criminals continue to prey upon people and commit murder while serving as informants. It happens all the time. In areas of organized crime, gangs, and the narcotics business, in particular, this tango between criminals and the law is how criminal cases are made. The scope of these arrangements can be vast and far-reaching. It exists at every level of the underworld, from low-level street criminals to mob bosses like Whitey Bulger and beyond.

Right now, somewhere in America, agents from the FBI, DEA, Bureau of Alcohol, Tobacco, Firearms and Explosives (ATF), or ICE are cultivating informants—maybe a Mexican assassin in the narco trade, or a young Muslim who could penetrate a suspected terrorist cell, or a member of the Aryan

Nations who is also a meth distributor. Deals will be made with these criminals that shall remain intentionally vague and clandestine. These criminals will utilize the arrangement to enhance their position in the underworld; that may be why they agreed to take part in the arrangement to begin with. The criminal and the agent will enter into a dance of mutual manipulation, and the wiliest man or woman shall come out on top. If the arrangement goes haywire, as they sometimes do, the agent, and most especially the agent's handlers within the system, will cut and run. They will deny involvement and seek institutional protection through the destruction of documents, bureaucratic smoke screens, or a skewed prosecution, as was the case in the disposal of the Bulger fiasco.

Unless this policy is called into question, and those who use and abuse it are held accountable, it will continue to metastasize, playing out on ever more grandiose levels.

Consider, for instance, the case of Jesus Vicente Zambada Niebla, the son of a powerful cartel boss in Mexico who was himself a high-ranking member of the Sinaloa Cartel.

At the same time that Bulger was on trial in Boston, Zambada Niebla was being held on racketeering, narcotics, and murder charges at a prison outside Chicago. In 2010, when Zambada Niebla was indicted and arrested in the United States, he claimed that he could not be prosecuted because he was operating under an immunity agreement with the DEA.

In legal papers filed in federal court, lawyers for Zambada Niebla claimed:

> Sometime prior to 2004, and continuing through the time period covered in the indictment, the United States government entered into an agreement with . . . the leadership of the Sinaloa Cartel. Under this agreement, the Sinaloa Cartel . . . was to provide information against rival Mexican Drug Trafficking Organizations to the United States government. . . . In return, the United States government agreed to dismiss pending cases against [the Sinaloa Cartel], not to interfere with drug trafficking activities of the Sinaloa Cartel, to not actively prosecute the leadership of the Sinaloa Cartel, and to not apprehend them.

The allegations were stunning but would have been familiar to anyone who had followed the Bulger case. Just as the FBI had done back in the 1960s when they played an incendiary role in the Boston gang wars, the DEA was accused of taking sides in the Mexican cartel wars. The results were similar, but on a much larger scale. In Ciudad Juarez, Mexico, located along the border with El Paso, Texas, narco violence reached unprecedented levels. The Sinaloa Cartel was engaged in a bloody war with the Juarez Cartel. According to Zambada Niebla, they won that war because they were being covertly protected by the U.S. Department of Justice.

After the dust had settled, Zambada Niebla played a role similar to that of Steve Flemmi. Just as Flemmi, upon arrest, had divulged his and Bulger's deal with the feds, Zambada Niebla claimed that he and his cartel had formed a similar deal with the DEA.

In 2014, the U.S. government reached a plea deal with Zambada Niebla. Rather than go to trial, which would have presented prosecutors with a containment challenge even greater than what Wyshak and Kelly encountered, the cartel underboss was allowed to plead guilty and accept a relatively light sentence of ten years in prison. This way, the gangster's tales would remain untold in a public forum.

The Bulger and Zambada Niebla cases, when placed against the larger framework of law enforcement strategies and DOJ policy, seem to suggest a long-standing pattern of U.S. agents acting not as lawmen but as players in the underworld, making secret deals, pitting one side against another, and protecting those who are deemed to be "on our side." Just as Bulger and Flemmi had supplied underworld intelligence to agents that helped them make cases against the Mafia, the Sinaloa Cartel would supply info to the DEA, helping them make major cartel-related narcotics cases in the United States.

The game goes on, and there is much collateral damage. Sometimes innocent people get killed, or framed for crimes they did not commit. There is a system of justice in the United States that is supposed to help protect the innocent and see to it that the law is applied with fairness and transparency. But the Bulger trial seemed to suggest that in some cases the pursuit of justice takes a backseat to the dictates of bureaucratic self-preservation.

Over the years, many people knew of or played a role in the coddling of

Bulger. That inclination was the ugly stepchild of an earlier generation of corruption forged through the handling of Joe Barboza, the Flemmi brothers, and untold other government-protected criminal informants. When these arrangements are exposed, those responsible have a tendency to disappear into the woodwork. The truth is buried or obscured. The facts are deemed inadmissible or not relevant to the matter at hand.

In the end, the System protects itself.

ALTHOUGH THIS BOOK is intended to be an account of the legal proceedings known as *The People of the United States v. James J. Bulger,* the narrative ultimately goes far beyond the trial. The result is a book based on sources, both human and archival, that I have accumulated while following the Bulger saga for more than a decade. Some interviews over the years have been off the record. More recently, the trial afforded an opportunity to revisit or interview anew individuals who lived aspects of this story. Among the key interview subjects: Kevin Weeks, Patrick Nee, Teresa Stanley, Joseph Salvati, Anthony Cardinale, Paul Griffin, Robert Fitzpatrick, Thomas Foley, Richard Marinick, Steve Davis, Marilyn Di Silva, John Connolly, and Janet Uhlar.

Requests for one-on-one interviews were made of the various legal parties involved in the Bulger trial. I was turned down by both the defense team and the prosecutors. As for Bulger, I twice wrote to him in prison requesting an interview, once before and once after the trial. I received no response.

To this date, Bulger has never submitted to a formal interview. In the documentary *Whitey,* directed by Joe Berlinger, he is recorded talking on the phone with Jay Carney, his attorney. He is asked questions by Carney that were designed to illustrate a central argument of the government's case, that Bulger never was an informant for the FBI.

Previously, Bulger had been able to leak self-serving versions of his life story to the media through a series of letters he wrote to a former fellow prison inmate named Richard Sunday. Bulger encouraged Sunday to divulge the letters to the media, which he did, creating a stir in the press in the months leading up to the trial.

In the letters and also the Berlinger documentary, Bulger proved to be skilled at finding ways to put forth his version of events without ever having to explain himself in detail or submit to questions that might challenge his version of the truth. Throughout the trial, Bulger's attorneys stated publicly that their client wanted "the full truth to be known," but what they really meant was that he wanted his version of the truth to be known. In his strategic leaks to the media and through his lawyers, Bulger put forth many incredible allegations, including that he was given immunity to commit crimes by Jeremiah O'Sullivan in exchange for protecting the prosecutor's life from retribution by the Mafia in New England. These allegations were sometimes reiterated in strategic letters sent to friends, which found their way into the press. Whitey seemed to have an interest in shaping his image in the public domain; this negated any desire he might have to submit to an honest interview the terms of which he could not control.

Since Bulger disappeared on the lam in 1995, there has been voluminous litigation on matters relating to his criminal exploits and also his time as a Top Echelon Informant. Evidence gathered for these trials and hearings, and the transcripts of testimony, have informed this book. The various legal proceedings are too numerous to mention, but two governmental hearings were essential in understanding the corrupt universe that helped to create Whitey Bulger. One was the Hearing of the House Committee on Oversight and Government Reform, which resulted in a report titled "Everything Secret Degenerates." The other was the memorandum issued by Judge Nancy Gertner, who presided over what became known as "the Limone matter," the lawsuit that resulted in substantial financial settlements for Joe Salvati and others who were framed on murder charges by the U.S. Department of Justice.

Finally, any understanding of the Bulger fiasco begins with absorbing the work of the many journalists who have covered the story over the years. Some of these reporters have gone on to write books about the case, as have innumerable people who were associates or rivals of Bulger. This includes people in law enforcement who played a role in trying to bring Bulger down. My opinions are my own, but all of these books and journalism accounts have contributed to a broader and deeper understanding of this complex, multilayered story.

ACKNOWLEDGMENTS

I AM INDEBTED to the following people for helping me locate sources, separate fact from fiction, and come to a deeper understanding of the hard truths surrounding the Age of Bulger: Raymond Flynn, Mary Lafferty, Ciaran Staunton, James Flynn, Kevin Weeks, Patrick Nee, Teresa Stanley, Bobo Connolly, Tommy Lyons, Joseph Salvati, Anthony Cardinale, Harvey Silverglate, Paul Griffin, Robert Fitzpatrick, Thomas Foley, Richard Marinick, Frannie White, John Martorano, Jimmy Martorano, Steve Davis, Marilyn Di Silva, John Connolly, Howie Carr, Michelle McPhee, Edward Mahoney, Richard Stratton, and Janet Uhlar.

My time living in Boston for the duration of the trial was greatly enhanced by people who helped with logistics, accommodations, and leisure activities, most notably Michael Habicht, Paul Spatachini, Charlie Lo Grasso, Jill Mantineo Macone, Frank DePasquale, David Duggan at the Bricco Suites, Guy Mirisola at Mirisola's restaurant in South Boston, David Riccio, owner of Caffé Vittoria in the North End, and Michael Wuschke, esteemed bartender at the Seaport Hotel. Also, special thanks to Sophia Banda, my personal assistant at the time, who tended to matters back in New York City while I was away.

Researching and writing a book that is complex and densely researched requires understanding and support from family and friends. At the end of writing a book like this, I am sometimes surprised I still have friends, given the all-consuming nature of the project. For hanging in there, I would like to thank Teresita Levy, Benjamin Lapidus, Mike English, Stephanie English, Christina Lorenzatto, Sandra English, Suzanne Damore, Chris Damore, Valerie Anne Garcia, Valentin Sandoval, Jack Brown, Patrick Farrelly, Kate O'Callaghan, and others who have stayed the course.

The journey from rough manuscript to finished book requires contributions from many people. My agent, Nat Sobel, and his assistants at Sobel Weber Inc. play an integral role in facilitating my work. At William Morrow, I am indebted to Cal Morgan and to David Highfill, who edited the manuscript with a steady hand. Thanks also to Danielle Bartlett and others in the Publicity Department.

Most everyone has some activity that helps him or her deal with the stress of a major project that seems as though it will never end. For me it is music, both as a listener and as an amateur percussionist. The spirit of the drum has a soothing power that serves as a soundtrack for many of my adventures, for which I sometimes turn to Elegua, the spirit of journeys and passageways, to guide me along the road to completion.

The People of the United States v. James J. Bulger

COMPLETE WITNESS LIST (IN ORDER OF APPEARANCE)

1. Robert Long—former Massachusetts State Police
2. Colonel Thomas J. Foley—former Massachusetts State Police
3. James Katz—former Winter Hill Mob bookie
4. Richard O'Brien—former Winter Hill Mob bookie
5. John Martorano—former Winter Hill Mob hit man, Bulger partner
6. William Doogan—Sergeant, Boston Police Department, Cold Case Squad, Homicide
7. Diane Sussman de Tennen—witness to the killing of Michael Milano
8. Donald Milano—brother of murder victim Michael Milano
9. Laura Mello—daughter of murder victim James O'Toole
10. Deborah Scully—former girlfriend of murder victim William O'Brien
11. Tom Angeli—nephew of murder victim Joe Notarangeli
12. Ralph DeMasi—shooting victim during killing of William O'Brien
13. Charles Raso—former Winter Hill Mob bookie
14. Nancy Ferrier—daughter of murder victim Alfred Plummer
15. Michael Colman—former Massachusetts State Police
16. Kenneth Mason—Bureau of Alcohol, Tobacco, Firearms and Explosives (ATF), Boston Division
17. Frank Capizzi—shooting victim during killing of Alfred Plummer
18. Joseph Costa—former Boston Police Department, motorcycle unit
19. Joe Angeli—son of murder victim Joe Notarangeli
20. Barbara Sousa—former wife of murder victim James Sousa

21. James Marra—Special Agent with the Office of the Inspector General, Department of Justice
22. Margaret King—wife of murder victim Thomas King
23. Joe Leonard—brother of murder victim Francis "Buddy" Leonard
24. Sandra Castucci—wife of murder victim Richard Castucci
25. Robert Yerton—Tulsa, Oklahoma Police Department, forensic lab
26. Celso Perez—former police officer, Miami-Dade Police Department
27. Paul McGonagle—son of murder victim Paul Charles McGonagle
28. John Morris—former FBI special agent, supervisor of the C-3 organized crime unit, Boston division
29. Joseph Tower—former South Boston drug dealer
30. Robin Fabry—Massachusetts State Police
31. Karen Smith—daughter of murder victim Edward Connors
32. Ken Brady—corrections officer, Plymouth County Correctional Facility
33. Billy Shea—former South Boston drug dealer, member of the Bulger organization
34. William Haufler—Bulger extortion victim
35. Kevin Weeks—former Bulger protégé, member of the organization
36. Ann Marie Mires—forensic anthropologist
37. Elaine Barrett—wife of murder victim Arthur "Bucky" Barrett
38. Thomas Daly—former FBI special agent, C-3 organized crime squad, Boston division
39. Paul Moore—former drug dealer, member of the Bulger organization
40. Kathleen Crowley—forensic dentist, Office of the Chief Medical Examiner, Commonwealth of Massachusetts
41. Anthony Attardo—former drug dealer, member of the Bulger organization
42. Patricia Donahue—wife of murder victim Michael Donahue
43. Barry Wong—unwitting accomplice in Bulger extortion of Bucky Barrett
44. Steven Davis—brother of murder victim Debra Davis
45. Kevin Hays—former bookie, extortion victim of Bulger organization
46. Dr. Richard Evans—former medical examiner. Commonwealth of Massachusetts

47. Patricia Carlson Lytle—former girlfriend of John Martorano
48. Gerard J. Montanari—former FBI special agent, C-2 labor racketeering squad, Boston division
49. Robert Barry Halloran—brother of murder victim Brian Halloran
50. Michael Solimando—extortion victim of the Bulger organization
51. Pam Wheeler—daughter of murder victim Roger Wheeler Sr.
52. Donald J. DeFago—former U.S. Customs agent, Boston division
53. Joe Saccardo—former Massachusetts State Police
54. Gina Pineda—DNA expert
55. David Lindholm—extortion victim of the Bulger organization
56. John Druggan—forensic chemist, Massachusetts State Police lab
57. Stephen Flemmi—former Winter Hill Mob member, partner of James Bulger
58. Brandi Braun—bank teller, Braintree Bank, Braintree, Massachusetts
59. Kevin O'Neill—owner Triple O's Lounge, member of the Bulger organization
60. Richard Buccheri—extortion victim of the Bulger organization
61. Sandra Lemanski—Internal Revenue Service, criminal investigation division
62. Scott Garriola—FBI special agent, fugitive task force, Los Angeles
63. Robert Fitzpatrick—former FBI special agent, assistant special agent in charge (ASAC), Boston division
64. Joseph L. Kelly—former FBI special agent, C-3 organized crime unit, Boston division
65. Joseph C. Crawford—former FBI special agent, Boston division
66. Fred Davis Jr.—former FBI special agent, supervisor of Electronic Surveillance Unit (ELSUR), Boston division
67. Todd Richards—FBI special agent, C-3 organized crime unit, Boston division
68. Matthew J. Cronin—former FBI special agent, C-7 stolen property squad, Boston division
69. Steve Johnson—former Massachusetts State Police
70. Heather Hoffman—real estate lawyer and title examiner
71. Desi Sideropoulos—former secretary to FBI special agent in charge (SAC), Boston division

JAMES
BULGER

STEPHEN
FLEMMI

JOHN
MARTORANO

JACK
CURRAN

SPORTS
GAMBLING
BUSINESS

PHIL
COSTA

SPORTS
GAMBLING
BUSINESS

PAT
NEE

BOBBY
FORD

BOBBY McCARTHY
(LOANSHARKING)

CHARLIE
RASO

JAMES
MARTORANO

KEVIN
O'NEILL

BOBBY
O'CONNOR

STEVEN PULEO
(NUMBERS)

THOMAS
RYAN

JOHN
CALLAHAN

JAMES
MANTVILLE

JOHN BAHAROIAN
(NUMBERS)

RICHARD
O'BRIEN

TOMMY
KING

JOSEPH
YERARDI

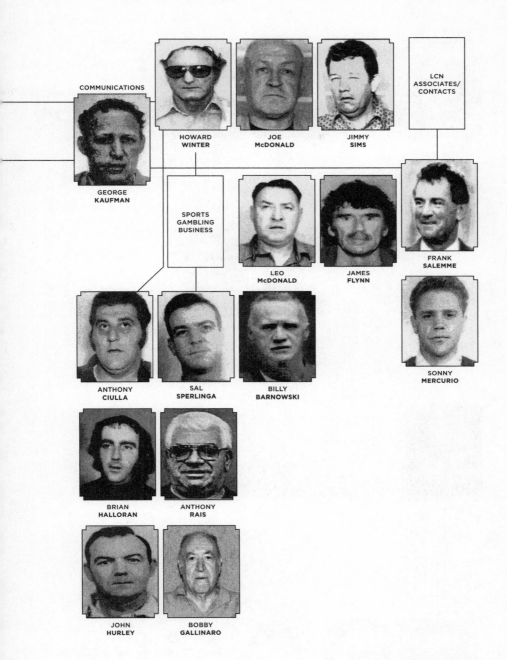

COMMUNICATIONS

GEORGE
KAUFMAN

HOWARD
WINTER

JOE
McDONALD

JIMMY
SIMS

LCN
ASSOCIATES/
CONTACTS

SPORTS
GAMBLING
BUSINESS

LEO
McDONALD

JAMES
FLYNN

FRANK
SALEMME

ANTHONY
CIULLA

SAL
SPERLINGA

BILLY
BARNOWSKI

SONNY
MERCURIO

BRIAN
HALLORAN

ANTHONY
RAIS

JOHN
HURLEY

BOBBY
GALLINARO

APPENDIX B

WINTER HILL ORGANIZATION
CIRCA 1975–1980

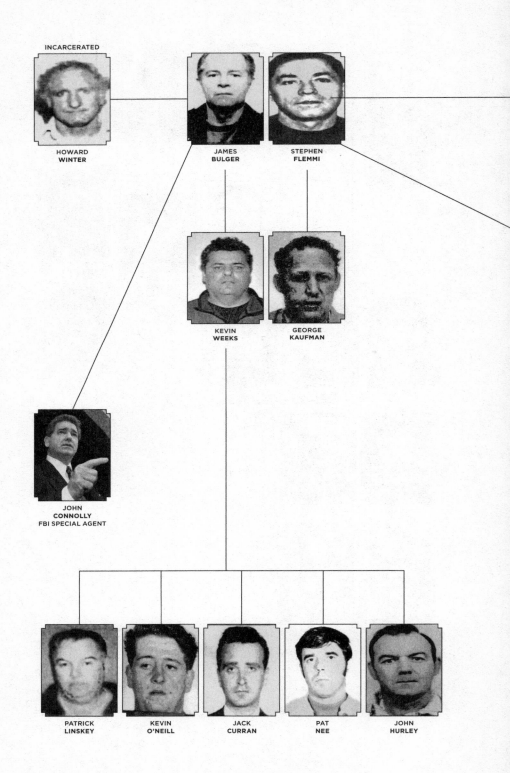

INCARCERATED

HOWARD
WINTER

JAMES
BULGER

STEPHEN
FLEMMI

KEVIN
WEEKS

GEORGE
KAUFMAN

JOHN
CONNOLLY
FBI SPECIAL AGENT

PATRICK
LINSKEY

KEVIN
O'NEILL

JACK
CURRAN

PAT
NEE

JOHN
HURLEY

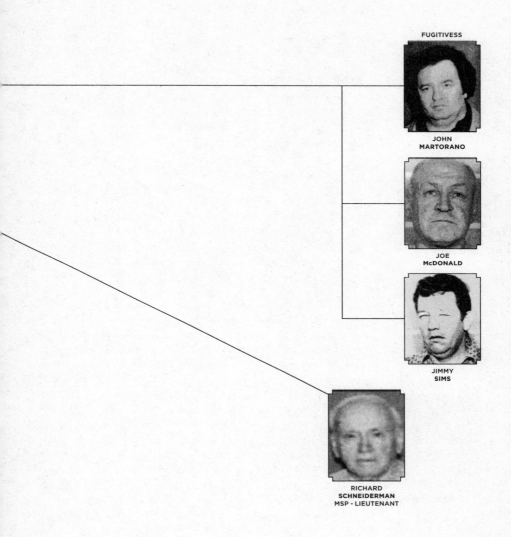

FUGITIVESS

JOHN
MARTORANO

JOE
McDONALD

JIMMY
SIMS

RICHARD
SCHNEIDERMAN
MSP - LIEUTENANT

APPENDIX C

WINTER HILL ORGANIZATION
SOUTH BOSTON ORGANIZED CRIME GROUP
CIRCA 1982

INDEX

Abe & Louie's, 139–40, 141
"accessory after the fact," 30, 30*n*
Ahearn, James, 369, 383–84
Albano, Michael, 205–7, 294
Alcatraz Federal Penitentiary, 78, 103
America's Most Wanted (TV show), 11, 250
Angiulo, Donato "Danny," 212–13, 281
Angiulo, Gennaro "Jerry," 112–13, 156,
   212–13, 277, 278–81
   arrest of, 364–65, 370*n*
   Deegan murder and, 105–6
   murder charge against, 92–93, 121,
   278
   racketeering charges, 280–81, 282, 362
   wiretap of, 198–99, 279–81
Angiulo, Michele "Mikey," 212–13, 281
Angiulo, Vittori Nicoli "Nick," 212–13,
   281
Animal (Sherman), 105*n*
Atlanta Penitentiary, 78–79
Attardo, Anthony, 275
audio interruption, 177, 179
Auerhahn, Jeffrey, 334

Bailey, F. Lee, 121, 277–78
Bangs, Joseph, 61
bank robberies, 61–62, 77–78, 113–14,
   117–18
Barboza (Barboza), 105*n*, 108
Barboza, Joseph "Animal," 103–13
   Angiulo and, 92–93, 105–6, 112–13,
   121, 278–79
   background of, 104
   Bulger trial and, 48–49
   in Carney's opening statement, 48–49
   as contract killer for Mafia, 6, 104–5,
   105*n*
   Deegan murder, 105–8, 117–19,
   121–22, 288–89, 344–46

as FBI informant, 2, 6, 7, 10, 48–49,
   108, 111–13, 115–19, 121–23,
   278–79
   McLaughlin brothers and, 109–11
   murder charge in California against,
   122–23
   murder of, 123
   nickname of, 104–5
   Patriarca and, 115–17, 121–22
   Salvati and, 2, 3, 5–6, 7, 49, 118, 119
Barrett, Arthur "Bucky"
   Depositors Trust bank robbery,
   61–62, 183, 255
   excavating and moving body, 260–62
   murder of, 36–38, 39, 234, 254–57
Batista, Fulgencio, 141
Bennett, Edward "Wimpy," 120,
   126–27, 394
Berlinger, Joe, 100, 274, 415
Beth Israel Hospital, 109
Betrayal (Fitzpatrick), 353, 358, 366–67
Black Mass (Lehr and O'Neill), 126,
   214–15, 215*n*
Boeri, David, 218
Bond, Theresa, 407–8
bookmaking, 44, 84–97, 179
Boozang, Steven, 320, 370–73
Boston (magazine), 60, 215
Boston, gangsterism in, 75–76, 80–84,
   105, 165–71
Boston Combat Zone, 111
Boston Edison, 284–85
Boston gang wars, 80–84, 93–94,
   105, 108–9, 111, 124, 164, 165–71,
   342–45
Boston Globe, 77*n*, 126, 193, 212–15,
   216–17, 320, 370*n*
Boston Herald, 137, 216, 273, 328, 404
Boston Marathon bombing, 31–32

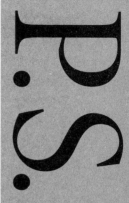

About the author

About the book

Insights,
Interviews
& More . . .

Read on

Meet T. J. English

THOMAS JOSEPH "T. J." ENGLISH comes from a large Irish Catholic family of ten brothers and sisters. Early in his writing career, English worked as a freelance journalist in New York City during the day and drove a taxi at night. He often refers to cab driving as a metaphor for what he does as a writer—cruising the streets, interviewing strangers, exploring the unknown, and reporting on what he sees and hears from his sojourns in and around the underworld.

English's first book was published in 1990. *The Westies* is an account of the last of the Irish Mob in the infamous Manhattan neighborhood known as "Hell's Kitchen." The book was the result of a series of reports English wrote for a weekly Irish American newspaper based in New York.

His second book, *Born to Kill* (1995), was an unprecedented inside account of a violent Vietnamese gang, based in New York's Chinatown, that operated up and down the East Coast. English's *Paddy Whacked*, a sweeping history of the Irish American gangster in New York, Chicago, Boston, New Orleans, and other U.S. cities, was published in 2005. In 2008, English hit bestseller lists with *Havana Nocturne*, his account of U.S. mobster infiltration of Havana, Cuba, in the years before the revolution swept Fidel Castro into power. The book became something of a publishing phenomenon, rising to #7 on the *New York Times* bestseller list and also making the following lists: *Wall Street Journal, USA Today, San Francisco Chronicle, Los Angeles Times, Boston Globe,* and Independent Booksellers. *Havana Nocturne* is currently in development as a major motion picture.

English's *The Savage City,* a blistering account of racial hostilities between the NYPD and the Black Liberation movement in the 1960s and early 1970s, was published in 2011. This book also became a *New York Times* bestseller. English's most recent book is *Where the Bodies Were Buried* (2015), an in-depth account of the Whitey Bulger scandal, with particular emphasis on the universe of corruption in the criminal justice system that helped to make possible the notorious Boston mobster's twenty-year criminal reign.

As a journalist, English has written for many publications, including: *Vanity Fair, Esquire, Playboy, New York* magazine, *Village Voice, Los Angeles Times* Magazine, and *New York Times.* In the mid-1990s, he wrote a three-part series for *Playboy* titled "The New Mob," which explored the changing face of organized crime in America. More recently, he wrote "Narco Americano," also for *Playboy* (February 2011), an investigation into the narco war in Mexico and how the violence has affected the Juárez–El Paso borderland. In 2010, his article for *Playboy* about a DEA agent alleged to have framed innocent people on bogus narcotics charges won the prestigious New York Press Club Award for Best Crime Reporting. These and other articles ▶

Meet T. J. English *(continued)*

were published in the book *Whitey's Payback* (2013), a collection of the author's crime journalism over a twenty-year period.

His work as a writer has taken him to Cuba, Jamaica, Hong Kong, Mexico, Ireland, and all around the United States. Most of his articles are on the subject of crime and criminal justice, though English writes on a wide variety of other subjects, including music, politics, and movies. He has published full-length interviews with actor Bill Murray, former Chicago mayor Richard J. Daley, director Martin Scorsese, and the late comedy legend George Carlin, to name a few.

In addition, English is a screenwriter and has penned episodes for the television crime dramas *NYPD Blue* and *Homicide*, for which he was awarded the Humanitas Prize.

He lives in New York City. ∾

Bullshit in Boston
The Persecution of Robert Fitzpatrick

THE CASE of the notorious Boston gangster James "Whitey" Bulger is not yet over. It is not over because a federal prosecutor in the District of Massachusetts does not want it to be over.

In April 2015, Assistant U.S. Attorney Fred M. Wyshak Jr. filed papers in the case against Robert Fitzpatrick, a retired FBI agent who, in the summer of 2013, testified on behalf of the defense at the trial of Whitey Bulger. Nearly two years after the trial was over, the U.S. attorney's office arrested Robert Fitzpatrick and charged him with six counts of perjury and six counts of obstruction of justice based on his testimony.

The charges had little to do with Fitzpatrick's testimony regarding Bulger's crimes. Rather, prosecutors were claiming that Fitzpatrick committed perjury by exaggerating certain aspects of his career as an FBI agent.

Fitzpatrick was seventy-six years old and in failing health. If convicted on federal perjury and obstruction charges, he faced fifteen years in prison—which for him would have been a life sentence.

I know Bob Fitzpatrick. I met and interviewed him numerous times while researching and writing *Where the Bodies Were Buried*. He is a good man. He was raised in the church-run Mount Loretto orphanage in Staten Island, New York. ▶

Bullshit in Boston *(continued)*

He served with distinction in the U.S. Army. He's been married for thirty years to a woman who works in hospital administration and has two daughters, recent college graduates, of whom any father would be proud.

Back in 1981, Fitzpatrick, a sixteen-year veteran of the FBI, was transferred to Boston and walked into a hornet's nest. The corruption Fitzpatrick encountered was astounding, not only within his own FBI division but also within the halls of justice. Among those who would later be exposed as playing a crucial role in the Bulger conspiracy was Jeremiah T. O'Sullivan, chief of the state's Organized Crime Strike Force and later U.S. attorney. O'Sullivan protected Bulger and his criminal partner Steve Flemmi, who, unbeknownst to the public, were serving as informants for the Department of Justice (DOJ) at the same time they were killing people with impunity.

At the Bulger trial, prosecutors Wyshak, Brian Kelly, and Zachary Hafer—working for the same U.S. attorney's office that once had a duplicitous relationship with Bulger and Flemmi— found themselves in a difficult position. Prosecuting Bulger for his voluminous crimes was the easy part; the evidence was overwhelming. Far more challenging was to control the narrative of the Bulger prosecution so that it did not reveal the historical continuity of corruption that helped to make Bulger possible.

Bob Fitzpatrick was not the only retired lawman who took the stand and detailed corruption that spread beyond the FBI into the U.S. attorney's office and all the way to DOJ headquarters in Washington, D.C. In many ways, the testimony of retired special agents Joe Crawford, Fred Davis, and Matt Cronin was even more devastating in its detailing of what happened to agents who smelled a rat in the Boston criminal justice system and attempted to do anything about it. But Fitzpatrick, it seemed, was being punished because he had the "audacity" to write a book about it.

In *Betrayal* (Forge Books, 2011), a book about Fitzpatrick's FBI career written by Fitzpatrick and Jon Land, the ex-agent vented his frustrations over his years as Assistant Special Agent in Charge (ASAC) of the bureau's Boston division. The internal law enforcement corruption that Fitzpatrick laid out in his book was corroborated many times over by others who published books and testified at the Bulger trial. But by testifying at the trial on behalf of the defense, Fitzpatrick—in the eyes of the prosecutors—stepped over to the other side and now had to be punished.

In motion papers filed in federal court in Boston, prosecutors Wyshak and Hafer cited that in his testimony Fitzpatrick mentioned that early in his career, while stationed in Memphis, he was among the first agents on the scene of the assassination of Martin Luther King Jr. Fitzpatrick noted that he, among other agents, discovered the gun that was used by James Earl Ray to kill King. The prosecutors sought to submit as evidence a transcript of an interview Fitzpatrick did for a CNN documentary in which he said, "Then I was transferred back to Memphis. Martin Luther King came to Memphis and I was told that King had just been shot. We found the gun and through the fingerprints we identified James Earl Ray, and we arrested him in London."

The prosecutors noted that nowhere in the official record of the King assassination was Robert Fitzpatrick mentioned as having been among those who found the gun.

And that was it: that was a primary count in the government's perjury case, that Fitzpatrick may have exaggerated this detail from his twenty-two-year-long law enforcement career about something that occurred nearly a half century ago.

Among other counts in the Fitzpatrick indictment was whether or not he accurately stated his managerial mandate when he was first transferred to the Boston FBI office, and whether or not he was present at the physical arrest of Gennaro "Jerry" Angiulo, boss of the Boston mafia, as he alleged in his book and on the witness stand.

Clearly, the reason Bob Fitzpatrick was indicted had nothing to do with these picayune acts for which he was being charged. His prosecution had to do with the U.S. attorney's office in Boston shoring up its legacy and attempting to rewrite the public record. By seeking to discredit Fitzpatrick, to bury him under the full weight of the U.S. attorney's office, they were attempting to reconfigure the narrative of institutional ▶

corruption that helped to make the long-running Bulger fiasco such a depraved and murderous reality.

Wyshak and Hafer got the conviction they wanted in the Bulger case. They helped to put away one of the most vile mob bosses in U.S. history. But the prosecution of Whitey Bulger also involved one of the most egregious whitewashes in the history of the criminal justice system.

The latest act in this ongoing whitewash was the attempt to destroy Bob Fitzpatrick, a man who served the FBI admirably for more than twenty years and now faced a prison sentence on charges that are beneath the dignity of federal prosecutors throughout the United States.

As it turned out, few of the particular crimes leveled against Fitzpatrick really meant much to the feds. They were merely a ruse designed to coerce Fitzpatrick into copping a plea on another count in the indictment, one that struck at the heart of the credibility of the criminal justice system in New England.

In his testimony at the Bulger trial, Fitzpatrick detailed—as he had in many other courtroom appearances—how he had met with Bulger. As ASAC of the Boston division, he had been sent to debrief Bulger and determine his "suitability" as an informant. During his meeting at Bulger's condominium in Quincy, the mob boss, in Fitzpatrick's retelling, made it clear that he did not consider himself an informant.

The offer the feds made to Fitzpatrick was this: if he would enter a plea stating that he lied when he recounted Bulger saying that he was not an informant, they would agree to a sentence in which he did no time in jail.

Through his attorney, Fitzpatrick said no. As he later told me: "I'm not going to lie about what I was told. I'd have to live with that the rest of my life. I'd rather go to trial."

In making their plea offer to Fitzpatrick, the same prosecutors who presided over the Bulger conviction revealed their true motives.

If there were to be any public legacy that the FBI, the U.S. attorney's office, or DOJ had allowed Bulger to operate within the fantasy that he was not an informant, then the criminal justice system had blood on its hands. The use of informants by law enforcement and the criminal justice system would have been exposed as a sham. By allowing Bulger to commit murders and other crimes free from any official informant relationship, free from any restraints, meant that the entire government had entered into a criminal partnership with a serial killer disguised as a gangster.

So, dig this. After meeting with Bulger, Bob Fitzpatrick told his supervisors: this guy does not believe that he's an informant. He believes that he's the one in charge.

No one listened to Fitzpatrick.

No wonder the system had now undertaken an internal mandate to criminalize Bob Fitzpatrick.

There were other factors at play. During grand jury hearings on the Fitzpatrick case, Assistant U.S. Attorney Hafer grilled a former FBI agent about Fitzpatrick's book, *Betrayal*, which the agent acknowledged that he had read. In his testimony, the retired agent/witness revealed that he had come away from reading the book with the perception that Fitzpatrick deserved some credit for having exposed and ultimately taken down Whitey Bulger.

Hafer took exception to that characterization. "Agent Fitzpatrick is not the person who took down Whitey Bulger," he said.

"Then who is?" asked the witness.

Hafer nodded to his co-prosecutor, Fred Wyshak, and said, "You're looking at him."

That, in a nutshell, is what the case against Fitzpatrick was all about. It was an attempt by the U.S. attorney's office to control and shape the legacy of the Bulger case.

Why should I care? you might ask. There are grave injustices perpetrated by the justice system all the time. On a weekly basis in America, DNA evidence reveals men and women who have been falsely convicted by state and federal prosecutors and sent to prison for crimes they didn't commit. In attempting to determine where you should focus your compassion and concern, why should you care about a man who was set up on perjury charges?

Well, consider this: until he arrived in Boston, Bob Fitzpatrick was an exemplary FBI agent who never once had any contentious dealings within law enforcement. He was a company man who ▶

Bullshit in Boston *(continued)*

believed in the system and carried out his duties with pride and diligence. Even when he began to smell a rat in Boston, he did not go outside the system to reveal what he knew. He sought to process it within the system because he was, as he had been in the U.S. Army and throughout his life, a team player. In seeking redress within the system, he became a threat, and he has been perceived as a threat to the system ever since. And for that, the system set out to destroy his reputation to salvage its own legacy.

Why should you care?

If the criminal justice system will do this to one of its own, just imagine what it would do to you or someone you know.

POST SCRIPT: On May 9, 2016, Robert Fitzpatrick walked into court in Boston and pleaded guilty to perjury charges stemming from the Bulger case. Though the U.S. Attorney's office touted the guilty plea as a victory, with U.S. Attorney Carmen Ortiz declaring that Fitzpatrick's plea made it clear that "there are consequences to lying in federal court," it was, in fact, a sad day for "justice" in the District of Massachusetts.

It is unlikely that Fitzpatrick was guilty of the charges to which he pleaded guilty. With pre-trial legal expenses in the hundreds of thousands of dollars, and health issues that included high blood pressure, loss of hearing, and kidney issues that required daily dialysis treatments, Fitzpatrick simply could not withstand the pressure.

Under his plea deal, the retired agent paid a $12,500 fine and was placed on probation for two years. He serves no time in jail.

The Fitzpatrick case is a lesson in how the system operates: a once proud agent, a true believer, has his reputation destroyed by the system to which he devoted his life. All because he had the audacity to publicly detail the corruption of that system.

The stench of the Bulger era is never-ending. Prosecuting Whitey should have been a triumph for the criminal justice system in New England. Instead, what remains is a legacy of deceit, self-delusion, systemic corruption, and the vindictive need to settle old scores. Whitey Bulger may be locked up and, at age eighty-six, soon to be deceased, but the ethos that helped to create Whitey lives on. ∾

Visit https://skullfragmentstjenglishonline.com/
for the latest updates.

Have You Read?
More by T. J. English

THE IRISH MOB TRILOGY

With *Where the Bodies Were Buried, New York Times* bestselling author T. J. English completes his unprecedented nonfiction trilogy of books that cover—collectively—the full sweep of the Irish Mob in America.

From the era of the Irish Potato Famine in the late nineteenth century, through the Prohibition years, right up to and including the trial of James "Whitey" Bulger in Boston, the Irish Mob held sway. The Irish Mob Trilogy lays bare this epic saga and presents a staggering cast of strivers, hoodlums, and crime fighters. The three books that constitute the trilogy—*The Westies* (1990), *Paddy Whacked* (2005), and *Where the Bodies Were Buried* (2015)—represent a major literary accomplishment and also happen to be entertaining as hell.

The story begins in the Five Points area of lower Manhattan, where destitute exiles from the Great Famine formed the earliest street gangs. These gangs partook of the various criminal rackets of their day—illegal gambling, thievery, prostitution, and extortion—but they also laid the groundwork for a criminal structure that was to become deeply embedded in the world of politics. Political organizations such as Tammany Hall utilized the financial bounty from criminal rackets and brute force to elect politicians and advocate for those represented by "the Tiger," as the organization was known.

This intermingling of underworld commerce, American capitalism, and politics would become the foundation for what is now referred to as "organized crime."

Prohibition was the heyday of the Irish American gangster, not only in New York but across the nation, in New Orleans, Chicago, Boston, Kansas City, and other municipalities. The Irish Mob became a force in the arenas of labor, politics, law enforcement, and gangsterism. At times, Irish mobsters worked in consort with the Mafia and other underworld factions; at other times, they were in competition with the Italians. This volatile and bloody subnarrative to American history is referred to by T. J. English as "the war between the dagos and micks," with a body count that surpasses many wars.

Through the Depression, the postwar years of the 1940s and 1950s, and right into the later decades of the twentieth century, the story of the Irish Mob remained largely a hidden history until author English devoted the better part of twenty-five years to uncoiling this yarn. His trilogy brings the story into modern times, through the especially violent era of the last Irish Mob in New York—*The Westies*—and the infamous story of Whitey Bulger in ▶

Have You Read? *(continued)*

Boston, which English chronicles through an account of the trial that brought Whitey down and in so doing signaled the end of a criminal tradition that had lasted more than a century.

The Irish Mob Trilogy, by T. J. English, stands as the most complete exploration of this history ever presented by an author, historian, or storyteller.

BORN TO KILL

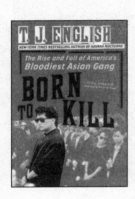

Throughout the late 1980s and 1990s, a gang of young Asian refugees cut a bloody swath through New York's Chinatown. They were the lost children of the Vietnam War, severed from their families by violence and cast adrift in a strange land. Banding together under the leadership of a megalomaniacal young psychopath, David Thai, they took their name from a slogan they had seen on helicopters and the helmets of U.S. soldiers: "Born to Kill." For a decade their empire was unassailable, built on a foundation of fear, ruthlessness, and unimaginable brutality—until one courageous gang brother helped bring it down from the inside.

To underworld kingpins Meyer Lansky and Charles "Lucky" Luciano, Cuba was the greatest hope for the future of American organized crime in the post-Prohibition years. In the 1950s, the Mob—with the corrupt, repressive government of brutal Cuban dictator Fulgencio Batista in its pocket—owned Havana's biggest luxury hotels and casinos, launching an unprecedented tourism boom complete with the most lavish entertainment, top-drawer celebrities, gorgeous women, and gambling galore. But Mob dreams collided with those of Fidel Castro, Che Guevara, and others who would lead an uprising of the country's disenfranchised against Batista's hated government and its foreign partners—an epic cultural battle that bestselling author T. J. English captures here in all its sexy, decadent, ugly glory.

THE SAVAGE CITY

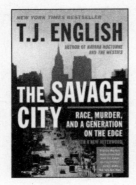

In *The Savage City*, T. J. English, author of the *New York Times* bestselling blockbuster *Havana Nocturne*, takes readers back to a frightening place in a dark time of violence and urban chaos: New York City in the 1960s and early '70s. As he did in his acclaimed true crime masterwork *The Westies*, English focuses on the rot in the Big Apple in this stunning tale of race, murder, and a generation on the edge—as he interweaves the real-life sagas of a corrupt cop, a militant Black Panther, and an innocent young African-American man framed by the NYPD for a series of crimes, including a brutal and sensational double murder.

If you enjoyed
Where the Bodies Were Buried,
look for the next book from T. J. English
on the Cuban mob in New York and
Miami, a continuation of the bestseller
Havana Nocturne

Available in hardcover in 2018
from William Morrow

Dramatic rights under development
by Paramount and Appian Way

Discover great authors, exclusive offers, and more at hc.com.